EFFECTIVE COMMUNICATION FOR ENGINEERS

McGRAW-HILL BOOK COMPANY

New York   St. Louis   San Francisco   Auckland   Düsseldorf   Johannesburg
Kuala Lumpur   London   Mexico   Montreal   New Delhi   Panama   Paris
São Paulo   Singapore   Sydney   Tokyo   Toronto

Library of Congress Cataloging in Publication Data
Main entry under title:

Effective communication for engineers.

    A collection of articles which were originally published in Chemical engineering.
    Includes index.
    1. Communication of technical information.   2. Technical writing.   I. Chemical
      engineering.
T10.5.E33   1975   808'.066'6021   75-16260
ISBN 0-07-045032-3

Effective Communication for Engineers

1234567890EBEB798765

Originally published by Chemical Engineering, McGraw-Hill Publications Company. Reprinted in 1975.
Edwards Brothers Incorporated was printer and binder.

CONTENTS

FOREWORD   v

INTRODUCTION: Are You Being Heard?   1

PART I: Making Engineer-ese Readable   5

  How Well Do You Inform?   6
  Watch Your Words   12
  Words: Chance or Choice   14
  Initials, Acronyms & Chaos   16
  The Jargon Jungle   18
  Poetry? For Engineers? Part I: The Best Word   20
            Part II: Words in Their Best Order   24

PART II: Receiving Communications   27

  Management—By Listening:

    Part 1: Listening for Feeling   28
    Part 2: Listening for Feeling   31
    Part 3: What's New in Listening   34
    Part 4: Learning To Listen   37

  A Quick Rapid-Reading Course   40

PART III: Presenting Ideas to Groups   47

  Improving Oral Communication   48
  Organizing Your Talk   51
  The Content of Your Talk   55
  Delivering Your Talk—I   59
  Delivering Your Talk—II   62
  Audio-Visual Aids Bolster Your Talk   66
  Techniques for Using Audio-Visual Aids   69
  The Q & A Period Can Make or Break Your Talk   72
  Oral Communication: Answering Audience Questions   75
  Challenges and Rewards of Public Speaking   78
  How To Hold an Audience   80
  Put Showmanship Into Your Next Talk   83
  Oratory Isn't Dead, But Many Speakers Are   86
  How To Run Better Meetings   90
  Conferencemanship   93
  Running an In-Plant Course   96
  How To Present a Technical Paper   99
  Going To a Meeting? Why?   102

CONTENTS

PART IV: Making Reports Work for You   105

What Managers Look for in Engineering Reports   106
Fast, Functional Writing   108
Six Guidelines for Fast, Functional Writing   115
Creative Report Writing—Part I   120
          Part II   123
Ten Common Weaknesses in Engineering Reports   126
Guidelines for R&D Reports   129
How To Keep Laboratory Notebooks   132

PART V: Producing Visually Effective Reports   135

Dress Up Your Technical Reports   136
Illustration Techniques for Technical Reports   139
Preparing Better Flowsheets   145
Drawing Effective Flowsheet Symbols   148
Putting Technical Illustrations To Work   157

PART VI: Communicating Within the Company   163

Effective Communications: Key To Promotion   164
Psychology in Your Communications   167
How To Write Better Memos   170
Writing the Appropriation Request   172
Communicate Your Designs   175
Communications Between Maintenance, Design and Production   179
Communicating Better in Research and Engineering   183

PART VII: Working With a Secretary   189

Operating Manual: Secretary   190
How To Be a Great Dictator   193
Dictation and the Engineer   196

PART VIII: Getting Your Material Into Print   201

Pleasures and Problems of Being Published   202
Writing for Publication   204
How Easy Is It for You To Write?   207
Engineers and the Technical Writer   211

INDEX   215

FOREWORD

Any reader, whether layman or engineer, keeps on reading a bit of writing he has picked up if the first words and ideas are concrete *and* interesting. This initial promise must be kept up (it's tough on the writer) if the reader continues willingly.

"Effective Communication for Engineers" is concrete, interesting, *and* engagingly illustrated. I have been impressed with this collection of articles to the point of reading right on through.

I found that the book spends its pages on *important* aspects of communication. It recognizes that both the book reader and the report recipient are busy persons, with the very human afflictions of preoccupations and distractions. And it impresses upon the would-be writer the self-defensive necessity of walking in the other Indian's moccasins: Who is the reader? What do they (and don't they) already know? What are they trying to find out? What can confuse them?

Most treacherous is to write well about good writing. In this collection, the editors and writers show that they know whereof they speak. They write from professional engineering experience, and hence with the right mixture of realism, humor, sensitivity, frustration, restraint, and thoroughness.

T. T. Woodson, Consulting Engineer
Director, Engineering Clinic
Harvey Mudd College

INTRODUCTION

Are You Being Heard?

You are a natural communicator, having practiced from birth. But do you get maximum benefit from your communicating? Probably not, unless you constantly strive to get the most out of language.

ROY V. HUGHSON, Associate Editor, CHEMICAL ENGINEERING

There is a famous character in a Moliere play who in middle-age discovers, to his surprise, that he has been talking prose all his life.* All of us have been communicating all our lives, yet few of us think we are expert communicators (and correctly so).

Every engineer is judged by the way in which he communicates. While relatively few people are qualified to judge how well you carry out the tasks assigned to you, everyone is qualified—or at least thinks he is qualified—to judge the way you write and speak.

You are also judged on the way that you listen. Of course, nobody really knows what goes on inside your head. But it is easy to see how well you pay attention to what is said, and the ways you respond. The final test of listening, of course, is in the way you carry out oral instructions.

Engineers tend to be bad communicators. Anyone who has been at a large professional-society meeting has suffered through the presentations of engineers who have never learned to speak in public. And any reader of engineering reports knows how few reports are even clear—much less, interesting.

There is really no reason why speeches have to be dull, nor is there any reason why reports have to be dull. There are techniques for giving a good, interesting talk,

as there are ways to write well. (This doesn't mean the fiction-writer's "well-turned phrase"—but it does mean clarity, accuracy and organization.) You don't need an inborn gift for speaking or writing. These things can be learned, just exactly as you learned mathematics or physics.

So far, we've talked about oral input (listening) and output (speaking), as well as written output (writing). What's left is written input (reading). But of course you already know how to read—otherwise this article won't be making much sense. But do you read really well? Well enough and fast enough to benefit from the mass of written material that comes your way?

In addition, there are hybrid inputs and outputs. For example, you can receive a written input aurally if someone reads aloud to you. This is a pretty inefficient way of obtaining information, unless you're blind. The converse of this is the oral output of written material. You've seen (and heard) this happen when someone "reads a paper" at a technical meeting. Unless the reader is very skillful indeed, the result is deadly dull. It's difficult to communicate your brilliant ideas to a half-asleep audience.

But there is one hybrid that is surprisingly useful—oral production of written material—usually called "dictating." Few engineers "write" their letters this way, and even fewer use the method for reports or articles. But it is a timesaving tool, once you get the hang of it.

*The play is Le Bourgeois Gentilhomme; the character, M. Jourdain; and the action takes place in Act II, Scene iv.

tions: 1—Handling Details; 2—Handling Ideas; 3—Abstract vs. Concrete Nouns; and 4—Passive vs. Active Verbs. In each of these sections, you'll find a "test" in boldface (heavy) type. Read through the first section, and for a week, apply the test to everything you write. Everything! Reports, memos, letters, instructions, class assignments, everything. By the end of your first week, you'll be writing better. By the time you've finished all four sections, you will have improved so much that other people are likely to notice.

That's only one chapter, of course. There are other chapters on writing, and each can help you to make an improvement. In fact, it would be worthwhile to come back from time to time to some of the chapters you studied earlier. You may find that you have slipped back into some of your old bad habits.

Well, What Shall I Do About It?

Obviously, you feel a need for improving your abilities as a communicator or you wouldn't be reading this book. You will find many suggestions to help you in these pages. While there is no easy way to learn to be a good communicator, some ways are more efficient than others. But there is no overall "best" way to study. The best will be that which gets you the furthest in the shortest time.

Where to start? That depends on your present skills and your needs. If most of your communicating is in writing, you can obviously leave the spoken word until later—except, perhaps, for listening.

If you spend a good deal of your time in conferences, you might want to brush up on speaking techniques first. You'll have to be the judge.

I suspect that most readers of this book are interested in improving their writing abilities. Certainly, surveys of recent (and not-so-recent) graduates frequently turn up an interest in learning to write better as one of the skills that the respondent most wishes he had been taught back in school. And more and more, engineering colleges are beginning to realize that the engineer who cannot communicate his (or her) ideas is only half effective; hence, half educated.

The best way to learn to write is to have your writing criticized and rewritten by a skilled writer. And the best way to teach engineering students to write would be to have every piece of paper that is turned in to their professors graded for writing style and structure.

The problem with this approach is that most professors just don't have the time. And few have the training for such work, either. If the job of correcting English gets delegated to a graduate assistant who can't write any better than the student, the results can be disastrous.

Since almost no engineers learn to write well in college, they have to learn later. Writing is a skill that is improved by practice—you won't ever learn to write just by reading about it. Indeed, it is almost impossible to do much writing without becoming better at it. However, you'll improve a lot faster if you consciously try to improve. Here is where this book can be a great help.

For example, take the chapter, "How Well Do You Inform?" on p. 6. You'll find that it's divided into four sec-

Make a Speech? Me?

It's surprising how many engineers get wild-eyed and dry-mouthed at the thought of standing up before a group to give a talk. Others are perfectly willing to speak at any occasion, but all too often they bore their audiences unmercifully.

Becoming a good speaker is rather harder than becoming a good writer. The problem is one of gaining experience, and there are many more opportunities to write than to speak.

If you really want to become a good speaker, the technique is to grab as many speaking opportunities as possible. If you are asked to report on the results of a new safety campaign, or to outline a proposed research project, you can treat it as an opportunity to speak. It is quite possible to practice the basic elements of speechmaking before an audience of three or four people.

Certainly it is worthwhile to consciously practice the techniques of speaking to small groups—some of the most important decisions that affect your professional career will be based on the oral presentations that you make to small management groups.

Since most of us have relatively few chances to speak, compared with chances to write, we must put more concentrated learning effort into each talk. It would be wise to go through all the chapters on speechmaking during the time that you are preparing your talk. Try to incorporate as many of the principles of organization, style and presentation as possible into the speech. After you are finished (but while the experience is still fresh in your mind), go over the chapters again—it will help you to see where you can improve.

Listening To Hear

This book devotes a great deal of attention to listening. Listening is probably the most neglected part of the whole communications process. It is a complex interrelation of hearing, understanding, analysis and retention. As such, it is one of the most important aspects of communications; perhaps the *most* important.

One thing that you will discover is that there is a great deal more to listening than merely letting the spoken word massage your eardrums. The author of these chapters calls it "listening for feeling," which describes the idea quite well. Learning to listen effectively isn't easy, but you'll certainly have enough opportunity!

And All the Rest

There are dozens more nuggets in this book. Whether you use them or not depends on you. For example, if you don't ever want to have an article or paper published, you can safely ignore the chapters on this subject.

Few people read as rapidly as they are potentially able to, so it would be wise not to ignore the section on speeding up your reading (the last chapter in Part III). The techniques involved are fairly simple. Like the techniques of listening, you will have many a chance to practice them.

Also, you may want to try to develop the techniques of dictating for your reports and articles. You can dictate to either a machine or a stenographer—the chapters in Part VIII point out the advantages and disadvantages of each. Once you pick up the knack, you'll find it a great time-saver—though the first few times you may find the going slow and the results demoralizing. But keep at it. Eventually, you too can be a great dictator.

Do you have to run a meeting? Or set up an in-plant course? You will find suggestions on how to do both. Indeed, you'll be hard put to spot any important phase of communications that isn't covered.

As engineer after engineer has discovered—as you climb the corporate ladder, communications skills become more and more important (and your technical skills become less so). Communications skills can be learned. The time to start is now. ■

Meet the Author

Roy V. Hughson has been an associate editor of CHEMICAL ENGINEERING since 1960. Prior to this, he spent about 10 years doing research and development work, mainly for the food industry. He holds a B.Ch.E. and an M.S. (in science education), both from New York University. His interest in technical writing was developed during his years in industrial R&D, when he discovered that the writing and editing of technical reports was one of the most important aspects of his job as a group leader and, later, as a department head.

His work at CHEMICAL ENGINEERING involves the writing and editing of technical and nontechnical articles. For over five years, he edited the magazine's "You & Your Job" department, which deals with the nontechnical aspects of an engineer's work. He also created the magazine's style manual.

He is the recipient of an award from the University of Missouri School of Journalism ". . . for excellence in reporting and interpreting business, economic and financial news," as well as the American Business Press' Neal Award for outstanding journalism.

Since 1970, he has been a lecturer at the Technical Writing Institute, conducted annually by Rensselaer Polytechnic Institute, and he is currently president of the New York Business Press Editors, Inc.

PART I

Making Engineer-ese Readable

How Well Do You Inform?

Here are some provocative tests that reveal how well you
are meeting the four criteria of informative writing—criteria
that apply to all types of reports and memoranda.

THOMAS P. JOHNSON, *Writing Consultant*

Probably no good engineer has ever been fired
simply because he was a poor report writer. Far too
often, however, good engineers have missed out on
promotions and other rewards because their poorly
written reports did not do justice to their technical
achievements.

Of course, older engineers find that writing skill
is vital in the transition to management responsibilities. But the ability to write may be even more important to the young engineer: Until he becomes a
participant at committee meetings, executive lunches
and other conferences, he may have to rely almost exclusively on the written report to present his work
and his ideas to higher management.

The four simple tests that I will describe are not
the solution to all technical writing problems. But they
will help the report writer answer the elusive question: "How well am I informing my readers?" Nothing else in engineering writing is nearly as important
as being informative.

Informative writing can be defined as being easy
to understand; it need not necessarily be "readable"
(i.e., easy to read). In recent years, many books and
scores of articles on the subject of readibility have
appeared. Written primarily to counteract the excesses
of ponderous, cautious, "academic" writing, these
publications seem to offer some rather simple solutions
to writing problems—don't use big words, and don't
use long sentences. Unfortunately, although short
words and sentences are desirable if they can be used
without oversimplification, they are not a panacea
for writing problems, and do not necessarily lead to
informative reports.

For instance, in a tabloid newspaper or popular
magazine, the announcement of a new lubricant will
be presented in very readable, perhaps even exciting,
prose. However, to obtain the information he needs on
the new lubricant, the engineer must turn to the manu-
facturer's brochure or to a business magazine, where
the language may contain such "unreadable" multi-
syllable words as "coefficient," "viscosity," and "pressure differential." If the chemical engineer becomes
confused or unhappy with this language, it will be because of the way these words are used, and not because
of the words themselves.

Actually, informative writing involves much more
than the lengths of words, sentences and paragraphs.
While it does not involve "style" in the sense of grace
or elegance, it does involve attention to sentence construction and choice of words. Also, the writer must
know how to present these details logically.

These requirements will become clearer as we proceed with the four tests. Essentially, the tests should
show the engineer not only what presentations are
usually best, but also why they are the best.

(A word of warning: The tests require some knowledge of grammar. Because time is unkind to memory,
grammatical terms will be redefined where appropriate.
If the reader is still hazy after finishing this article,
he should run, not walk, to the nearest grammar text.
A few minutes of intensive study should be enough
to clarify things.)

1—Handling Details

In technical reports, where detail must play a far
more significant role than in most other forms of writing, the goal of the engineer must be too present pertinent details—major and minor—in an informative
way.

Basically, there are two ways to present details in
a sentence; let us first examine the bad way:

> The unlikelihood of meeting orders from the majority
> of its new customers is of concern to the company,
> due to tardiness in the installation of its new manu-
> facturing line.

Here is a good example of what might be called
catalogical writing, in which the writer has cataloged
or equated all his details, so that minor details become
as important as major ones. In other words, there is
no discrimination among details, so that the sentence
is more difficult to understand than it should be.

Catalogical writing of this sort abounds in technical
reports; in fact, more poor writing can be traced to the
cataloging of details than to any other source. Happily,
there is an infallible clue to the cataloging of details:
There is an inordinate use of the prepositional phrase.
By way of proof, let us repeat the example, this time
with prepositional phrases—there are eight of them—
in parentheses:

> The unlikelihood (of meeting orders) (from the ma-
> jority) (of its new customers) is (of concern) (to
> the company), due (to tardiness) (in the installation)
> (of its new manufacturing line).

In sentences, prepositional phrases act as adjectives
or adverbs, that is, they add qualifying detail. (Adjective: The writer *of technical reports* is intelligent.
Here the phrase modifies the noun "writer." Adverb:
The book is lying *on the table.* Here the phrase modified the verb "is lying.")

When the qualifying details in a sentence are put
into prepositional phrases, they are all treated in precisely the same way, technically speaking. But some
details obviously are more important than others;
hence the cataloging of details clearly is a detriment

to informing, because the main details simply do not have the impact on the reader they should have. To repeat, the cataloging of details is the most serious error in most poorly written reports.

How can the technical writer eliminate as many prepositional phrases as possible? The following rewrite of the example says essentially the same thing as the original:

> The company does not know whether it can meet most new-customer orders, because its new manufacturing line is not yet installed.

Here is a good example of *analytical writing*, which is the chief asset of good informative writing. If the clue to catalogical writing is overuse of the prepositional phrase, the clue to good analytical writing is *a judicious use of the dependent clause*. In the rewritten sentence, there are two dependent clauses: "whether it can meet most new-customer orders" and "because its new manufacturing line is not yet installed." There are no prepositional phrases.

For at least three good reasons, dependent clauses help make sentences more informative:

• They analyze detail, highlighting what is important. The very words that introduce clauses strengthen this analysis, because they tell the *when, if, because, who* and so forth of the clause. These are strong words that help the reader interpret what is being described.

• They force the writer to break up the equating of detail that is characteristic of a series of prepositional phrases strung together.

• They make writing sound much more natural. Anyone who doubts this, should reread the examples in the section aloud.

In analytical writing, dependent clauses act as adjectives or adverbs in a sentence; in addition, they may act as nouns. Here are some examples:

I heard *what you said* (noun, object of the verb "heard").

The book *(that) I read* was very interesting (adjective, modifies the noun "book").

He sings *when he takes a shower* (adverb, modifies the verb "sings").

With a little practice, anyone can learn to recognize dependent clauses quickly. These three points need to be remembered: (1) A dependent clause is not a complete statement; (2) It must have an introductory conjunction or relative pronoun (*if, when, which, that, because, since* and the like), although the relative pronoun *that* can often be omitted, as in the second example above. (3) To qualify as a clause, it must have both a subject and a verb, such as *you said, I read,* and *he takes* in the above statements.

Here is another example of the difference between catalogical and analytical writing; prepositional phrases are in parentheses, dependent clauses are italicized:

CATALOGICAL: The need (in the company) (for great increases) (in space), caused (by a steady growth) (in research work), has necessitated the addition (of a new wing) (to the laboratory).

ANALYTICAL: *Because its research work has been*

Why taxpayers get gray

The following excerpt is from the booklet **"New York State Income Tax Forms and Instructions for Filing,"** published by the New York State Income Tax Bureau. The excerpt does not inform as well as it might, chiefly because of the way it presents details. To determine why, readers are invited to subject the excerpt to Test 1.

The return for the period before the change of residence must include all items of income, gain, loss or deduction accrued to the taxpayer up to the time of his change of residence. This includes any amounts not otherwise includable in the return because of an election to report income on an installment basis.

Stated another way, the return for the period prior to the change of residence must be made on the accrual basis whether or not that is the taxpayer's established method of reporting. However, in the case of a taxpayer changing from nonresident to resident status, these accruals need not be made with respect to items derived from or connected with New York sources.

growing steadily, the company is adding a new wing *that will greatly increase its laboratory space*.

Once again, the rewritten sentence eliminates every prepositional phrase. In most catalogical sentences, however, it is difficult if not impossible to eliminate every prepositional phrase, nor should a writer strive to do this. Yet it should be possible to reduce the number of these phrases by at least one-half. The report writer's tool for doing this is, of course, the dependent clause.

Here is a longer example of catalogical writing; the subject matter has to do with two-phase flow systems:

Variance of the mechanism for momentum transfer with respect to the flow pattern is to be expected, but this is not too well understood. Uncertainty even surrounds the correctness of reliance on visual description of flow patterns as a means of identifying the regions involved in possible changes in the mechanisms for momentum transfer. Consideration, in addition, of entrance effects, as well as the possibility of transient or unsteady-state behavior being of importance, makes the relative efficiency of existing correlations seem even more remarkable. Knowledge of the flow pattern and all the physical and geometric properties of the system enables one to predict, in the best correlations, pressure drop within an accuracy of about 25%.

This four-sentence paragraph contains a large number of prepositional phrases: 24, to be exact. There are no dependent clauses. This is a dull, uninformative catalog of details, which the reader must interpret if he is to extract concrete meanings. After wading through several paragraphs of this sort, most engineers would be ready to head for the hills.

A more analytical approach would have benefitted the reader immensely. Actually, the original version of this passage was more analytical; the above excerpt represents this writer's catalogical version of a well-written paragraph that appeared in an article published in CHEMICAL ENGINEERING. Here is the original paragraph, with its analytical approach restored:

It is to be expected that the mechanism for momentum transfer might vary with the flow pattern, but this is not too well understood. It is not even clear whether visual description of flow patterns is sufficient to identify the regions where the mechanisms for momentum transfer might change. When, in addition, entrance effects are considered, as well as the possibility that transient or unsteady-state behavior is of importance, it is remarkable that the existing correlations work as well as they do. If one knows the flow pattern and all the physical and geometric properties of the system, the best correlations will predict the pressure drop within an accuracy of about 25%.

The statistics here are much more encouraging: The number of prepositional phrases has dropped from 24 to 12, and there are now eight dependent clauses, listed below by introductory word, subject, and verb only:

that mechanism might vary
whether description is
where mechanisms might change
when effects are considered
that behavior is
that correlations work
as they do
if one knows

Because each passage is quoted out of context, and because some technical terms might not be familiar to everyone, the passages cannot inform completely. But few persons would deny that the analytical version is much more informative than the catalogical one; it is also much more natural.

The report writer who has begun to suspect that his writing is more catalogical than it ought to be should take the following simple test:

Test 1: Take a short passage from one of your reports (one typewritten, double-spaced page is long enough). In the passage, blot out every prepositional phrase with a red pencil and every dependent clause with a green pencil. Blot out the whole phrase or clause, not just key words. If, when you have finished, there is more red than green on the page, you can be reasonably certain that you are not handling details as informatively as you might.

2—Handling Ideas

If details within a sentence must be presented carefully, it is equally important to concentrate on presenting ideas—sentences themselves—in an informative way. As with details, sentence construction can be catalogical or analytical. Learning to connect ideas or sentences analytically is a major step toward more informative writing.

In any paragraph, some ideas obviously are more important than others. But the writer who catalogs ideas refuses to recognize this fact of life. As a result, his technical reports are apt to follow the pattern of the following paragraph (in each sentence, the main subject and verb are in italics):

This expanding drum *brake* for motors *has* shoes made of electrical steel laminations, mounted on a common anchor pin. *They/serve* as armatures for the brake release solenoid. The *drum/is* aluminum. The brake *lining/is bonded* directly to laminated shoes. The release *solenoid/is connected* across electric motor terminals. *It/is energized* when the motor starts, holding the shoes away from the drum. *Interrupting* current to the solenoid automatically *applies* shoes to the drum, with brake pressure applied by a helical spring between the shoes. Manual *release/is* by a cam, applying pressure below the pivot point of the shoes. The drum *brake/is* available for mounting on NEMA C frames or independently housed and foot mounted. *It/is* available with 2 to 20 foot-pound ratings.

A quick examination of this ten-sentence paragraph reveals an interesting fact: Almost every sentence begins with the main subject and verb. What we have here is a tedious catalog of ideas, each technically constructed in precisely the same way. By limiting himself to this approach—subject-verb, subject-verb, subject-verb—the writer has made informing virtually impossible. In this paragraph, the main ideas simply don't get through clearly to the reader, because minor ideas are given the same construction. Too, it is extremely difficult to tie ideas together when this pattern predominates; this sort of writing doesn't "track."

In informative writing, sentence construction is much more varied. Consider the following excerpt from another article that was published in CHEMICAL ENGINEERING (once again, the main subject and verb only of each sentence are italicized):

Operating and maintenance *supervisors* of an oxygen generating plant *were* quick to credit polyelectrolytes with increasing plant-operating efficiency, reducing downtime, and eliminating manual mud removal.

The *plant*, located on the site of a steel mill, *supplies* oxygen for steel making. Although it has a closed cooling system and makes up with clean water, a sticky *mud/was settling* in its pipes, heat exchangers and compressor jackets because atmospheric dust from the mill was entering the water through the cooling tower.

The *mud* greatly *reduced* heat-exchanger efficiency, *caused* power consumption to go up and operating efficiency to go down. Because the operating temperatures of the oxygen compressor ran high, the *compressor/had* to be shut down every two months and manually cleaned to restore temperatures to design levels. Besides the expense of cleaning, *oxygen/ was vented* when the compressor was down.

In this passage, arrangement of main subject and verb is much more varied, as it should be. Some of the main subjects and verbs are preceded by dependent clauses, others by phrases. The writing does "track," and, incidentally, is much more natural than the catalog of ideas previously quoted.

Test 2: In a passage from your writing, underline the main subject and main verb in each sentence. (In this test, ignore the subjects and verbs of dependent clauses.) If the main subject and verb appear at the beginning of more than half the sentences in the passage, you have good reason to believe that you are not presenting ideas informatively.

The percentage (one-half) given in this test is of course arbitrary and perhaps a bit high, but it does give you a goal to strive for. If it does nothing else, it should provoke you into making a few thoughtful changes, such as putting a few connective phrases or clauses between ideas.

3—Abstract vs. Concrete Nouns

We can define the ideal engineering report as one that every reader will interpret exactly the same way.

Very often, engineering reports are hard to interpret not because they are too technical but because they contain too many ordinary, everyday words of a certain kind: abstract nouns. Abstract nouns are by definition ambiguous, and the more often they crop up, the less informative the writing.

Admittedly, abstraction appears in all forms of writing, including technical reports. Words like *profits*, *industry*, *economics*, and *manufacturing* are as abstract in their own way as words like *truth*, *love*, and *justice*. Whenever a writer has to make a general statement (and he often does), abstract nouns are likely to creep in. The following statement, for example, is open to several interpretations, chiefly because of the abstract nouns (italicized) that are present:

> The *question* of where the company will locate its new plant depends upon such *factors* as the employment *situation*, local tax *conditions*, and transportation *facilities*.

Here is one concrete interpretation of this statement: "The company wants to build its new plant near a major rail center, where local taxes are low and skilled labor is plentiful." This is, however, only one interpretation—not necessarily the correct one. No one except the actual writer of the statement can hope to know precisely what is meant.

In many technical reports, there are sentences that could be expressed more concretely. Generally, the main subjects of these sentences are abstract nouns. Here are some examples:

Leave abstraction to the philosophers

The excerpt below, taken from John Dewey's "The Quest for Certainty" (1929), is a good example of the abstraction that is typical of philosophical writing. Readers who subject the passage to Test 3 will discover that 17 of the abstract nouns and awkward constructions listed in the text appear in the excerpt.

There is one common character of all scientific operations which it is necessary to note. *They are such as disclose relationships.* A simple case is the operation by which length is defined by one object placed end upon end upon another object so many times. This type of operation, repeated under conditions themselves defined by specified operations, not merely fixes the relation of two things to each other called their *length*, but defines a generalized concept of length. This conception in connection with other operations, such as those which define mass and time, become instruments by means of which a multitude of relations between bodies can be established. Thus the conceptions which define units of measurement of space, time and motion become the intellectual instrumentalities by which all sorts of things with no qualitative similarity with one another can be compared and brought within the same system. To the original gross experience of things there is superadded another type of experience, the product of deliberate art, of which *relations* rather than qualities are the significant subject-matter. These connections are as much experienced as are the qualitatively diverse and irreducible objects of original natural experiences.

The condition of the centrifuge is such that it re-requires replacement.

The problem of increasing production was resolved when the company purchased an additional machine.

The use of a computer will help a company to process its payroll faster.

Corrective surgery on sentences of this sort, to eliminate abstract nouns like *condition*, *problem*, and *use*, is not difficult. Usually, all the writer need do is look immediately behind the abstract noun, where he will

Avoid these pallid, passive verbs

The passive verbs in the following list are especially weak and should be avoided whenever possible by one of the three techniques described on the opposite page.

is accomplished	is facilitated
is attained	is featured
is based	is involved
is considered	is made
is designated	is observed
is effected	is permitted
is employed	is provided
is enabled	is used
is enjoyed	is utilized

find a prepositional phrase with a concrete noun as its object. Promoting this noun to main subject produces a more concrete sentence:

The centrifuge needs to be replaced.

Production increased when the company purchased an additional machine.

A computer will help a company to process its pay-roll faster.

Sometimes the concrete or real subject of a sentence does not come immediately after the abstract main subject. But with a little practice, any writer can learn to spot the real subject of a sentence quickly.

Abstract nouns are bad for informative writing in another respect: They often attract awkward construc-tions that have no place in good writing. If the writer replaces an abstract noun with a concrete one, he often will find that the awkward construction disappears au-tomatically. Here are some examples (abstract nouns and awkward constructions are italicized):

ABSTRACT:

The *nature* of helium is *such that* it is a gas at room temperature.

The *reason* production stopped was *due to the fact that* the workers went out on strike.

The *use* of the new compounds *in connection with* the

cleaning of boiler tubes will result in the *elimination* of scale.

CONCRETE:

Helium is a gas at room temperature.

Production stopped because the workers went out on strike.

The new compounds will eliminate scale from boiler tubes.

The following abstract nouns should be eliminated, if possible, from technical reports:

ability	effort	order	relation(ship)
activity	employment	persuasion	respect
basis	extent	policy	responsibility
case	facility	position	result
character	factor	possibility	situation
circumstance	instance	practice	standpoint
concept(ion)	intent	problem	substance
concern	interest	prospect	system
condition	manner	purpose	type
connection	measure	quality	use
course	method	question	utilization
degree	nature	reason	view
effect	necessity	reference	

Some of the nouns in this list can, of course, have concrete meanings at times. But there is a great deal of difference between the concrete "The instrument *case* is in *use*" and the abstract "In the *case* of the missing instrument, the *use* of our insurance policy may minimize the loss." The objection here is to the abstract usage of these nouns, which results in need-less verbosity.

Here is a list of awkward phrases that crop up with great regularity in technical writing. These should also be eliminated:

according as to whether	in the course of
as far as....goes	in the form of
as regards	in the interests of
associated with	in the light of
as to	in view of
by means of	on the basis of
due to the fact that	on the order of
for the purpose of	on the part of
for the sake of	relative to
from the standpoint of	such that
in a manner of	to the extent that
in connection with	with reference to
in order to	with regard to
in relation to	with respect to
in the case of	with a view to

The above lists of abstract nouns and awkward con-structions suggest a third test for the report writer:

Test 3—In the passage from your writing that you are analyzing, draw a circle around every abstract noun and awkward construction that appears. If more than six circles appear on the page, your writ-ing probably is more abstract than it should be.

4—Passive vs. Active Verbs

In informative writing, active verbs usually out-number passive verbs by a large ratio. When too many passive verbs creep into writing, prose tends to be-come unnatural, less direct, and far less forceful than it should be.

Passive verbs are easier to recognize than to avoid. Any verb that consists of some form of the auxiliary *to be,* followed by the past participle of the verb, is passive. In sentences, the subject of an active verb initiates the action described by the verb ("Jones *drives* his car to work."); the subject of a passive verb, on the other hand, receives the action described by the verb ("The car *is driven* to work by Jones.").

The following passage, in which every verb but one is passive, is typical of the unnatural writing that appears in many reports (verbs are italicized):

> This handbook *has been written* to provide an authoritative single source of information on all facets of temperature control in these systems. It *is issued* for use by all who *are concerned* with design, development and utilization of components and/or complete systems. This revision, as *will be* the case when future revisions *are considered* to be appropriate or necessary, *is based* on experience gained in usage of the handboook over a given period of time during which certain advancements *have been made* in the state-of-the-art. This book *is* not *intended* to supersede any regulations, contracts, or documents referenced therein.

The contention here is that at least half the passive verbs that appear in technical writing can and should be replaced by active verbs. When this happens, writing almost always becomes more natural than the passage just quoted, and more informative. Our argument is not with the passive verb itself—no one can hope to avoid it completely—but with its consistent overuse.

There are, of course, many ways to rewrite sentences so that passive verbs become active. The three following techniques, however, accomplish this goal perhaps more easily than others:

1. In a sentence, look immediately behind the passive verb, where you will often find an infinitive that can be converted into an active verb that replaces the passive verb. Examples:

PASSIVE: Coal is used to heat the plant.
ACTIVE: Coal heats the plant.

PASSIVE: Tests were made to verify the hypothesis.
ACTIVE: Tests verified the hypothesis.

PASSIVE: In the process, a catalyst is provided to speed the reaction.
ACTIVE: In the process, a catalyst speeds the reaction.

2. If an infinitive does not follow a weak passive verb, try converting a noun that appears in the sentence into an active verb. Examples:

PASSIVE: Sulphuric acid was employed in the removal of surface impurities from the specimen.
ACTIVE: Sulphuric acid removed surface impurities from the specimen.

PASSIVE: Completion of the process is effected by a rust-preventive coating.
ACTIVE: A rust-preventive coating completes the process.

PASSIVE: Correction of production errors was obtained through laboratory tests.
ACTIVE: The laboratory tests corrected production errors.

3. Switch from an impersonal style, which is usually passive, to a personal style, which is usually active. Examples:

PASSIVE: Several laboratory tests were conducted on the specimens.
ACTIVE: We conducted several laboratory tests on the specimens.

PASSIVE: After installation of the new equipment, production was doubled.
ACTIVE: After installing the new equipment, the company doubled production.

PASSIVE: Procedures were initiated to reduce plant accidents.
ACTIVE: They initiated procedures to reduce plant accidents.

Some report writers do not favor a personal style. The tone of technical writing, these people feel, is objective and impersonal. There is, of course, nothing wrong with an impersonal style, except that too much of impersonal writing is passive, abstract and catalogical. Also, there are times when the reader will want to know who did what. Note, for instance, that the statement "The reactor that was ordered was inspected" is not only more awkward but also less informative than "the materials engineer inspected the reactor that Dept. X had ordered."

Although impersonal writing can be informative, most professional writers prefer to be personal, simply because it makes the task of informing easier. In personal writing, people do something, but in impersonal writing something is done to things. The writer who is consistently impersonal tends to become consistently unnatural in his use of language.

In seeking to reduce the number of passive verbs in his writing, the report writer should try first of all to eliminate the really weak passive verbs that appear in the box on page 10. These verbs almost never carry their own weight in sentences. When they appear, sentence construction is likely to become awkward and overly indirect.

Here is a fourth test that will show the report writer whether he is informing as well as he might:

Test 4—In a representative passage from your writing, underline the first 20 verbs. Count two points for each passive verb that appears in the list on page 150, one point for all other passive verbs. If your total score is more than 10, you have evidence that your writing is more passive than it should be.

What the Tests Show

From the examples that appear here, the reader should see that the four tests are intimately related. Almost always, catalogical writing is passive, abstract and impersonal. Analytical writing, on the other hand, is usually concrete, active and personal. Very often, making corrections in one area will automatically improve writing in other areas. Thus, the writer who consciously avoids the cataloging of details is likely to present ideas informatively, actively and concretely.

Watch Your Words

Engineers, and particularly engineering managers, have to be familiar with many specialized vocabularies. For better communication, make words your hobby.

VINCENT VINCI, Lockheed Electronics Co.

The engineer usually has special problems in communicating effectively because he is a specialist operating in a world of generalists. Sometimes he uses ordinary words with specialized neanings—mass, velocity, mole, free energy. This can cause many difficulties. To illustrate in somewhat different context:

"There's glory for you!"

"I don't know what you mean by 'glory,'" Alice said.

"I meant, 'there's a nice knock-down argument for you!'"

"But, 'glory' doesn't mean a 'nice knock-down argument,'" Alice objected.

"When I use a word," Humpty Dumpty said in a rather scornful tone, "it means just what I choose it to mean—neither more nor less."

So wrote Lewis Carroll in "Through the Looking Glass," illustrating what is usually called today, a breakdown in communications.

Communications, by its very nature, requires both a sender and a receiver; its medium is a language (or code) composed of a system of symbols based on the experiences of two or more people. However, the experiences of people (just as in the case of Alice and Humpty Dumpty) are never exactly the same. Therefore the symbols often have an individualized character, rather than having the same meaning for all people.

Symbols (or words) of language, then, have varied meanings and usages. And yet there is a common ground or body of agreement associated with words. All of us, without fully realizing it, enter into an agreement through everyday usage. But, because of the dual character of words, as we will discuss, communication is never precise or exact. Both the interdependence of the communications process and dual nature of our code of verbal symbols put a responsibility on the speaker and the listener. They must learn to manage meanings, selecting and combining words with utmost care if they really wish to be understood or to understand.

Words—Dual Meanings

Meanings assigned to all words possess two distinguishing characteristics—denotation and connotation. Denotation, sometimes referred to as extension, is the meaning or idea conveyed by a word through common (widespread experience and agreement) usage, while connotation (intention) is the many thoughts, emotional and personal, which are attributed to a word. Certainly the word democracy has a distinct (denotative) meaning; however, its connotative aspects encompass a broader base. Russians, Swiss and Englishmen would definitely attach widely varying emotional and personal meanings to this word.

In both formal and informal communication situations, all of us run the risk of being misunderstood because of an ill choice of a word or combination of words. Since there are hundreds of thousands of words in our language and each word has dual meanings, we cannot hope to master even a majority of them.

What each of us can do is to attempt to know the common or agreed meanings of many of our often-used words. Even this task is not a simple undertaking. If we strive to know the common meanings (denotative) of frequently used words and if we succeed to some degree, then part of the problem of effective communication is surmounted. Then, hopefully, as Hamlet said, you can suit the word to the action; at least, the action you expect of the listener (and not the gesture, as Shakespeare meant).

Why Choose

To tailor your words, you must be intimately familiar with the fiber of their cloth. Though a particular word, uttered in a particular manner, during a particular circumstance, may have completely changed its color, weight, and size, it has as its foundation a rather precise, commonly understood or conventional, meaning. A word's uniqueness must be known if it is to be chosen to convey an idea. Perhaps John Ruskin in Education Means Knowing Words, from "Sesame and Lilies, I," expressed this conviction best.

"I tell you earnestly and authoritatively (I know I am right in this) you must get into the habit of looking intensely at words, and assuring yourself of their meaning, syllable by syllable—nay, letter by letter. You might read all the books in the British Museum (if you could live long enough) and remain an utterly "illiterate," uneducated person; but if you read ten pages of a good book, letter by letter—that is to say, with real accuracy—you are for evermore in some measure an educated person.

The entire difference between education and non-education (as regards the merely intellectual part of it), consists in this accuracy. A well educated gentleman may not know many languages, may not be able to speak any but his own, may have read very few books. But whatever language he knows, he knows precisely; whatever word he pronounces, he pronounces rightly; above all, he is learned in the peerage of words; knows the words of true descent and ancient blood, at a glance, from words of modern canaille; remembers all their ancestry, their intermarriages, distant relationships, and the extent to which they were admitted, and offices they held, among the national noblesse of words at any time, and in any country."

A Word to The Engineer

At this point, you might be asking, what has all this to do with engineering, chemistry, or any other scientific profession?

The scientist has more problems in communicating than the non-scientist. There are perhaps four hurdles placed in the scientist's path to effective expression. First, he generally receives less total schooling in the humanities, particularly English, literature, composition, and speech, than his fellow liberal-arts classmate. Secondly, regardless of his discipline, the scientist has to contend with the terminology of his specialty. From the atomic expert's "barn" to the computer designer's "byte," there's a world of words in technology alone. It's difficult enough to keep abreast of the acronyms. Additionally, a third element of his society plagues the scientist; that is, the fast changing and expanding technology with its concomitant birth of new words to describe new breakthroughs, processes and products. A fourth influence on the scientist's vocabulary is his role as a manager. If he is both manager and scientist, he needs to deal with terms widely used by management, such as overhead, return on investment, accounts receivable, and inventory.

Putting it all together, we then have the man-scientist-manager who must communicate effectively with other men, other scientists, other managers, subordinates, peers, and superiors—all of whom know and understand various words according to their experience and education. Just about every scientist or engineer has sat in on a meeting and observed two people arguing over a point expressing their ideas in different terms while he realizes they are really saying the same thing. Because the speakers place different meanings on various words, they see only disagreement.

In similar fashion, you have undoubtedly listened to a convention speaker describe a process and noted how easily the speaker could have improved understanding had he exercised greater care in selecting his words.

Words, Words Everywhere

Just as Sousa states in "Poetry? For Engineers?"*, scientists need to realize the impact of words. Sousa recommended that engineers write poetry. I recommend that you make words your hobby. Words can be a portable hobby, for you find them everywhere—in newspapers, magazines, books; on billboards, emanating from radios, televisions, and recorders; flowing out of the mouths of babes, geniuses, dumb blondes, beggars, salesmen, hippies, democrats, republicans, musicians, secretaries, presidents and janitors. Each word is discovered clothed in a variety of colors and dress, intoned in anger, desperation, humility, hate, desire, love and indifference. Some words are savored, sputtered, squashed, caressed, abandoned and abused—some are pregnant with meaning, punctuated with delight, or stripped of any sense and denied their dignity.

All are subjected to this barrage of words. But few do more than let the stream of words flow past. To make a hobby of words, you must pluck specimens from the stream. You must examine the ways in which the meaning of the word differs from that of the last speaker (or writer) who used it. Has the speaker used the best word to express his meaning, or do you know a better one? Did he pronounce it differently from the way you would? (If he did, you had better make a note to check later—one of you is probably wrong.) Is a word used in a particularly apt way? You may want to remember it for your own use later.

Regardless of where you find a word, Proverbs† states, "A word fitly spoken is like apples of gold in pictures of silver."

*"Poetry? For Engineers?", A. J. Sousa, p. 20.
†Prov. 25.11.

Meet the Author

Vincent Vinci is Manager of Public Relations for Lockheed Electronics Co., U. S. Highway 22, Plainfield, NJ 07060. Before joining public relations, he was supervisor of presentations, proposals and reports. He is a graduate of Seton Hall University, and has been a member of its staff, teaching courses in speech. He has also taught effective writing at Newark College of Engineering.

ROB

ROBBED OF A HOME RUN

STEAL

STOLE SECOND

Words: Chance or Choice

Careless choice of words makes for misunderstandings and bad communication.
Pick the word that means exactly what you want to convey.

VINCENT VINCI, Lockheed Electronics Co.

If you arrived home one day and said to your wife, "Dear, you have a face that would stop a clock!", you could wager that statement would produce at least one lump on your head. If, however, you walked in and said, "Dear, when I look at you, time stands still!," you might receive an appreciative smile. The reactions produced by these statements take place because most listeners assume that a statement or word carries the meaning they would attribute to it if they had said it.

This simple story illustrates the use of diction. If I were to ask the reader to define "diction," the most likely response would be something like "vocal expression, enunciation or manner of speaking." That reply is the secondary definition; the primary meaning of "diction" is the "choice of words to express ideas."

Selecting the Right Words

Effective communication, regardless of medium, requires the communicator to master both voice and diction. No matter how well pronounced his words,

a speaker will be ineffective if he hasn't selected them carefully—tailoring them to the meaning he desires to convey to his audience.

The first burden in the communication process then rests on the speaker or writer. He must select the correct words or combination of words based on his knowledge of the words' accepted or commonly held meaning. A speaker should not use a word or words that have a private or exclusive meaning (unless his audience is limited to those who also share the private meaning). Using a word that has a private meaning is about as effective as trying to dig a tunnel with a table fork.

Words of a Feather

In most social, conversational situations (that is, nonbusiness), there is the tendency to choose words with less communicative care than in a business exchange. Because of this, we often find ourselves explaining what we mean, in order to correct a misunderstood concept. In business situations, however, we exercise greater care in selecting words, attempting to avoid misinterpretation of instructions or information.

Choosing the correct word (or is it "right" word?) sometimes becomes difficult because there are a number of words that seem to have the same meaning. Correct and right, for instance, for the most part are used interchangeably. Yet, these two words do have distinct meanings. If they had exactly the same meaning, there wouldn't be any need to have two words when one would suffice. "Correct" denotes absence from fault when compared to some standard, while "right" signifies conformity to truth or fact. It is "correct" that two plus two equals five if that is the standard established by the teacher. Since two plus two equals five does not conform to fact, it is not "right." In almost every instance of ordinary usage, however, we could readily substitute one for the other and be understood.

Equal understanding is not the case with "ambiguous" and "equivocal." In the second statement of the opening story, the speaker utters, "Dear, when I look at you, time stands still." Was he being ambiguous or equivocal? The answer lies in his intent. When the speaker inadvertently obscures the meaning, he is being ambiguous. When he attempts to cloud or confuse, he is being equivocal.

In baseball parlance, a runner "steals" second while a batter is "robbed" of a home run. Why aren't the terms reversed? Why doesn't the runner rob second base and the outfielder steal the home run? True, they don't seem to sound right that way, but there is more than "ear" involved in correct usage. Although both rob and steal are felonious acts, rob usually is accomplished through fear and the victim is aware (and helpless) of the (as the police say) perpetration. Steal, on the other hand, conveys stealth; it's a furtive act of appropriation. Since the runner cannot take a base without getting the "jump" (surreptitious lead) on the pitcher, he then steals, not robs, the base. The outfielder accomplishes his felonious act in full view of the victim—there is nothing clandestine—therefore, he has committed robbery. Within the act of stealing there are specific types of thievery including filching, pilfering and purloining.

In a tense moment of a courtroom drama, the prosecutor asks the defendant, "What's your excuse for committing this odious crime?" A defendant versed in diction would simply reply, "I have no excuse, I have an alibi." If his answer were different, he would be admitting he committed the crime. An excuse implies that he did commit the offense but he had a reason, while an alibi is a statement of being elsewhere than the place where the crime occurred and is tantamount to saying, "I'm innocent." On the other hand, colloquially, an alibi is regarded as a flimsy excuse.

Two other words often interchanged without causing misunderstanding are sofa and couch. But you would be concerned if your analyst told you to lie down on the sofa. You would wonder if he realized the difference—a sofa is designed primarily for sitting (even though probably everyone has taken a nap on a sofa) and usually has a back and arms. A couch is used for reclining and does not have a back or arms. Along with sofa, there are upholstered items such as settee, chesterfield, davenport, lounge ,and dos-a-dos.

Choose or Confuse

It is easy to confuse a listener just by choosing the wrong word. Manufacturers of detergent and toothpaste do it every day. Do you know that the "large" tube of toothpaste isn't really so large. Although the economy size is smaller, both the jumbo and family size are larger than the large.

The Russians say we are "capitalistic," implying that big businesses govern the economic future of the people. They never consider it as meaning a free-enterprise system.

In Wonderland, the March Hare said to Alice, "You should say what you mean." "I do," Alice hastily replied: "At least—at least I mean what I say—that's the same thing, you know." "Not the same thing a bit!", said the Hatter. "Why, you might just as well say that 'I see what I eat' is the same thing as 'I eat what I see!'"

Just as Lewis Carroll's Hare advised Alice to say what she meant, you should say what you mean. If you mean a bungalow, don't say house. If you mean a German shepherd dog and not just any dog (or even a German shepherd), say it.

It is the speaker's responsibility to choose his words with care and not leave them to chance. He must watch his words. Then, as the Duchess replied in Alice in Wonderland, "That's nothing to what I could say if I chose." ■

Meet the Author

Vincent Vinci is Manager of Public Relations for Lockheed Electronics Co., U. S. Highway 22, Plainfield, NJ 07060. Before joining public relations, he was supervisor of presentations, proposals and reports. He is a graduate of Seton Hall University, and has been a member of its staff, teaching courses in speech. He has also taught effective writing at Newark College of Engineering.

Initials, Acronyms & Chaos

DOD · AIChE · TEMA · FORTRAN · TAPPI · SOCMA · NASA

FYI (for your information), the use of pronounceable and unpronounceable sets of initial letters has muddled communication. Let's stop ASAP (as soon as possible).

ROY V. HUGHSON, Associate Editor

Everyone knows what the initials AIChE and ACS mean. AIChE is always the American Inst. of Chemical Engineers. And ACS is always the American Camellia Soc. Right?

Well, not always. Sometimes ACS is the American Ceramics Soc. And if you're in the military, it's the Asst. Chief of Staff (unless you happen to be in the Royal Navy, in which case it means Admiralty Computing Service). For electrical engineers, it's Alternating Current, Synchronous—except for the computer branch of the trade to whom it means Adaptive Control System.

(Sorry about that, American Chemical Soc.)

We're so bombarded by initials and acronyms, that half the time we're lost. Quick now, just what government organizations are these: FAA, FCC, ICC, FPC, FDA?*

Too hard? Well, let's try a few that often appear in this magazine: TAPPI, TEMA, ASTM, SOCMA, AIME (be careful of that last one, there's more to it than meets the eye).†

Acronyms Are a Puzzle, Too

An acronym is a pronounceable word that is formed from initial letters or parts of words. You can't very well pronounce FCC (and it's better not to try), so that is simply an initialism. But you can pronounce NASA (Natl. Aeronautics and Space Administration), so it is an acronym.

There were few acronyms in common use before World War II (WW II), though ANZAC (Australian and New Zealand Army Corps) dates back

*Federal Aviation Administration, Federal Communications Commission, Interstate Commerce Commission, Federal Power Commission, Food and Drug Administration.

†Technical Assn. of the Pulp and Paper Industry, Tubular Exchanger Mfrs. Assn., American Soc. for Testing and Materials, Synthetic Organic Chemical Mfrs. Assn., American Inst. of Mining, Metallurgical and Petroleum Engineers.

about a half-century or so, to WW I (World War I).

The real budding of acronyms came from the military, which gave us radar (radio detection and ranging), sonar (sound navigation and ranging) and SNAFU (situation normal, all "fouled" up).

The Navy has long had a penchant for acronyms. The Navy Bureau of Personnel, for example, is known as BUPERS (pronounced B'YOU-pers). At the start of WW II, Admiral King (the Navy's top officer) was CINCUS (Commander-in-Chief, U.S.). In best Navy style, it was pronounced "sink-us." After the debacle at Pearl Harbor, "sink-us" seemed less than apt, so the acronym was hurriedly changed to COMINCH (Commander-in-Chief).

The Army has fallen into the same evil habits. Gen. Creighton W. Abrams, for example, was known as COMUSMACV (Commander, U.S. Forces, Military Assistance Command Vietnam).

Most of us know that "radar" is an acronym. But how many realize that "gestapo" is too? Gestapo stands for Geheime Staats-polizei (secret state police).

While we're on foreign languages, here's a poser. What does LSD stand for? Sure, any chemical dictionary will tell us that it's lysergic acid diethylamide, but that's LAD. Where did the "S" come from? It took me two years to find the answer to that one. It seems that the drug was first investigated in the German-speaking part of Switzerland. They tagged it LSD because the German word for acid is Säure. In German, the chemical is called Lyserginsäure Diäthylamid—LSD!

Acronyms of Acronyms

Probably the worst addiction to acronyms* is found in computerese, that strange jargon of computer engineers and programmers.

*Some nine years ago, CE's (Chemical Engineering's) copy editor, Henry Gordon, coined a name for this strange addiction. He calls it "acronymphomania." Someone has since called it "acronymania," in print, but I like Henry's word better.

Most everyone knows about the acronym FOR-TRAN (formula translator) but how about an acronym that contains that acronym—GRAF (graphic additions to FORTRAN), which is a language designed to facilitate the use of graphics on the computer.

Then there's NELIAC (Navy Electronics Laboratory international ALGOL compiler) which contains the acronym ALGOL (algorithmic language).

I'm not sure how to categorize L⁶ (Bell Telephone Laboratories' low-level linked list language).

The simplified computer language BASIC is supposed to mean beginner's all-purpose symbolic instruction code, but I'll bet that "BASIC" came first and they made it into an "acronym" later.

My favorite, though, is JOVIAL, an unfunny language widely used by DOD (Dept. of Defense). It came about when a programmer, Jules Schwartz, drafted a modification for IAL (international algebraic language). So JOVIAL is Jules' own version of international algebraic language.

Pronouncing the Unpronounceable

Initialisms are generally unpronounceable, but people try to pronounce them anyway. For example, during WW II, the high-frequency direction finder (HFDF) came to be pronounced "huffduff."

The Federal National Mortgage Assn. has the initials FNMA, and the financial community usually pronounces it as "Fanny Mae." Indeed, you'll find Fanny Mae in print more often than FNMA in the financial columns of newspapers.

And electrical engineers have taken to "pronouncing" the abbreviation "pf." (picofarad or 10^{-12} farad). So if you hear an EE speaking of a "50-puff capacitor" you can translate it as 50 picofarads.

Companies Go To Initials

International Business Machines Corp. is known as IBM to most people. But this is colloquial.

Now, though, companies are using initials as their official corporate names. For example:
- FMC Corp. (formerly Food Machinery Corp.).
- PPG Industries (formerly Pittsburgh Plate Glass).
- TRW Inc. (formerly Thompson Ramo Wooldridge).
- EG&G Inc. (once Edgerton, Germeshausen & Grier, Inc. (EG&G is certainly easier to pronounce).

Societies

Engineering societies are generally known by speaking their initials, even when they can be pronounced as words like NACE (Natl. Assn. of Corrosion Engineers). And IEEE (Inst. of Electrical and Electronics Engineers) is usually spoken as "eye-triple-e." (It is possible to pronounce IEEE—the sound has been described as the one a man makes when falling off a cliff.)

A Plea for Information

After WW II, the Allies set up an organization called AMGOT (Allied Military Govt. of Occupied Territories). Shortly after, this was shortened to AMG (Allied Military Govt.). The reason, as reported in magazines and newspapers, was that "amgot" was an obscene word in one of the Middle Eastern languages. Now, almost 25 years later, I still haven't found out what the word really means. If any reader knows, I'd appreciate a note explaining it.

Help for the Reader

CHEMICAL ENGINEERING (*CE*) has a rule that requires that the editors define most initialisms and acronyms the first time they appear in an article. But, often, this isn't enough. A few months ago, we ran a news story with 11 acronyms. Each was defined when first used, but I couldn't keep track of them, and had to continually flip back through the pages to find their meanings. If more than two or three are used, I feel that the writer owes it to the reader to collect them in a nomenclature box. I did this, for example, in my article on standards that appeared in the issue of Nov. 17, 1969.

There's another problem that editors face: When is a term so well known that it isn't necessary to define it? For example, there's the new system of metric units known as SI units (Système International d'Unités). How long will we have to keep on spelling out the meaning of SI?

In this case, there's the added problem that spelling it out doesn't explain anything. Even the engineer who knows no French can figure out that the words mean "International System of Units," but knowing this doesn't help much. And if he knows what the system is all about, he probably knows what SI means. It's a puzzlement.

Towards Chaos

There is no doubt that initialisms and acronyms serve a purpose. They save us from having to repeat long strings of words.

But the proliferation of these terms makes for trouble in communicating because the reader has to stop too often and try to remember what each queer combination of letters stands for.

If we keep on at the rate we've been going, our technical literature is going to become incomprehensible. This may lead to CHAOS (*Committee for Halting Acronymic Obliteration of Sense*). ∎

Meet the Author

Roy V. (Victor) Hughson is an associate editor of CE (CHEMICAL ENGINEERING). He edits feature articles, and the YYJ (You & Your Job) department. He has B.Ch.E. (Bachelor of Chemical Engineering) and M.A. (Master of Arts) degrees from NYU (New York University). He is a member of AIChE (American Inst. of Chemical Engineers), ACS (American Chemical Soc.), IFT (Inst. of Food Technologists), NASW (Natl. Assn. of Science Writers), and AAAS (American Assn. for the Advancement of Science).

The Jargon Jungle

Jargon tends to obfuscate meaning and so inhibits communication. Generally,
you will do better by avoiding it. But first you have to recognize it.

W. H. WEISS, Professional Engineer

How often have you read something like this?—"It is believed that these data, particularly those with regard to the ethical considerations of the problem, may be interpreted as not entirely unrelated to the questions raised concerning it, and justify the investigation undertaken in this respect to the extent that the data are worthwhile in reaching a satisfactory solution to the problem."

Understanding what the writer of the above had in mind is very difficult because his sentence is a form of jargon—here, a lot of words are used to say little or nothing. Unfortunately, similar words and sentences sometimes appear in the memos and reports of professional people, including engineers. Jargon is the name for verbal fuzziness of various sorts, such as wordiness and abstract words that add nothing to the meaning of a statement.

Have you ever started explaining an engineering problem to some friends (or perhaps workers from another department) only to have them ask questions that indicated they didn't know what you were talking about? Too many of us talk and write over the heads of others. Most of the time, we are unaware that we are not being understood. By watching our language, we could do a much better job of communicating.

Forms of Jargon

There are several kinds of jargon users that we must contend with both on the job and in our relations with persons who are not engineers.

One type makes simple ideas obscure by using specialized and technical words. It is too much to expect a janitor to understand that hydrochloric acid would be hard on drain pipes if he were told that "the corrosive residue is incompatible with metallic permanence." How many nonengineers know what the Reynolds number indicates? The production super-

visor should not be expected to be familiar with interaction parameters. These matters can be explained in simpler words, ones which nonengineers understand.

Another type overuses words. This style is favored by the long-winded person who uses several words to say what can be said in one or two: "My trend of thought leads me to the conclusion that . . ." instead of "I think that . . ." "This is in reference to . . ." in place of "This refers to . . ." and "did not succeed in achieving its objective" instead of "failed."

Then there is the type of jargon that substitutes fancy or "respectable" expressions for those that might suggest something unpleasant or of low level. For example, the titles of menial jobs change for the better: janitors become "custodians," garbage collectors graduate to "sanitary officers," and reporters rise to "publicity directors." We develop "thermonuclear devices" instead of hydrogen bombs.

Why Use Jargon?

Why do people use jargon? There are several reasons.

First, a person may become so accustomed to the words of his profession that he simply forgets that not all people use and understand them. Jargon is the talk of the man who is so wrapped up in his job or hobby that only another person having the same interests knows what he is talking about. Bankers and lawyers continually have this problem, and engineers may also. Unless these individuals try to use words of the layman, watch their listeners for understanding, and realize that their words may not be understood, they will probably fail in their communication efforts.

Second, a user of jargon may be trying to impress others with his knowledge or experience. He's the amateur acting like a professional. He may have heard scientists discussing a theory and now uses some of their terms. He may imply he's an authority on space travel by using the words of the experts in this field. And he may use specialized words that will mislead his supervisors about his knowledge of a particular subject.

Third, the user may feel that talking jargon gains him acceptance and cooperation. If you want to be accepted by a special group, must you not speak their language? A supervisor may try to use the worker's slang in hopes they will consider him "one of the boys." And an accountant may use (and sometimes misuse) engineering terms in asking for help from an engineer on a cost problem.

Fourth, jargon may serve to cover up a person's lack of anything important to say, or to say things in a way that makes it difficult for others to disagree. He does this by deliberately making his meanings and intentions unclear. A consultant might try to avoid being clearly understood in order that his client will not see his incompetence. A writer may be unable to reason logically or to present interesting material; he may use pretentious language to conceal these facts.

Fifth, using jargon is a way of avoiding direct statements. The politician likes it because he can give stock comments on issues to gain a desired effect with a minimum of intellectual effort and without committing himself to a definite program. An engineer might use it to explain a design difficulty to management when he isn't quite sure of himself or hopes to cover up his inability to cope with the problem.

Jargon's Pitfall

Using jargon makes us become lazy communicators. Look how easy it is to start letters by saying, "We appreciate your apprising us of this matter and certainly will give it due consideration." "You are advised that . . ." "As a matter of interest, we shall be interested in knowing . . ." Such writing is cold and stiff. The reader may feel the lack of true concern on the part of the writer.

Avoiding Jargon

How do we avoid jargon in our talking and writing? How can we communicate to be more easily understood?

We can express ourselves as simply as possible. We can try to let facts speak for themselves instead of giving them more emotion and dramatics than they deserve. We can stay away from clever and cute expressions; we can eliminate words that have fancy or "smart" connotations. And we can cut unnecessary words. Simple words and sentence structure are easier to understand and far more effective. We can forget about trying to impress others when all we are asked to do is inform them.

The conditions and situations under which communications take place should be considered. Circumstances should determine the tone and style of words we use. Is the setting formal or informal? Will simple words or slightly uncommon words be most appropriate? It is equally bad to say "it ain't so" among college professors as it is to say "that is a prevarication" among ditch diggers. In the first case, you will be accused of talking like a ditch digger, and in the second of talking like a professor. Unusual words may express our message more accurately but not everyone may understand them. Also, we should not use difficult terms merely to display our mastery of such words.

There Is a Place for It

Jargon, nevertheless, does have its place. Actors put across their part by using expressions typical of the people they're portraying. The Englishman drops a few "bloodys" here and there, and the Southerner must come out with "you all" now and then. Writers have their characters talk true to life. Every specialist uses a language of his own. And why shouldn't professional people in *conferring with one another* use their technical language? There may actually be less chance of being misunderstood if they do!

It pays off to learn the other man's language. You can understand what he's talking about. When he realizes this, he's going to be more willing to cooperate and help you with your problems.

There's proof that jargon is going to be here for awhile. A government agency in referring to its use has this to say:

"Much of the work of the Revenue Service depends on the use of legal and technical terms; we are obliged to phrase our letters in such a way that there are no loopholes for possible misinterpretation."

The writer hastens to add, however:

"We have no choice in this matter of legal language—we have to live with it. There is, however, no rule that says we are forbidden to add translations of passages into language taxpayers can understand."*

The inefficiency of jargon is also recognized by other agencies. Several years ago, the State Dept. started teaching elementary composition to its officers so that they would be able to understand each other's messages.

Jargon is a colorful means of expression that will probably always be with us. We may as well accept it. We can, however, avoid using it to bloat our speech and to impress rather than inform.

Don't you concur with this cerebration? ∎

---

* "Effective Revenue Writing," U.S. Treasury Dept., Internal Revenue Service, Training No. 82-0 (Rev. 5-61).

Meet the Author

W. H. Weiss is Manager of Engineering and Maintenance of the Chemigum Plant of the Goodyear Tire & Rubber Co., in Akron, Ohio. He has a B.S. in Ch. E. from the University of Illinois, and an M.B.A. from Kent University. He is a registered professional engineer in the State of Ohio.

Poetry? For Engineers?

Part I—The Best Word

Engineers often feel the need for more education. That usually means more technical courses. But do you really need to grow technically? Or is it that you need something else? Our author suggests poetry. Don't laugh. See what he has to say.

ANTHONY J. SOUSA, Consulting Engineer

I believe that men enter engineering because they seek an environment that is not subject to human vagaries; where they are judged for their true worth. So, it is a letdown when the engineer finds human politics determining his future growth despite the hopes that all those beautifully exact courses in math, physics and chemistry offered.

When an engineer has a problem, his usual answer is to learn more, to brush up on his science and technology. Will that help?

No, the problem isn't technical. Then what is it? It's summed up by that TV comic, Rodney Dangerfield, who turns to the audience with his popping eyes and clownlike face and says, "You know my trouble, I don't get no respect."

You know what I mean: like when they moved your desk into a room with four other engineers and gave you one-eighth of a secretary; or when they left you out of a meeting with the client on your research results; or when the electrician came to the pilot plant and boasted that he was making more than you and he never went to school; or when they brought in that new man at your level and you had to train him, and now they bypass you. Yes, engineers don't get much respect, and although they take it as a joke, they don't think it's funny.

Like it or not, your real problem is that you are missing an inner something that is preventing you from winning friends and influencing money—and reading technical journals this summer is not going to find it for you. Then what will? Anything that will develop the inner you, like Yoga meditation, painting, philosophy, music, turning hippie, or practicing any art that will help you to find yourself.

But I have a specific recommendation that I'll tell you about if you promise not to laugh too loudly—engineers, spend some summer writing poetry! What?, you say. Suppose somebody catches me? Then deny everything and say it's a plot to discredit you. What if you don't write anything worthwhile? I guarantee that you will not write anything worthwhile; but attempting to achieve such a goal will start you on a path of inner development that will produce real changes in the years to come.

In case you didn't notice, I said *write* poetry, not read poetry; of course, you'll have to read it as a minimum to accomplish the almost impossible task of writing it. I recommend it over other arts because when one practices poetry, one is writing—and few will argue with me when I state that engineers are very weak in writing. Poetry will definitely strengthen you in this art and your increased sensitivity to words will decrease spelling errors and grammatical mistakes, and in short diminish any hangups that interfere with successful communication through writing. This alone is sufficient reason for studying poetry.

Poetry will do more. It could bridge the generation gap, since it is now so often used in rock and roll music. Poetry can sensitize one, and provide the image that a man is educated and not merely someone with a degree. Poetry can only be dug out of one's self and is therefore self-educational (and in the words of the poet Robert Frost, "The only worthwhile education is self-education."

But even after finding yourself, you may still remain one of the seduced instead of the seducer;

there is just so much room at the top. And, if you were destined to fail in this world—then create an inner world where you win. If this is not sufficiently satisfying to you, then you'll require a personality transplant; develop the arrogance of a flamenco dancer, the voice of a trial lawyer, and the presence of a Shakesperean actor—anything that will assist you in getting your own way.

But even with all this, you may still miss "making it," since in the words of Peter's Principle, one rises by pull from above rather than by push from below. Or, as the poet Emily Dickinson put it:

> We never know how high we are
> Till we are asked to rise
> And then if we are true to plan
> Our statures touch the skies.

Poetry as a Key to Writing

The poet Coleridge of *Ancient Mariner* fame, wrote: "Prose—words in their best order; poetry—the best words in their best order."

Obviously, poetry has fewer degrees of freedom and is the more difficult to write. I like to think of poetry as the calculus of writing, and prose as the algebra of the art. Engineers all have experienced the improvement in their grasp of algebra after calculus. I propose a similar improvement in their (engineering) prose from a study of the higher art of poetry. It is analogous to taking graduate courses to do routine engineering, or jogging just to occasionally catch a train, or as Robert Browning put it:

> "Ah, but a man's reach should exceed his grasp,
> Or what's a heaven for?"

After the proper development, we may find engineers making entries in their lab notebooks in a manner similar to Coleridge:

> My hands are scarred with scratches from a cat, whose back I was rubbing in the dark in order to see whether the sparks from it were refrangible by a prism.

The entry is clear as written and has the added feature of some artistic beauty. Would it have been easier to read a shortened version of the entry written in the third person to conform with modern engineering report writing? I think not.

Poetry is very much "first person," with lots of I's, and very much in conflict with the accepted third-person method of reporting. But why should there not be I's in engineering reports. The work of an engineer is very personal and possesses distinctive character for each individual, and should not be lost in that infinite gray heat sink "it."

What Do I Mean by Poetry?

Poetry is a difficult thing to define in words; one must feel how it differs from other writing. Poetry need not rhyme—it can, but there is the danger that it will deteriorate into verse. Verse is easy to write. For example, if I begin, "There once was a man named Fred" (which is a line that already lacks poetry), I know that the next line must rhyme with Fred, and could be dead or lead. Then, I merely put words in between that have about the same rhythm, and I have a second line. Take the following poem, which was an attempt to visualize the kind of poem a young engineer might write to his secretary:

> Your eyes are like offsites
> Your teeth equimolar
> Your hair is cold reflux
> On my shoulder.
>
> O what's the reaction
> Improved entropy?
> In a fixed or a fluid
> Bed down by the sea.

Most engineers like this verse because it uses engineering words, all the lines rhyme, and the meaning is clear. But this is *not* what I mean by poetry. (Please don't get the idea that I mean that poetry isn't fun.)

Poetry is magical—a memorable grouping of words that put forth a whole mood, express a truth with great impact. It need not be complete as in most poems. It could be a single line, or as little as a few words. Poetry is produced almost accidentally, and results in ordinary words that mathematically model magical, mysterious, joyous, and always interesting and moving, thoughts. Great poems are seldom achieved and one must search hard among the greatest writing to find them. Unlike engineering, there is hardly agreement on the merits of a given work. You must decide on the poetry that is yours! What pleases others is of little interest.

Consider these lines of Emily Dickinson:

> Hope is the thing with feathers
> That perches in the soul,
> And sings the tune without the words,
> And never stops at all.

Could you begin to describe the human feeling "hope" better. Poetry dares to communicate feelings, the most elusive of things, yet not unimportant—even in engineering. For example, what is your answer when the V.P. asks you whether you feel the catalyst will have as long a life in the commercial reactor as it did in the bench-scale unit. He is not asking for facts, he is asking for the feelings you have. The exact answer is that you really don't know because no one can predict what exposure the catalyst will receive in the real plant; and as it is, you are not even sure what the catalyst life is in the bench-scale unit. But you may feel that it will hold up, or can be easily regenerated if it doesn't.

But what has poetry to do with engineering? You may be aware of the Mond process for purifying nickel, which consists of passing CO gas over a crude nickel to form gaseous $Ni(CO)_4$, which is then decomposed into pure nickel. Feel more on home grounds again? Lord Kelvin hailed this process as "one which gives wings to a heavy metal." I would say that he described it poetically without loss of scientific accuracy, and was a rounder and more interesting man for it. The scientist Sir Humphrey Davy dabbled in poetry, and Coleridge is said to have remarked of him, "If Davy had not been the first chemist, he would have been the first poet of his Age."

Writing Poetry

How does one go about writing poetry? They say a poem starts with a lump in the throat. I say it is a joy or a depression that fills the mind to capacity, then supersaturates the brain until something insignificant occurs, a word, some small event, and the solution precipitates in a shower of crystals that show up as words with excitement and tension. One must experience it to understand.

What's in a Word?

What's in a name? That which we call a rose
By any other name would smell as sweet.

The above lines from *Romeo and Juliet* must be favorites for engineers. If the rose were renamed "sludge flower," most would sense little loss of beauty and would be quite satisfied with the change, after having made the proper correction in their dictionaries.

Engineers are notoriously uninterested in words. Take the engineer who just returned from an exciting four-month startup near the Tibetan border:
"How was the trip, Jim?"
"All right."
"Understand you stayed with the Dalai Lama."
"Yep."
"What's he like?"
"He's O.K."
To most engineers, one word is as good as another, as long as it gets the job done. Does the new product have an odor? a smell? a scent? an aroma? Will any word do?

Engineers need a great deal of work in the area of developing an inner sense for the feel of words irrespective of their dictionary meanings. Words are notorious liars; they are all two-faced at best, and while they stand conveying their dictionary meaning on the one hand, they are sticking their tongues out on the other hand and conveying secondary meanings and feelings. It is these subtle secondary perturbations that allow the poet to achieve heights of compact meaning from ordinary words. Control of this secondary feature is the key to the art of writing, and this control can be developed only through feeling, which ultimately culminates in a "taste" or sense for good writing.

The Art in Words

I suggest that you play with words in order to sense their feeling, their inherent rhythm, their aes-

---

A List of Random Engineering Words Based on Their Feeling and in My Opinion

Poetical

melamine	tie lines
cascade	tunnel caps
risers	liquid seal
enthalpy	Teflon
modulus	cathode
poromeric	cooling curve
ilmenite	downspouts
polyisoprene	Murphree
ethanolamine	capillary
selectivity	colloidal
fuller's earth	electrolyte
Elgin Tower	flights
	laminar

Non-poetical

leaching	sludge digester
blowdown	slurry valve
eddy	chelating
batch	pesticides
equimolar	fungicides
thickener	coking
sieve	mother liquor
osmosis	flocculator
raffinate	wetted wall
berl saddles	hysteresis
entrainment eliminators	reflux
sliding vane	Fenske
coagulator	cash flow
	crud

---

thetic poetry and their beauty; that which is independent of their proper or dictionary meanings. But let me explain what is not readily explainable in words, but readily understood by feeling.

Cathode is a word that senses smooth, mysterious; while its ever-present companion, anode, is short, stifled and uninteresting. I prefer cracking to pyrolysis. Pyrolysis reminds me too much of paralysis. I prefer HTU to HETP as a combination of letters, whatever they mean. I prefer catsup to ketchup—the *k* is too strong.

Take the periodic table. The latest element discovered is eka-hafnium. Can you think of an uglier name? Compare it to beryllium. Listen to the music, sense the brightness, the brilliance. And selenium—say it slowly, feel its smoothness, its slipperiness. Sense the heat in hydrogen. Helium feels not only light but giddy to me. Germanium is rhythmical and has the sense of germination, which gives it a kind of earthiness. Don't you think so? Yes, I want your opinion. Don't give me that "whatever you say is O.K. with me" jazz. And stop fingering "Perry's" and looking in your old English notes. There are no teachers around—this is an exam where you correct your own paper. I'm asking you to look inside yourself. Take your time. Take a week. Sense the word, feel it. Clank it against other words and ask yourself, "What is it about the word that appeals to me?"

Some words have been perfectly named. Acetylene is both incendiary in reality and in feeling. One poet wrote, "The sky was bright acetylene," which says nothing but conveys the feeling of a brightly heightened and active sky. Here, acetylene was used not for its proper meaning but for its feeling.

Engineering is filled with beautiful and not so beautiful words. A partial list is shown in the box that, in my opinion, can be divided into two categories: poetical and nonpoetical. As an example, imagine the pretty girl next door whose name is Polyisoprene; or sense the elegance of the Elgin Tower, or the richness in fuller's earth.

On the other hand, visualize this typical outcry emanating from the plant disposal group, "Cut off the slurry to the sludge digester before the crud coagulates in the thickener." An entrainment eliminator may be important to efficient plant operation, but it sounds more like some kind of laxative. Heap leaching is a little-used unit operation, thank heavens, and mother liquor has many secondary meanings.

The Best Word

If one has the time, the genius, or the luck to find the best word, it can greatly strengthen one's writing. Engineers should develop the patience to wait for inspiration to provide them with the best word. Suppose you wish to express the feeling that brain-storming sessions are useful because one man's idea stimulates another man to create a new idea, and so on. We might say in our report that ideas tend to breed new ideas, but a better statement might be, "ideas tend to germinate," which says it all.

In his poem *The Hollow Men*, T. S. Eliot wrote,

> This is the way the world ends
> Not with a bang but with a whimper.

How did Eliot ever find "whimper"? The choice was truly inspired and adds greatly to the interest and activity in these lines.

The Smothers Brothers have a routine in which they sing about a man who falls into a vat of chocolate; when asked what he did, he replies "I shouted Fire. What should I have shouted? Chocolate?" In this case, the best word was "fire," since it produced the desired result of his being rescued.

A famous World War II novel was originally named *Catch 17*. For weeks the publisher looked for a new title that would be more appealing, and finally arrived at *Catch 22*. The difference is significant. The word seventeen has a downturning pessimism in it, while the word twenty-two has a lift at the end that peaks* one's interest.

The choosing of a name can be an important event in the engineering field, especially since the return on a huge research project may depend on the final appeal of the product's name. Du Pont pioneered fluorocarbon refrigerants, using the name Freon, and was later followed by Allied with its Genetron fluorocarbons. Which name do you prefer? Teflon is an excellent name for a plastic; it is neuter and yet pleasing. Corfam is not quite so pleasing. Qiana, Du Pont's latest fiber, is not appealing—even if it was chosen by computer to avoid conflict with other tradenames. And it is also often misspelled by people who insist on putting a u after the Q.

I feel fortunate in finding a poem by a great poet that exemplifies the art of using the best words. It is a sonnet by Elinor Wylie.†

Pretty Words

Poets make pets of pretty docile words:
I love smooth words, like gold-enamelled fish
Which circle slowly with a silken swish,
And tender ones, like downy-feathered birds:
Words shy and dappled, deep-eyed deer in herds,
Come to my hand and playful if I wish
Or purring softly at a silver dish,
Blue Persian kittens, fed on cream and curds.

I love bright words, words up and singing early;
Words that are luminous in the dark, and sing;
Warm lazy words, white cattle under trees;
I love words opalescent, cool, and pearly,
Like midsummer moths, and honied word like
    bees,
Gilded and sticky, with a little sting.

The reason for all this discussion on words is to make us well aware of the tricky devils we are dealing with; to loosen up the viselike grip of using words only for their meanings; and to call up words more on feeling than on meaning, since they come quicker by that route.

Try letting your wife read this article. I find women, by nature, have a deeper sense for the feeling of words than men do. ∎

---

* Poets can be a problem. I can't figure out if this is an imaginative use of a word, or a misspelling of "piques."—Ed.

† Copyright 1932 by Alfred A. Knopf, Inc. and renewed 1960 by Edwina C. Rubenstein. Reprinted from COLLECTED POEMS OF ELINOR WYLIE, by permission of the publisher.

Meet the Author

Anthony J. Sousa, 140 Seventh Ave., New York, N. Y. 10011, is a consulting engineer specializing in process evaluation and licensing. He claims to be a generalist, being not particularly good at anything . . . or bad. Prior to this, he worked for Chemical Construction Corp. under the title of Information Engineer. He has a B.S. in Ch.E. from City University of New York, and an M.Ch E. from New York University. Also, he has taught (evenings) in the Ch.E. department at Cooper Union.

Poetry? For Engineers?

Part II—Words in Their Best Order

Choosing the best words for your poetry is hard enough, but then you must put them in their best order. Can you do it? "'Tis a consummation devoutly to be wish'd."

ANTHONY J. SOUSA, Consulting Engineer

In the first part of this article, we studied words themselves, their external qualities, their hidden characteristics and how the best words are chosen by feeling rather than by meaning alone. In this section, we are concerned with the effect that the order of words has on the desired communication or, as poetry was defined by Coleridge: The best words in their best order.

The Best Order

The engineer may immediately notice that words in the best order indicates an optimization, and optimizations are best handled by computer. Unfortunately, the criterion for optimization is not the relatively simple economic optimum we are all used to, but is based on that order most pleasing to the programmer's or writer's taste.

This is not unusual when one considers that many reports we write have similar criteria. The annual report is an optimum based on an executive's opinion of what the stockholders will tolerate; research reports are tailored to suit the whims of certain supervisors; our own resume is written in a form that we consider optimum for the mind of the reviewer. But rarely is that optimum reached! Running out of patience, we usually settle for a product somewhere along the way to a converging solution.

Professional writers literally have to have their manuscripts torn from their hands since some revise their work ad infinitum. Dylan Thomas, in the prologue to his collected poems, writes, "If I went on revising everything that I now do not like in this book, I should be so busy that I would have no time to try to write new poems." If engineers could develop this persistence to rewrite and rewrite, there would be no problem in their ability to communicate in writing.

Visualize the tremendous difficulty in putting words

in their best order. Let us take three words for simplicity: silver, berry, light. We have the following possible combinations for these three words:

1—silver berry light   4—berry silver light
2—silver light berry   5—light berry silver
3—berry light silver   6—light silver berry

Arrangements 3 and 4 feel ugly since they give the sense of burying light silver or silver light. Arrangement 5 has a rhythm that is defeated by the middle word, berry. Arrangements 1, 2 and 6 have beauty, and the choice of the best arrangement becomes more difficult; differences in taste between individuals begin to take precedence. In my opinion, the optimum arrangement is number 6, but don't quote me, because there is no right answer—only successful and unsuccessful writing. The choice of the best order is also dictated by the direction the author is headed, the effect he wants to produce. Arrangement 6 has an upward trend that leaves one with expectations to follow. From the above, we can readily understand Edgar Allen Poe when he wrote of poetry, "Its sole arbiter is taste."

If we increase the number of words to be optimized, the possible combinations become astronomical. Can we use a computer to rid ourselves of this mental effort in the same way we have removed much of the drudgery in distillation and heat-transfer calculations? The answer is yes, to some extent. Computers have been used to write poetry, and they do surprisingly well, but they hardly approach the great masters. One computer was programmed with 100 words and some basic rules so that it poured forth poetry at the rate of 150 stanzas per minute—hardly a converged solution. The real effort comes in deciding which stanzas to keep, which is quite similar to distillation programs that leave the engineer to make all the important decisions. I would imagine a poet might find a computer helpful since it could eliminate much physical writing, and its random combinations might stimulate ideas. The thought of a computer poet is slightly repulsive when I compare it to the warm image of a man huddled over an antique desk writing by candlelight, near a fireplace. But the old way may prove uneconomical; a poor reason to drop beauty, but then we lost our lovely zeppelins the same way.

One should not fall into the trap of running words in the same order as they have generally appeared in the past, or in the order in which they fall in natural speech. This is all too easy, and results in dull writing, such as, "Sorry I took so long to answer, but . . ." Stay away from cliches and try to break the language in new ways that please. To help you in this endeavor, I offer a practice rule.

Write without a conscious attempt to convey meaning, then step back and read the meaning that has accidentally evolved and see how closely it approaches what you wish to convey.

It seems paradoxical, but it is difficult to put words down on paper that do not convey some kind of meaning. Witness the poem "Jabberwocky." Meaning springs forth in a way that is difficult for the novice

writer to foresee, but the ability to write meaningfully improves with time, as one improves in any art. With a great deal of work, a writer eventually achieves the quality of control—the ability to feel his way to his desired meaning by using words to mathematically model meaning. Benjamin Franklin is said to have learned writing by cutting words from the newspapers and arranging and rearranging them to achieve a desired effect. In later life, he is said to have been able to write finished work directly (an idea I find difficult to accept).

Is Writing Difficult?

Yes, writing is difficult. Indeed, it is almost impossible and rarely successful, but of course this depends on how high one sets his goals. One poet has said that writing poetry is like pulling hairs, the ends of which must be bloodied. This thought may give joy to Dracula, but it gives the shivers to me and has therefore communicated successfully the pain of writing. Analogously, after the fifth rewrite, it takes great courage to redo the entire report; it is simply easier to take your chances and issue it, since chances are that no one will read it, although it will always remain as a record of your effort and ability.

Writing is very much like growing a crystal, each word is more difficult to add without producing a fault. Joseph Conrad, whose writing appears so flawless, had no formal education. When he first began writing, he would sit at his desk for an entire day, write a single word, and then tear it up. The time was not wasted; he was searching, deciding, evolving his style, so that when he finally crystallized, he wrote lines like:

> The ship, a fragment detached from the earth,
> went on lonely and swift like a small planet.

There is another analogy that indicates the difficulty in writing. Imagine a bell ringer with hundreds of thousands of bells, a bell for each word of the English language. But the ring, or the sound, or the tone of each bell (or word) is independent of the meaning written on it (its dictionary meaning). We now give the bell ringer the problem of communicating. If he merely wishes to pass on a given meaning, as most engineers do, he chooses the appropriate bells based on meaning and rings them in a certain order. The resulting tune may have the sound of falling dishes, but the meaning is still received and noted.

Now we ask that the message be optimized to produce the most pleasing sounds and also convey the desired meaning—the best words in the best order, and we begin to approach the writing of poetry. The bell ringer must now play around by trial and error, and search in hope that luck will reward him; he may have to compromise if no combination seems to succeed. The problem is difficult and requires a strong motivation to justify the pain required to resolve this problem. But man is an exceptional creature and is capable of developing skill in the art of handling this complex musical instrument (the English language), and as a writer and poet, he is able to ring the bells pleasingly and still control the meaning conveyed.

William Shakespeare, I'm sure, has discouraged as many writers as he has excited. We must all despair in the presence of great art. Yet in school, we are exposed to his and other great writing and to some extent it may be harmful in being inhibiting. A finished piece of writing is like a completed cathedral, one has little idea of how it was constructed but is left awestruck at its beauty. It is similar to viewing a huge chemical complex from the plant manager's window before discussing salary and having him turn to you and say, "Now what can you do for us?" It is a humbling experience, and similar to taking a plant trip without being in on the original design; one can hardly appreciate the development work that went into the plant.

The Problem of the Writing Engineer

Robert Louis Stevenson wrote, "But the truth is one it has first to be discovered, then justly and exactly utter." This would indicate that one must first discover truth, then convert it into beauty through the art of writing—a two-step process. To accomplish this, the engineer first goes to the lab, pilot plant, literature etc. During this stage of discovery, he seems useless to management, which cannot comprehend why it is taking so long, and also notices that the engineer is not doing very much except staring into space. Where's the production, where's that damn report? Soon the engineer succumbs to the pressure, and a kind of truth is uttered long before the truth is discovered.

Engineers often write reports before the results are conclusive. In fact, the most typical report submitted by an engineer concludes that further work is necessary and more money must be allocated—hardly something to impress management. What will determine whether a report is going to be judged good or bad? The answer is the writing art put into the report, whether the writer's intelligence shows through, and whether pleasure is received by the reader in absorbing the information.

Yet, management demands more; it demands conciseness because it is very busy and wants the engineer to summarize a year's work in a moment. Management is unsatisfied unless the report strikes it into brilliance, which rarely happens. One cannot say for sure whether management or the engineer is at fault, but for the record, the engineer is always blamed.

Poetry uses conciseness to achieve impact and could help the engineer to better meet this demand from management, although it would also help if management would try to meet the engineer halfway.

Practical Uses for Poetry

How about some practical uses for poetry. Many engineers tell me they find it difficult to keep pace with their technical reading. They get bored by it, they find their minds wandering. This is because technical writing is read for meaning only and can hardly provide the incentive one needs to plow through such material unless one is following up his own idea or is on a hot motivated project. Poetry can improve your reading incentive. You will find yourself reading via the feel of words. Your mind will play games with the dull words, switching them around, etc., and the reading will give delight instead of being merely the somber duty of keeping up to date. I think Walt Whitman expressed it when he wrote about being depressed by the learned astronomer, and how he wandered off by himself ". . . and from time to time/ Look'd up in perfect silence at the stars."

Many engineers have difficulty spelling. If they learn to sense words for their artistic feeling, they will feel a misspelling since it will show up as odd in their constant search for beautiful words; the very architecture of the word will look wrong.

Take wisdom. I find many times that a poet can be wiser than an engineer. I have seen articles advising an engineer on how to plan his career that lay out, in block flowsheet fashion, the development of his career from bottle washer to V.P. of Research. The engineer with poetic sense will feel the hopelessness of such logic. For support, he may even turn to Robert Burns, who wrote that man was made to mourn. He may turn to Robert Frost to support his contention that there are no truths per se, when Frost wrote ". . . why abandon a belief/ Merely becaues it ceases to be true/ Cling to it long enough, and not a doubt/ It will turn true again . . . Most of the change we think we see in life/ Is due to truths being in and out of favor."

Can I recommend books on writing poetry? That is like asking if I can recommend any good books on swimming or golf. Certainly there are books on the subject, but I cannot recommend any of them; one has to dive in the water, or get out on the course and swing; to learn one has to feel it for himself and self-develop his own style.

The most difficult principle to understand in poetry is that meaning is unimportant. Once this is understood, the walls are down and one is free to fly out in any direction.

Next one must learn that poetry is written without conscious effort to express a meaning. Think of all those hours we spend in school trying to decipher what Masefield meant when he wrote that "the wind's like a whetted knife." He said it that way merely because he could not say that "the wind's like a sharp knife" without killing the flow and artistic value of his poem "Sea Fever."

I can recommend many great poets to read, but one must be careful. Take Alfred Lord Tennyson; out of a book of his collected works of several hundred pages, I find only about ten pages of great poetry. The poet Edwin Markham wrote hundreds of poems but only one has been judged great, 'The Man With the Hoe." Yet the completion of a single poem of such magnitude in a lifetime may rival the rewards of a lifetime of only engineering. You must decide! ■

PART II

Receiving Communications

Management—By Listening
Part I: Listening for Feeling

This is the first of a series of articles on listening—listening for comprehension, and listening for feeling.

GUY E. WEISMANTEL, Western Regional Editor

Listening is not an esoteric art. It is an ability. To become a competent, skilled listener, a person must spend extra effort in studying good listening techniques and applying them to his own listening program. It must be a conscious program—that, it is hoped, will become automatic, like driving an automobile.

Unfortunately, most of us think we already know how to listen, and this can be a very false assumption. Few have ever had a formal course in listening, and even in the "communication" courses we have taken, the topic of listening is sadly overlooked. When one begins to investigate the subject of listening, however (as this writer did) one notes a void in the literature—a void that even the experts seem to have overlooked.

For, while most of the information on listening puts stress on how to remember facts (and emphasizes retention), there is a very important aspect of listening that deserves study in its own right, that is, listening-for-feeling, or listening with the third ear, the ear of sensitivity.

Yet, this overlooked, and often completely forgotten, part of management-by-listening is an important part of the communication cycle. These articles shall not attempt to tell why listening-for-feeling is overlooked or ignored, but rather will talk about why it is important, and how and when one must listen for feeling.

To begin with, I'd like to comment on listening in general. Total listening-comprehension involves both listening-for-facts and listening-for-feeling.

There are individual cases (such as a lecture) where listening for facts may predominate. This may involve 85% listening-for-facts and 15% listening-for-feeling.

In another case, however, say, in counseling, listening-for-feeling may play the major role—maybe 85% listening-for-feeling and 15% listening-for-fact.

It is the feeling aspect of listening that I hope to emphasize in my first two articles.

Management-by-listening, indeed, relies on listening-for-feeling. Listening-for-facts is definitely important as an educational role, but a manager must play the part of the instructor and not the student. Managers are always involved in formal or informal counseling and this necessitates listening. Perhaps a remark heard as you walk down the hall will reflect 95% of a person's feeling but very little fact. So, first it is necessary to stress the importance of proper listening.

The need for such emphasis may seem amazing because any conversation, lecture or talk involves at least two parties, the speaker and the listener. One begins to wonder, if anyone is listening, or making an effort to develop an honest listening ability.

Is Anyone Listening?

In discussing this subject with communications people, many comments substantiated my own belief, namely that listening-for-feeling is greatly overlooked.

These thoughts were confirmed in conversations with people like Norman Sigband, a professor in the Graduate School of Business Administration, University of Southern California, Los Angeles. He has devoted considerable time to the subject.

Dr. Sigband explained that his "biggest gripe with the whole area of listening is that so much emphasis is placed on listening for facts." He thinks that, "more attention should be given to listening for feelings. If you don't respond to what people *don't* say, then communication breaks down."

Take the engineer who started talking to his boss about how he had sweated and slaved to meet a design deadline, stayed up until midnight to get computer time, and then hand-carried the final report to the airport post office to assure the material would make the midnight plane. After hearing the story, the boss curtly replied, "Yeah, that deadline was an important one to meet."

This is an exhibit of a breakdown in communication. For the engineer was searching for more. What he really wanted was a pat on the back, and the response could easily have given him that pat. The boss must, in his everyday routine, make a habit of listening for feeling.

A listening workbook (soon to be published) has recently been completed by Elias H. Porter, Technomics Inc., Falls Church, Va., author of "Introduction to Therapeutic Counseling" (Houghton Mifflin, 1950). In his new workbook, Dr. Porter presents a set of exercises, with examples from business and industry, to develop skill in listening for feeling and disregarding content. If you decide that you want to learn more, here is one way to go about doing it.

Reacting to Reality

Dr. Porter points out that: "One of the biggest problems for the listener, whether a manager or a counselor, is the problem of trying to see people's worlds as they see them. This isn't necessarily reality, but it is reality to them. It is the reality to which they are reacting. If a listener wants to listen with feeling, he must first understand the speaker's reality."

Problems can occur when a young manager deals with foremen and employees at the lowest management level. Often he doesn't listen to feeling, and particularly is not able to create the reality within which a minority-group employee is living.

Your Own Listening Program

While talking to Dr. Porter, I asked him what he did to improve his own listening habits. (This will be discussed in detail in a later article of the series.) He felt that "although a few people may have the ability naturally, most must make a conscious effort to form listening skills until they attain an involuntary habit of listening." Porter said, "to stay in tune and not be bothered by noise and distractions requires a lot of hard work. I used tape recordings of speeches, compared these with notes and sought help from my colleagues."

A Listening Tool

Many people don't have tape recorders and won't develop or take time for a formal listening-comprehension program, yet they want to improve listening habits. For these, I'd like to recommend something that they can begin immediately. It is a concept I call *triggering.* Triggering involves choosing two or three words that immediately trigger your brain to listen for comprehension—i.e., both for fact and for feeling.

One way of doing this is to choose trigger words that relate to the topic you want to remember. My own trigger words are: *listen, hear,* and *ear* in all their forms (*listening, hearing,* etc.).

Become conscious of your own trigger words so that whenever you hear them, you tune in to listen for both fact and feeling. Once you've been triggered a couple of times you'll begin to go off automatically even without noticing the word.

Good trigger words that are diametrically opposite of listening (like *talk, speech, speak*) can act as catalyst to give you a gentle nudge to shut up and to listen.

There is another triggering mechanism that doesn't involve a word, but rather a cliche or quote. It is surprising how many sayings creep into the conversations—choosing to use them as a stimulus to listen whenever you hear them will make you a better listener. Some of those commonly used are:

Speak up	See no evil, hear no evil, speak
Play it by ear	no evil
Lend an ear	Speak softly but carry a big
Listen here	stick
Hear ye, Hear ye	In one ear and out the other

But, for the moment, let us turn again to identifying the speaker's world of reality.

There are several styles of listening according to Dr. Porter, and a study of these styles is important to listening ability.

First, there is the conclusion jumper. This man hears part of a statement, or all of it and, without analyzing feeling, jumps to a conclusion.

Then there is the man who sits back and spends all his time developing believability data about the speaker. In the process, he fails to listen.

Finally there is the person who answers a question by asking one. In this case, he (the listener) actually thinks he is answering.

When listening for feeling, be cautious of exaggerations. People, particularly the person needing therapy or counseling, in order to obtain understanding, will often exaggerate. Once understanding takes place (or he thinks it takes place), the speaker will generally tone down his exaggeration.

It Can't Be Done

Managers who listen will eventually run into an employee who says something can't be done. In this case, the reply and the manager's action is ever so important. A sensible reply like, "I gather that you think this is impossible," will in effect say: "Am I understanding you?"

The employee's reply might be, "that's right, it's impossible, and here is why." Once he begins to try to prove it, he'll often work his way right into the solution. The task of the listener (manager) is to perceive how the talker views his real world by constantly asking forms of: Am I understanding you?

Trend to Group Dynamics

In our culture, the person held responsible for understanding is the speaker and not the listener— yet, this may be changing.

According to Bob Braverman, Director of Management Development, ITT, those getting involved with the question of listening are "plugged into a live wire."

Training and development seems to go through cycles, and presently the ideas of human relations and group relationships are hot spots within many a company's training program. There is considerable emphasis on listening.

This new emphasis came about at ITT because training programs were apparently producing students who returned to their jobs without applying what they learned. The importance of teaching the dynamics of group activity became apparent. Case work and efforts were applied to problems that demanded the cooperation of the group. One of the prime requisites for successful group operation is understanding the relationships among the individual members. This comprehension requires total listening activity by each individual—both for feeling and for fact.

Although ITT (and this is characteristic of many large companies) is still using the older training techniques, it is also running a workshop known as the "family group." Here, employees concern themselves not with what is going on outside, but rather with the dynamics of the group itself, and how things are done *by* the group. "The critical skill," according to Braverman, "is listening."

Unlike the older methods, personnel get feedback from one another—from the other members of the family. People's talk is like music; there are often several themes running simultaneously.

Wining, Dining, and Listening

Many managers in today's dynamic organizations do a lot of traveling, and they are not always in a position to record what they hear. Listening-for-feeling cannot be easily recorded anyway. Yet, when visiting or inspecting a facility, talking with employees, having lunch with field managers or managers of the other firms, listeners must continually be aware of feeling. Feedback not possible through correspondence is often noted during trips.

One such listening trip made headlines recently. The *Wall Street Journal* (WSJ) on Feb. 21, 1969 stated: "Nixon's Trip—President Will Stress Listening as He Makes Delicate Mission Abroad." That same week, the *National Observer* described: "The Nixon Trip: To Say Little, Listen a Lot." This is a good lesson for industrial travelers.

Feedback

A lesson in feedback comes out of the Detroit, Mich., Catholic Archdiocese. A recent WSJ article (March 28, 1969) described how a "soft-spoken, unassuming prelate committed himself to a deep plunge into . . . listening."

Archbishop John Dearden, according to the article (Listening in Church) discovered a method to bring vast numbers of the rank-and-file members into the decision-making process without surrendering his responsibility.

In an attempt to include laymen, as well as priests and nuns, in running the church, he ordered nine commissions—one for each area of church activity— to open their proceedings so that anyone in the diocese could make suggestions and recommendations to the bishop.

Skeptics labeled the proposal unworkable, but the bishop's decision was "vindicated by an overwhelming response. . . . About one out of every five adults participated in six weekly speak-up sessions."

The mechanics of Bishop Dearden's listening experiment, the filtering of good and bad suggestions, and the ultimate outcome, are open to close scrutiny, but for the present, critics are not saying much.

According to the article, the biggest complaint is that "speak-up" sessions did not last long enough. "Undoubtedly the format the Detroit diocese used to get people involved was too slow and unwieldy for many institutions . . . yet it is intriguing to speculate just what might have happened if Ford dealers had had a chance to vote on the Edsel. . . ." ∎

Meet the Author

Guy E. Weismantel is Chemical Engineering's Western Regional Editor, based in Los Angeles. He has a B.S. in chemical engineering from the University of Notre Dame. Prior to coming to CE, he worked for the O'Brien Corp., manufacturers of paint and varnish, where he was Western Div. Production Manager and Technical Director.

Management—By Listening
Listening for Feeling: Part 2

More on listening (even to silence),
including a list of commandments for
listening and a plea to listen to yourself.

GUY E. WEISMANTEL, Western Regional Editor

An important aspect of listening-for-feeling is listening to silence.

How a man remains silent can indicate *how* he is listening and *what* he is thinking. For example, a man who is generally outspoken about new ideas usually shows enthusiasm or criticism and will work them over either for their good or bad points. If during a meeting the man remains completely silent, it is meaningful. Listening to his silence is important.

Such a man once worked for me, and on one occasion he remained totally silent during a client's presentation—even when his name was mentioned as an authority on a subject.

It happens that the reason for his silence *was* very meaningful. The presentation contained boldface lies, that, because of the situation, would have embarrassed our company had my employee said anything at the time. Since an immediate decision wasn't necessary, the speaker continued without interruption and embarrassment.

When the speaker had left I asked my employee why he was silent, and he told me of the problem, and the situation was handled without embarrassment to either the company or the client. So, listening to silence is important in judging audience reaction.

Perhaps this last example is best summarized in a quote from Dr. H. Francis, of C. F. Braun, when he said that "listening involves the whole personality and requires a certain empathy that is not the same as talking."

Connie Moon, who teaches business management courses at Mobil Oil Corp. says: "Listening is an activity. It requires attention, concentration, deduction, effort, openmindedness, memory—and the knack of knowing how to put yourself in the other person's place."*

Researchers at Loyola University in Chicago spent 18 months contacting thousands of workers in order to answer one question: What is the single most important attribute of an effective manager? The answer came in one short paragraph.*

"Of all the sources of information a manager has, by which he can come to know and accurately size up the personalities of the people in his department, listening to the individual employees is the most important. The most stereotyped report we have received from thousands of workers who testified

* Moon, Connie, Want to do a better purchasing job? Learn to become a better listener, *Chem. Purchasing*, Sept. 1967, p. 15.

they like their supervisor was this one: 'I like my boss, he listens to me. I can talk to him.'"

Being liked doesn't necessarily mean the boss is actually a good manager. However, an employee respects the manager and his judgments when he does listen.

Employees take note of the listening personality of a manager. But, do you appreciate the importance of your listening personality?

Employees will draw an impression from your manner, facial expression and your suggestions. Response techniques are very important. Avoid common and mechanical words and phrases such as "that's interesting." Usually that remark is taken to mean "it's important to you, but I don't have time for it."

It is easy for a manager, especially a plant manager, to spend so much time in rushing from place to place that he can't take two minutes to listen to an employee on the line. Yet, a curt conversation with an employee can do more irreparable damage than one can imagine. If an employee wants to talk and feels he has something to say, letting him get halfway with his remarks and then rushing off to what you consider more important business is very harmful.

I've had my own assistant say: "If you want to put words into my mouth, go ahead; on the other hand, if you want to hear what I have to say, that's something else." At a time like this, you know you were not a good listener.

You may want to consider changing your listening personality, especially when you are under pressure. If you are really going to stop for a moment, to talk to an employee, say to yourself: "It is important that I listen." Ask yourself why the employee wants to talk and whether allowing him to do so can be useful to you and to him.

And, oh yes, sometimes your boss wants to talk about trivia—it happens to all of us. Listen to his feeling. It may be he is just trying to be a nice guy but sometimes needs a shoulder just like anyone else.

I'm not recommending that you put a "listening post" sign on your desk, but I am saying it is important to develop a listening personality to know especially when it is important when not to listen.

I'm reminded of one of the listening-for-feeling dangers, namely, listening too honestly. If you are a good listener, you will recognize that in the communication cycle one may listen honestly and, in so doing, walk right into the trap of believing that the speaker is honest. I'm not talking about exaggerations, but outright lies.

This problem suggests caution in listening for feeling whenever you suspect dishonesty.

Wanted: Good Listeners

Probably the best listener I've met was Jerry Crowley, President of the O'Brien Corp. I recall my

first visit with him, after I had taken a tour through the company's South Bend, Ind., facilities.

I had never been through a paint plant before. My visit was related to a scholarship given to sophomore chemical engineers at Notre Dame, and I was applying for the grant.

I still can't remember Jerry asking a question, yet he was able to let me expound on my visit and my background to the point where I realized I was doing all the talking, until I flatly remarked that I had nothing more to say unless he had some questions. I ended up getting the scholarship and spending many enjoyable years with the company. Perhaps this illustrates that "A Closed Mouth Gathers No Foot."

During my childhood, I remember my grandfather using this expression, "shut up and say something." Any listener will understand its value, and meaning. Nothing is more frustrating to a listener than someone who presents nothing in the way of fact or feeling. On the other hand, a modification of my grandfather's adage may be: "Shut up and listen."

Engineers are accused of having hushmouth disease. This doesn't mean they are automatically good listeners, but perhaps they have taken the first step.

Commandments for Good Listening

In Keith Davis' book, "Human Relations in Business," published by McGraw-Hill, he presents ten commandments for good listening.

1. Stop talking.
2. Put the talker at ease by creating a permissive environment.
3. Remove distractions.
4. Make a determined effort to see the speaker's point of view.
5. Show the speaker you want to listen. Listen to understand and not to reply.
6. Be patient. Allow the speaker plenty of time.
7. Hold your temper.
8. Go easy on criticism. If you win, you stand to lose.
9. Ask questions that show you are paying attention.
10. Stop talking again.

Although one can memorize these ten steps and think about them, here is a practical suggestion to begin your own Better Listening program.

Ask one of your colleagues for lunch specifically to talk about the subject of listening. You can probably draw up (in your mind) some guidelines for the conversation, but make sure that both of you go into the meeting with the idea of listening.

If you are like me, you'll experience a rather eerie feeling, for you'll know that the other party is really listening to everything you say. To begin with, he'll be listening for facts (and will be ready to pounce on you if he thinks you are saying something wrong) and, secondly, he'll listen to feeling, analyzing not only what you are saying but why. To be sure, there is a continual credibility factor—credibility for facts and for the reasons. You'll find yourself thinking twice before you say something, and you'll be careful to pick and choose what you say and how you say it. Bluntly, you'll begin to listen to yourself.

Another possibility would be for you to write a short article for the company house organ—one that would require interviewing a few people. If you want to learn your listening faults fast, make the interviews short, but with the intention of a followup phone call. When you return to do the writing, analyze what you missed and why you missed it, then take corrective measures as to your listening habits.

Listening to Yourself

I'd like to return to the concept of listening to yourself; this happens both while you are speaking and while you are listening.

An actor on a stage, a speaker on a platform, or a manager in a meeting listens to himself and to his audience. *Time* magazine quoted Alec McCowen (starring in Hadrian VII) as saying, "It's marvelous to hear an audience listening." A speaker watches the response of his listeners and can often tell when they are in the palm of his hand or when he must concentrate on gaining their attention.

Another example of listening to yourself is in extemporaneous speaking. There, you are thinking of what you are going to say, listening to the thought while saying it in your mind, evaluating it for credibility and accuracy, and then spouting it out.

Listening to yourself during any normal workday might be a good habit to get into. There are little things that can make a big difference in attitudes and morale, such as mentioning an important appointment that prevents you from doing something, rather than using a terse, "I don't have time."

Listening Techniques

Becoming attuned to someone listening requires practice and presumes some feedback. Dr. Norman Sigband (a professor in the Graduate School of Business Administration, U. S. C.) told me, "On one occasion, I was speaking to a women's group, including some elderly ladies. They were all nodding their heads and I'm sure they heard every word I said, but they weren't listening."

This can be a disappointing experience. I'm sure each of us has fallen in the trap of agreeing with a speaker so much (or disagreeing) that we quit listening. This has led me to the belief that there is no such thing as a dull speaker, only a poor listener.*

The importance of listening is evident, for when a speaker knows you are listening, and understanding, he is forced to become more precise. This is easy to experience in a personal situation where you are getting continual feedback, but it is also possible to

*Want to bet?—Ed.

attain this condition even as part of an audience.

More on Not Listening

What does one do when he listens? To begin with, the average man does a lot of not listening. Speaking and listening speeds are quite different (to be discussed in later article), so the mind is left with idle time. One thinks about other things, like, "what am I going to have for lunch; why doesn't the speaker get a haircut."

If you are involved in a conversation, you begin to think of your return remark. In this case, it is possible for the speaker to trigger an idea. After that idea pops into your mind, you are on the edge of your chair waiting until it is your turn to speak, and in many cases you'll start even before the other fellow is through.

Of course, this is discourteous, but even worse, there may have been some significant facts presented after you quit listening (while thinking of your reply). Dr. Elias Porter calls this a "bilateral monologue" where each person mutually goes off in his own direction. Abraham Kaplan, Professor of Philosophy at the University of Michigan, calls it "duologue," and suggests that the "perfect duologue would be two TV sets tuned in and facing one another."

When speaking at Minnesota's Gustavus Adolphus College in January, *Time* magazine (Jan. 24, 1969), quoted Dr. Kaplan as saying: "An honest dialogue is never rehearsed. 'I don't know beforehand what it will be. I don't know beforehand who I will be, because I am open to you just as you are open to me.' Dialog involves serious listening—listening not just to the other, but listening to oneself."

"It seems to me impossible to teach unless you are learning. You cannot really talk unless you are listening."

When a person listens, there are thinking considerations that parallel the thinking used when a person counsels. You think *about* a person, *for* a person and *with* a person. For example, almost everyone has stumbled in a conversation, trying to think of a word, only to have the listener say it.

Multiple Listening

Relatives sitting around the dining room table after a large family dinner seem to be able to listen to several different conversations at once. The Xerox efficient listening course* attacks this problem directly. Its thinking is that whenever there is a discussion among three or more people, the task of listening effectively becomes more complicated.

It may be a highly realistic situation that many conversations go on at the same time with each person trying to listen to the others; however, a business man can't or shouldn't use this technique. The ideal listening manager would not permit conditions that would allow such a condition to exist or persist. ■

*See page 35.

Management—By Listening

Part 3: What's New in Listening

How to improve your listening skills by in-house training, tape-recorded listening courses and non-verbal "listening."

GUY WEISMANTEL, Western Regional Editor

Seven out of each ten minutes that you and I are awake, we are communicating in one form or another. This time is devoted 9% to writing, 16% to reading, 30% to speaking and 45% to listening.

Noting these figures, an engineer may decide to evaluate his own listening ability or institute a listening program for his subordinates. While much of the listening literature simply warns against poor listening, there are several fine new programs now available, and others are in the planning stage, which offer the

engineer a chance to enhance his listening ability.

Dun & Bradstreet, Inc., Business Education Div., New York, recently introduced a "Complete Course in Listening." Developed by Dr. Ralph G. Nichols, University of Minnesota, Minneapolis,* the course focuses on one's own Central Listening Ability (CLA).

Central Listening Ability

There are four parts to CLA: overcoming distraction, detecting central ideas, maintaining objectivity, and evaluating the message. The Dun & Bradstreet course tackles each of the points via a series of cassette tapes, various exercises and workbooks, and a conference leader's manual. A company is able to administer the program in-house without using outside instructors, or an individual can take the course on his own. Exercises teach you to overcome distraction despite noise, interruption, or the speaker's jargon, pomposity, dialect and alliteration.

If you can detect the central idea of a message, you can understand and retain it better. Identifying the main idea involves fastening the facts to framework; this is known as the structure of the message.

Dr. Nichols told CHEMICAL ENGINEERING that "a person who sees the message sees a skeleton and uses this to hang on similarities. If you listen like a sponge, you don't get much. There are four basic structures a listener can use, on which to hang things:

1. Time sequence: utilizing past, present, future concepts.
2. Space sequence: ladder of success, five tributaries, jungle gym.
3. Enumeration patterns: 1,2,3, etc.
4. Problem-solution aspect: subdividing what one hears into halves and pairs.

"I have a deep conviction that facts are only retained on a type of fastener," says Dr. Nichols.

An angry listener is a bad listener, therefore it is important to maintain calm. Dun & Bradstreet tape cassettes contain drills that bombard you with every kind of emotionalism—outrageous statements about race, religion, politics, personalities. No matter how

---

* Dr. Ralph G. Nichols is head of the Communications Program, University of Minnesota, and is a well-known speaker and writer on communication problems.

hard you try to keep cool, you can become upset and miss key points.

Evaluating the message enables you to cope with emotional harangue, test the speaker's evidence, and evaluate conclusions and implications.

The cost of a corporate-wide license for the listening course, including tape players, cassettes, leader's manual and 100 workbooks cost about $1,300. Other options are available.

More Listening Courses

Xerox Corp., New York, charges a similar fee for its "Effective Listening" program. This is an older course that has been recently complemented by a booster series, "Advanced Effective Listening." Several CPI companies have used the Xerox approach (Lummus, Combustion Engineering, Institute of Gas Technology, Dow, Sinclair, and others) with listening effectiveness improving up to 45%.

Employees are confronted with a series of realistic listening situations (using tapes, texts, response books and administration instructions) designed solely to increase listening ability. Instruction tapes include background noise, speaker bias, emotional overtones and distractions in every normal listening situation.

The advanced course digs into the more complicated problem of listening to multiple speakers, listening and note taking, and writing memoranda—the focus is on deriving greater value from the time spent in meetings.

Toastmasters International, Santa Ana, Calif., is about to introduce an easy, practical, inexpensive (dues are only $12/yr.) way for an individual to improve listening skills. The course is called "The Communication Leadership Program."

Industrial Situations

Frank J. Jasinski, Director of Career Development, TRW, Redondo Beach, Calif., says: "The chief element in communication is to create an environment or condition that is open and honest, where people work together to solve problems—it is really more of a process than a program. People are constantly moving in and out of projects,* and on occasions we have to build, in a day and a half, a team that works like it has been together for three and a half years. The key element is to make the individual aware of what he must do, and this involves active listening."

So, the question arises: How do you teach one to listen? And at TRW the answer is pretty simple—you don't teach it, you experience it. In project-team building, men are put together with the job of solving a real live problem. By creating an openness, members of the group have the experience of listening for feeling and facts.

The Industrial Relations Dept. is called in whenever a new project team is formed in an attempt to create openness among the group. This involves receptiveness (where a person hears you) and expressiveness (where a person "levels" with you). One might consider this a type of on-the-job sensitivity training.† Listening is not concentrated on *why* a person manifests a certain behavior but, rather, *what* his behavior is, and what he is saying. This kind of awareness is based on a system of act and critique, act and critique, act and critique, instead of act, act, act. Employees begin to critique themselves when problems occur, with comments like: "You look angry." "Yes, I guess I am." "Do you know what you just did to that guy?" "Yes, I didn't realize it."

Nonverbal Listening

Did you ever hear a person smile? Listen carefully to the other person—his face, his mouth, his eyes and his hands. Listen to his walk, his posture and the clothing he wears—each transmits a message.

The body is full of silent signals from an angry frown to raised eyebrows. These signals were discussed in a recent issue of the British journal, *New Scientist,* and described later in *Time* magazine.[1]

According to the *Time* article, a team of doctors under Dr. Michael Chance, Birmingham, England, "has catalogued no fewer than 135 distinct gestures and expressions of face, head and body. This human semaphore system, they explain, is not only capable of expressing an extraordinary range of emotions, but also operates at a lower—and sometimes different—level of consciousness from ordinary speech."

Apparently such nonverbal language is easily observed in children who are far less restrained than adults; and subtle traces of posturing and gesturing are still evident in adulthood. These are activated at times of stress. The movements "may be quite inconspicuous and unconscious."

"By reading such unconscious gestures . . . the psychiatrist . . . may get more valuable information on the progress of therapy from the silent signals than from the spoken word."

Perception of the nonverbal langauge requires a listening skill perhaps even more intricate than understanding words. Dr. Seth Fessenden has described this aspect[2] of listening by saying that language is an abstract use of symbols:

- There is a language of gesture and movement.
- There is a tonal language.
- There is a phonetic language.

Readiness to listen includes the above, as well as a "mental set" and intent to listen and understand. Sound can indicate mood. Just like the sound of a jet warming for takeoff, the body can give off similar signals.

So, to really listen, it is necessary to put all your senses on alert; true listening involves more than

---

* TRW uses a systems approach to management. Personnel belong to a functional group (with a functional boss who is responsible for salary, etc.), and project managers tap any or all of the functional groups whenever a project team is needed to accomplish a task. One person may belong to several project teams at once.

† Over 6,000 TRW employees have been through "team building" and over 1,100 have been through actual sensitivity training.

BETTER LISTENING for effective interviewing is taught here by instant-playback videotape recording.

hearing. A smile (as one walks down the street) may receive a smile in return, and communication can take place without a word being spoken.

Len L. Lasnik, Director, Almeda County, Calif., Schools Dept., is responsible for many of the new ideas in nonverbal communication.[3] The work, pointed at helping the teacher, will find industrial significance. It involves use of space (certain territorial rights are traditional in the classroom), when and where a teacher can travel in a classroom, and the use of time. Students receive certain nonverbal actions of the teacher without deliberate reflection, and this behavior by the teacher can be symbolic or nonsymbolic, spontaneous or managed.

McGraw-Hill Inc. is also active in the schools, and has published a "Programmed Approach" to listening. In this course, the behaviorial objectives of the student include: listening to a sample of public speaking, stating the main idea in one sentence, listing main divisions and pattern of ideas, identifying illustrations and statistics, and examining the speech for emotional content.[4]

Listening is still not being taught in the majority of colleges because of academic politics and course requirements of the curricula, but there is evidence that consideration of this topic is appearing in the lower grades; this is where it could be most important anyway.

Ripple Effect

In industry, listening techniques are taught to purchasing agents,[5] salesmen, college recruitment per-

sonnel, and engineers. Also, listening is a part of almost every management development program.

Joseph A. Robinson Associates, consultants in management communications, San Francisco, does not separate listening from the total communication process, but on several occasions has used videotape to record observed behavior of listeners. This technique is unusual because the cameras have essentially been turned around—instead of focusing on the speaker, the lens is on the listener. Kaiser Industries and Standard Oil of California are companies in the chemical process industries (CPI) that have used this technique.[6]

One of the most complete programs focused on listening is at the graduate (MBA) level at the University of San Francisco, San Francisco, Calif. Dr. Edward Nolan has introduced a curriculum called: Professional Development at the Graduate Level. The courses have a strong organizational behavior flavor and are patterned to include such things as group reaction. A commercial-manager skill lab is designed for constant feedback to the individual and includes videotaping and interviewing; students also do a thesis on themselves that includes an in-depth analysis of their own strengths and weaknesses as managers. The whole emphasis is on "participation management," and successful completion definitely is keyed to a person's listening.

Two other organizations deserve mention:

NASA (Natl. Aeronautics and Space Administration) has devised a decision-making game that involves listening and group decision-making. One can see the importance of this exercise as it applies to survival or other critical elements within the space program. Quite often a team will be thrown together to work on a crash project, and immediate listening to, and understanding of, one another is important to success.

Finally, there is a "supervisory kit" used by Bell and Howell. Some may feel that its use is a bit superficial, because role playing is involved, and players put on Negro masks or glasses in a real attempt to involve human relations with one's listening ability. Yet, this is an honest attempt to manage minority groups or the new generation by "letting them do their own thing toward contributing. As managers we must be sure we know the difference between hearing and listening, perceiving and seeing."[7] ■

References

1. The Body, Man's Silent Signals, *Time*, June 13, 1969, p. 86.
2. Fessenden, Seth A., "Ace Listening Manual," printed at California State College, Fullerton, Calif.
3. Lasnik, Len L., Some Ideas About Nonverbal Communication, *The Instructor*, Apr. 1968.
4. Erway, Ella, "Listening—A Programmed Approach," McGraw-Hill, New York, 1969.
5. Moon, Connie, Want To Do a Better Purchasing Job? Learn to Become a Better Listener!, *Chem. Purchasing*, Sept. 1967.
6. Robinson, Joseph, A., Videotape in Training, *Training Develop. J.*, Nov. 1968.
7. Neal, H. R., Can Industry and Youth Find Happiness Together, *Iron Age*, May 15, 1969, p. 62.

Management—By Listening
Part 4: Learning to Listen

Here are some tips and techniques for learning to listen better and faster.

GUY E. WEISMANTEL, Western Regional Editor

I know of no studies showing that engineers are worse listeners than the average American, but I do know that many engineers do not always realize when they are being too technical and are talking over the heads of their listeners. This is true not only in person-to-person conversation; I've seen engineers have major communication problems in front of judges, city councils and in conferences—they often don't listen to the feedback an audience is giving.

For the moment, let's forget about the communica-

tion and listening problems involved when an engineer addresses a nontechnical audience. Most people are aware of that problem even if they are sinners themselves.* Instead, let us concentrate on a method engineers can use to improve their ability to listen to each other.

Planned Listening

The concept of triggering (having a specific word initiate a listening response) was described in an earlier article.† While triggering presumably is a personal technique for tuning in, there is a broader concept, "prepared triggering," that creates a rapport between speaker and listener even before a speech begins. "Prepared triggering" is based on the adage Proper Prior Planning Prevents Poor Performance.

Engineers are often required to attend staff meetings or conferences that have a specific agenda; and one goes into such a gathering armed with his own contributions. But, it is not unusual to attend a lecture, seminar or meeting where you will know only the title of a speech or the topic to be discussed. It is in these situations that "prepared triggering" offers benefits. Here is how it works.

Once a topic or title is chosen, both the speaker and the listener prepare themselves for the meeting (instead of just the speaker himself). The speaker writes his manuscript and chooses two or three

*Haakenson, Robert, Delivering Your Talk,
†Weismantel, Guy E., Management—by Listening, Part I: Listening for Feeling, p. 28.

trigger words that he will use whenever he wishes to stress a point or assure audience attention. Then, he sends these trigger words to the attendees. They, knowing of the triggering concept, will acquaint themselves with the trigger words so that the word will work when it is supposed to.

This doesn't take a long time; in fact, it is possible that a speaker could hand out a little sheet of paper (listing the trigger words) right before he begins to speak.

The advantage of the "prepared triggering" technique is that it provides for continuation of a central thought or idea without a physical interruption or call for attention. And, if interest lags, the speaker can always throw in the trigger word to wake people up.

It is entirely possible that prepared remarks should also include one-minute periodic pauses that would permit listening review time. A speaker could give an explanation and announce use of effective listening pauses prior to beginning his presentation.

Tips and Techniques

Most of the listening books are loaded with how-to-improve-listening lists, but some don't receive attention. For example, an older book by Nichols and Lewis* is sometimes overlooked, yet it has a very good section on note taking.

In meetings where one can't take notes, listening becomes a very important factor. Nichols has found that the average person remembers only 50% of what is said no matter how carefully he was listening. Two months later, the remembrance percentage drops to 25%.

Consequently, listening for facts involves attention and receptivity, a person's conscious attempt to concentrate and memorize. Adding to the problem of concentration is the listening barrier created by differences in listening and speaking speeds. "People usually talk at between 100 and 150 words/min. Thinking time varies greatly, depending somewhat on intelligence and the brain's operational speed, but also on one's knowledge of the subject. It can vary from just a few words to over one thousand words/min. although it cannot be measured accurately."

It seems probable that our failure to listen well also stems from an inability to quickly classify and weigh the importance of what a speaker is saying—this is particularly true in a disorganized talk that is not well outlined, e.g., in off-the-cuff remarks. Thus it becomes very hard to use the listening structures described in the previous listening article.

Speed Listening

When speed reading, a person normally dismisses the irrelevant and passes to the key words and phrases as he scans a page. Thus evolves a central theme or idea. A person can't speed listen because there is dependence on the word rate of the speaker. So, what one must do is fill in the voids (spare time) with items that relate to what is talked about, while continuing to hear what is said. This is analogous to playing the piano and singing at the same time. How do you do it?

One way is to hear for awhile and then very quickly repeat back in your mind everything that the speaker has said, emphasizing key elements and tying them to a listening structure. "We can also use spare time to analyze what we hear, to consider the quality of thought, the validity of evidence, the accuracy of illustration, and adequacy of idea development. We can learn to add examples of our own to those given by the speaker and to wonder why the speaker failed to talk about some aspects of the topic that might be considered important. We can think ahead of the speaker, guess how he will develop a point, and compares our guess with what he actually does."†

Listening to Jabber

Bell Telephone Laboratories, Murray Hill, N.J., has developed an electronic device to enable speed hearing of recorded speeches at word rates comparable to speed reading. The device, called an harmonic compressor, permits making recordings of the human voice that are played at twice their normal speed while retaining normal voice pitch. It eliminates the high pitched "Donald Duck" babble that results when an ordinary recording is speeded up. The faster word rate made possible by harmonic compression approximates the speed at which many persons speed-read printed material.

The harmonic compressor divides in half the frequency components (harmonics) in a voice recording, while preserving the original time duration. By doubling the speed of this half-frequency recording, the frequency components are restored to their original values. The result is a normal pitch, double-speed recording. This naturally eliminates some of the spare listening time one has when listening to normal speech.

Because the device would permit blind persons to listen to recorded material at the same rate as material is read by many sighted persons, the American Foundation for the Blind is studying possible applications in its programs of providing tape and disc recordings.

Research on speed listening has yielded a very interesting and unexpected finding. Emerson Foulke, University of Louisville, and head of the Center for Rate Controlled Recordings, has found that a listener does not necessarily prefer the word rate that yields the most information. For example, one of his studies showed a preferred listening rate of 207 words/min., with profound loss of comprehension at 350 words/min.

* Nichols, Ralph G., Lewis, Thomas R., "Listening and Speaking," McGraw-Hill, New York, N. Y. 1957.

† Fessenden, Seth A., "A Program for Listening Development," California State College, Fullerton, Calif. (an internal school publication).

Listening Tests

Intelligibility of speech and comprehension are not the same thing. Dr. Foulke has stated,* "A word is termed audibly intelligible if, when heard, it can be repeated accurately by a listener. Comprehension, on the other hand, is demonstrated by the listener's ability to show a knowledge of the facts and implications of a listening selection."

Some methods of measuring comprehension are more sensitive than others, and it appears that testing for recognition (e.g., by multiple-choice tests) produces higher results than those obtained from a test aimed strictly at recall. It has been suggested that information-retrieval problems arise from incomplete encoding (in the brain) of stimulus material. Consequently, such an incomplete message may be released (from the memory) in a recognition test, but may prove irretrievable in a recall test.

A "tape-and-test" technique was developed by a Los Angeles group. The program consisted of listening to five-minute tapes, followed by a written test for comprehension; such a test was given one day a week for six weeks. After the fourth week, there was no improvement in listening. As with all things, there is a point of diminishing return.

Importance of Importance

The prerequisite to real listening is an honest determination to make whatever a speaker says important to you.

In some listening, it is the event that is important, e.g., the Nixon-Kennedy debates. The impact caused by Kennedy's acceptance speech ("Ask not what your country can do for you, but what you can do for your country.") came from the personal identification of what the listener was hearing. There was a personal important meaning regardless of agreement or disagreement.

Importance and personal sublimation go hand in hand whenever there is an honest attempt to listen. Developing importance is especially necessary when listening to poor speakers, or topics that are old hat, mundane or of little concern to the individual.

One example that backs up the importance of importance is described by Seth Fessenden, California State College, Fullerton, Calif.

"After giving half of a lecture, students were informed that there would be a test on the material covered. Six of the test questions were taken from the first half of the lecture and six from the last.

Always there are better scores on the last six questions, even though all the questions are equally difficult."

In terms of dollars, there is no way to estimate the money lost due to poor listening. Anyone could list myriad examples. Yet, I still advocate the principle of: "Don't write it—say it."

People have got into the habit of writing memos for everything, and many of these are so lengthy it is impossible to find the important points. Some letters never need to be written. Cases occur where an engineer will write a letter in longhand, and give it to his secretary who types it (twice) at a total time of half an hour. A phone call to the person involved (even long distance) would save the company money, and perhaps a week's delay in receiving a reply and ultimate action on a project. If a company considers these values, listening becomes much more important.

The Listening Bonus

Once you develop the listening habit, it is surprising how often you will shut up while other people show their ignorance. Proper listening improves decision-making prowess by promoting thinking and evaluating instead of talking. While temptations to give a verbal salvo always exist, one will find a different satisfaction in listening opportunities. You can also develop a listening etiquette that should bring meaningful enjoyment. This will be characterized by:†

1. An interest in people.
2. Patience in hearing the other person out.
3. Respect for the other person's right to express opinion.
4. Interest in comparing points of view.
5. Interest in broadening a viewpoint rather than defending a position.

† Wagner, Guy, others, "Listening Games," Teachers Publishing Corp., Darien, Conn., 1960.

Suggested Additional Reading

Wagner, Guy, others, "Listening Games," Teachers Publishing Corp., Darien, Conn., 1960.
Nichols, Ralph G., Stevens, Leonard A., "Are You Listening," McGraw-Hill, New York, N. Y., 1957.
Morris, Jud., "The Art of Listening," Industrial Education Institute, Boston, Mass., 1966.
Barbara, Dominic A., "The Art of Listening," Charles Thomas Pub. Co., Springfield, Ill., 1958.
Hayakawa, S. I., ed., "Language, Meaning and Maturity," Harper and Row, New York, N. Y., 1954.
Hayakawa, S. I., "Language in Thought and Action," Harcourt Brace and World, New York, N. Y., 1939.
Fessenden, Seth, "Ace Listening Manual," California State College, Fullerton, Calif., 1969.
Proceedings of the Louisville Conference on Time Compressed Speech, Oct. 19-21, 1966, University of Louisville, Louisville, Ky.

* Foulke, Emerson, Comparison of Comprehension of Two Forms of Compressed Speech, *Exceptional Children*, Nov. 1966, p. 166.

A Quick Rapid-Reading Course

If it takes you about 15 minutes to read this article, you're only an average
reader—and learning about rapid reading could help you. If, on the other hand,
you need only 5 minutes, you shouldn't bother—you're already a fast reader.

MICHAEL G. SHELDRICK, McGraw-Hill World News Bureau

You probably needn't look any further than the top of your desk for a reason to read faster.

If you think you are shuffling more paper and wrestling with more books now than ten years ago, you're very likely right. At the same time, your reading has probably become more narrow and specialized. Yet, you must be finding it difficult to keep up with your own field, let alone with chemical engineering as such, or more broadly with engineering in general.

There are only two solutions to this problem: either spend more time reading or increase your reading efficiency.

Defining Efficient Reading

What does more-efficient reading mean? Two things really: faster reading and greater comprehension. (Tests show that comprehension increases with speed—to a point, of course.) The two may seem contradictory; but imagine trying to understand this sentence if you were forced to read it letter by letter; not only would it take you a long time to get through, you also probably wouldn't be able to make much sense out of it. You'd have: B...u...t...... i...m...a...g...i...n...e....etc.

Now, let's say that you're going to read it word

by word: But...imagine...if...you...etc. This takes much less time, but the meaning is still locked within the words.

Finally, if you read the entire sentence in a glance —assuming you are intelligent, and the words are not unfamiliar—you would get the meaning of the sentence (there can be, of course, an infinite range of meanings).

You were able to absorb the meaning when you read the entire sentence at a glance, but at the same time, you probably would be unable to exactly recite the sentence shortly after reading it.

Reading, then, is not a process of examining words, but of extracting meaning and information.

Efficient reading is the extraction of information and meaning as rapidly and completely as possible. Individual words are important only insofar as they contribute to information and meaning. By reading faster, you will avoid being bogged down by words. Instead, you will read ever larger groups of words.

How Fast Can You Read?

One component of more-efficient reading, as we have said, is greater speed. But as you shall see, what we are really striving for is probably best called greater variable speed: you will flash through some material, barely crawl through other. It's a good guess that you are reading this article at a speed of somewhere between 250-300 words/min., if you are an untrained, average reader.

There is considerable controversy over how fast people can read. Some say 1,800 words/min. is the limit imposed by physiological barriers. Others claim to have trained students to read at 5,000, 18,000, 40,000, and in one case, 80,000 words/min.

Obviously, a careful examination of what is meant by reading is required. A person might breeze through a light novel at a remarkable pace, but unless he knew something about chemical engineering, he would get almost nothing out of reading a unit operations text at the same speed.

Why You Read Slowly

If you're going to improve your reading—a reasonable goal would be increasing your speed about three times your normal rate—your first step will be to examine your present reading habits. You read the way you do because of the sum total of habits you began to build up from as long ago as the first grade. For awhile, your habits could be easily molded.

But at some point, your habits became ingrained. All your experiences up to that point combined to form your present way of reading.

When you first began to read, you probably did it out loud. The teacher spoke the words and pointed to them, and the class responded. Later, the words were put together in stories, and you stood up and read out loud before your class.

This method of teaching reading will have left you with a habit of saying the words to yourself under your breath, silently moving your lips or vocal cords. This is called subvocalization or inner speech. It has two effects, and overcoming them will be an important part of your attempt to read faster and better.

First, subvocalization slows you down, because your speed is limited by how fast you can say each word to yourself. Secondly, this emphasis on individual words keeps you from taking in large groups of words with your eyes.

How to Read Faster

To the extent that you can overcome this subvocalization, you'll become a better reader. Because it is such a powerful, longstanding habit, you'll probably never overcome it completely.

If you gain confidence in your ability to assimilate information without "monitoring" it by subvocalizing, you will not be so reluctant to let go of an old habit. Also, by forcing yourself to read at triple your present speeds, you will not be able to subvocalize.

You may not be aware of it, but you are already taking in large amounts of information, digesting it, and retaining or acting on it—all without subvocalizing. As an engineer, you are probably an expert equation reader. Think about how you read equations. Certainly not term by term, saying each super- and subscript to yourself as you go along. You simply read it all at once.

Soon, you'll find an equation. Stop! Cover this part of the page with a piece of paper or your hand before you look at it. Expose the equation, and immediately re-cover it. You probably recognized it. Write it out.

$$N_{Re} = \frac{LV\rho}{\mu} = \frac{DV\rho}{\mu} = \frac{DG}{\mu}$$

The preceding paragraph, among other things,

was a good test of your visual span. If you looked at the equation before you saw the word "stop," the chances are good that you were concentrating too much on individual words.

The equation was, of course, the Reynolds number. You were probably able to write it down without subvocalizing the parts. If you examine the equation, you'll see that it's packed with information. You probably read the equation without saying it to yourself because no one ever taught you how to read equations. It's unlikely that you read it: N sub R . . . e . . . equals. . . .

You might object that only a few sets of terms make up the Reynolds number, but that a sentence, which is the equivalent of an equation, can contain an infinite number of terms. Yet, it is also true that you are familiar with all the words (terms) in a sentence. And just as you don't read a derivation term by term, you shouldn't read sentences word by word.

Reading sentences is vastly more complicated than reading equations. Even so, you can develop the same rapidity and efficiency in reading the former as you now have in reading equations.

The Two Main Skills

Good readers have a wide visual span. Their eyes only stop on a line once or twice, and they take in large groups of words. If you watch someone read, you will see that his eyes alternately move and stop. The fewer stops made, the faster the reader.

These two skills—taking in information without saying it to yourself, and having a wide visual span—are developed through long experience, but can also be sped along by purposeful development. The following exercise is valuable for developing both skills.

Find yourself a typewriter and type any three numbers in a form something like:

4   3   5

Then gradually increase the distances between the left and right numbers:

4   3   5
7   2   1
3   6   8
2   7   4

Keep your eyes focused on the center number. Without vocalizing, add the numbers and say the total, either to yourself or out loud. When the letters are so far apart that you can just about see them with your eyes focused on the center number, fill a sheet of paper with various combinations of numbers at this space interval.

This exercise consists simply of reading off the totals of each combination as you move your eyes down the center, keeping them focused on the middle number. At this stage, it's a good idea to get someone to watch you, to be sure that you're not moving your eyes.

You'll find that you'll go slowly at first and make

The Learning Techniques

Some teachers rely heavily on mechanical devices to force the student to concentrate, as well as to make him read faster and faster. One student observed that these devices actually worked because, "we were driven to keep up with the idiot machine."

The "pacer" system, in which the hand or a mechanical device keeps the student's attention on a given group of words, blocking out everything else on the page, is used in many courses. The idea is to gradually increase the visual span so that whole areas of a page can be absorbed instead of a few words at a time. Another method encourages scanning the first and last sentences of a paragraph to get the content and identify the salient points.

many mistakes, but after awhile, you'll be able to see the outer numbers more clearly. If you find yourself remembering the totals, rather than adding them in your head, simply type up a new sheet. After you've mastered the first width, type up a new list, with the numbers spread even wider.

Eventually, you'll reach number sets of a width somewhere between the size of a typical column of print of a paperback book and a typical hardbound book's column of print.

Practice this exercise often, but only for short periods.

As an extension of this, you can take publications having narrow columns of print, such as newspapers or some of the news magazines. Draw a light line down the center of the column and keep your eyes fixed on it as you move down the page. At first, you won't understand much at all; practice, therefore, on material you're not in the habit of reading, so you won't be concerned about not comprehending. Save the issues, because you can go back over them. If you persist in this exercise, you will find you will be able to read straight down newspaper columns.

Now, Your Speed

It should be clear to you by now that speed is variable. Your highest will be with light material. Therefore, start by assembling all the light novels, mysteries, superficial biographies and other easily read material you can get hold of.

Read through these at a speed that's comfortable, and time yourself. This will give you an idea of how fast you normally read this type of material. If anything, when doing this, rate your speed on the high side.

Now triple your normal speed. For the duration of this practice, read all this light reading at this speed. Nothing less. Don't include material that you normally would read at work.

At first, your comprehension will plummet. As you charge though an Ellery Queen mystery, the most you will pick up will be a few words, possibly some dialogue, and some impressions. Don't let this slow you down. If you keep practicing, you will find yourself understanding more and more.

The addition exercise described previously should be pursued independently of your speed-reading practice. And both should be carried on separately from any reading you do as part of your job. This cannot be emphasized too much. Right now, you are not ready to go out and speed read "for keeps."

While you're reading, do not consciously try to overcome subvocalization, or direct your eyes in any way. These things will come naturally.

The best way of practicing is to set side a specified time, say one hour per day. You can practice more than that if you wish, but don't extend the sessions too long.

If you get interested in a passage, don't get bogged down. Simply note it with a check mark and go back to it later.

One final note: Don't get tied up by timing yourself with precision. Just make good estimates of your speed.

Although you've mastered speed in light material, you're still not a speed reader. You're only a speed reader of light material. And you're not an efficient reader yet.

Organizing Your Reading

The final component of efficient reading is the ability to dig out information and meaning—and this depends largely on two things: your awareness of the type of material at hand and your knowing what you want out of it.

Your awareness of the type of material at hand

Consider Your Reasons

Evaluating your reasons and comparing them to the reasons that motivate others to study rapid reading can be helpful. Most people feel they can't read as well as they should. Whether this is actually true is debatable because while the majority of those interviewed believed they didn't read as well as they should, they found they were well within the average range when tested during their first class session.

Many said they took one particular course because it was highly publicized and guaranteed that the individual's reading speed could be tripled. In addition, it promised that they could go back for a refresher or even repeat the entire course at a later date at no additional cost. Generally, they found the basic course quite laborious.

will depend largely on your reading experience; there is really no other way of teaching people to recognize what they have. But digging out what you want from the material is within your control. The problem is that most people are lazy and don't bother to examine what they do before they do it.

The first, and most critical, decision you will naturally make on any piece of writing is whether or not you will read it at all.

If you can make a decision not to read something, you've gained a lot of time and haven't filled your head with useless information you'll only forget.

Despite the trend to snappy, uninformative titles, most books' titles still give you some idea of their contents. Dust covers, despite their puffery, also present information, and should not be ignored.

In addition, read the preface or introduction of a book closely. Either will usually tell you what the author had hoped to do. You can avoid starting a great number of books this way.

You should also check the date of publication to see if the book has been revised, and if the edition you have is out of date.

Indexes are not always prepared by the author; but even if not, those subjects the author considers important are usually extensively indexed.

Read the footnotes and check the bibliography. Authors have the disconcerting habit of putting some of their more important information into footnotes. If the bibliography refers mainly to works you are familiar with, the book may not contain anything new for you. On the other hand, it may use as jumping off points those books referred to.

Now to the Table of Contents

Only at this point are you ready to tackle the table of contents. From it, you can see how the author handles his material, and whether he's covered the things he and his publisher have claimed he does. You can get a feel for his interpretation of the material. Note the relative lengths of chapters and sections within chapters to see what is given the greatest weight.

Now leaf through the book itself to see how it's laid out, and to get a feel for the author's style. Note all graphics and derived equations. There are times when you can get all you want out of a book, paper or report simply by looking at the charts, tables and equations.

At this point, you're ready to read—that is, if you've decided the book contains something useful or interesting. You also have probably found that some chapters or sections are of greater interest than others. When you finally begin to read, there's no reason that you can't read these parts first.

All of this may sound like a tortuous process, but you probably go through many of the steps already. The idea is to raise the process to a high art. Whatever you're reading, all of the above should never take more than 10% of the time you would spend on the entire book. If you're really good, you can work it all down to a few well spent minutes.

Let's assume you've made a decision that the book will be useful to you. Now you plunge right in and start reading it, right?

Wrong! If you think about your progress to this point, you'll see that you've worked from the outside in, from the general to the specific. There's no reason not to continue this approach.

Write down what you're after from this book, and then devise a plan to read it. It may turn out that you'll read the last chapter first and work your way backwards through the book.

Add details to the skeletal structure you've built up. At first, you'll have to do this in writing; later you'll be able to do it mentally.

Is Taking a Course Worthwhile?

"I thought, why not? What can you lose?" an engineer who took a popular course confided. "They promise your money back if you don't triple your speed. But what really happens is that you're embarrassed to say that you're not getting as much out of it as you expected. And it follows that you don't ask for your money back at the end of the course. All I really got out of it was a few calluses on my fingertips, but at least they were tax deductible."

He raised his reading rate from 299 words/min. with 60% comprehension to 925 words with 75% comprehension. This may sound fast, but he seriously questions the real comprehension of anything deeper than Mickey Spillane. He adds, "For engineers who are dealing with precise technical data, I just can't see how such a reading program would be adequate."

If the book is well organized or you don't know too much about the field, you'll most likely simply follow the author's structure. If you are concerned that the method just outlined will get you into trouble, keep in mind that there's no rule against reading a book again.

The second time, if it makes you feel better, you can read the book straight through from the beginning.

Above all, avoid reading passively. Inject yourself and your background into the material. If the author's line of reasoning isn't clear, question it. Don't hesitate to go back over the material. (It should be mentioned that it is forbidden in any kind of speed reading to go back over lines just read; if there's something you don't understand, push

The Class Should Be Small

"Be sure there are no more than 25 students because individual instruction is imperative," one chemical engineer advised. "A class of 25! Fifteen would be better," another responded. "The more chance you get to practice in class, the more you learn."

The composition of the class, as well as its size, is important. Almost everyone interviewed mentioned that his class was heterogeneous, a hodgepodge of different ages, interests, occupations and reading abilities. Each felt he might have made more progress had the class been more homogeneous.

on until there's a natural break in the material; it may be subsequently explained; if not, go over the whole block of material.)

Reading Papers and Articles

The techniques of efficient reading are the same whether applied to nonfiction, fiction, technical books, meeting papers, or articles in journals. However, there are tricks involved in reading each.

An important advantage of technical papers: Because the author is not concerned with the number of copies he can sell, he will generally give you a descriptive title, which often permits you to immediately determine whether or not the paper is of interest to you.

Having made the decision as to whether a meeting paper is worth reading, your next step is to read the abstract. Don't spend too much time on it (most authors misuse abstracts and fail to include any of their results or conclusions) before turning to the conclusions of the paper itself. If these, combined with the fast reading of the abstract, still maintain your interest, read the abstract again, now carefully.

After this, still don't plunge into the paper yet. Go through it rapidly, reading the first line of each paragraph, If you find a break in the continuity of the logic, continue on. If the point isn't cleared up later, go back and read (still quickly) until it does become clear.

About now, you should have a good idea of what the author is doing, how he does it and what he found from what he did. You are now ready to actually read the paper. It is tempting to plunge right into papers because usually they are rather short. But don't do it! The time you save by sorting out the chaff permits you to read other papers and get an overall view of the meeting.

Techniques in reading technical articles vary according to the nature of the magazine. Articles in society journals are likely to be pretty much like the papers given at the society's meetings, and should be read accordingly. Editors of these journals often remove the abstract (a considerable loss to the reader), and change the descriptive title into something snappy and uninformative. So read the conclusions first, then the blurb or "deck" (below the title), which takes the place of an abstract.

Some of the "commercial" magazines are well edited and contain fine articles. Others contain material whose only purpose appears to be fulfilling postal regulations for an inexpensive mailing rate.

In any case, a well-edited article should be read by first reading the blurb (or deck) carefully; then, the crossheads (the larger, generally bold-faced, phrases that break the article into sections).

Editors generally organize articles according to the classical inverted pyramid, or some variant of it. This means that the whole story is at the beginning, with details following in order of importance. This structure corresponds very well to efficient reading techniques, but because the editor and writer are aiming at a wide audience (while you have a special interest), you should not simply start at the beginning. ■

Acknowledgement

The author wishes to acknowledge the contribution of June Ranill (of CHEMICAL ENGINEERING's Los Angeles office) to this article. Parts of her survey of the opinions of engineers about rapid reading courses appear in the boxes. Unfortunately, space limitations did not permit more of her report to be presented.

Meet the Author

Michael Sheldrick, as chief of McGraw-Hill's Chicago News Bureau, directs news coverage of industry and business in the Chicago area for more than 40 McGraw-Hill magazines. Prior to that, he was, successively, assistant editor and Midwest regional editor for CHEMICAL ENGINEERING. Before joining CE, he worked as a process engineer for Allied Chemical Corp., having received his degree from New Jersey's Newark College of Engineering.

PART III

Presenting Ideas to Groups

Improving Oral Communication

Although we spend a large part of our lives in talking and listening, we don't do either very well. This series will tell how to do better.

ROBERT HAAKENSON, Smith Kline & French Laboratories

A few years ago, alumni of Purdue University were polled regarding what had been most conspicuously lacking in their education. The responding alumni, predominantly engineers, declared overwhelmingly: "communication."

The engineers had discovered that technological proficiency is not enough. The professional person must also be able to explain what he does, and why, and how; and to understand what others are saying to him.

For reasons that will be given in a moment, we will concentrate on the spoken word in this series and entitle it, "Improving Oral Communication." Further, we will concentrate on formal settings—oral reports, public speaking—but will not minimize conversation, interview, committee meeting, conference, etc. Essentially what is effective in platform presentation is also effective in the less formal modes. The challenge is to find and apply the universal principles.

Embarking on "Improving Oral Communication," then, let us attempt to answer briefly these questions:
- How much of it do we do?
- How important is it?
- How good are we?
- How do we improve?

In this installment, we will discuss the first three questions and offer a beginning on the fourth. But the full discussion of the fourth will be the subject of several ensuing articles.

How Much Oral Communication?

In 1926 a young man named Paul Rankin offered a dissertation in support of this Ph.D. candidacy at Ohio State University. His study produced surprising results. He concluded that the typical person spends 70% of his waking hours engaged in some form of verbal communication. This suggests that more than 11 of the normal 16 waking hours are spent in exchanging words.

Rankin went further. He analyzed the 11 verbal communication hours and came up with this apportionment:

9% writing
16% reading
30% talking
45% listening

It is interesting that we spend 75% on the spoken medium (talking and listening) and 25% on the written (writing and reading). Our formal schooling, incidentally, exactly reverses the commitment of time.

Other studies paralleling Rankin's have been conducted at various times and in various places since, yielding similar results.

The December 1966 *Communications News* proclaims boldly that the computer rapidly is dominating communication—men talking to computers, computers to men, computers to computers, and computers to machines. Yet the article freely admits that spoken communication has grown steadily, and will continue to increase.

Thus we conclude that we spend a lot of time talking and listening—substantially more than a quarter of our lives.

How Important Is It?

There are many ways of responding to this question. One is to consider the time, energy and resources we pour into the endeavor. Loren Reid of the University of Missouri wrote:

A General Electric official reported that management spends half a billion dollars annually in communication to employees. Vance Packard estimated that the 100 largest corporations spend 50 million dollars each year on public relations. *Fortune* in 1952 reported that American business spent 100 million dollars a year selling free enterprise to Americans . . . The financial editor of the New York *Herald Tribune* gave 168 lectures in two years. The president of the U.S. Chamber of Commerce makes 100 speeches annually; Kenneth MacFarland of General Motors makes 200. The Dale Carnegie company teaches 50,000 students a year from General Motors, RCA, Coca Cola, and other corporations and businesses.

There are now more than 3,600 Toastmaster clubs in 50 countries and territories throughout the free world. *Toastmasters International* describes itself as a "nonprofit, nonpartisan, nonsectarian educational organization which has helped more than one million men through its program of self-expression and self-improvement."

A club is described as "an organized group providing its members with opportunities to improve their abilities to speak in public, conduct meetings and develop executive abilities. In congenial fellowship, ambitious men help each other through practice, mutual constructive criticism and the assumption of responsibilities within the organization."

Another way of considering the importance of spoken communication is our intent. We talk and listen primarily to exchange messages: to achieve understanding. This is basic to any sort of efficiency in getting on with the world's work.

Less obvious, but powerfully important is morale. Because personality is brought directly to bear, spoken communication has special potential in elevating human relationships. One authority suggests that the finest thing one human can do for another is to listen—fully and empathically.

Edward Annis was a fine but unsung surgeon of Miami, Fla., until the American Medical Association discovered his speaking talents at a time when the Medicare issue was flaming. Dr. Annis vaulted into the presidency of the AMA and became its forceful number one spokesman.

Again, listening comes into prominence. Pfizer Laboratories entered into a contract with Basic Systems, Inc., to develop programmed instruction in listening. When the course was written the first employees to use it were the sales representatives.

Dr. Robert T. Oliver, Professor of Speech at the Pennsylvania State University, addressing the Annual Convention of Toastmasters International, New York City, Aug. 20, 1965, stated:

"Winston Churchill with a rifle in his hand, crouched behind an earthen rampart along the Dover coast, might have repelled two or three Nazi invaders. But the same Winston Churchill, speaking with his matchless oratory, was able to marshal the global resources and inspire the will to victory that toppled Hitler's empire and preserved the democratic civilization of the Anglo-American world."

Let us not minimize the individual's selfish reasons for polishing his oral skills. A chemical engineer experienced slow but steady progress during several years of employment with a firm. Suddenly he received a handsome promotion with expanded responsibility. Befuddled, he analyzed his meteoric rise. He traced it back to an important oral presentation he had made to the firm's top management.

In his talk to the Toastmasters convention, Robert Oliver cited experiences of some great Americans:

"... Henry Ward Beecher, America's greatest preacher, traced his intellectual awakening to the speech class taught by John Lovell in Mount Pleasant Academy, in Amherst, where for the first time he encountered a kind of teaching that was less concerned with the input of information into his mind than with the outflow of influence from his whole personality.

Henry Clay attested that whatever he was and whatever he achieved he owed to his early and constant training in the art of public speaking. Andrew Johnson could not even read and write at the time of his marriage, but he educated himself by hiring a boy to read aloud to him the great orations of Burke, Fox, Erskine, and Pitt while he worked busily at his sewing in his tailor shop. Lucy Stone left her farm home to enter Oberlin College where, as a mere girl, she was not allowed to give speeches but prepared herself for leadership as an eloquent advocate of women's rights by sitting as a mute auditor in the young men's public speaking class.

Woodrow Wilson wrote his first published essay on oratory and organized a debating society because he was convinced that skill in speech was the basic requirement for intellectual development and personal leadership."

In summary, then, we can say there are many compelling reasons for improving oral communication: for getting on with the world's work—to enhance understanding, to dignify human relationships and elevate morale, and to strengthen persuasion, both for convincing and motivating; for the individual—to possess the powerful tools of good speaking and listening and to enjoy the rich pleasure of confidence in one's self-expression.

How Good Are We?

Both as talkers and listeners we are, in a word, poor. After conducting a series of studies, Ralph Nichols of the University of Minnesota concluded that in the typical audience situation, not more than 25% will be able to report accurately even the speaker's central idea. This reflects badly on both speakers and listeners.

We are insensitive—to ourselves and to those with whom we are supposedly communicating. Our messages are poorly conceived in topics, amplification and support, and organization. Our words, inflections, gestures and audio-visual aids are either inadequate or overdone. We fail to exploit the power of felicitous language to clarify and motivate. We are not wise in the choice of media (e.g., speech, discussion, interview, telephone call) and in timing. We fail to elicit feedback and use it to refine ensuing transmissions.

Loren Reid told of a two-part Civil Service examination used to create a manpower pool of young men and women to fill important junior posts in the federal government. Though the need for personnel is great, only one of five passes the written portion. Then, alas, of every five who survive the written test, only one passes the oral.

How Do We Improve?

If as a result of what we have said up to this point, we have a new appreciation for oral communication—its reach, its importance, and our general ineptness—we have already begun to improve.

Above all, we will wish to conceive of (and cast our) communications in the form of dialogue: Mr. A and Mr. B striving for a meeting of minds in an ongoing series of verbal exchanges.

One theorist conceived of communication as "helical" in its formation and suggested the "Slinky" toy as a communication model. One tip end of the coil might represent an initial transmission. A point diametrically opposite would represent the receiver, whose "feedback" response would be represented by the "return" semicircle. But the response does not return to the precise point of origin, but to a point just "above" on the coil, showing the process nature of communication.

R. W. Revans, Director of the European Association of Management Training Centers, published in the Aug. 26, 1965, issue of *New Society*, the report of a study by Manchester University:

Ten courageous mathematics teachers in ten different secondary modern schools, in and around Manchester, volunteered each to give five lessons of 40 minutes upon a subject of their common choice. They met together several times and decided upon the use of logarithm tables; as far as it is possible to standardize the presentation of this subject among 13-year-old B-stream pupils, they agreed among themselves to do so. Each of the lessons was then photographed at three second intervals by two cameras, one facing the class, one the teacher; each lesson was also tape recorded.

Each class had about 35 pupils; since each class was photographed 800 times per lesson and since 50 lessons were observed, the total number of child photographs was well over one million. We used 16 mm. film with a wide-angle lens, and were able to work under normal classroom lighting; the children got familiar with the apparatus and, in our subsequent scanning of the films, we found it very rare indeed, not once in a thousand times, to observe a child distracted by the camera.

The students' achievement in learning the logarithm tables was measured and the pictures analyzed painstakingly, searching for important clues. The major conclusion reached was that the most signicant factor in the students' learning achievement was entering into dialogue with the teacher. Revans concluded:

Is this result not perhaps an illustration of a more general law, that institutions in which subordinates feel free to ask questions of their superiors are those that adapt best? . . . May it not be that one of the more important inalienable rights of small children is to be both seen and heard? Is it not intelligibility rather than happiness that most of us are after in this life? What, after all, is education other than learning how to ask questions? . . .

In future installments, we will forge ahead—improving our oral communication by discussing these topics:

A. Oral reports and public speaking
   1. Composition: content (topics, supports) and organization.
   2. Audio-visual aids.
   3. Language.
   4. Delivery.
   5. Question and answer.
B. Group leadership and participation.
C. Listening.

Summing Up

In summation, how much talking and listening do we do? A lot; typically more than eight hours per day. How important is it? Critically important: for understanding of messages, for morale, in persuasion and in individual development. How good are we? Most of us are poor talkers and listeners. And even the good ones can improve. How do we improve? Lots of ways.

We begin by attempting to communicate in the form of ongoing dialogue. We will aggressively seek feedback from our receivers, and use this response to improve our succeeding transmissions. Then, in the months ahead, we will develop some principles on speech content, organization, audio-visual aids, language, delivery, handling the question and answer period, discussion methods and listening.

Meet the Author

Robert Haakenson is Community Relations Manager of Smith Kline & French Laboratories, 1500 Spring Garden St., Philadelphia, Pa. 19101. In 1959 he launched the company's nationwide Speaker's Bureau which now has 500 members. He has taught at the University of Iowa (where he received his Ph.D. in Speech), Temple University and the Universities of Missouri and Minnesota. He is past president of the Pennsylvania Speech Assn. and a member of the National Council of the National Society for the Study of Communication as well as numerous other organizations.

Organizing Your Talk

Good organization makes your talk more effective and easy for the listener to follow, plus making it easier both to write and deliver.

ROBERT HAAKENSON, *Smith Kline & French Laboratories*

"First I tell 'em what I'm gonna tell 'em; then I tell 'em; and then I tell 'em what I told 'em." This is the reported success formula of a backwoods speaker.

"A strong proposition based on three compelling reasons." This is the reported success formula of interscholastic debaters.

Put the two formulas together and we have the basis for a functional pattern of speech and report organization.

Simple, hard-hitting organization is the basis for versatility, eloquence and effectiveness in communication. We will speak of:

- The basic plan (schema).
- Patterns of analysis.
- Introductions and conclusions.
- Sample outline.

Good organization is helpful first to the listener. With a clearcut matrix, he has a frame of reference in which to fit the particulars as they come to him.

But do not minimize the value to the speaker. If he is working from a simple, well-conceived outline, he is freed from the memory burden of intricate sequences, and is able to concentrate on winning from his listeners the desired response.

Schema

Actually, we may think of any well-organized communication in this simple schema:

_____

_____

_____

The long first line represents the *central idea*. The shorter lines represent the *main points* that undergird the central idea. There should be not fewer than two nor more than five main headings.

The central idea may come instantly and automatically to the speaker, or it may present a very difficult challenge. If we are asked to speak in behalf of joining the civic association, or to explain the new data processing installation, the central idea fairly well declares itself. If, however, we are asked to speak on civic reform, or to advance ways in which corporate procedures can be streamlined, the selection of this central idea may be a long, even agonizing, procedure. If the subject area is emotionally explosive—civil rights, partisan politics, moral standards—the assignment may be even more trying.

When decision on the central idea is difficult, there is no easy way out. The speaker simply must commit the necessary time and thought. One consideration might help: We know that as any experience, including listening to speeches or reports, fades into history, it narrows to a sort of unified single impression. If we can decide, when the tumult and the shouting, the sound and the fury have died away, that *this* is what we would like to persist in the minds of the listeners, we have a good clue to the central idea. What, above all else, should be retained? If we can phrase this in a simple declarative sentence, we probably have a good statement of the central idea.

Patterns of Analysis

Having selected the central idea, the main headings ought to come more easily. There are five basic patterns of analysis, with certain stock designs in each category.

We say "not fewer than two main headings and not more than five" because if there are fewer than two we have not subdivided. If there are more than five, we have not discovered natural groupings and have lost the major benefit: ease of remembering by both speaker and listener.

Many speakers are fond of 10-point expositions. Who can remember 10 points? Five is a sort of upper limit. Also, as will be evident in examples to follow, natural groupings are found in two, three, four and five. Interestingly, the most popular number of main headings is three. Some persons attribute this to the

SPENDING TIME on organizing your talk pays off later.

religious trinity; others feel that it derives from the concept of continuum: two extremes and a middle ground.

Here, then, are the five major so-called "patterns of analysis," with illustrative "stock designs" for each:

1. Chronological or Time Pattern—There is only one stock design here: past, present, future. It is probably the most used stock design. This is understandable. As we approach any topic we ask: How did it start? Where are we now? Where do we go from here? All of this is fine, except that when it comes time to report our analyses, there are probably much more significant relationships.

2. Spatial, Topographical or Geographical—Following are some stock designs in the spatial relationship:

Federal	Metropolitan	Left
State	Suburban	Center
Local	Rural	Right

Top	Near	Inside
Middle	Mid-distant	Outside
Bottom	Far	

3. Topical or Distributive—Here the basic relationship is neither time or space but is substantive, e.g.:

Who	Theory	Background	Criteria:
What	Practice	Problem	Quality
Where		Methodology	Price
When		Results	Service
How		Implications	Beauty
Why (sometimes)			

A very useful device both for analysis of topics

and synthesis of outlines is the so-called "decachotomy" (a ten-way breakdown):

> Political
> Social
> Economic
> Scientific
> Educational
> Religious/Moral
> Military
> Psychological
> Cultural/Esthetic
> Philosophical

Using the "decachotomy," the speaker can determine which facets of any subject are the most important to the talk. Indeed, when he organizes his speech or report, he may use the self-same considerations as his main headings.

4. Logical Pattern of Analysis—There are basically two stock designs here: problem-solution and cause-effect. We commented earlier that past-present-future is the most-used stock design and probably overworked. Instead, the most-used should be problem-solution. This is because we are a purposeful people. We communicate to meet needs, solve problems and, in general, advance the human condition. Further, the stock design should include "damage":

> Problem
> Damage (consequences)
> Solution

If, for example, we deal with the problem of air pollution, demonstrating undeniably that the air is being polluted, and demanding that laws be passed and enforced, the member of the audience might say to himself, "Sounds reasonable. I agree." But all of this is detached, at arm's length.

If, on the other hand, the speaker demonstrates that so long as the problem of air pollution exists, there is direct damage, dire consequences, to these *immediate listeners*, their families and heirs, then the member of the audience becomes involved, ready to respond actively, no longer arm's length, but shoulder-to-shoulder, ready to move.

Remember, we tend to rely most heavily on past-present-future, but because Americans, above all others, are progress-oriented people, we should be employing problem-damage-solution. We wish to identify problems and needs, and to move forward purposefully to resolve them.

5. Psychological—The psychological pattern of analysis takes into account the psychological set of the listener as a member of the audience. One of the most famous of the stock designs is Richard Borden's "Ho-hum" formula:

> Ho hum
> Why bring that up?
> For instance?
> So what?

First the speaker must catch the listeners' attention, then demonstrate that his topic has relevance, then demonstrate its validity, and finally carry it over into the action phase.

A combination of psychological and logical (problem-solution) designs is the "motivated sequence" of professor Alan Monroe of Purdue University:

Attention step

Need step

Satisfaction step

Visualization step

Action step

The famous format of advertising is "AIDA":

Attention

Interest

Desire

Action

Thus we have five basic patterns of analysis, with illustrative "stock designs" in each. These, obviously, are merely suggested ones. The speaker or writer of the oral report may create his own main headings and can use these stock designs as patterns or suggestions.

Introductions and Conclusions

In one of Plato's dialogues, Socrates comments to the effect that a speech should be like a living being with head, body and feet, and all parts complementary to the whole. Ever since, it has been fashionable (and properly so) for a talk to have an introduction, body and conclusion.

The body of the talk is the fulfillment of the schema, i.e., the central idea and two to five main headings. In a long or complicated talk or report, the speaker may develop subheadings and even sub-subheadings. In most presentations, however, the simplicity of the central idea and the two to five main headings is advantageous.

What about the introduction and conclusion?

In the introduction, our speaker will want to "tell 'em what he's going to tell 'em." He does this with a preview. He reveals his pattern or outline by announcing his central idea and main headings. If he wishes to build suspense, he will do this in an abbreviated or perhaps somewhat mysterious fashion. At the very least, however, he will provide good clues to his central idea and main headings.

In his conclusion, our speaker will want to "tell 'em what he told 'em." He does this in the summary. After a preview in the introduction and development in the body, the speaker leaves nothing to chance, and recapitulates his schema emphatically.

What else remains?

SAMPLE OUTLINE for a talk on the drug industry follows the suggestions given in the outline. Note the introduction with its icebreaker and preview, the body with its three main topics, and the conclusion with its summary and haymaker.

Sample Outline

I. Introduction
A. Icebreaker
  1. Story of mass production of pencillin in World War II
B. Preview
  1. Challenging criteria in chemical production
    a. Quality
    b. Economy
    c. Safety

II. Body
A. Criteria in chemical production
  1. Quality
    a. Translating chemical process into chemical production
    b. Solving the challenge of faultless production of massive quantities
  2. Economy
    a. Chemical engineer strives for lowest possible unit cost consistent with quality and safety
    b. Efficiency is critical where throughput is enormous and profit margin slim
  3. Safety
    a. Production workers
    b. Community
    c. Subsequent handlers and consumers

III. Conclusion
A. Summary
  1. Chemical engineer must fulfill demanding standards in chemical production
    a. Pinpoint-accuracy in massive quantities is first requisite
    b. Production economy may determine market life
    c. Safety concern extends beyond production workers to ultimate consumers.
B. Haymaker
  1. Genius of American chemical engineering, which produced enough penicillin to treat all Allied casualties in Normandy landings, is working for us round the clock.

Our speaker will begin artistically with an "icebreaker." Its purpose is to call attention to, and rouse interest in, the speaker and his topic, and, secondly, to create a pleasant communicative rapport between speaker and audience.

The best type of icebreaker is the case-history type of narrative that illustrates the central idea, or at least leads into it intriguingly. Audio-visual aids are often useful in breaking the ice and in previewing. Audience participation, e.g., show of hands, guessing answers, also is good. Sensational statements, "shockers," should be used with caution. If jokes are relevant and well told, they are fine. Spontaneous spur-of-the-moment humor is better. Definitions may be used. The speaker may quote scripture, maxims or poetry. References to the audience, occasion, speaker, or all three, are fine.

Thus, to call attention to, and arouse interest in, the speaker and his topic; and to create a pleasant rapport between the speaker and audience, any one of a variety of icebreakers is available. If time is plentiful, the speaker may use several, e.g., reference to audience and occasion, humor, participation ("Who will tell us what material this container is made of?"), a case history.

The speaker then offers his preview ("tells 'em what he's going to tell 'em"), e.g., "I want to share with you some of the miracles of chemistry in health. We can get a pretty good idea in brief time if we cover: First, discovering the molecule's health-giving properties; second, synthesizing the molecule; and, third, quality-control manufacturing in quantity. Or, in brief: one, discovery; two, synthesis; and three, manufacture." Now both speaker and listener have a plan of attack, an orderly approach.

Occasionally, some concept or term is so basic to the entire talk that it should be defined in the introduction. If the speaker is to report, for example, on "Information Sharing in Decentralized R & D Locations," and he plans to make extensive use of the concept of "telecommunications," obviously he should define the term early, probably immediately after the preview and just before getting into the discussion proper.

At the other end of the talk is the conclusion. Here, the speaker first summarizes ("tells 'em what he told 'em"). We know that we forget 50% of what we hear in one 24-hour period during the ensuing 24 hours.

In our speaking and reporting, we wish to do everything we can to improve retention. One aid is restatement. Therefore, the speaker recapitulates central idea and main headings. If there has been true development in the body of the speech, and if the speaker has any artistry whatever, there will be steady growth from preview, through development, to summary. The final summary can be hard-hitting and emphatic because of this growth. It will not seem to the listener to be mere repetition. Listeners will accept more redundancy than the speaker might at first think possible.

Finally, the speaker will wish to end climactically. The orators of ancient Greece and Rome called this peroration. Here the speaker made his final impassioned plea for his cause. Today we are less flamboyant but the principle stands. The "haymaker" may be almost any one of the items suggested for "icebreakers": Narrative, instance, quotation, participation, humor, audio-visual aid, etc.

A particularly pleasing touch, though not essential, is for the "haymaker" to refer back to the "icebreaker," bringing the talk 360 degrees, full circle. If the "icebreaker" is a case-history-type narrative, for example, and the "haymaker" brings the narrative right to the moment, there is a sort of esthetic completeness that is artistically satisfying. Obviously, the "haymaker" above all should give impact to the central idea.

In the "telecommunications" example just suggested, for instance, the "icebreaker" might be an interesting narrative of the amount and variety of information on a given topic a computer can produce in a matter of seconds.

The "haymaker" might be the posing of an R & D problem confronting this immediate group that might be susceptible to the information potential of the data processing installation. The talk has come full circle, the central idea is reinforced, and a challenge is put to the listeners.

Summary

We have said, then, that clear-cut organization is the basis of versatile eloquence. It enables the listener to proceed methodically and frees the speaker to concentrate on winning the desired audience response. Effective organization usually multiplies the speaker's efficiency in his preparation. If he can quickly decide on his central idea and main headings, he then can go about completing the talk and creating audio-visual aids methodically.

The basis of functional organization of any communication is the *schema:* Central idea based on two to five main headings. The main headings will reflect one of five major patterns of analysis: Chronological, spatial, topical, logical, or psychological. Well-known "stock designs" (past, present, future; federal, state, local) may be used themselves, or may suggest main headings the speaker creates himself.

The speaker opens artistically with an introduction that "breaks the ice" and then previews. He concludes artistically and emphatically by summarizing and by landing a "haymaker."

Henceforth, we will combine the genius of the backwoods speaker who "tells 'em what he's gonna tell 'em, etc." and the inter-scholastic debater who advances his proposition relentlessly on the basis of "three compelling reasons."

The Content of Your Talk

Once you've chosen your topic, you are faced with the problem of just what items to include in your talk, and what to omit. Here are some hints for solving the problem.

ROBERT HAAKENSON, *Smith Kline & French Laboratories*

Late in the 19th century, Dr. Russell Conwell gave a talk at a reunion of some of his old Civil War comrades. Entitling it "Acres of Diamonds," Conwell considered it a good effort, but not outstanding. He described it as "a mere accidental address." To his surprise, it was requested again and again.

The upshot: Over the next many years, Dr. Conwell delivered "Acres of Diamonds" more than 6,000 times, for revenues of $7 million. Most of the money, incidentally, was plowed into the education of needy young men and the founding of Temple University in Philadelphia.

Perhaps the outstanding feature of the talk is that it develops a highly unified theme by narrating one illustrative instance after another. The theme is simply that opportunity lies everywhere about us if we will but scratch the surface.

The supporting instances range the breadth of human experience. They begin with the legendary Ali Hafed spending his life in search of the fabled "acre of diamonds" and—on returning home, old and exhausted—dying, just before the treasure was discovered on his own land. Additional instances, actual and more current, include the discovery of gold at Sutter's Mill, California; the discovery of oil at Titusville, Pennsylvania; the millinery venture that launched the fortune of John Jacob Astor; and dramatic success stories in trout farming, toys, and hatpin design.

This famous talk illustrates several principles of speech content, notably topics and supports. Let us discuss:

- Analysis of audience and occasion.
- Delimitation of topics.
- Amplifying and supporting particulars.

Audience Analysis

As he begins to prepare, the first thing the potential speaker should do is focus on his target. And as he continues his preparation, he should keep refining his aim. For example, while gathering materials, he will continue to analyze the audience and the occasion. His principal source of information will be his sponsor —the program chairman, president, or other officer— but he will not stop there. He will contact prospective members of the audience and former speakers, and consult published descriptions. He may be able to attend intervening meetings of the group. His objective is to get in his mind's eye as comprehensive and accurate as possible a picture of his forthcoming speaking engagement:

Who will be present? How keen is their interest in his topic? How much do they know about it? What is their concentration span?

What are the circumstances of the occasion? Is it a serious meeting, or largely social? What precedes? What follows? Will a long program have fatigued the listeners? Will a lengthy agenda worry them about preserving vitality for what is to follow?

Delimiting Topics

Often a recommendation is made to: "Narrow the topic; don't try to cover so much."

This advice is doubtless well intended and often good. But it is not infallible. Simply narrowing a topic endlessly may not necessarily achieve the desired result: e.g., chemistry, synthetic materials, plastic, plastic toys, plastic flying saucers, and so on. As the topic is narrowed, to be sure, the speaker is permitted to delve more deeply in the specified length of time. But what is the most meaningful for the audience? Perhaps exposition on the broader theme of "synthetic materials" may be best for this audience at this particular time.

In delimiting the central idea, therefore, the speaker will realize that he can interpret it broadly and provide limited coverage. Or he can shrink the central idea and plunge in depth. Or he can choose a middle course.

At the outset, then, the speaker must make the basic decision: Is it more useful for these listeners at this time to say more about less, or less about more?

Amplifying and Supporting Particulars

Amplifying and supporting details fill out the speech outline. They supply clarification for understanding, support for belief, stimuli for action, and interest to attract and sustain attention.

Following are some of the chief types of such specifics:

> Definition.
> Description.
> Comparison/contrast.
> Figure of speech.
> Example or illustration: real or hypothetical.
> Instance.
> Case history.
> Date/event.
> Enumeration/listing.
> Narrative/anecdote: true or fictitious, serious or humorous.
> Figure/statistic.
> Quotation: witness testimony, authority opinion, maxim, scripture, poetry.
> Humor: quip, pun, repartee.
> Audio-visual aid.

Case History

The case history is a first-rate type of amplifying particular. It attracts attention, holds interest, and persists in the listener's memory. Properly selected, it clarifies, convinces and motivates.

Members of the Smith Kline & French Laboratories Speakers Bureau have addressed more than 14,000 audiences in the past 8 years. One talk, "Prescription for Tomorrow," in its various revisions, accounts for more than 6,000 of the talks. The speakers consistently report that the case histories explain the popularity. Here is an example:

"Most of us have had prescriptions that call for taking medicine every three or four hours. We all sometimes forget or think it a great inconvenience, especially when we have to get up at 4:00 a.m.

"A team of our scientists searched for a method of solving this problem. They thought it would be possible to make one dose that would provide continuous, uniform medication for 10 to 12 hours. They reasoned that this could be accomplished by dividing a single does into a number of very small parts that would disintegrate at different times. But this took some doing. Month after month went by without finding the proper combination of size and ingredients.

"Finally one of our scientists, while shopping in a grocery, spotted those brightly colored candy beads used to decorate cookies and cake icings. These were the size particles he was looking for. An idea clicked in

his mind, and candy beads like these, *coated with intricate patterns of medication*, became the basis of an entirely new pharmaceutical form.

"We now have 18 products in this special form called 'Spansule' capsule, indicating that the medication is released over a long *span* of time. In each capsule are more than 600 tiny pellets, each of which will release its medication at the proper moment. That simple project —from candy beads to finished product—simple though it seems today, took seven years or 35,000 man hours to complete.

" 'Thorazine,' that pioneer tranquilizer, is available in 'Spanule' capsule form, and in several strengths. Think of the advantages when this medication can be given only once, or at most twice, a day and bring continuous tranquility to a once-disturbed mental patient."

Source

There are four fruitful activities for gathering amplifying and supporting particulars:

> •Inventory: taking stock of what one already knows.
> •Talking.
> •Reading.
> •Observation.

A frequent tendency is to depend chiefly on reading to gather materials. This is regrettable because it overlooks many vital data, and, secondly, misses a great deal of the fun of research. The communicator should read, to be sure, in a wide variety of published sources and in great quantity. But he should also give himself credit for already possessing vital and useful information. And he should certainly interview others—formally and informally. This provides not only firsthand specifics, but is a kind of audience analysis, yielding insight into the way the ultimate audience may react. Finally, in all topics, wherever possible, nothing is more valuable than direct, firsthand observation. What, after all, is more convincing than, "I was there. I saw it with my own eyes."

The speaker should gather an abundance of particulars. A good rule of thumb is that he should begin his outlining with not less than four times the amount of information he can possibly include in the talk. And not only should we have such copious quantities, but they should be of varied types and from varied sources.

Criteria

Now the outlining—and perhaps drafting—of a manuscript can begin. The speaker applies these demanding criteria:

• Relevance. Irrespective of any other merit, the particular is worthless if it is not germane. It must amplify or support the point under consideration.

• Accuracy. Truth must be served.

• Human interest. Richard C. Bates, M.D., writing in the February, 1967, *Hospital Physician*, on "How to Keep Medical Audiences Awake," suggests, ". . . unadorned traffic statistics will put an audience to sleep; . . . details of specific accidents in the community will do the opposite."

• Quantity. Are there adequate details to clarify the point and make it convincing, but not so many as to labor it?

• Proportion. Are the specifics nicely arrayed in terms of type, length and source? One good suggestion is to "balance the specific with the general," i.e., illustrate the point by citing an actual instance, then demonstrate that the instance is typical, representative of the general situation, by citing statistics or quoting authority opinion.

Successful meeting of many of these criteria is illustrated in a recent lecture. Dr. Hubert Alyea is professor of chemistry at Princeton University and a celebrated lecturer who addresses audiences all over the world in all sorts of circumstances. He has presented one talk on the atom 2,800 times, and another, "Unlikely Accidents: Great Discoveries by Prepared Minds," 500 times.

On this recent occasion, he was introducing a new talk, "Curiosity and Satisfaction." Its theme is the romance of science, and it is intended for after-dinner audiences who may be groggy from food and drink and sweltering in a banquet hall that is too hot, too dark, too smoky, too noisy. Dr. Alyea faced up to the challenge with an admixture of amplifying and supporting particulars worthy of any rhetorical alchemist. He knows well the time-honored factors of attention: surprise, shock, humor, narrative, emotion, conflict, novelty, the familiar in a new setting, personal data.

Dr. Alyea led off with surprise, reversing the ordinary situation by handing his speech outline to the audience. He quickly revealed that he would intersperse his commentary with demonstrations. He admitted that these laboratory pyrotechnics would be more for recapturing flagging interest than for teaching science.

His commentary consisted of one narrative after another, much in the fashion of Dr. Conwell's "Acres of Diamonds." But Alyea went Conwell one better: Almost every one of Alyea's instances involved him personally, providing interest and identification.

An example: Alyea told of Albert Einstein's visiting him in his research room at the Kaiser Wilhelm Institute in Berlin. There, Alyea had a Rube Goldberg device for the investigation of certain optical phenomena. The device consisted of a pipe closed at one end and, at the other, two lenses unequally lighted. Experimentation included twisting the lenses to measure light ray interaction. Curious, Mr. Einstein approached the device and peered into it. Furious, he complained, "Can't see! Can't see!"

Professor Alyea noted that he was peering into the closed pipe, explained that he was at the wrong end and directed him to the lenses. Einstein was elated, "Wonderful! *Wunderbar!*"

Alyea reported that in later years, with both men resident at Princeton, Einstein frequently attended his lectures. During his explanation of a point, Alyea would watch Einstein. If he found a frown, even immobility, he would try another explanation, and another, keeping it up until he saw Einstein's head begin to bob up and down and a smile to spread across his face. Then Alyea knew he had made it clear.

At this point, it may seem that the Alyea lecture was exclusively gimmicks—human interest stories and laboratory sleight of hand. But along with this, the professor had imbedded a very solid message in his discourse. His point regarding Einstein, for example: a true scientist does not hesitate to admit his ignorance.

The Larger "Message"

The larger "message": Alyea was very caught up in the project of bringing chemistry education to the disadvantaged people of the developing nations. He described and demonstrated the ingenious steps taken to reduce costs of a workable audio-visual projector from $400 to 25¢. He described and demonstrated the "unicell," in an inexpensive Plexiglas container that alone does the work of 200 audio-visual devices formerly required.

There are millions who need science education but their circumstances permit only penny expenditures. The selfsame science they need to learn may nevertheless make possible the achievement of their educational goal.

Alyea states that laboratory costs for a chemistry

student in a U.S. university total around $500 a year. With devices like those described above, he has brought this down to $5. He points out that this is significant not only to the students of the impoverished, developing nations, but also to students of overcrowded schools everywhere. The miniaturization makes it possible for each student to have his laboratory on the folding arm of an auditorium chair. This project, called TOPS (for Tested Overhead Projected Series) is described in an article, "Microchemistry Projected," in the June, 1967, issue of *Journal of Chemistry Education*.

Documentation

A specific piece of information has a way of being about as good as the source from which it comes. The matter of divulging sources of information we call "documentation." This is a study in itself. There are rules: legal, moral and stylistic. We will suggest here some rules that reflect—at least informally—those regulations:

• Reveal the source when credit is due: The ideas belong to another; the information or the data are the fruits of another man's toil. If the material is copyrighted, of course the source must be acknowledged, the limitations of quote and paraphrase respected, and —for extended passages—permission obtained.

• Reveal as much information about the source as necessary to give the listener a clear idea: Who said it? When? Under what circumstances? Is it a direct quote? Paraphrase? Where is it published? Use language precisely, to distinguish clearly what is quoted or paraphrased.

• Accentuate the positive. Wisely handled documentation adds interest and credence; awkwardly handled, it invites inattention and reduces credibility.

Summary

Speech content, then, consists of the topics we select for our talks and reports, and the amplifying and supporting particulars that give body to those themes.

The first step in preparation of speech content is careful analysis of the audience and occasion: Establishing as comprehensive and accurate a picture as possible of the persons who will attend and the circumstances that will prevail.

We delimit topics effectively when we define that breadth of scope that will permit desired depth of treatment in the time available.

We marshal amplifying and supporting particulars effectively when we know all the types available, use all methods of gathering them, analyze audiences and occasions perceptively, and employ functional criteria in selecting details for inclusion: relevance, accuracy, human interest, quantity and proportion.

We employ documentation (revelation of sources).

Russell Conwell gave a talk 6,000 times and netted $7 million. Hubert Alyea launched a new talk that exalted the first audience, and doubtless will do the same for hundreds more. Each of these talks illustrates critical considerations in speech content: wise delimitation of topics, and moving use of amplifying and supporting particulars.

Delivering Your Talk—I

Even the best thought-out talk can be ruined by poor delivery. Here's how to make the audience sit up and take notice.

ROBERT HAAKENSON, *Smith Kline & French Laboratories*

Which is more important: what the speaker says, or how he says it?

This battle has raged for years but is needless. Obviously, the speaker should have something well worth the saying, then must say it well enough to gain a fair hearing.

It is true that many persons with fine ideas go unnoticed because of colorless presentations. Other persons, gifted in expression, often attract more attention than their thoughts truly deserve.

Our objective here will be to perfect our skills in delivery and then to use them in behalf of worthy causes and sound ideas. In order to do this, we will consider four points:

1. The challenge.
2. Goals.
3. Options.
4. Success formula.

We will use the words "delivery" and "presentation" interchangeably. Further, we will differentiate "delivery" and "presentation" (how the speaker says it) from "content" (what the speaker says) and "organization" (how he structures the talk). "Content" and "organization" have been covered in previous articles.

The Challenge

Talks are given under widely varied circumstances. They differ in numbers of persons attending, length of presentation, formality of occasion, setting, etc. A typical community audience numbers 40 persons. A typical setting is a meeting room that is little more than adequate: noisy, modestly to poorly outfitted, fairly to poorly ventilated and illuminated.

The speaker would like to believe that when he opens his mouth to expound, a hush will fall over the group and a magic spell will prevail. This is rarely the case.

There are always certain factors present that compete with the speaker as he strives to stir his listeners. These factors may be broadly classified as internal and external.

Internal competitive factors are within the intended listener. Each member of the audience brings his own collection of concerns: ill health, physical or intellectual fatigue, preoccupation, worry, overindulgence in beverage or food. Wrap them up and they become a great bolus, a sizable barrier separating the speaker from the desired listener response.

External competitive factors: even in the newest, most ingeniously designed meeting rooms, there are sources of distraction: excessive noise, traffic, other extraneous activity, excessive heat or cold, humidity or aridity, smoke. Air-circulating equipment often is amazingly noisy.

Stop for a moment, wherever you are, ask everyone to remain silent, and listen. You will be surprised and distressed to hear the roar. This is just one of the many external competitive factors that get between the speaker and the listener.

The foregoing description may seem to be overdrawn and morbid. There are some settings, true, that approach the ideal. But the safest thing for the speaker to do is to assume the worst. He should, in fact, prepare himself to survive a "Roman Circus."

Another precaution is to assume there are present greater competitive factors than meet the eye—especially, the internal. The human attention or concentration span is notoriously limited. Further, the things that unfold in the report or talk often will remind listeners of old worries, or stimulate thought in peripheral or unrelated areas.

The challenge, then: Win the desired response while operating in the arena of the "Roman Circus."

Goals

One good definition of communication is "an endeavor by one individual through a system of symbols to win a desired response from another." We can state these goals in a progression of aspirations, i.e., for the speaker to be:

- Heard.
- Understood.
- Believed.
- Inspiring.

One should be heard. Many individuals are concerned —and properly so—about "acoustic pollution." For years, the noise level has been rising, especially in the big-city complexes. In the 15,000 talks by members of the Smith Kline & French Laboratories Speakers Bureau, the most pervasive single problem has been that of being heard. Even where public address systems are available, speakers find it difficult to rise above the clatter of dishes, the uproar from the adjoining room or the din of traffic outside. In short, being heard is no minor aspiration.

Secondly, the speaker strives to be understood. Wishing not to demean his audience, and wishing to present himself as an authority in his field, the speaker is naturally motivated to provide challenging ideas and information. But even with sophisticated audiences, it is easy for him to get beyond his audience conceptually and in vocabulary. Today's increasing specialization complicates matters. Despite our very best intentions, it is easy to fail to be understood.

In much, perhaps most, of our speaking there is an element of controversy. In some cases, the audience response is openly hostile. In others, it is simply one of resistance to change. Therefore, much of our speaking is dedicated to achieving change (we think of it as "progress"). Thus we strive to influence attitudes and belief. We strive to change convictions and that is a challenge.

Finally, we strive for the ultimate objective: action by our listeners. Possible actions include: to carry forward the message, to initiate a project (or cancel or modify it), to sign a petition, to vote in a certain way, to campaign, to become a candidate, to enroll as a volunteer, to make a financial contribution, to join an organization, to endorse a proposal, to approve a budget.

Options—Four Modes of Delivery

There are four modes of delivery for presenting our reports and speeches: memorization, reading, extempore and impromptu. Each has certain advantages and disadvantages. The truly "compleat speaker" is effective in any of the four, and knows when to use each.

Memorization has the advantage of detailed preparation, exact timing, and freedom from any memory aid (manuscript, note cards, visual aids). It has the great disadvantages that (a) it is hard work, (b) few speakers recite well, and (c) memory is fickle—the chain is as strong as the "weakest link"; if it snaps, the whole presentation has an air of fraudulence.

Reading from manuscript has many of the advantages of memorization plus the greater security of the manuscript—almost anyone can read aloud so long as there is proper lighting. The major drawback of reading is that few people are communicative in this mode. The manuscript becomes a barrier between speaker and audience. This barrier, however, is not insurmountable.

In extempore speaking, the speaker is fully prepared, except that he stops short of putting his ideas and information into final words. This is done on the platform. Thus this mode has the advantages of full preparation (including rehearsal), adaptability or flexibility, and spontaneity. The disadvantages are that:

- The word supply, which was abundant in rehearsal, may fail before the audience.
- Sometimes the inspiration of the moment stimulates the speaker to say things he didn't intend to and later regrets.
- It is easy to lose track of time—particularly, to talk too long.

The speaker may use memory aids—notes, an outline, visual aids, or even a manuscript as an outline. It is particularly effective to speak extemporaneously, while free from any notes or other aids.

Impromptu speaking is completely off-the-cuff or ad lib, and is therefore different from the three preceding modes in that it is not prepared. It is splendid when it is the only option available, but unforgivable otherwise. Occasionally a speaker will procrastinate, failing to prepare and forcing himself to speak impromptu. The inspiration of the moment may bring resounding success and he will resolve never again to undergo the agony of preparation. Such success without preparation is rare and, therefore, a snare and delusion. The few successes in such impromptu speaking are outweighed by thousands of dismal failures.

There is a current trend toward reading from manuscript: speeches must be approved by employers or sponsoring organizations—sometimes, indeed, by representatives of the group to be addressed. Timing must be exact; occasionally, visuals must be coordinated with a projectionist. Often the text of the talk must be released in advance to the news media and other publications. There is increasing attention to this secondary (reading) audience, and properly so. For these reasons, today's effective speaker must learn to talk communicatively from manuscript.

Success Formula

To overcome the competitiveness of the internal and external environmental factors that make up the challenge; to fulfill the objectives of being heard, understood, believed and inspiring so the desired audience response is won; and to be successful in all four modes of delivery—memorization, reading, extempore and impromptu—a success formula must be found. In a single word it is "impressiveness"—impressive content, impressive organization and impressive delivery. Content and organization have been discussed elsewhere. Impressive delivery can be described by considering the speaker's duty at the lectern step-by-step.

Getting under way

(1) Focal or initial pause
(2) Salutation

(3) Smooth transition into the discussion proper

Under way*

(1) Authority

(2) Involvement

(3) Communicativeness

(4) Vocal expressiveness

(5) Physical expressiveness

Climactic finale*

(1) Hard-hitting windup

(2) Terminal pause

Getting Under Way

Focal or Initial Pause—When the amateur speaker hears his name called by the program chairman making the introduction, his immediate inclination is to begin talking—even before he has risen from his chair. He is self-conscious and over-eager. The veteran speaker, on the other hand, will proceed to the lectern deliberately, even slowly. With a pleasant facial expression, hopefully a smile, he will look out over his audience.

At a convention in New York City, Bishop Fulton Sheen was introduced to an audience of more than 2,000 persons meeting in the grand ballroom of a major hotel. He was given an ovation. Then, as the audience settled down to hear him, he looked out over the assembly, smiling serenely. Even after the last chair scrape had quieted, he continued this initial pause. It may have been as long as 30 seconds. Because he was seemingly comfortable in silence, his audience was comfortable. It gave them the opportunity to ready themselves to listen and to anticipate what he might say. It gave him the opportunity to feel the stimuli of this anticipation.

If a speaker begins to jabber immediately, his words are competitive with the visual stimuli he is transmitting. Listeners have to satisfy their visual curiosity. If words are emanating simultaneously, they are in conflict.

Thus the speaker serves both the audience and himself by indulging himself lavishly in this silence. It is the initial pause to permit the listeners to focus their attention on the speaker and specifically on what he is going to say. The veteran speaker will use this time to sense the audience anticipation, to compose himself, to get his notes, manuscript, visual aids, microphone, drinking water in order; or perhaps, he will simply look out over the group making visual contact or enjoying the pleasant scene before him.

The self-conscious amateur who finds this hard to do can occupy himself with certain business, e.g., running through a little checkoff list: Jacket buttoned? Manuscript in order? Microphone at right height?

*These subjects will be covered in the second part of this section, beginning on p. 62.

First words (salutation) clearly in mind?

Salutation

The salutation should be full, spontaneous and as free from cliches as possible. First, the speaker will want to acknowledge the nice introduction he has been given. He should state his thanks spontaneously, using the title and name of the person who introduced him. Then he will wish to acknowledge the others present by name and/or title, and most especially the name of the organization that is the basic audience.

Sargent Shriver addressed a large banquet gathering in Philadelphia. After his focal pause, he said, "Thank you, Mr. Chairman, Judge Reiml, for your glowing comments and lively introduction. President and Mrs. Gladfelter . . ." At this point, Mr. Shriver was faced with a head table that stretched the width of the ballroom. How could he keep the "pecking order" straight in a lineup of this sort? He resolved it by starting at his extreme left, graciously acknowledging each individual, with an occasional impromptu comment for some, and working his way naturally and easily across the width of the head table.

When we are introduced socially around a living room, we try to respond, repeating the name of each individual to whom we have been introduced. Public speaking protocol follows basically the same principle. The program chairman has introduced us to this group assembled and we respond by acknowledging the presence of the program chairman, the dignitaries, the organization and guests.

The salutation should be natural, spontaneous and cordial. That protocol be respected is far less important than that there is honest awareness of persons present and their identities.

If the situation is informal and time is limited, the salutation will be trimmed accordingly. At the very least, it should be an acknowledgement of the program chairman and his introduction and most important, the identity of the group itself.

Smooth Transition Into Discussion Proper

Next our speaker should have "parry and thrust" ad libs. Unless time is pressing, he should make references to the occasion, to the audience, to himself, and to his topic. His purpose is to seize attention, arouse interest, and weld common bonds in a nice, easy, communicative rapport. Humor is wonderful if appropriate and deftly put, but unnecessary and downright bad if heavy-handed.

This ad-lib parry and thrust should provide a smooth transition into the text of the talk. The speaker should know the opening paragraphs of the manuscript "cold" so he can slide smoothly into the discussion proper.

Delivering Your Talk—II

Once your talk has started, the way that you handle yourself has a marked influence on the audience. Here's how to do it right.

ROBERT HAAKENSON, *Smith Kline & French Laboratories*

In the last article, we discussed how to get a talk under way. The speaker's next responsibility is to present the talk itself with impact. To do so, he should fulfill the five essentials of impressive delivery:

- Authority.
- Involvement.
- Communicativeness.
- Vocal expressiveness.
- Physical expressiveness.

Authority

Here we speak not of content expertise, but of the speaker's frame of mind or psychological set.

Members of audiences empathize with speakers. If the speaker radiates assurance, the audience reposes its confidence in him.

Perhaps the best phrase to express what we mean is that of the military: "situation well in hand." In speech terms, this means that the speaker need not be absolutely free from stage fright or apprehension but that he is present, determined to communicate. He reveals that he has control of fears and has adequate confidence to get on with the job of communicating.

A couple of alphabet-soup expressions might be helpful:

PTP: "Prime the Pump"—Thousand of speakers report that they lack authority in the opening moments of a talk, but once under way gain confidence and assurance. The challenge then is to bolster performance during those first minutes.

Speakers who have tried it report that they can successfully "prime the pump." By exhibiting a little courage or bravado that they may not actually possess, the desired effect can be achieved. It might be described as making an extra effort, or, in theater parlance, assuming the posture. One might say that the speaker can "psych" himself into an attitude of confidence that will strengthen his opening and give him continuing authority.

If, at the beginning, the speaker reveals that he is in fact taking charge, and that he is at least that confident, he has requisite authority. If he can also

radiate his comfort with this responsibility—i.e., natural confidence, self-assurance, poise — effective communication will be enhanced.

KBF: "Keep a Bold Front"—There are really two dimensions here. One is at the outset of the talk. Speakers often open with apology. They didn't know until 11:00 last night that they were to speak. Their health is deserting them. (It is true, of course, that apprehension about a speech can bring on or aggravate symptoms.)

The speaker opens his talk by saying, "I didn't know until 11:00 last night that I was to be your speaker. As you can hear, I am having an attack of laryngitis but, if you will bear with me . . ."

Having said this, the speaker has experienced catharsis. Verbalizing his feelings of inadequacy provides a kind of purge.

The member of the audience does not feel the same relief. Instead he thinks, or senses subconsciously, "Here is a man who did not know until late last evening he was to be the speaker; here is a speaker who by his own admission is not in tip-top condition; and yet he has the gall to take up a precious half-hour of my life." Thus we see what a masterpiece of destructive psychology the speaker's alibi is.

What is often demonic is that the speaker, no matter how sorely tried by tardy invitations, poor health, or other circumstances, secretly expects to do all right. But with his alibi he has protected himself. Should he flop, then the blame is on the dilatory program chairman or the doctor responsible for his poor condition. On the other hand, if he does all right, as he expects to do, he will look all the better because he has labored under such trying circumstances.

The second dimension of "Keeping a Bold Front" is in the handling of mishaps under way. The tendency of the amateur speaker is to magnify his mistakes by calling attention to them. True, such verbalization probably reduced his tension, but it also spotlights inconsequential errors such as an incorrectly pronounced word, a transposition of phrases, a lost place. If the error is insignificant, the speaker should KBF and sail right on, not even bothering to correct it. If the error muddies understanding or disserves truth, then, of course, it must be corrected. In a quiet, workmanlike way, the speaker goes back, rights the situation, and resumes his presentation.

No matter how trying or unfair the circumstances, we should not prejudge our talk, or the audience's reaction. We should sail in and do the best we can. And, happily, the chances are very good that we will do all right.

Involvement

Involvement is the speaker's sensing deeply the meaning and emotion that his words are intended to convey. Involvement slips away very easily when the speaker speaks from memorization or reads from manuscript. And when it does, there is no panacea. If the speaker realizes that he is merely parroting words, he can only draw himself up short, pause, and work his way back to the meaning and emotion.

Several things will help. One is *pause*, frequent use of pause—either for emphasis (holding eye-contact) or simply for speaker and audience to reflect over what is being said.

More alphabet-soup may be helpful:

TTT: "Think the Thought"—If the speaker is involved, he will himself be thinking the thoughts that he is attempting to share. If he is thinking the thought, he is almost certain to reveal his involvement to his listeners. TTT is helpful to the speaker under way. He asks himself, "Am I 'thinking the thought'?" If not, he must do something about it: Pause, and deliberately work his heart back into his work.

LKF: "Little Known Fact"—This is a special kind of ad lib. The "Little Known Fact" is something known to the speaker alone or perhaps also to one or a few of the audience. The little known fact demonstrates that the speaker has a personal connection with the subject, thus a substantive involvement. His spontaneous expression of this fact communicates involvement in delivery.

The reason the ad lib reinforces involvement is that while the speaker is talking, free association may trigger recall of some pertinent item, possibly something in the day's news or something said by his luncheon partner just preceding the talk. The speaker is so deeply immersed in what he is saying that these relevant experiences are spontaneously brought to mind.

Many speakers will deliberately mark the manuscript at places where they can ad lib if circumstances permit.

Communicativeness

Think of yourself in your last act of "friendly persuasion." You were endeavoring to persuade some friend to some belief or course of action for your friend's best interest as you saw it. Here is what you were doing, probably subconsciously:

You were bringing into play every argument, every contention, every emotional appeal, every shred of evidence, every piece of description that would make your case persuasive. In short, you brought into your campaign everything in the way of *content*.

Secondly, you structured your campaign. You might have said, for example, "Okay, we're agreed up to here, are we not? All right, then." And you would launch off into "no man's land." You would penetrate as deeply as you could, until you thought you could penetrate no deeper, being rebuffed. Then you would fall back and regroup, consolidating your gains. After a summary, you would launch off on a new tack into "no man's land."

Thus you were structuring intuitively. You were using *organization* for maximal persuasiveness.

Thirdly, your personality ran its full gamut, from overpowering forcefulness to humble supplication. All facets of presentation varied dynamically, persuasively: voice, articulation, bodily expression, language. Your vocal inflections varied from thundering to whispering. Certain words were enunciated with compelling precision. The words and phrases themselves were your most persuasive. You circled about your friend and may have towered over him or even drooped before him. Your face was alive with expression. Your eyes did not leave his. In short, your personality and presentation ran the gamut, intuitively, without deliberate or self-conscious intent. Thus, the maximum of your potential in *delivery* was exercised.

Fourthly, you were so caught up in the act of communicating, striving to elicit the desired response from your friend, that you were totally oblivious of self. Your total attention was riveted on response, noting when you had made headway, when you had to amplify, to reinforce, or to offer more supporting detail.

Vocal Expressiveness

It is said that Madame Eleanora Duse, a great Italian actress, once brought an audience to tears merely by her moving recitation of the alphabet in her native tongue. Properly used, the voice by itself can be powerfully persuasive. Most of us use only a fraction of the potential.

The greatest danger is that we will not be heard. Next, our voices will be dolefully monotonous. Thirdly, there is the danger of artificiality, forced inflection changes.

There are four variables with which we work:
- Pitch—soprano, alto, tenor, bass.
- Loudness—ranging from whisper to shout.
- Rate—rhythm or tempo, how fast and how slow and how much pause.
- Quality—timbre.

Over the first three variables, the speaker has a great deal of control.

The fourth variable, timbre or quality, is harder to change. This factor is best defined by negative characteristics: strident, hoarse, husky, harsh, breathy, excessively nasal, etc. Favorable attributes include resonance and mellifluousness. Timbre is in fairly large part hereditary, and improvement therefore may require clinical attention, or perhaps cannot be improved at all. But proper use of the first three variables can compensate for poor quality, and may sometimes actually overcome timbre problems.

The best assurance, however, is that each of us, even though his voice may be quite ordinary, has enough control over pitch, loudness and rate, to make it effective.

To overcome monotony, the simple counterpart is variety. To overcome artificiality, the inflections must be generated genuinely, spontaneously. The speaker freely lets his voice give expression to his true feelings. To overcome speaking too quietly (or too loudly, rapidly, slowly, shrilly or rumblingly), the speaker merely avoids the extremes.

Remember that your voice is spontaneously expressive in your "friendly persuasion." A good rule is: "Bring to the lectern your conversational manner with close friends, only put a little more energy into it."

Since the most frequent problem is that of inaudibility, a wise procedure is for the speaker to recruit someone to serve as monitor. This should be arranged before the speech begins; but, if necessary, the speaker may ask in his introductory comments, "Can you hear me? May I ask the gentleman in the middle of the back row—you, sir—to give me a signal if I should become too quiet or too loud?" Always the gentleman in the middle of the back row is happy to oblige. The speaker then must see to it that he watches for any signal, and responds promptly and fully.

Microphones and public address systems add whole new collections of problems. The speaker can do several things: (a) observe what works for the speakers who precede him; (b) recruit the monitor described above; (c) throw himself on the mercy of his audience: "Can you hear me? What do I need to do?"

There is another dimension of vocal expressiveness: *articulation.* This consists of accurate pronunciation, the right syllables in the right order, and crisp, distinct enunciation.

There are occasional problems of mispronunciation, e.g., "nuculer" for "nuclear", "appraised" for "apprised", "revelant" for "relevant," but for the most part speakers do well. A wise practice is to always look up the pronunciation if you have the slightest doubt.

In the second aspect, *enunciation,* however, most of us are mediocre at best. We are typically lip-lazy, slovenly. Actually, on the public platform, the speaker should exaggerate the crispness and precision of his enunciation.

Physical expressiveness

Meaningful bodily action includes movement about the platform, stance, gesture, facial expression and eye contact. The best general rule for physical expressiveness is: "Plentiful, meaningful and spontaneous". When we think of such pantomimists as Charles Chaplin and Harpo Marx, we realize how eloquently communicative bodily action can be.

The speaker should move about the platform as freely as the setting allows. Perhaps the worst circumstance, and a frequent one, is when the speaker is locked between program chairman and president, with wall behind him and lectern in front of him. Yet, with no more than a two-foot square in which to move, the speaker can shift from side to side, step backward or forward, or lean purposefully across the lectern, thus enhancing his effectiveness.

Such bodily expression is helpful to the audience because it freshens the visual stimulus—making attention easier, interpreting meaning, and providing emphasis. Such movement helps the speaker because it relaxes his tensions, helps him use up additional energies his emotional stimulation has created, and gives him greater total expressivity. Movement about the platform can be overdone, of course, as is often illustrated in the caricature of the professor who paces back and forth in front of his class, sentry-duty style.

The second opportunity for the speaker to use effective physical expression is in stance or posture. The basic rule is "erect, yet comfortable." The speaker should stand tall, leaning slightly forward while balancing his weight on the balls of both feet. He should not clutch the lectern, but might rest his hands lightly on the edges of it.

A good basic position is to rest the wrists lightly on the hips. With elbows thus bent, the speaker's arms are cocked, ready immediately to respond to the impulse to gesture. If, however, his hands are clutching the lectern, the paralytic grip must be relaxed before the impulse can be followed, and then it might be too late. Also, good gestures must have some lead time.

With the speaker's arms across his mid-section, and his elbows bent, the fingers of one hand might lightly touch the fingers of the other; but one hand should not grasp the other for the reason just given. The speaker may prefer to bend only one arm which, of course, is perfectly all right. Some speakers will bend the arms so sharply that the hands are in front of the chest, at the lapels. This initially might seem awkward to the speaker, but, suprisingly natural to the audience; and in this position it is almost impossible *not* to gesture.

The emphasis on taking a stance that will facilitate gestures indicates the importance of the latter. Gesticulation at its best is a visual aid. If the speaker draws an imaginary diagonal, this is an effective visual aid to depict an upward or downward trend. Tallying on the fingers visualizes enumeration. Relationships of size, placement, growth, diminution, speed, direction, and many other concepts can be effectively visualized by good gesture.

Gesture, like proper stance and movement about the platform, helps give rise to total expressiveness.

The fourth factor of physical expressiveness is facial expression. The general rule is "alert and friendly." Do you recall the wire service photo of General Eisenhower when he was given the news of General Douglas MacAuthur's recall from his Pacific Command? Here was a mobile facial expression that communicated worlds.

The speaker's facial expression should be essentially friendly. Most speakers are friendly; but many, perhaps most, appear to be unfriendly. This is because they are apprehensive, and fear shows up less as fear than it does as unfriendliness: brow furrowed, eyes narrowed, corners of eyes and mouth pulled down, etc.

The problem is simply how to bring to the surface the friendliness the speaker feels. The answer: the speaker must smile. Yes, the best way for the speaker to bring his friendliness to the surface is to smile. Although a smile is not infallible, it is a universal sign. A way of brightening the facial expression without smiling is simply to raise the eyebrows. The speaker may also employ: (a) humor; (b) melodic vocal inflections; and (c) jovial cordiality with the other people who are present. A lively, pleasant interaction suggets a friendly speaker.

The fifth and final factor of physical expressiveness is eye contact. A general rule is that the speaker should maintain eye contact 90% of the time—eye contact with all his listeners in an irregular, roving sweep.

Genuine eye contact is not achieved by a blank-eyed stare in the direction of the audience. The speaker must not only see his listeners, but he must note their reactions and adapt to them. If they appear bored, he must spark his presentation; if confused, he must amplify; if disbelieving, he must offer support; if unmoved, he must offer inspiration.

Closely related to physical expressiveness is the problem of what to do with the manuscript itself. There are two alternatives: (a) when possible, keep the manuscript inconspicuous. It is merely a memory device and the speaker who is fully prepared will refer to it only in infrequent and swift glances. "True art conceals art"; communicative reading conceals reading. (b) When references to the manuscript are unavoidably conspicious, e.g., the speaker has not had opportunity to steep himself in it, or there is no lectern available, the speaker should display the manuscript boldly. It is reported that Winston Churchill said the speaker should virtually flaunt the manuscript, figuratively beating the listeners about the head with it.

Either way, the important consideration is that the speaker emerge predominant and the manuscript only as an aid.

A verse by an unknown poet sheds light on the problem:

> Of all the kinds of lecturers
> The one I most detest
> Is he who finishes a page
> And places it behind the rest.
>
> I much prefer the kind who takes
> The pages as he finishes
> And puts them in a mounting pile
> As pile the first diminishes.
>
> But I like best the lecturer
> Who gets them in confusion
> And halfway through he lets escape
> The phrase, "And, in conclusion . . ."

Climactic finale

Hard-hitting windup—The speaker should conclude as smoothly as he began. He should know the last several paragraphs of his talk "cold." This should free him completely from both the manuscript and the lectern.

His "haymaker" (peroration) should be a truly climactic finale, positive, resounding, inspiring. He may wish to come around in front of the lectern, closer to his listeners.

Terminal pause (holding eye contact)—When his final word is said, he should begin a terminal pause, holding eye contact with his audience. He should challenge himself to make it a matter of artistry that he can end thus climactically without limping off on the weak crutch of "thank you." Employing this phrase to end a talk is such a cliche that the artistic speaker should vow never to use it.

If the speaker can't think of anything else to do during the terminal pause, while he is waiting for his audience to applaud, he can count silently to himself: "1000-1, 1000-2, 1000-3." If he gets to "1000-8" and the audience still has not begun to applaud, he may contemplate abandoning his speaking career. The terminal pause obviously is the counterpart of the focal pause. At the outset we emphasize the smile; at the windup we emphasize eye contact.

Summary

Assuming that our speaker has ideas and information well worth his audience's hearing, he will set about providing proper expression. He begins by realistically facing up to the challenge—an abundance of internal and competitive factors that may add up to a Roman Circus. He "goes for broke" in his aspirations: to be heard, understood, believed, and inspiring to the point that the listeners take the desired action. He develops expertise in all four modes of delivery and selects that which is most appropriate for the occasion: memorization, reading, extempore or impromptu. Ultimately, he delivers the speech impressively with "situation-well-in-hand authority;" "think the thought involvement;" "drive for the desired response communicativeness;" melodic, crisp vocal expressiveness; and plentiful, spontaneous, meaningful physical expressiveness.

Cicero described the ideal orator as "the good man speaking well."

Audio-Visual Aids Bolster Your Talk

Nothing but talk can be dull. Visual aids can make points clearer and add interest, too.

ROBERT HAAKENSON, *Smith Kline & French Laboratories*

A speaker was talking about molecular manipulation in chemical research. He explained that tiny modifications can mean extreme changes in the chemical's effect. The point was reasonably clear and the generalization accepted by the audience.

On another occasion, a speaker advanced the same point. He, however, displayed a molecular model of the benzene ring, the so-called "wedding ring of organic chemistry." He described the properties of the industrial solvent benzene, represented by the molecular structure. Then he added a group of atoms to the model, explaining he now had benzoic acid, a food preservative. Finally, he added a third group of atoms, explaining that the new compound has pain-killing qualities: *aspirin.*

The description by the second speaker obviously was clear and vastly more memorable because the visual aid was employed. Additionally, this particular story illustrates many principles of effective audio-visual (a-v) aids usage, as we shall soon discuss.

It would be wrong to imply that a-v aids are good *per se.* Properly used, they strengthen the impact of the talk; improperly used, they detract.

To develop the principles of effective a-v aids usage, let us discuss:

1. Rationale for their use.
2. Types available.
3. Criteria for selection.
4. Techniques.

A basic consideration in effective a-v aids usage is determining and stopping short of that point where the aids begin to dominate, reducing the speech to mere demonstration, and the speaker to the role of narrator. Proper use keeps the items as *aids,* i.e., they bolster the presentation but do not take over.

Rationale

It is reported that 85% of what we retain in our minds is gained from visual stimuli. What we gain through listening, therefore, is only a portion of the remaining 15%. This means that the oral-aural medium is a fickle one indeed. On the other hand, it is widely reported that the medium of communication that has the greatest impact is the spoken word, especially that described as "eyeball to eyeball." The

reconciliation of these apparently contradictory statements may be found in R. Benschofter's article, "In-Service Training Aids" published in *Proceedings of Nebraska's Inservice Training Conference,* Oct. 21-22, 1964, Omaha, Neb., Psychiatric Institute:

Methods of Instruction	Recall 3 Hr. later, %	Recall 3 days later, %
Telling (when used alone)	70	10
Showing (when used alone)	72	20
When a blend of telling and showing is used	85	65

A-v aids enhance the communication process in various ways. First, members of the audience are served. Their attention is attracted, interest aroused, understanding benefited and motivation stirred by good aids.

Secondly, the speaker—especially the amateur—is served. Preparation of aids tends to sharpen preparation over-all. Attractive aids give the speaker confidence. Handling the aids provides opportunity for purposeful "stage business"—something to do with one's hands, good reason for making direct contact with the audience.

Thirdly, good aids serve the sponsor of the meeting by fostering more-satisfactory treatment of complex topics in less time.

Types

A-v aids are almost limitless in type. The box contains a classification that is illustrative, not exhaustive.

This list cannot be exhaustive because virtually anything to be found in our universe may become an aid. Think of the variety of items that have been "Exhibit A" or "B" or "C" in courtroom trials.

There is a broad classification that may be useful: (1) items as they exist in their natural state, e.g., an ear of corn; (2) items modified for a-v usage, e.g., an ear of corn halved and specially mounted to show (in section) ideal proportions at full maturation; and (3) items specifically created, e.g., stop-action motion-picture visualizing the maturation of an ear of corn. Wise use of a-v aids, then, requires awareness of the limitless variety of types available.

Criteria

Eyes opened to the array of possibilities, we must now have some guidelines for judicious selection. Criteria may be summarized as "RSVP"—*Relevance, Subordination, Visibility* and *Portability.*

Relevance—A speaker who was to describe the new technology in oil refining made a special effort to include visual illustration. Splendid. But he fell victim to the lure of "interesting scenes," the temptation of irrelevance. He showed slides of company officers, foreign offices, oil depicted in art classics, oil in cartoon humor—some amusing, the majority interesting, but too many *irrelevant.* His central idea and main points were obscured by the scrapbook display.

The speaker must resist this temptation to include visuals simply because they are attractive, novel or "cute gimmicks." Aids should be relevant. They should underscore the central idea and main points. They should help the speaker lead the listeners in the right direction. One good way to assure relevance is to use one good aid for each main point.

Further, among the two to five aids thus employed (one for each main point), it is a good idea to use different types. In a speech to reveal the impact of synthetic textiles in our lives, the speaker illustrated (1) *comfort* by balancing the weight of several garments against one made from natural fibers, and using an electric fan to show air penetration, (2) *convenience* by demonstrating ease of cleaning, (3) *cost* by showing large swatches of synthetic and natural fiber fabrics on which were painted expenditure-per-hour-of-service figures, (4) *variety* by a brief motion-picture clip of range of textile applications, colors and patterns, and (5) *industry growth* by a graph portraying growth in dollar volume.

Once in a great while, it is okay to toss in an a-v "gimmick" to interject variety, recapture interest or relax the audience with a little humor.

The real test of the aid is that it amplifies and supports the point under consideration. For example, a Colorado psychiatrist projected a humorous cartoon to introduce each of five major types of disorientation he was describing.

Subordination—Characteristic of the scientific meeting is the speaker stepping to the lectern, saying, "House lights off, please; first slide, please"; then droning on in the darkness through 45 slides in 45 minutes; and concluding, "Last slide, please; house lights on, please; thank you very much."

The member of the audience has only the scantiest notion of even the speaker's looks. The talk was a *spoken* aid to a visual presentation; in short: a demonstration. The speaker was no more than a voice. This is not speaking. Most of the all-important impact of the speaker's *person* is lost. A good rule to follow is: *The speech must be able to stand by itself, yet be a better speech because the aids are used.*

If a person is present as the speaker, or the maker of the oral report, his personality must merge with the thought-content in order for his theme to make its unique impact.

Visible (audible)—A-v aids should be large enough for all to see, or loud enough for all to hear. To be visible to an average-size audience of 40, an aid about the size of a full newspaper page is satisfactory if illustration and text are proportionately large and simple. For big audiences in big auditoriums, aids may have to be the size of a large motion-picture screen.

To make sure audio aids will be heard by all, the speaker should check acoustics and amplification system before he begins his talk. Since audio aids are predominantly electronic, the nontechnical person should consult with a specialist.

Visuals should be properly displayed. Ideally they will be in sight only when in use. Otherwise, they may be a distraction, competing with the speaker for audience attention. If a large visual has to be mounted in advance, it can be covered by paper or cloth except when in use. Handouts should be distributed *following* the talk, perhaps simply made available at the door.

A notable exception to the out-of-sight-except-when-in-use rule is the organizational visual: a visual presentation of the talk's structure, i.e., key words or phrases that signify the central idea and main points. This may be in view throughout the talk. Speakers of the Smith Kline & French Laboratories

---

I. Visual aids

  A. 3-dimensional
    1. Persons
    2. Objects
    3. Models/mockups

  B. 2-dimensional
    1. Photos
    2. Drawings: schematic, cartoon
    3. Maps
    4. Posters: graphs, charts, enumerations
    5. Devices: blackboards, flannelboards

  C. Projected
    1. Slides/filmstrips
    2. Motion pictures
    3. Overhead projector ('Vuegraph')
    4. Opaque projector

II. Audio aids

  A. Human voice: imitations, songs
  B. Sound instruments: musical, electronic
  C. Phonograph records
  D. Tape recordings
  E. Radio

III. Audio-visual aids

  A. Sound motion pictures
  B. Video Tape recordings
  C. Television

Bureau use this in all talks. In a talk on chemotherapy in the treatment of the mentally ill, "The Silent Revolution," the card lists "Bedlam, Banishment, Breakthrough, Bridge." As the speaker develops his theme, he refers to the visual at appropriate points along the way.

Reasoning that a speaker's face will be in view for all hearers, we can generalize that visuals should be displayed at head height, and near the speaker's head. A poster-card visual, for example, fits nicely into the angle formed by head and shoulder. With an aid that is easily handled, the speaker can avoid using a long pointer, or turning his back on his audience. The speaker himself should look at the aid one-fourth to one-third of the time to focus audience attention on it; the rest of the time, he should look at the audience. Use of a miniature pointer, such as a pen or pencil, adds a touch of precision.

A major part of visibility or audibility is simplicity. Let us say we were going to make an organizational visual for our present discussion. We could present the outline verbatim:

> Improved Oral Communication
> Through Good A-V Usage
>
> Reasons for using a-v aids
>
> Types of a-v aids
>
> Criteria for selection
>
> Techniques of good usage

Using letters of reasonable size, our card or screen would have to be enormous.

Instead, we would abbreviate, perhaps as follows:

This, or Even . . .   **This**

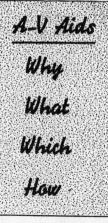

A-V Aids Usage	A-V Aids
Rationale	Why
Types	What
Criteria	Which
Techniques	How

It is not bad, indeed it is good, to abbreviate, to be cryptic. This enhances the spoken word that will explain and fulfill the visual impressions. The same principles of abbreviation and simplification apply to projected visuals and audio aids. Keith W. Sehnert, M.D., in his article, "Your Slides: A Visual Aid or Annoyance?" (published in the September-October, 1966, issue of *The Journal of New Drugs*) includes the following items as five of his "Ten Commandments for Speakers":

• Thou shalt not use slides with blue or black background.
• Thou must be able to read 2 x 2 in. slides without a magnifier . . .
• Thou shalt not use more than three comparative results per slide, or have multiple-line graphs.
• Thou shalt make graphs tell a story at a glance.
• Thou shalt add color or pictures to slides whenever possible.

Portable—A-v aids should be portable. The advantages of being able to carry them any place, any time, and without special transportation, are obvious. Free from bulky briefcases, portfolios, clumsy easels, or other display equipment, the speaker avoids much inconvenience. What may be lost in size and impressiveness is gained in mobility.

Dr. Hubert Alyea, professor of chemistry at Princeton University, developed a remarkable projector by silvering a 25¢ auto-headlight lamp and connecting it with a car battery. He also developed a companion Plexiglas cell with which chemical reactions can be projected.

The overhead Vuegraph projector is very versatile. Its present design is compact and lightweight—easily portable. Its light source is so intense that clear images may be attained on an ordinary wall while room illumination is normal. Facsimile transparencies may be made speedily on a photocopier machine. And the speaker, with a grease pencil, can modify the visual as he speaks—adding, deleting, underscoring.

Techniques for Using Audio-Visual Aids

Audio-visual aids are so important a part of your talk that it's essential to use them correctly. Here are details on working out your own visuals, providing the needed action and variety, and avoiding practices that detract rather than help.

ROBERT HAAKENSON, *Smith Kline & French Laboratories*

Audio-visual aids have become a veritable art form. Educators were using them increasingly when World War II began. Then the Army and Navy, faced with the job of teaching millions of persons new tasks in a short time, relied on every known a-v aid. The lowly comic book became an educational institution. Before invading North Africa, for instance, the military supplemented its lectures with a comic book travelog featuring Donald Duck.

Today, educational institutions, industry, advertising agencies and the military have full-blown a-v departments and conduct far-reaching research. Television stations use aids for newscasts, commercials and speeches.

Speeches are becoming shorter and visual aids more numerous. The typical address is now closer to a half-hour than the hour or more of 50 years ago. Time limits imposed by radio and television have influenced this, as has the pace of modern living. A-v aids help the speaker say more in less time.

Principles of a-v aids, and corresponding techniques, have evolved. Here are some:
- "Roll your own."
- Variety.
- Action.
- Projected visuals.
- Audio devices.

"Roll your own"

The speaker is wise to prepare his own visuals, at least to participate aggressively in their design. Here are some of the reasons: (1) he can select aids to rein-force exactly those points he chooses; (2) aids can be kept free from distracting details; (3) size and complexity of aids can be made appropriate to the occasion; (4) the speaker will be intimately familiar with the aids and able to use them better; and (5) the speaker will be strengthening his over-all mastery of the talk.

Artists' show cards or poster boards make excellent visual aids. Or, using a large art tablet on a sturdy easel, the speaker can sketch lightly with pencil before the talk, then while speaking "create" his sketch with bold strokes of crayon or felt-tip pen. Large blackboards with colored chalk offer good possibilities.

Crayons, marking pencils, india ink and other materials are now available in most colors. The basic visual may be black on white, but color should be used generously to provide interest and emphasis. Dark green on a light green background is said to be the best color combination for legibility.

Variety

Where several a-v aids are to be used, different kinds will be particularly suited to making different points; variety heightens interest.

A medical speaker described the human heart with the aid of a skeleton, a ceramic heart, a schematic drawing, and an oscilloscope portrayal of heartbeats. In a music appreciation expert's talk designed to inform the audience about musical cadence and tempo, the speaker used enlarged time-signatures from musical scores and two audio aids: a metronome and the humming of well-known tunes.

A speaker comparing the success of two competitive

products used: (1) samples, (2) a tabular presentation of the makeup of the two, (3) a line graph of sales trends, (4) statistical tables comparing sales and profits, and (5) writing, on a large paper pad, possible reasons for the differing success of the two products being compared.

Action

Changing the a-v aid while in use is desirable. "Creating" the drawing from the near-invisible sketch, described above, is an example. Or a speaker might start with an item prepared for some totally different purpose—for example, a highway map—and adapt it to his purpose, such as by designating an area scheduled for industrial development. In presenting statistics, one prepared figure, line or column can be boldly circled or otherwise marked for special attention. The same can be done with a list.

Blackboards and flannelboards almost always involve action; stripcharts do also, by the speaker's peeling the cover off specific portions at appropriate times during his talk.

Projected Visuals

Projected visuals are both the speaker's joy and despair: slides, filmstrips, transparencies, motion pictures, videotapes. In varying degree, they are expensive, weighty, bulky and "demanding," i.e., they need a darkened room, projection screen, power supply, operator, etc. But they can provide vivid illustration, distinct images even for vast audiences, rich artistry, lively animation, etc.

Thus we must weigh the advantages carefully. Here are some tips to supplement those of Dr. Sehnert, quoted in the previous article:

Projected visuals must be kept simple just as any other visuals. Because the screen is big, speakers are inclined to cram their slides with data. The result is a screen full of barely legible symbols. *Abbreviate, simplify.* Cut to the bone and leave the rest for the audience to imagine, or the speaker to verbalize.

Cluster the slides and filmstrip sequences so the house lights need be darkened only once or twice (maximum three times). Only under rarest circumstances should lights be down for the entire talk.

Special Projectors

The opaque projector is elephantine in its bulk and weight, but it is swift, powerful and economic. Any printed material may be fed into its breech; it will accommodate more than a full-page in width and the thickness of an encyclopedia. Indeed, encyclopedia illustrations are often projected. A toggle permits the operator to manipulate an arrow-shaped beam of light to single out items in the projected image.

The so-called "overhead" projector overcomes many of the objections to other devices. Some models are costlier, bigger and heavier than a slide projector, yet most are compact and portable. Transparencies can be made as quickly and easily as ordinary photocopies. The light source is so powerful that a blank wall is a satisfactory screen and the image is sharp even in normal room illumination.

Because the transparency rests on an easily accessible deck, the speaker can stand right up front, facing the audience, near the image on the screen, and add, delete and alter to his heart's content. He can provide on-the-spot artistry with his grease pencil or felt-tipped pen, supplying the "action" recommended earlier. The "buildup" technique of one transparency overlay superimposed over another, and another, and another, is very useful in portraying complicated relationships.

Integrate With the Image

The speaker should try to integrate himself with the projected image. Ideally he will stand right alongside it and physically point out items of interest. The worst is when the speaker is totally remote, perhaps the width of the stage or the length of the room away. Then he is no more than a narrator. The least he can do here is to employ a flashlight, with its beam masked into an arrow shape, so he can do some visual designating.

The principle is unity of stimulus. If voice and visual are physically separated, they tend to be divisive and competitive. If they are together, the audience can focus its attention. If the speaker must be his own slide-projector operator, he should obtain a remote control cord and switch.

These problems seldom occur when using the overhead projector. It is quite near its projected image, and the sense of unity of stimulus is achieved further by the speaker marking up the transparency as he progresses.

Audio Devices

There should be no long stretches of tape or phonograph recording. It is very difficult for the speaker to integrate himself into an audio aid unless he is supplying a share of the dialog "live," with responses on the transcription. During "pure" listening to such transcription, the audience ideally should close its eyes, because any visual stimulus is unrelated and distracting. Short audio excerpts, however, offer novelty and limitless possibilities: interviews, speeches, discussions, sounds of all types—nature, music, warfare, industry, electronics, languages. A speaker who was describing the communications program of a great U.S. corporation included in his presentation tape-recorded excerpts of interviews with employees' families, and a sample of a "canned" message-of-the-day available to executives by picking up their phones and dialing a number.

Finally, audio aids should, if possible, be pretested in the auditorium in which the speech will be delivered. Tested in an ordinary room or office, a tape recorder or phonograph might prove sufficiently loud, with lots of gain remaining on the volume control. Later, in the meeting room, however, when the volume is turned up for the larger room, distortion might be introduced because the recorder or phonograph speaker simply is not large enough for fidelity at high volume.

Under these circumstances, the speaker will have to play his tape or phonograph record using the auditorium's public address system, or connect his own machine into it.

Summary

Today's public speaker recognizes the value of audio-visual aids. Audiences tend to be less patient and more fickle than they were in generations past. A-v aids can help capture their attention, sustain their interest, clarify their understanding, bolster their conviction, and motivate their action.

Types of aids available—persons, objects, 2- and 3-dimensional representations, projection and other devices, audio-aids—are limited only by the speaker's imagination. By making certain that his aids are relevant, subordinated, visible (or audible) and portable; and by making certain that they are well-conceived in terms of the speaker's "rolling his own," injecting variety, incorporating action, and making intelligent use of projected and audio aids, the speaker can enhance his content, organization and delivery.

Confucius is reported to have said that a picture is worth 1,000 words. Who can estimate the worth of the right pictures *combined* with the right words?

The Q&A Period Can Make or Break Your Talk

The question and answer period lets you emphasize main points and clear up problems.

ROBERT HAAKENSON, *Smith Kline & French Laboratories*

Do you recall the University of Manchester experiment in teaching logarithms to junior high school students?* From test scores and thousands of classroom photos, the experimenters concluded that the students who learned the most were those who entered most freely into the classroom dialog.

R. W. Revans, who reported the research, commented:

Is this result not perhaps an illustration of a more general law, that institutions in which subordinates feel free to ask questions of their superiors are those who adapt best? ... May it not be that one of the more important inalienable rights of small children is to be both seen and heard? Is it not intelligibility rather than happiness that most of us are after in this life? What, after all, is education other than learning how to ask questions?

In platform presentations—public speaking and oral reports—our best opportunity for such dialog traditionally is the question and answer period (Q&A).

Some speakers, it is true, are able to field questions as they go along. Properly handled, this is ideal. The speaker receives continuing indicators of audience response: interest, understanding, acceptance. But he must be skilled. Otherwise such audience participation may squander his time and lead him astray.

If the speaker has this skill, or if time is plentiful, he should at least experiment with handling questions as he goes along.

Traditionally, however, the Q & A session is saved until the conclusion of the formal presentation. Whichever form it takes, let us say:

• We *want* the Q & A.
• We will *obtain* the Q & A.
• We will *exploit* the Q & A.
• We will *follow up* the Q & A.

*Described in the first article in this series, p. 50.

Although the Q & A is often translated as the question-and-answer "period" or "session," it is good to think of it as Q & A *discussion*. A good Q & A promotes lively and widespread participation.

Some people foolishly think that to question a speaker elevates them in the eyes of others. Some wish to show off their knowledge. Whatever the motivation, the speaker should accept brief statements, for they provide him an opportunity to expand his own message by refuting or amplifying the rejoinder. "I will be happy to respond to your comments as well as your questions, but please keep them brief."

Therefore, in the pages which follow, when the word "question" appears, please add silently "or comment."

We Want the Q&A

More than one veteran member of the Smith Kline & French Laboratories Speakers Bureau has said, "Keep the speeches brief. Make them just long enough to stimulate a Q&A. If we do any persuading, it's apt to be in the Q&A. This is where communication really happens."

Here are some benefits of the Q&A:

• People can ask about those aspects of the topic that interest them most.

• The speaker reinforces his message through recall and elaboration of main points.

• The speaker gets to demonstrate that he knows his subject and can handle himself on his feet. (How many speakers fumble in formal speaking, but flourish when fielding questions!)

• Speakers and their sponsors glean valuable feedback on audience reaction to the speech subject.

Therefore, we want the Q&A. In a moment, we will take up the subject of getting the Q&A.

First, however, let's put the shoe on the other foot. Let's put ourselves in the audience. Here, too, we should want the Q&A. As questioners, alas, we typically range from mediocre to poor. We don't raise questions promptly. When we do, we grope and mumble. (Usually it is good practice for the questioner to stand.) We phrase questions poorly. We don't listen to the answers.

The worst fault is wasting the opportunity to raise questions. As members of the audience, we should want the Q & A for many of the same reasons as the speaker. Also, if we have grievances on the topic, here is a fine forum. We can enjoy the emotional hygiene of a little public ventilating. We can give the speaker a boost, introducing topics he skipped, or reopening issues where his support was weak. And we can even drop some bombs for the speaker to lug back to his sponsor.

Thus, the speaker and audience should be equally eager for the Q & A.

We Will Obtain the Q&A

It is important that the Q & A be planned, and not be a hit-or-miss, afterthought venture. If there will be barely enough time for comfortable delivery of the speech itself, no Q & A should be scheduled. If five minutes or more can be made available, however (perhaps by shortening the talk), it is worth planning the Q & A. This involves (a) letting others know, and (b) getting yourself ready.

Letting Others Know

A good place to start is the moment the speaking engagement is nailed down. As the topic, date, time, place are confirmed, simply ask, "Will there be a Q&A?"

The answer is usually, "If you wish."

Then your response should be, "Yes, indeed!"

Next there are advance announcements of the speech. Ask the program chairman to include mention of the Q&A. Audiences like to know they will have the privilege of asking questions, even if they do not exercise it later.

Before the actual program begins, the speaker should arrange the details of handling the Q&A with the chairman. The chairman, when introducing the speaker, should state clearly that the Q&A will follow the talk. Completion of such an arrangement should not put the speaker at rest, however. Chairmen have human frailties and in the excitement of the introduction may fail to mention the Q&A. If the speaker notes the omission, he will make the announcement himself. For example:

At the outset, I thank you for providing time for a question and answer period. I admit I will be disappointed if you don't have something for me. I welcome comments as well as questions. Please feel free to jot down items as I speak.

This makes a good icebreaker comment, of course, even if the program chairman has *not* forgotten, e.g., "I am happy you allowed time for Q&A discussion. I second Chairman Hulbert's suggestion that you have some questions and comments ready."

The speaker's noting whether the chairman has brought up the Q&A is just one of the many reasons why a speaker should be a very good listener, totally attentive to what is going on about him throughout the duration of a speaking engagement. This is not easy to do when one is preoccupied with his own

speech, but it is important. First, it is simple courtesy to one's hosts. Secondly, the environment will provide valuable clues for audience analysis and adaptation in introductory comments, ad libs during the talk, and illustrations in the Q&A.

Getting Yourself Ready

Piling up the ammunition is half the battle in a well-planned Q&A. The speaker will know, from earlier experience with the speech topic, from what is prominent in the news, and by the nature of his audience, the kind of questions he is likely to encounter. With such prospective questions in mind, he should do a little reflecting, reading, talking and observing to have his answers sharp. He may wish to bring with him to the lectern some critical supportive materials. He will be wise to organize them in a ring binder or some other indexed, easily consulted form.

Most questions raised during a Q&A are surprisingly easy. Facts obvious to the speaker because of his specialized knowledge often mystify and intrigue audiences. These simple questions virtually answer themselves and require little discussion here. But, inevitably, there are other types: complex questions that challenge a speaker's intellect, hostile questions that challenge his tact, partisan questions that challenge his persuasive skill. We will have in mind these tougher ones, particularly as we move on to exploiting the Q&A.

We Will Exploit the Q&A

First, we must get the questioning started. The transition between speech and Q&A should be made smoothly and without delay. After concluding the talk, the speaker acknowledges the applause gratefully and modestly, pauses briefly, yields the lectern to the chairman to open the Q&A, or opens it himself.

A speaker should be prepared to wait several seconds for the first question. If, after a good long wait, silence still prevails, the speaker has a decision to make. First he should remember he controls the mood: the audience will be only as embarrassed as he shows himself to be.

In this situation, the speaker asks himself, "Is there really enough interest to go ahead with a Q&A?" If members of the audience are looking at their watches or slinking toward the door, there is little to be gained by further wooing. The speaker wraps things up gracefully and calls it a day.

On the other hand—and this is frequently the case —the audience is interested but inhibited. No impatience is evident, but neither is there a question. There are several alternatives. One is to wait, comfortably, for what may seem to be an interminable time. Given that time, some member of the audience will get his nerve up, or get his question phrased.

In another approach, the speaker may comment:

Almost invariably, people will come to me after a talk to ask questions. I am pleased to

respond and hope that this will happen today. What often disappoints me, however, is that the questions would have interested the entire audience. So, if you are planning a question or comment, let's hear it now while all can share.

Perhaps the surest alternative, and a justifiable one, is to use a "plant"—someone primed in advance to raise the first question. The plant, preferably in the audience rather than at the head table, should hesitate momentarily to see if questioning will begin spontaneously.

If it does, he need not seek recognition unless he is genuinely interested in raising his question. The justification for this seemingly dubious practice of using a plant is that the Q & A often will flourish if someone will break the ice.

The speaker should recognize questioners with precision: "The gentleman halfway back on my left." "The lady at the far table." The sharply pointed index finger is efficient, but since artist James Montgomery Flagg created the Uncle Sam "I want you!" recruiting poster, it may be considered threatening. The questioner can be designated accurately with a gentler gesture or perhaps by nodding the head and looking directly at the person.

In conducting the Q & A, as in spoken communication generally, use names whenever possible. It demonstrates the speaker's personal interest in the members of the audience. And it offers greater precision than even the intimidating index finger.

It is the speaker's responsibility to make certain that a question has been heard and understood by all before he begins his reply. He should ask the questioner to repeat it only if he got no part of it. If he got any part, then he can say, "Let me see if I understand. Is what you're saying . . . ?"

If the speaker has any doubt about the audience hearing and understanding—and he should remember that a questioner in the audience is directing his voice *away* from all those behind him—he, the speaker, should restate the question, simplifying it if necessary. Thirdly, it gives him a little extra time in which to collect his thoughts and frame a reply. Amazingly, the very restating of the question often gives the speaker the thought he wishes to begin his answer. If the question obviously is heard and understood by all, however, the speaker should begin his answer promptly. Blatant delaying tactics will offend the audience.

Analyze the Question

In the few seconds that pass between the speaker's first hearing a question, repeating or rephrasing it,

and replying, he must get in some fast thinking. What kind of question has been asked? Is it "loaded" or otherwise hostile? Does it have more than one part? Is it really a question in the first place?

Spotting the Loaded Question

The loaded question is one based on false premises or assumptions. It may be the innocent result of ignorance. Or the questioner may be baiting the speaker. In either case, tact is the order of the moment.

For example, an agricultural chemicals speaker was asked, "Since your pesticides are killing off all the birds and fish, why don't they control insects?"

The speaker replied by first pointing out, firmly but pleasantly, that he could not accept the premise that pesticides are killing off all the birds and fish. He said that except for a few highly publicized exceptional instances, birds, fish and other wildlife are far better off *because of* biochemicals. Then he went on to the remainder of the question (on the effectiveness of insecticides), dignifying it by giving his best possible answer. Note two things the speaker did. First, he killed the "load" so that the audience would not be left with a false impression. Then, he went on to speak forthrightly on a controversial subject.

Divide Complex Questions

Many questions raise two or more points. When the speaker detects this and divides such a question into its component parts, he helps both himself and the listeners.

An SK&F speaker was asked, for example, "All I want to know is: Are those delayed action capsules manufactured so I get even results, no jolts or blanks, so I really get some benefit?" The speaker responded—properly: "Are you not asking two questions—first, does the medicine cure, and secondly, is it reliably manufactured?"

Dismiss Irrelevant Questions

Occasionally a question is clearly out of place. It may have nothing to do with the subject, or be unfairly personal. Such questions should be quickly dismissed: "I believe that is another subject. Next question, please."

Or, "I'm sorry that I can't respond to that question as it is outside my field of competence."

Or, "That is a very involved, personal question. If you wish to discuss it with me after the meeting, however, I will be happy to do so."

Or, in the case of outright or implied insult, simply: "No comment. Next question, please."

Oral Communication: Answering Audience Questions

For some speakers, the question period can be a trying time. Here are some hints on how to keep things moving, how to handle hecklers and sticky questions, and how to end smartly.

ROBERT HAAKENSON, *Smith Kline & French Laboratories*

After you have given a talk, you are faced with questions from the audience. Many will be easy to answer, but others pose difficulties. The speaker should welcome—not dread—stickler, heckler questions.

A British political scientist noted that prime minister candidates' formal campaign presentations were dull as dishwater but that give-and-take with hecklers not only aroused interest but bolstered the candidates' performances. He suggested in all seriousness that a heckler should be a regular member of the campaign retinue.

A large measure of the speaker's over-all success will rest in the way he handles "hot" questions and comments. In all cases, his answers should be straightforward. There is a tendency to evade controversy. Don't. Meet it head on.

There is a danger of going on the defensive unnecessarily. The speaker or his sponsor is accused of wrongdoing, or otherwise impugned. Even if the charge is justifiable, the speaker should "accentuate the positive": "I know the instance of which you speak. I must insist that that unhappy case—and I assure you we are doing everything in our power to prevent its recurrence—was a rare exception. The over-all record is one of competence and dedication."

Answer forthrightly. Take a partisan stand. One warning: don't look for trouble. Do not conclude that because a question seems hostile and the questioner a heckler, that this is necessarily the case. Assume no worse than neutrality until you have good reason.

On the canvas of contemporary persuasion the advocate must make bold strokes with a broad brush. Forceful assertiveness is expected of him.

Factual Support

In the final analysis, that speaker will prevail in the Q & A period who has his "meat and potatoes." If he has his facts, common sense will probably keep his reasoning from going too far wrong, and the facts will impress his listeners. Thus there is no substitute for the speaker's knowing his subject.

For amplification he will want an abundance of definitions, descriptions, figures, comparisons, anecdotes, figures of speech, visual aids. For support he will want case histories and other specific instances, statistics, statements by experts and firsthand observations.

In some instances it is helpful to document the specifics, i.e., to cite their sources. This is called for when the information is hard to believe or when the source itself will add credibility: ("This is directly from the commissioner himself"). Documentation should include the name of the speaker or writer quoted, the place where the words were spoken or published, the date and page number, right down to chapter and verse.

The speaker who can toss instances and statistics right off the top of his head is to be envied. Most of us, alas, can keep only limited information on the tip of the tongue. For this reason, many experienced speakers refer to printed reference materials during the Q & A.

Ideally the speaker will review his Q & A reference material just before the meeting. He then can give the gist of it from his head, while he inconspicuously turns to the actual supporting data.

What must be avoided is delaying an answer altogether while searching for a page. The speaker *must not* say, "I have an answer for that here somewhere; just a minute," and then, after a deadly pause, proceed to draw the entire response from the printed material. If he cannot locate his place while making the initial reply, he should complete his preliminary response and say, "I have some specific data that support my answer; one moment, please."

Avoid Cliches

Traditionally the Q & A is shot through with cliches: "Did everyone hear the question?" "Will you repeat the question?" "That's a good question." "I'm glad you asked that question." "That's the $64 question." "As I said in my speech. . . ." Each of these has a place in isolated, and infrequent cases. But they become meaningless and insulting when parrotted over and over again.

In controversial questioning, one should avoid, "Does that answer your question?" Give your answer; do the best you can; move on: "Next question, please." If the answer did not in fact satisfy the questioner, leave it to him to renew his inquiry.

There is, however, one expression which is pardonable: "I don't know." Into every speaker's life comes that awful moment when, to put it bluntly, he's stumped. When the speaker doesn't know, even when he should know, he should say aloud what he is saying to himself: "I don't know." These can be the three most eloquent words in our language. The speaker who uses them need not fear losing the respect of his audience. If anything, listeners will admire him for his candor.

When the speaker doesn't know it is often a good idea for him to offer related thoughts he has on the subject. Another solution, especially if the speaker really should know, is to say: "I'm going to find out and I'd like to share the answer with you. Please jot your address on a scrap of paper."

Help From Allies

"There's a temptation for a speaker to offer his views on anything that comes up in a Q & A. Don't succumb. Stay within your area of expertise. Don't attempt to answer questions that are in the province of others. On the other hand, don't ignore the possibility of calling for help from brothers-in-arms in the audience. Phrase the invitation as tactfully as possible: For example, "I notice that Professor John Doe is with us this evening. I know him to be an expert in the field about which you are inquiring. Dr. Doe, do you wish to comment?"

Or even more cautiously, "This is a ticklish matter requiring some thought. It isn't fair, therefore, to put anyone on the spot. I notice that Professor John Doe is in the audience, however, and I know he is experienced in the area. Dr. Doe, would it be fair to ask you if you have comments?"

Make it easy for Professor Doe to wave you off if he wants to decline. He may be pleased at your attention but might also have several reasons for declining.

Share the Wealth

If you have sat in an audience during a Q & A, waving your hand in vain for recognition, you support fair play by the speaker. It is his responsibility, as moderator, to give everyone a chance. He should respect: (1) *time* and (2) *geography*.

The speaker is fair in the distribution of time when he keeps answers brief—two minutes at the absolute maximum, most less than a minute in length.

The speaker is fair in terms of geography when he acknowledges questions from all parts of the room: left, center, right, front, back, head table, balcony. When an area is ignored that portion of the audience begins to feel left out. When several hands are raised simultaneously, the skilled speaker will set up a "batting order": "You, ma'am; then you, sir; and you, sir"; and carry it out faithfully.

Allow any given questioner no more than one follow-up in succession. If the Q & A degenerates into a wrangle between the speaker and one member of the audience, the whole situation is apt to fall apart. If the questioner persists after two turns, the speaker can say, "I'm very pleased by your interest, but in all fairness we must hear from others."

As a matter of general principle, when the speaker has rough going, he properly should invoke the common good. He deals with any nasty situation not to save his skin, but because *the responsibility rests on*

him to protect the best interests of all assembled. This is justification, for instance, for squelching a heckler or a filibusterer.

Keep Things Moving

There is a rhythm to a good Q & A: questions and answers volley back and forth in a brisk, staccato fashion. The speaker does not prolong an answer, even though he might have more to say, because he is confident that if amplification is desired, another question will elicit it. Brief questions, brief to-the-point replies, with many of the audience actively participating—this is the essence of a vigorous and productive Q & A.

"Quit while you are ahead." It is much better to end with questions unanswered, even if it means stopping short of the allotted time, than to respond to an interested few, or stand waiting, when most of the listeners have had their fill.

Conclude Smartly

Anticipate the windup of the Q & A. Keep an eye on the clock, or ask the program chairman to signal you when time has almost run out. Then announce, "We have time for one more question. Whose will it be?"

Be prepared with some appropriate closing remarks. The speaker might acknowledge the audience's interest in the subject, comment on his own enjoyment at responding to their questions and comments, and offer to meet anyone interested in further discussion following adjournment. It is effective to end with a *summary statement* that wraps up the essential message. For example:

As you could see, your interest in this vital subject of citizen participation in community government has been exhilarating for me. Government begins at the grass roots level. The happy reward for active participation is threefold: (1) improved government, (2) pride in civic service, and (3) old-fashioned sociability and fun. I hope you will discuss these ideas with your acquaintances.

Keep the Q & A moving briskly; stop while you are ahead; anticipate the end; and wrap it up with a summary statement.

We Will Follow Up the Q & A

An informal Q & A frequently develops spontaneously after adjournment. If time and circumstances permit, make yourself available for this type of discussion and be cordial and polite to everyone who stays to talk.

Frequently the problem arises that many wish to file by and simply express thanks for the talk. To hold them up while discussing another's point of concern is awkward. Try to sort out the "discussants" and

the "leavetakers." A comment such as the following may work: "Let me quickly shake hands with those who have to run, and then we can give uninterrupted attention to the points you wish to discuss."

This postadjournment discussion offers many advantages. For one thing, it may lead to another speaking engagement. Then, too, this is a good opportunity to talk at greater length on controversial topics raised during the Q & A. Skeptical questioners often can be more easily persuaded through informal, personal give-and-take.

With the main program completed, there is a natural tendency to feel relaxed and casual. The evening is over, you've done well, and you feel good about it. This is fine, providing discretion is not tossed to the winds. Keep in mind the same guidelines that helped make the regular Q & A so successful: be fair, avoid arguments, stay within your area of competence.

If you've promised members of the audience additional information, be doubly sure you have names and addresses. If you found your expertise thin in spots, scribble yourself a reminder to shore it up. If you agreed to communicate certain items to appropriate authorities, follow through. Promise only what you can deliver, and deliver as promptly as possible.

Summary

We want the Q & A session whenever we can get it because we know what it does for audience understanding, message reinforcement, the speaker's personal impact, and feedback for the speaker's sponsor.

We get the Q & A successfully launched when we let others know it is going to occur and we get ourselves, as speakers, ready.

We exploit the Q & A when we assure that questions and comments are clearly understood by all, when answers are forthright and factually supported, and free from cliches.

Q & A "field strategy" is properly exercised when we utilize help from allies in the audience, share speaking time among all interested persons and keep the session moving to a smart conclusion.

We round out the Q & A ultimately when we follow through on promises we made—to obtain information, initiate inquiries, pass the word along, etc.; and we report feedback to our sponsors.

In the Q & A session in the Rocky Mountain states, a distinguished-looking member of the audience arose and said, "All right, sir, that's a very fine talk you have given us on this remarkable health progress. Adding 10 years to the life span may be just fine, but have you thought about me? I am a mortician." Laughter erupted.

The speaker was ready as soon the laughter subsided: "Please understand, sir; we don't prevent death; we merely postpone it."

The Q & A will not prevent failure. But it certainly can help.

Challenges and Rewards Of Public Speaking

There is a constant need for speakers who can present industry's side on such problems as pollution to service and educational organizations. By his participation, the engineer can benefit his industry, his company and himself.

W. DONALD LIEDER, Sun Oil Co.

A desire to meet people, an ability to speak sincerely, together with some skill in fielding a wide variety of questions—these can be developed into an avocation that should appeal to many chemical engineers. It can benefit his industry, his company and his career.

Engineers Have Much To Contribute

Chemical engineeers are conversant with many subjects that would be of interest to luncheon, service, educational and similar organizations.

A desire on the part of your employer to project a favorable community profile would dictate your participation in such an activity. Your company's encouragement is obviously necessary, just as its opposition would be reason enough for you to forego participation. In any case, various phases of the chemical process industries are now in considerable disrepute, and could use some positive image projection.

Of course, public speaking is not everyone's forte. It is not easy for many people to get up in front of an audience. To make matters worse, audiences can sometimes be extremely hostile. A case in point, the board chairman of a major oil company was drenched with sludge oil by an ecology enthusiast in the audience he was addressing. A sense of humor and an outgoing personality are desirable traits. Still, such speaking becomes easier with practice.

Wide Interest in Technology

Over the last 18 months, I have given about 40 talks on pollution control, emphasizing the economic impact of various environmental actions. The groups I addressed have been diverse, and the talks ranged in length from 15 to 60 minutes. The questions asked have varied widely and the motivating interest behind them posed definite challenges. In all cases, I detected a sincere desire on the part of many people to learn something of industry's point of view. How science and technology are affecting their lives is of interest to audiences.

Sometimes, for instance, it is the generation of electricity that must be explained. Another matter often brought up are the flare stacks of the three refineries in and around Toledo. (Apparently, the public is interested in such visible phenomena that could be considered as polluting and wasteful of a natural resource.)

The ultimate economic impact of environmental actions on the public is quite a revelation to many persons. The main point of my talks and discussions is that the public will pay for all environmental actions, whether publicly or privately undertaken. These costs, I point out, will appear in the market price for goods and services, and as higher taxes.

Why You Must Have Backing

Because your talks will be criticized at times, and they will frequently be misunderstood, the wholehearted backing of your employer is necessary if you are to reply. For example, during one talk, I described the nature of some air pollutants and mentioned that about 50% of the manmade SO_2 discharged into the atmosphere in the U.S. came from the generation of electrical power. I noted that, to control this emission, power companies would have to bear many new capital and operating costs.

After the talk, an accountant-type executive from a local power company took me to task for daring to mention any other industry (other than the oil industry) and for attempting to "place all the blame for air pollution on the electric utilities." He later called and complained to my plant manager, who fortunately backed me up completely.

A careful review of the talk and discussion with others in the audience failed to turn up any other adverse response. In fact, the audience felt that I had actually defended the power companies, especially in their requests for a nuclear plant and some rate increases. However, this incident indicates the type of criticism that can arise, and which should be expected.

Some Qualities You Need

The audience response has been varied in all of my presentations. It is necessary to have a large measure of patience and the ability to candidly answer a wide range of questions. And it is much better to simply reply "I don't know" rather than invent an answer to questions you truly do not understand or cannot answer.

There also are always people who ask very general, philosophical questions, sometimes to lead you into a trap. In addition, some people will not be convinced by any arguments you might advance. In their eyes, you are a spokesman for industry and as such cannot be trusted. Such a person will often insist that all the nation's environmental and economic problems are solely caused by industry. Such responses are usually best politely ignored. But they will try your patience.

Panel discussions that present supporting and conflicting viewpoints are a format that require almost no formal presentation but do call for an ability to express oneself extemporaneously. Questions that evoke philosophical discussion, rather than technical consideration, are especially prevalent with generally, rather than technically, oriented audiences.

The immediate personal benefits of making such presentations are usually limited to perhaps a free lunch or dinner, and sometimes a token gift or certificate. It is perhaps the longer term benefits that are more important, including the recognition you will receive as a spokesman for your employer and your industry. This recognition often produces tangible rewards from many employers. Of course, there is also the ego gratification, and the development of your self confidence, which will help you sell yourself and your ideas to your management.

How To Get Started

Many corporations, as well as local Chambers of Commerce, maintain active speakers' bureaus and your willingness to participate can generate a very busy schedule. Various public utilities generally promote this activity to project a favorable community image. After a couple of successful presentations, the awareness of your willingness to talk will spread among program chairmen, and they will quickly fill up your available time.

You can begin by making presentations to groups within your plant, then within your division and company. Initially, you might find it easier to speak to a group of your coworkers. Their responses will be easier to solicit and accept, and would constitute an excellent training ground. A talk at your church or your child's school could initiate your activity. Participation in a

Toastmaster's club can also provide training in public speaking.

Don't be disappointed at a poor turnout, or turn down a speaking engagement because a small audience is anticipated. Program chairmen have their problems getting people to meetings and usually those who do attend are worth addressing.

You might also be surprised by the response. I was once approached to speak to a luncheon group. It sounded as if an audience of 15 or 20 would be there. I went through with it though, and found myself in front of about 200 retired Shriners. Needless to say, an audience of this size can make a speaker feel good.

What To Talk About

Industries, trade organizations, societies and corporations have a large variety of essentially ready-made talks that are available for presentation. Some of these come equipped with visual aids.

An example of the type of data sources and topics available is the American Petroleum Institute's "Magic Barrel" presentation, which outlines the many benefits of petroleum, and its "Voice" program, which includes a vast array of material on many aspects of the oil industry.

Talking about industry's pollution problems, because of the current ecology fervor, is not easy. Possibly, a better subject for an engineer to deal with is some of the problems related to the current energy shortage, such as defining the various forms of energy used in the U.S. and their relationships.

Defining things (such as volumes) in terms that are easily visualized can add spice to a talk. For example, when talking about the quantity of oil consumed in the U.S. and the world, I found it useful defining volumes in terms of a swimming pool the size of a football field with a depth equal to its width, 300 ft. x 120 ft. x 120 ft., and saying that such a swimming pool would hold about 700,000 barrels of oil, or a little over 1 hour's supply for the U.S. This gives the audience something to which they can easily relate.

School audiences are generally interested in potential technical careers. Problems that face the U.S. and the world, where technical knowledge is needed, is a subject I try to impress upon school audiences—such problems as how to feed the world (protein substitutes, efficient food production), provide sufficient water (seawater desalting) and adequate fuel in the world. In such presentations, care must be exercised not to talk over their heads.

Talking about subjects of personal interest makes the research easier and your presentation far more sincere. An extemporaneous talk is much preferred to one that is read verbatim. And because an audience responds to a speaker's enthusiasm, a positive approach is desirable. ∎

Meet the Author

Don Lieder is a Senior Refinery Process Engineer at Sun Oil Co.'s Toledo Refinery (P.O. Box 920, Toledo, OH 43693), where he is engaged in operational planning, economics and operations research. He holds a B.S. in chemical engineering from the University of Cincinnati and an M.S. in engineering administration from Case Western Reserve University.

Active in AIChE (pollution solution chairman for the Toledo section) and the Toledo Management Assn., he is also a member of the World Future Society. He also serves on the Environmental Committee of the Toledo area Chamber of Commerce and acts as industry representative to Toledo's Solid-Waste Task Force.

Do you ever get the feeling that people aren't listening to you?

How to Hold an Audience

THOMAS W. CARLIN, *Alexander Hamilton Institute, Inc.*

We all spend many of our waking hours in conversation, but most of this is idle, pointless chatter. However, we cannot assume that just because we spend so much time talking we can automatically stand up and give an effective speech.

When a successful speaker talks, things happen. He has harnessed the power of speech and can use it to start a flood of action. His talk has purpose.

Therefore, in planning for any kind of talk, whether for a small group meeting or a roomful of Wall St. analysts, your first job is to determine precisely what you want to accomplish. Your objective should be stated in terms of the action you want the listener to take, or the emotion you want him to experience. You can then shape your material around this objective.

Take the Listener's Point of View

Once you have decided what you want to accomplish, you must then turn around and approach your subject from the viewpoint of the listener's own self-interest. To take a simple example from everyday experience, suppose you are trying to gather some special figures from a staff department in your company. Someone balks at giving you what you want, and you are tempted to bawl out the recalcitrant staffer, his boss, and anyone else who will listen.

But if you are more interested in getting the information rather than venting your spleen, you had best adopt another approach. Try to point out why complying with your request will also benefit him. If the staff department has been coming under fire, for example, you might say that you will point out in your report how helpful the department was in providing the needed information.

Pride is the root of effective motivation. If you appeal to a person's pride in the right way, he'll react positively and do what you want. Destructive criticism will hurt his pride, the reaction will be negative and it's likely you'll never get what you want.

Marketing specialists have long lists of appeals that motivate people to action. Among them are sex, survival, superiority, approval, comfort, curiosity and the like. Some appeals are logical, some are emotional; each can be helpful in particular circumstances.

Selecting a Theme

So far, we have established two basic principles about oral communication: it should have a clearly stated objective and should be slanted to motivate a specific audience. The third essential ingredient is a theme.

A theme fulfills two important functions: (1) it determines what material will be used and what will be discarded; (2) it unites the elements into a coherent whole. Without a theme, a talk is nothing but a hodge-podge of different thoughts.

When a speech flops, the most common reason is that the theme was not even clear to the speaker himself.

Put succinctly, your job as speaker is this: to tell the listener what you are going to say, to say it, and then to tell him what you have said. Obviously, this repetition should not be word-for-word, but each element of your talk should reinforce your basic theme. In the box below are some suggestions for organizing your talk once the theme has been selected.

Choosing Your Vocabulary

A speaker's language should be vivid and quotable. This means he must walk the line between extremes of being hackneyed on one hand vs. being overblown on the other.

A talk sounds stilted when the speaker tries to be profound. He uses two-dollar words to express two-bit ideas, fills his talk with nouns like "implementation" and "utilization," and expressions like "it should be noted that . . ."

Many textbooks are available to help you correct stilted language (many of the suggestions for brightening up technical writing can also be used for speeches). Here are a couple of hints:

• When you find nouns ending in "-ion," "-ation," and "-osity," change the sentence around to convert the nouns to verbs. For example, "selection of the topic" would be changed to "selecting the topic."

• Whenever possible, use the active rather than the passive voice. Rather than use "it was observed," say "we noticed."

• Substitute short words for long ones whenever possible. There are a lot of short colorful Anglo-Saxon words (not necessarily the four-letter kind); put them to work for you.

A trite vocabulary springs mostly from lazy habits in the use of similies and metaphors that are now cliches, e.g., "pretty as a picture." Try to make up your own figures of speech, create your own descriptive style. You may not come up with a literary gem every time but at least you can be sure your audience hasn't heard it before.

Should You Read, Memorize or Extemporize?

Some of the finest speeches ever delivered have been read; others have been memorized and delivered verbatim; still others have been spoken off-the-cuff. In

---

Elements of an Effective Talk

1. Introduction. The introduction should catch the listener's attention and set the mood for the rest of the talk. This can be done only if the material is relevant to your theme; in fact, in a good talk the introduction and statement of theme are usually indistinguishable. To catch the audience's attention you can:

• Relate an anecdote. People would rather listen to a pointed anecdote than to a generalization. If the anecdote is told in such a way that the listener can identify with the situation described, the audience will be spellbound. But an anecdote does not mean a canned joke. Some speakers can introduce a talk with a joke and make it come off. Too often, however, the joke is old-hat to the audience. This establishes the wrong mood and brands the speaker as an amateur.

• Pose a problem. Posing a problem with which the audience can identify is a good opener—as long as the speaker intends to offer some solution.

• Startle the audience. Any statement that startles an audience will assure its attention. This can be done with: a paradoxical statement ("One of the great myths is that mother knows best"), a challenge ("There isn't a man in this room who can solve the problem I'm going to describe"), a pointed statistic ("Nine men in this room will be dead of lung cancer in five years").

2. Statement of the Theme. A theme should never be implied; it should be stated clearly and precisely. What's more, the mood (the feeling to be conveyed to the listener to make him proud, elated, angry, indignant, amused) should be consistent with the theme.

3. Body of the Talk. The body should contain a distinct number of thoughts. As a rule, a five-minute talk should contain three thoughts, a ten-minute talk six, and so on. The thoughts should be clearly distinguished from one another and developed in sufficient detail to make their significance to the theme appreciated by the listeners. These thoughts should be introduced and concluded with transitions that tell the listeners exactly where they are in the development of the talk they are hearing.

When possible, the points made in a speech should be introduced in ascending order of importance.

4. Conclusion. Your speech should build toward the conclusion so that it comes off with power and emotional impact, which will in turn elicit action. Like the first sentence in a speech, the final sentence is important because of its position. You should plan it with care so that it will echo in the listeners' minds.

other words, there are no set rules. Much depends on the ability of the speaker and the type of occasion.

In general, a man must be an accomplished speaker to read a speech and yet make it interesting. Too often, the sheets of paper occupy the speaker rather than the audience, and a spark never gets lit. A novice may think that reading a speech offers him an escape from his fear of facing an audience. But it is better to refuse a speaking invitation than to accept and waste the time of an audience with an insipid presentation.

Memorizing a speech also has its pitfalls; it takes weeks of practice before a memorized speech can ring with sincerity. And there is always the danger of going blank in mid-talk and having to grope for a new place at which to continue your delivery.

On the other hand, most speakers would profit by memorizing at least the main points in the body of their address. This allows you to polish key points so that they are consistent with the mood and theme of your talk and enables you to build logically to your conclusion.

The value of an extemporaneous address is that a good one establishes rapport with the listeners, holds their attention and heightens the drama of the occasion. But these things are possible only if the "extemporaneous" talk is carefully prepared. The danger is that a speaker may try to fill in as he goes along with spur-of-the-moment remarks.

Most good speakers outline an extemporaneous talk and practice the speech aloud several times, experimenting with variations in content and emphasis. Then they commit key parts to memory and rely on small cue cards to remind themselves of the basic outline.

Delivering the Speech

Even though he is talking to a large audience, the speaker should think of his listeners as individuals. He should speak to one individual after another, not to an impersonal mass of humanity.

After he has reached the rostrum, the speaker should look slowly over the audience before starting his speech, establishing eye contact with as many individuals as possible. So as not to neglect any section, he should pick out people to his right, left, center, up front and in the rear. As he talks, he should shift his gaze slowly from one listener to another.

The speaker's hands should move naturally and unhurriedly, except at such times as he is making a gesture for emphasis: pointing with his finger when he is giving advice, pounding with a clenched fist to show anger. The important thing to remember is that hands will make natural movements if you let them. But you must avoid mannerisms and nervous gestures that can be as distracting as the total absence of bodily movement.

If you are a novice at public speaking and expect to be nervous, it's best to try to stick to a topic with which you are thoroughly familiar and about which you have strong feelings. This will help you forget yourself and think about the subject matter. And, of course, the better you prepare and rehearse your speech in advance, the more at ease you will be when facing the audience.

Naturally, your voice should be loud enough to be heard by everyone and clear enough to be understood. Practicing with a tape recorder can be a big help in correcting faulty speech patterns. A conscientious speaker will also, if possible, check the acoustics in the place where he is to speak, having someone listen to him at the farthest corner of the room. If he is going to use a microphone, the speaker should determine in advance how far away he should stand and how much he should project his voice to be heard.

Join the Toastmasters

The only way to become an outstanding speaker is to first learn the proper techniques and then practice as much as possible. Practice, however, can be a problem for most professional people. Unlike college professors, they do not have frequent opportunities to speak before an audience.

One way to practice is to take a course in public speaking. Another, and perhaps better, way for professionals is to join a Toastmasters Club.

A Toastmasters Club is an organized group of men over 21 who seek to improve their speaking ability by meeting regularly and delivering speeches to one another. As an integral part of the training, members evaluate one another's speeches.

There are no occupational, educational, racial or religious bars to membership in the Toastmasters. The cost of joining is modest—initiation fees are from $5 to $10 and the monthly dues are small. Many groups meet at places like the YMCA, so the cost of the weekly or biweekly luncheons (the sessions are conducted in a banquet atmosphere) is reasonable.

Information about Toastmasters clubs in any locality can be obtained by sending a postcard to Toastmasters International, Santa Ana, Calif. Visitors to the meetings are always welcome, so you can attend a few sessions before deciding to join.

Meet the Author

Thomas W. Carlin is editor-in-chief of the Alexander Hamilton Institute, Inc., 235 E. 42nd St., New York, and is responsible for texts and newsletters in the Institute's executive training program. Mr. Carlin, who has an M.B.A. from the Harvard Business School, has recently authored the book "Business and the Man" from which this article has been adapted.

Put Showmanship Into Your Next Talk

*You can hold your audience's attention, in lectures and conferences,
by imaginative use of visual aids and group-participation techniques.*

JOHN SCHERBA, *Pittsburgh Plate Glass Co.*

There was a time when many people found something not quite respectable about the stage and its performers. In the same way today, many engineers find disreputable the thought of introducing a little showmanship into the technical meetings or courses they may conduct.

Remember, however, that executives, engineers and hourly workers alike share a common frailty—they have a limited attention span. Their minds have a natural tendency to drift in and out as you present your material, and, no matter how well you know your subject, you will have trouble getting your points across unless you use some of the proven techniques for holding an audience's attention.

We all know that engineers are frequently out of their element when called upon to address or lead a group. They behave like ducks out of water—able to cover the ground, but in an ungainly fashion. Academic, conventional and rigid are usually the best adjectives to describe their performances. This is how they lose their audiences.

There are many techniques that have proved to be exceedingly effective in industrial teaching or conferences, and many of them have ingredients that smack of showmanship. Gimmicky presentations that lack a solid foundation or have no message to deliver are certainly of little value. But honest methods that hold the audience's attention, make a dramatic impact on them, and make them retain what they hear are used far too rarely by engineers.

What are some of these techniques, and how can they be applied?

Don't Just Stand There, Move Around!

Nothing is more deadly than standing still at a lectern and talking in a monotone. Get away from the lectern, walk among the listeners, point your finger at them, use natural gestures, raise and lower your voice, be spontaneous. Most important, use variety; try to make the audience wonder what you'll do next.

Shock your audience, get them angry at you, or make them laugh, but be sure that you've awakened them and that they are rolling with you. Remember that your activity and enthusiasm will be contagious.

Accentuate the Visual

Too frequently, a presentation dealing with complex equipment, processes or statistical data is delivered without the slightest semblance of a visual aid. Some people seem to think that their eminence or expertise exempt them from the requirements of being interesting. But as they talk, without adequate illustration, they bore and then lose their audience. Words, hand gestures or blackboard sketches are just not as effective as the wide range of audio and visual techniques that are available today.

Here are a few of the more common tools, which can be dramatic and yet do not require elaborate preparation or artistic skills:

The Flannel Board—This is a flexible tool and can give special impact and emphasis to a verbal presentation. The board is a flat surface covered with flannel that is mounted on an easel. Words, phrases, pictures or graphs are printed or drawn on cardboard, cut to size and backed with flannel.

As the speaker presents his material, he places the prepared cards on the flannel board to emphasize points or to illustrate his talk. The cards easily adhere to the board. This technique draws attention and imparts an air of preparation and professionalism to the program.

The Pad Board—This is a metal tripod holding a pad of paper about 2 x 3 ft. in size. It is used like a blackboard but has the advantage of allowing you to prepare material in advance. You can expose individual sheets to the audience at appropriate intervals without having them distracted while you write out the material. Changing these previously prepared pages at regular intervals also helps recapture wandering attentions. A variation of the technique is to loosely tape independent strips of paper over sections of a chart and remove them at appropriate points.

Material on the pad board can be as simple as ordinary handwriting, or you can use sketches or cartoons to make the material more appealing.

The Overhead Projector—One of the most versatile pieces of visual-aid equipment is the overhead projector, which uses 8 x 10-in. transparent slides. It can handle material from simple handwritten notes up to the most elaborate precision color visuals. It is even possible to suggest motion on the slides by means of polarization that depicts flow of materials or reactions.

The projector is placed at the front of the room with the speaker, who himself places the slides on the machine's horizontal glass plate. The resulting image is projected over the speaker's head onto the screen. Because the projector is close to the screen and has a high-intensity bulb, the images can be seen in a lighted room.

Slides are prepared by making a master consisting of black impressions on translucent paper. This master is then exposed to special photo-sensitive acetate, which is developed in a large jar containing ammonia, or in an ammonia-process blueprint machine.

Don't make the mistake of using ordinary typewritten copy on these slides if they are to be shown to large audiences. Either have the typewriting enlarged, or use large transfer letters or hand lettering. Also avoid long sections of written material—key words supplemented by your verbal statements are far more effective.

Another useful technique that can be done on the overhead projector is to use overlays to show machinery, flow diagrams or any complex material in step-by-step fashion from simplest to most complicated form.

The overhead projector, then, has an audience impact that is readily apparent to the speaker. Each new slide refocuses attention and lends emphasis to the speaker's words. What's more, the transparencies are easily prepared, with only a modest investment in equipment.

The Tape Recorder—A much neglected tool of showmanship, the tape recorder can not only record sound but it can also dramatically broadcast material to your group. A message from an executive, the sound of a machine, statements of hourly operators, or just plain attention-getters can all effectively stimulate interest or help to drive home a point.

When using this tool, however, don't send a boy to do a man's job. Small, economy recorders will probably not be able to transmit a clear audio message to a group. A quality tape recorder is usually necessary to project sound clearly across a room.

Slides and Movies—These are familiar media in most companies and, when available, they add considerable emphasis to a program if properly used.

There are now many film-processing firms that offer one-day developing service for certain types of 35-mm. color slide film. This makes the medium practical for meetings and classes, even on short notice. The Polaroid Corp. has a process in which 2¼ x 3¼-in. black and white slides can be developed in seconds if necessary. Services are also available for preparing 35-mm. slides with polarization to suggest motion.

The high-speed color films now available lend themselves well to many industrial photography problems in which light conditions may be marginal. When you are photographing plant equipment with these films, get right on top of the subject and frame only those sections in which you are interested. If the lighting is not ideal, take several shots at slightly varying exposures. The cost of a few extra pieces of film is negligible compared with the cost of the time you are probably giving to the project.

You may wonder when selecting visuals whether to use 35-mm. slides or the 8 x 10-in. overhead projection slides discussed earlier. The 35-mm. ones can be handled more easily than the larger slides and they are better for color photography. But the overhead slides can be shown in a lighted room, which allows the speaker to supplement his voice presentation with facial expressions, gestures and animation. Also, he can use overlays with the overhead slides, or even write on them.

Exhibits—All too often, class discussions or conferences are held on specific machines or processes without showing samples to the group, even where it is practical to do so. Nothing is more effective in teaching than to have the actual item, models, or cutaways of the equipment for the group to examine.

A particularly good item to get hold of if you can, when instructing new operators, is the model that was built during design and construction of your plant.

Make the Audience Work Too

There are many non-lecture techniques that you can use in a class to make the students actively participate. These methods are supplements to, not substitutes for, the lecture itself and, when properly used, they spur interest, increase retention and reduce dozing.

The Case Study—Nothing is more interesting to a class than an actual problem drawn from their own plant or company. Labor problems, human relations incidents, production problems and scores of other topics can easily be researched and adapted for class study. If you don't have time to do this research yourself, there are many excellent books available that feature typical industrial cases.

The Incident Process—An extension of the case study, this method is a fascinating technique of problem solving based on actual incidents. The class is presented with an incident, and they then ask questions of the group leader. He fairly and completely answers questions although volunteering nothing, until all the facts are gathered. Each student then organizes the facts, makes a logical decision and defends his position.

A typical case that can be studied in this manner is a labor grievance. The class members are presented with a simple statement of the dispute and they then ask questions in the light of the labor contract, precedents and the people involved, just as they would in a real grievance on the job.

The incident technique is particularly effective in the areas of labor problems, human relations and safety, but can be adapted to other subjects as well.

The In-Basket—Still another variation on the case study, this method involves collecting actual problems that would be common to the daily activities of the class. The students, who might be foremen, salesmen, technical service representatives or executives, are given a pack of correspondence, memos and incidents.

In a workshop period, they individually decide what problems are to be handled immediately and what ones are to be delayed. They record their decisions and take action just as they would in a real work situation. During a later stage of the class, the students discuss their decisions as a group.

Be Prepared

Everyone, no matter what his position, experiences a leveling when he speaks before a group. The group, particularly if they are subordinates, will appear to be listening attentively, courteously and quietly. But they will shut out the speaker from their attention, no matter what his position, unless he is prepared, lively and interesting. The techniques we have discussed will help you to be just that.

Meet the Author

John Scherba is director of training at the Barberton, Ohio, plant of Pittsburgh Plate Glass Co.'s Chemical Div. He holds a B.S. in industrial relations from Illinois Institute of Technology, and an M.S. in industrial management from University of Illinois. He joined PPG in 1955 as a personnel assistant, was named communications manager in 1958 and assumed his present post in 1962. Scherba is vice president of the Northeast Ohio Chapter, American Society for Training and Development.

Oratory Isn't Dead But Many Speakers Are

You can command attention and sell your ideas—whether lecturing at a meeting or talking to a small group! These tips from a professional on the art of public speaking can help make you a more skillful and dynamic speaker.

JAMES GRAYSON FORD, Speech Consultant

Some speech authorities will tell you that public speaking is simply enlarged conversation. This may be why so few people *listen* to so many speeches.

The average person listens to the average speaker one minute and fifty seconds, then his mind goes off on a tangent, says Ralph Nichols, professor at the University of Minnesota and an authority on listening. If the speaker tells a story or shouts, he may attract the listener's attention for another minute or two before his mind wanders again.

Many a speaker thinks that because his audience is looking at him, it must be listening. But don't you believe it. A listener can be staring directly at a speaker while his mind is miles away.

What Makes an Audience Listen?

To be effective as a speaker, you must command the attention of your audience; you must make them want to listen; you must earn their attention. How do you do it?

Making speeches is a skill, just as playing good golf or painting masterpieces is a skill. And what is skill? Webster says skill is "the ability to use one's knowledge effectively and readily in execution or performance;" or "a learned power of doing a thing competently: a developed aptitude or ability." You will note that nothing is said about talent.

People will often say that a person is talented in a particular skill. They often forget that the talented person has been motivated by a strong desire to excel in his particular interest, that he has spent countless hours receiving instruction, and practicing.

History tells us that the outstanding leaders in business, politics, education and religion have been excellent public speakers and communicators. They have been able to influence the emotions, attitudes and actions of their listeners. History also tells us that they have spent many, many hours preparing and practicing their presentations.

Why Reading a Speech Doesn't Work

Many executives who, because of their position, are asked to make speeches, and have been doing so for many years, think that they are good speakers. Often enough, however, their speech is written for them by somebody else. And, all too frequently, they do not practice reading it.

As a result, not one percent of an audience will listen continuously when such a speech is read. Yet, because nobody has the courage to tell Mr. Bigshot that he is a rotten speaker, he thinks he is good. Unless he gets professional instruction, he never realizes that he has been making the same mistakes over and over.

When a golfer hits a ball, he can see where it goes. If he consistently hooks or slices, he goes to the club pro for help in correcting what he is doing wrong. The speaker who reads his speech cannot see where his words are landing. A polished speaker will always speak from an outline or notes. He does this because he wants to watch his audience; he wants each member of his audience to feel that he is speaking directly to him. And he wants to sense how he is going over; he wants feedback from his audience. When that feedback tells him his words are being received about the same as a mother-in-law's advice, he knows he has to do something: turn on more steam, change his tone of voice, make more gestures, place greater emphasis on important words, shout, ask a question. He knows he has to make changes in his delivery if he is going to recapture and hold the attention of his listeners.

The person who reads a speech does not get audience feedback because he spends most of his time looking at his script. All he has to do is read words. Consequently,

SPEECHES lasting over forty-five minutes are too long.

he goes too fast; he does not express any emotion; he uses few if any gestures; and his audience stops listening after about the first ten seconds.

A speaker must express thoughts and ideas. Words in themselves do not always convey a thought. Words have different meanings and can be interpreted different ways. It is your attitude, the way you say words, that gives them meaning. The emotion in your voice, your facial expressions, the gestures or body movements that accompany your words—all of these convey meaning and give impact. Abraham Lincoln said, "If tears to the eyes of others you would bring, yourself the signs of grief must show."

Human beings are creatures of emotion; how we feel controls our attitudes and actions. And how we feel is transmitted to those we come in contact with. If there is enthusiasm in our voice and actions, our listeners will also become enthusiastic. This is empathy, which means "feeling into," or the transference of emotion from one to another.

If you want to sell your ideas, win acceptance for a proposal, or persuade others to follow some course of action, you must be enthusiastic yourself. You must be sincere and believe wholeheartedly in your presentation. If you have these qualities, your words and actions will transmit the same feeling to your listeners.

How Long Should a Speech Be?

When a person is asked to make a speech, it is usually because he is considered an authority on a subject. He is expected to bring to the audience new information of in-

terest. No audience wants to listen to something it has already read about in the newspaper.

When asked how long it would take him to prepare a ten-minute speech, Woodrow Wilson replied, "two weeks." When asked how long to prepare a one-hour speech, his response was, "I can start now." A person who is an authority on a subject can talk for hours and still not cover it completely. However, most audiences will not sit for hours and listen to one speaker. Any speech that exceeds thirty to forty-five minutes is too long. For this reason, even the authority must carefully plan and practice his presentation.

Preparing a Presentation

The experienced speaker does not wait until the day before he must make his speech to prepare it. He starts thinking and planning almost from the minute he receives the assignment.

Nobody knows all there is to know about any subject. In any given field or occupation, ideas and techniques are continually being changed. Because of the rapid advances being made in all areas of knowledge, no one person can even read all of the new information being published about his specialty.

So, if you are to bring new information to an audience, you must research your subject. You must collect new data, check the latest developments, and explore what other people are saying about the subject. You should put the newly acquired information on cards, a separate card for each fact, point, or bit of information. Also, you should carry a notebook and jot down ideas as they occur to you. You must write down the information so you can retrieve it later when you start to prepare your presentation.

Organizing Your Notes

If you made notes on small cards, these can simply be laid out on a table. If you did not put your information on individual cards, take a large sheet of paper and draw horizontal lines on it one and a half inches apart. Next, draw vertical lines one and a half inches apart. In each square, write one fact or idea that you might include in your speech. After you have put all your facts and ideas into the boxes, start organizing your speech. Evaluate the points— those that are important and should be included, and those that are less important and should be eliminated or made subtopics. Shuffle the elements around until you find the best order.

Are there more points than you can cover in the allotted time? Should you narrow your scope and talk about only one aspect of the subject? Wouldn't it be better to cover three points thoroughly rather than ten superficially? There is a limit to how many points the audience will retain, and three is about the limit.

If you can impress three points upon your audience in thirty minutes, you will have done a good job. If they cannot remember your three points, you will have failed to put across your message.

Listeners often misinterpret what speakers say. Words mean different things to different people. If a listener has

REHEARSALS are imperative when using visual displays.

to ponder on the meaning of some of your words, he is going to miss some of your speech. So keep your words simple.

Practicing Your Presentation

The more professional the speaker, the more certain it is that he will repeatedly practice his presentation beforehand. And with every trial, he will make improvements.

As you practice, consider reorganizing your talk, making changes in your choice of words, putting greater emphasis on important words or phrases, or more enthusiasm in your voice and gestures. Add an anecdote that will emphasize a point you want to make. Try standing in front of a full-length mirror to check your posture, facial expression and whether your gestures are vigorous and from the shoulder instead of half-hearted wig-wags from the elbow. A tape recorder can tell you if you are talking in a monotone, or too fast or too slow. If videotape equipment is available, you can use it to get a preview of how you will look and sound to your audience.

If you are planning to use audio-visual equipment, rehearsals are imperative. Not only will it polish your presentation, but you can time it to ensure staying within your limits. This also applies if you will rely on charts, graphs, illustrations or other props. Learn if they are suitable and how to use them.

Are your visuals on the best kind of material; i.e., flip chart, cloth, cardboard, transparency or slide? Are they too "busy," too much data or information on any one? Is the print large enough to be read by the people in the back of the room? Are colors intense enough to be seen from the rear? Never use light colors or pastels. Stick to the primary colors.

Practice using mechanical equipment beforehand. This includes projectors, recorders, television and audio or visual equipment. If equipment is going to fail, it will during your presentation, so be prepared to fix it or have somebody present who can.

Set the Stage in Advance

Always arrive well in advance of the program. Check on the room arrangement, adequacy of seating and sufficiency of lighting. Note where the controls are and how they operate. If you will use a public address system, make sure it is working and know who will control it. If you will have to move around, see if there is a chest microphone with a long enough cable.

Set up and test any equipment that is to be used. Arrange any props, charts or other visuals in the desired location and in the correct order, but keep them covered until the right time for exposing them.

Delivering Your Speech

There is no substitute for self-confidence when making a speech. Two or three quick drinks may quiet your nervousness but they will also dull your mind and impair your speaking ability. Self-confidence comes with preparation and practice. Knowing what to say and how to say it does not come spontaneously, "off the cuff." Even what appear to be "ad libs" on the radio or television are usually carefully practiced and rehearsed.

Most professional speakers or actors will readily admit that they are nervous and apprehensive before starting a performance. It is a normal emotional state. Nervousness provides energy and makes a speaker more dynamic and forceful. It also motivates the speaker and increases his desire to do a good job.

To do a good job, you must capture the attention of your audience with your first words. Some speakers will stand at the lectern and remain silent until every eye is on them and the audience is waiting for their first words. Others will start with a question and pause as though expecting an answer.

Still others will open with a startling statement. An attractive young lady once walked to the lectern, looked at the audience and said, "I am a prostitute." From the resulting uproar, you can be sure she had captured the attention of her audience. After the uproar subsided, they were waiting with anticipation for her speech. She then explained that she was a copy writer for an advertising agency and that some of the copy she had to write to sell products was often less than truthful. By writing statements that could not be proven, she felt that she was prostituting her profession.

Your first words must convey to your audience that you have information that will be of interest to them. You must arouse in them a *desire* to listen.

Once Started, What Then?

Not only must you capture the attention of your audience, you must hold it, and that depends on how you deliver your talk.

John Wesley, the founder of the Methodist Church, was once asked how it was that he could attract such large audiences to hear him speak. He said, "I set myself on fire and they come to watch me burn."

Another word for this kind of performance is enthusiasm, probably the most effective tool of any speaker.

Enthusiasm is derived from two Greek words, "en" and "theos," which literally translated mean "in God" or "God in us," or to be inspired. Enthusiasm is an emotion, an inner feeling of strong belief in what we are saying. Someone once said, "If I could give my son but one gift, it would be enthusiasm."

Enthusiasm for a subject is demonstrated by tone of voice, the words that are used, the passion with which they are spoken, and the facial expression that accompanies the words and the gestures.

Abraham Lincoln is quoted as having said, "When I listen to a preacher, I like to have him act as though he is fighting bees." Your gestures and movements convey more meaning than the words you speak. The cliche "your actions speak so loudly, I cannot hear what you are saying" applies to every speaker, whether he is talking to one person or a thousand. Sir Richard Paget, a noted English scholar, spent many years researching the subject of nonverbal communication. He determined that there are more than seven hundred thousand signs, signals, gestures, body movements and motions that have meaning. In all written language, there are approximately six hundred and twenty-five thousand words.

But gestures must be spontaneous. They must come from an inner desire to communicate—to give emphasis to our words, to illustrate points we make, and to add vigor and dramatics to our presentation.

What Makes a Compelling Speaker?

There are three types of speakers, those you can listen to; those you can't listen to; and those you can't *help* listening to.

What makes the difference? It is the delivery of the speaker. If the speaker talks in a conversational manner, chances are the listeners will turn their ears on and off. They will listen to portions of a talk and lose interest intermittently. The speaker who drones on in a monotone turns everybody off.

If you would compel the attention of your audience, you must use all of the tools at your command. The first requirement is that you be heard. Your voice must carry your words clearly to the most distant person in the audience. To do this, you must have good articulation, and this requires having breath control, so that you can breathe while talking. You must form and resonate your words by means of your vocal chords, your tongue, lips and jaws. To articulate clearly and project your voice, you must use all of these parts. To clearly pronounce or enunciate words, you must open your mouth, and the wider you do the further your words will carry.

A tired speaker makes a tired audience. A dynamic, energetic, ethusiastic speaker wakes up his audience. A lawyer, making his summation to a jury, noticed that one of the jurors had gone to sleep. He stepped to the bench and said, "your honor, one of the jurors has gone to sleep, will you please wake him up and order him to stay awake." The judge looked down at the lawyer and replied, "You put him to sleep. So *you* wake him up—and keep him awake!"

A speaker starts to communicate with his audience the instant he stands up and approaches the lectern. His bearing, appearance, posture and facial expression all send signals to the audience, and these signals start to form impressions. If he grasps the lectern with both hands or leans on it, he is telling his audience he is tired, lazy, uninterested or unsure of himself. If he strides confidently to the lectern, stands firmly on both feet, his hands at his sides, and looks around at his audience for a few seconds before starting to speak, he creates the impression that he is confident, knows what he is going to say and how to say it, but that he is going to wait until he has attention.

Occasionally Try Table Thumping

A skillful violinist achieves a variety of tones by varying the tension on the strings.

The skillful speaker does about the same thing. He may at times raise his voice to a shout, or lower it almost to a whisper. He will vary his rate of speaking, fast at times, then very slowly to give emphasis.

Pauses between words or phrases are extremely effective. After an important statement, a pause lets the words sink into the minds of the listeners. Pauses also hold an audience in suspense, waiting for the next words.

The meaning of words also determines how they are expressed. If a person says "I love you," it will probably be said slowly. If the words are "I hate you," they will be snapped out quickly.

The emotion the speaker is feeling controls the tone and level of his voice. If he is angry about the subject, he should speak angrily, and contrarily if he is happy. Emotion is contagious and is transmitted from the speaker to the listener. Emotion adds realism to words and enforces the sincerity of the speaker. We are usually taught from childhood not to display emotions. This is fine when playing poker. But, if we want to be persuasive and win people to our way of thinking, we should let our strong feelings come through.

All of the foregoing may seem like a great deal of work, and it is. Nothing worthwhile comes easy. But the rewards can be great for those who can present their ideas persuasively. ■

Meet the Author

James Grayson Ford (41 Deer Ridge Rd., Basking Ridge, NJ 07920) is acknowledged as one of U.S.'s foremost trainers in public speaking. Previously Manager of Professional Personnel at Johns-Manville Products Corp., he has also served as Public Relations Representative, Sales and Traffic Training Director and Sales Manager for Pan American World Airways, and as President of the Speakers Bureau of the Junior Chamber of Commerce. He has trained thousands of upper and middle management personnel in advanced speech. He graduated from the University of Nebraska.

If the last meeting you ran ended up in chaos, perhaps you can use this advice on . . .

How To Run Better Meetings

It's no secret that many people think meetings are a waste of time. They probably feel this way because many meetings *are* a waste of time.

But this need not be the case if the meeting organizer follows a few basic rules. It's a shame to allow poor technique to build up anti-meeting sentiments, because in many instances meetings are the most efficient way to deliver information, resolve conflicts, solicit ideas or solve problems.

Your first step, as organizer, is to decide what type of meeting it will be, for this will determine your approach. The majority of all meetings fall into three categories—tell, sell or solve.

The Tell Type—Purpose of this meeting is to pass information along to a group, such as explaining the company's new life insurance plan.

This type of meeting is the easiest of the three—about the only time there will be discussion is when someone asks you to clear up a point that he doesn't understand.

The Sell Type—This meeting is supposed to win the group's acceptance of the leader's proposal. Example: selling a new cost-reduction compaign.

A sell-type meeting usually divides equally into two parts: presentation by the leader and discussion by the group. Discussion is essential because people tend to believe that something is true, valuable or necessary if they can arrive at the same conclusion after general discussion, particularly with their associates.

The Solve Type—The goal here is to solicit help from a group in solving a particular problem—prob-

ably the most difficult type of meeting to run. For example, a production superintendent may be seeking ideas from his subordinates on ways to cut down on the amount of raw-material inventory.

The leader's role is to present the problem, then to keep things hot after the group gets warmed up. The group should do 80-90% of the talking in order to ensure that everyone's special knowledge is utilized.

Once you have determined the type of meeting you are going to conduct, there are three things to prepare: yourself, the room, the group.

A good way to start preparing yourself is to review notes or minutes of the last meeting (if there was one). Refresh your memory on exactly what happened and how things stood at the end of the session.

Next, know precisely what your meeting is to accomplish, then determine the best way of attaining your objective. Suppose the problem is to reduce waste coming from the A unit. Set a realistic cost-reduction goal and a reasonable time for its attainment. Then figure out the simplest, most convincing way to present the problem to your people. This means having at your fingertips background information, facts and figures, pertinent questions to stimulate discussion, provocative statements.

Prepare a complete agenda and plan to make the meeting as brisk as possible. A 30-min. meeting is ideal; an hour-long session is OK—but never let a meeting run over an hour and a half.

A final must is to check the list of persons you intend to invite to make sure no one is left out who can contribute to the solution—and to make equally sure no one is invited who has no business there!

Physical Arrangements

Advance checking of the meeting room can prevent chaos later on. On your checklist should be such things as ventilation, heat, lighting and chairs. If your meeting involves discussion, always arrange the chairs in an informal circle rather than in schoolroom rows, which suggest a lecture rather than free exchange.

Among the other items to check:
- Plenty of ash trays, paper and pencils.
- Name cards.
- Visual aids (e.g., charts, slides).
- Blackboard with an eraser and plenty of chalk.

Another important item is the time of the meeting. Remember that late-afternoon hours are tricky because a man's thoughts are likely to be devoted to worrying about missing his car pool. Meetings scheduled too close to noon put your words of wisdom in competition with lunch.

A successful meeting leader gives his people plenty of advance notice—not only because they may have other commitments but because he wants them to have enough time to do some thinking about the subject of the meeting.

Be sure to emphasize *promptness*. One company recently found that about three out of ten meeting goers were from two to thirty minutes late. As a result, leaders must repeat what the slowpokes missed, hold up the starting time of the meeting, or be stymied because three out of ten are only partially informed.

Whenever possible, the best policy is to ignore latecomers. Make no attempt to bring them up to date. This is one of the best ways to cure chronic tardiness.

Make a Fast Start

Whether you call it a "warm-up" or "motivating the participants," you've got to capture the group's interest in the first few minutes or they start to doodle. This process is especially important for the solve-type meeting where you want the group to come forth with constructive suggestions.

The burden rests with the leader; he should play his part to the hilt just as an actor does. Forget all your personal problems and give the group the kind of performance that will send them away reacting the way you want them to.

A relaxed, informal style is the most productive. Greet people by first name as they come in, make small talk as they settle down. As soon as everyone is ready to begin, be sure to welcome the group as a whole; this clearly establishes your role as host.

Plunge right into the purpose and objectives of the meeting. State goals concisely; preferably emphasize them by writing on a blackboard. Express objectives in terms of the group's self-interest. If each man realizes that a satisfactory solution is important to him, he will be more apt to take an interest

ANY OF THESE AT YOUR LAST MEETING?

Proper care and feeding of these creatures can prevent a meeting from degenerating into a zoo-house nightmare.

Loud-Mouth

Don't squelch him right off the bat. His volubility may come in handy later —and he really may have something to contribute. If he just wants to hog the spotlight, however, try tactfully ignoring him. If, as a last resort, you have to squelch him, do it firmly and make it stick.

Tough Guy

He loves to argue and has a talent for making other people furious. Don't lose your temper; try to find something in his argument with which you agree, then move on. If his statements are clearly inaccurate, toss his remarks to the group and let them handle the situation. If he gets completely out of line, talk to him privately. If you can't win his cooperation, exclude him from future meetings.

Eager Beaver

Before you can finish a question, he is springing forth with an answer—without taking enough time to think it through. Because he is sincere, your only resort is to sidestep his eager proposals, thank him, then ask for answers from the others.

Fuzzy Thinker

His conversation follows so many paths that he gets lost in irrelevant issues. When he stops to catch his breath, restate the subject and try to get him back on the track.

Antagonists

Clashing personalities can destroy a meeting by splitting it into factions. Try to separate duelists by playing up points of agreement, playing down disagreements. Sometimes throwing the question to a third party can produce a compromise that will neutralize bad blood. If the clash gets personal, tell both to leave personalities out.

Buzzer

He is forever whispering in his neighbor's ear. There's no point in giving the offender dirty looks, or stopping until the dead silence reprimands him. Best way to end the side show is to call one of the talkers by name and ask him a direct question.

Silent Type

If he's merely bored or indifferent, fire a direct question at him. If he's shy, direct a question to the man next to him, then ask the timid soul to tell his neighbor what he thinks of it. When asking his opinion, phrase the question as though it were a two-man conversation rather than a case of airing views to the whole group.

in what's said and to participate actively in the discussion.

Remember also that conducting a good meeting is a little like "show biz." Use dramatic effects—like a good film or recording, colorful diagrams, or some other audio-visual aid. Try a shock treatment—like greeting your listeners with "adjustment costs on Product X are 300% higher than two years ago. We have exactly 30 days to cut these costs down to par. I need *your* ideas on this subject."

Especially for solve-type meetings, such a beginning makes three facts crystal-clear:
• The meeting is a *group effort*.
• Everyone is expected to take part because he has a personal stake in the problem.
• The leader's role is simply to explain the objective and keep the discussion moving.

Pitching Questions

Once you have outlined the objective, throw the ball to the group. If someone doesn't pick it up, call on an articulate person and ask: "What do you think, Joe?"

If Joe lets you down, try another member of the group. If after a couple of tries the question approach doesn't work, suggest a solution that you know in advance no one will agree with. Someone is bound to challenge it—and the discussion is on. Remember that the purpose of the meeting is not to air *your* opinions; if someone asks you a question, toss it right back to the group.

Use "what, why and how" questions. If someone says, "I agree with Charlie," ask him why. Ask debatable questions, avoiding those that can be answered with just "yes" or "no." Ask three or four people the same question. To assure full answers, clamp down on interruptions, like saying, "Just a minute, Ray! Don has the floor." Don't hesitate to rephrase anybody's answer in the interest of brevity and clarity. But be sure to keep the same thought.

While many of your questions will come spontaneously from the discussion, don't push your luck. Think up some good questions *before* the meeting and fire them into the discussion when things slow down.

Disagreements are healthy; if there isn't a single dissenting voice in your meeting, the chances are that some of the people are too disinterested to care or else the group is loaded with yes-men. Don't attempt to gloss over disagreements but rather try to define exactly what the objection is and, if necessary, explain why the majority decision must prevail. In this way, the dissenters will still be encouraged to contribute on other topics since they feel their objections have been neither ignored nor steam-rollered.

When one topic is exhausted, make a 30-second summary and move on. Summaries act as a score-card on progress and let everyone know exactly where you are

in the meeting. By moving through your agenda point by point, you break the subject up into blocks of information that can be easily digested by everyone.

Critical Time: the Wrap-up

The most important part of the meeting is the end. After all of the decisions, solutions, and conclusions have been discussed, it is still up to the leader to solidify the results.

Whatever the decisions were, be sure to repeat them and hammer them home to the group. Otherwise, you'll be saying, "Thank you for coming, gentlemen," to a lot of men who are uncertain as to what was decided and who accepted what responsibility.

Don't hesitate to spotlight some of the rugged aspects of the meeting: tough assignments, unpopular decisions, possible conflicts. The leader who shies away from these hard facts reveals that the meeting probably was a failure and the follow-up will be weak.

Group decisions are like passing the plate in church: some put in more than others. Individuals who have contributed the most to your meeting deserve credit—out loud. Joe will be even more helpful at your next meeting if he hears you say: "Joe Jones kicked in with a fine suggestion for handling the XYZ problem."

On the other hand, if no major decision was reached, don't let the group leave with a sense of failure or irritation. This takes a bit of doing and you sometimes must play it by ear. Some obvious devices are: emphasize what *was* achieved; express appreciation for valuable suggestions; announce need for another meeting to dig deeper into the problem; nail down definite follow-up assignments—"Joe, you're going to dig up such-and-such information; Bill, you're to have figures on XYZ by next Monday."

If you fail to follow through on your promises to the group they will be less enthusiastic about contributing the next time a problem crops up.

If you have promised your people a brief summary of the meeting in writing, get it into their hands at once. This is doubly important if you depend on certain individuals to act on your report.

If you have saddled some of your group with operating details, do some personal follow-up. Make certain that they deliver what they were supposed to.

If a report is to be made to top management, get it written as soon as possible. Outline the objectives of the meeting, the decisions reached, and the action required as a result of those decisions. Here again, give credit where credit is due.

Following through on meeting decisions will show everyone that meetings really *can* accomplish something and will make your people more eager to participate next time.

About This Article

Material in this article is taken from a booklet "Let's Hold Better Meetings" published by Goodyear Tire & Rubber Co. as a guide for its employees.

Conferencemanship

Mastery of the art of participating in conferences has always been vital
to job advancement. This has become more important for engineers, now that
they are being urged to become involved in environmental and "social" issues.

DENNIS J. CHASE, McGraw-Hill World News Bureau

The art of conducting oneself at conferences neither comes naturally nor is easily acquired. Good conference participants are made, not born. The glibness, the facility with language, the ability to say little while appearing to say much, to disagree while appearing to agree—all takes practice. For chemical engineers, who are accustomed to preciseness and a certain no-nonsense frankness, conferences often appear to be another dimension entirely.

The techniques of "conferencemanship" (as one writer calls it) have one objective: to keep the conference going. The proceedings—which usually involve presentation of papers, give-and-take among panel members, and audience questions—must never be stopped or allowed to bog down in detail, confusion or vituperation. The show must go on—and keep moving.

Because of the functional limitations of such conferences, the most successful participants are those who obey the rules. It takes savvy, and those who do not plan ahead usually end up the object of comments like: "Who invited *that* guy?" Because representation at these conferences is in high demand, such savvy is indispensable to the rising engineer, or to any upward bound professional. According to Andrew M. Greeley, director of the Center for the Study of American Pluralism of the National Opinion Research Center, and lecturer in the University of Chicago sociology department:

"Our occupational prestige is increased not only by our salaries, our cars, our homes and the kind of coats our wives wear, but increasingly by the number of prestigious meetings we attend. A sure sign of a slip in prestige is the absence of a name from a conference list. It is pathetic to see a man who was once a giant at conferences look puzzled and hurt when a colleague says, 'Of course I'll see you at next week's meeting,' and he must perforce reply in embarrassment and confusion, 'What meeting?' "

III

Greeley's Suggested Statements and Translations for Conferencemen

Statement	Translation
"I'm confused . . ."	I'm not really confused at all, but you people are trying to confuse me.
"I don't exactly see what our objectives are in this discussion . . ."	You people wandered away from the point at least 3 hours ago.
"I don't understand what's being said . . ."	I understand damn well what's being said, but I don't think you people know what you're talking about.
"I'm very naive, but . . ."	I'm really not naive at all, but I see things clearly and the rest of you don't.
"I don't know much about this subject, but . . ."	I may not be an expert, but I know more than you people do.
"I've been bothered for the last several hours (days) by . . ."	I can't believe how irrelevant everything you people have said is.
"I think we ought to ask ourselves again what we're here for . . ."	If the chairman had any sense at all, he would have got us back on the track hours ago.
"It seems to me that what we need is more action and less talk . . ."	Isn't it about time we adjourned for the coffee break?

IIIIIIIIIIIIIIIIIIIIIIIIIIIIIIIIIIIIIIIIIIIIIIIIIIIIIIIIIIIIIIIIIIIIIIIIIIIIIIIIIIIIII

Preparation: What Not To Do

Do not do the typical research and familarizing yourself with position papers—such efforts will merely contribute to keeping the conference on its assigned topic, which is awkward. boring, and not what people come to conferences for anyway. Remember: the "medium"—the conference—is the "message." People attend conferences not just to obtain information on a particular topic (they probably know all the information anyway), but rather to make an appearance there.

Some things that a conferenceman can do to prepare for the meeting:

1. Master conferencemanship-ese. Says Greeley: "Choice of vocabulary is extremely important in establishing one's reputation as a conferenceman, and one must expend considerable amounts of effort keeping one's vocabulary up to date." The language of conferences consists of opening gambits (see box), and avoidance of unacceptable words. Among the latter are: "United States," "middle-aged," "white," "past," "dialogue" and "liberal." Recommended substitutes are: "third world," "young," "black," "future" "confrontation" and "radical." However, "bad" words are not verboten, says Greeley, "provided they are always used in the pejorative sense."

2. Establish a "line." Such a line or "ax" should be all-purpose enough to fit into every conference at some point, regardless of the conference topic. It should be something like: "We need a radical restructuring of our thinking," or "The future belongs to the young." It is important, says Greeley, that the speaker not get bogged down in nuances or qualifications, or attempt to define terms like "future" and "young." This is the sure road to oblivion for a conferenceman, who will end up with a discredited line and fewer conference invitations.

3. Be aloof from the conference topic. The conferenceman must never forget that conferences are organized not to solve a problem or generate additional insight but just to . . . have a conference. Says Greeley: "The problems that society faces are so complex, in any event, that no conference is going to solve them." Conferences are organized for a variety of social, political, and attention-gaining reasons, and the sooner this attitude is ingrained the better. You might even allude to this during the conference—if you think it will be appreciated—but don't push it.

William Avrunin, executive-vice-president of the Jewish Welfare Federation in Detroit and an experienced conferenceman, asked one group: "How is all this fancy conference talk related to how you feel about the campaign worker who, two weeks after the closing date, finds he has mislaid the prospect cards you sent him two months ago?" The fact is that it *isn't* related, and Avrunin—who treads on dangerous ground by saying things like: "Conferences are conferences and work is work"—quickly dropped the point and got on with his talk. But the ploy can be effective, as was another that Avrunin used at a conference on "local services," which he opened with: "Why are we meeting here today to discuss 'Who is for Local Services?' My guess is that the program-makers don't particularly care about the answer . . ." Carried any further, that kind of talk could of course mean disaster for the conferenceman.

Other short-lived attitudes that are proper under certain conference conditions are: moral righteousness, profound guilt, and utter despair (this last must be carefully controlled).

4. Know your audience. This is necessary not so you can gear your message to them (remember, your *real* message never changes) but because the religious, social or political affiliations of the audience may make, say, moral righteousness totally out of place. Even the code words discussed earlier must be judiciously used, and they by no means exhaust the possibilities. According to author and attorney Bernard Siegan, it is self-destructive to refer to "free enterprise" or the "market system" in one Chicago suburb—"they look at me as if I were talking about evil things," says Siegan—but references to how the "poor" or "less affluent" will benefit from a particular proposal is acceptable. However, in another suburb, with a different ethnic and economic makeup, the situation could be reversed.

Execution: Try These Ploys

Some ploys for establishing your conferencemanship:

1. Discover which group has been excluded from directly participating in the conference, and promote this group. For example, a general conference on the "energy

crisis" might not include sufficient representatives of the "poor," the black or the female—each year's annual meeting of the American Assn. for the Advancement of Science is disrupted for this reason. It is best to get on the bandwagon early. The very first panel of a journalists' conference last year in New York was disrupted by a group of "underground" journalists who demanded representation on *all* panels, and promised to seize the microphones if they were refused. Within minutes, quick-thinking panel members on stage were expressing sympathy for the protestors, and by the end of the opening session, conference officials had reorganized all subsequent panels.

Incidentally, there is no way for conference officials to stand off such challenges. "Reality is completely irrelevant . . ." says Greeley. "If anyone does raise the possibility that a minority group may indeed be present in appropriate numbers, the obvious response is to insist that because of the importance of the given group, it should be *over*represented . . ."

2. Be humble. Explain how your group has made many errors ("We're just beginning to understand the problems" is a good one), but still has accomplished many worthwhile goals—which you may then enumerate *ad infinitum*. Don't be fooled into thinking that conference attendees appreciate brief, to-the-point talks; try that approach and you won't be invited back.

3. Be stern, if necessary. If all else fails, and no one is agreeing with your position, try lecturing the conference attendees on the virtues of action over talk. Tell them it is necessary, says Greeley, to "make a stand" and to avoid "mere semantics." Warn them that people expect solutions, not just talk, and then add the clincher by saying that they are all "irrelevant"—a sure-fire guilt-producer. Don't worry about contradicting yourself during the lecture—no one will notice.

At all costs, conferences must never be permitted to go nowhere. This is especially true when engineers are involved, with their slide rules and precise calculations—people expect some attempts to find solutions, and go home grumbling if no point is made. A recent conference on stack-gas sulfur removal quickly reached that point of no return—and no "answers"—largely because the scope of the problem and design of possible solutions are just in the beginning stages. Consequently, the identical set of figures can be used to draw the conclusions that sulfur removal technology is available and that it is not available. But the answer in such conferences can never be: here is information, but no decision. Come prepared with *something*.

Counter-Conferencemanship for Engineers

Chemical engineers have an added problem. "Engineers don't know how to deal with people," says one who has attended many conferences. "I went into engineering because I didn't want to have anything to do with people, but rather to deal with nice, neat little subjects—in mathematical terms—where nobody can disagree." On top of this, he says, engineering societies are "scared of controversy; they don't know how to handle it. When someone comes from the floor with a question that tends to upset the speaker, you look around and everybody is gulping. They are afraid of the disapproval of their peers."

Inevitably, someone at a conference will say something with which you disagree, and it is important to master what Greeley calls "counter-conferencemanship." This consists of demolishing the opposition in the appropriate manner. "If you'd take the wax out of your ears, you'd know that I already said exactly what you've said, in three different ways," is one example of the meat-ax approach. The engineer advises that a different— and better—approach is to carefully rephrase "in the best possible manner" your opponent's argument, and then quickly "make mincemeat out of it."

During all such encounters, always guard against displaying emotions, and never get sucked into someone else's counter-conferencemanship. Remember the superior position you occupy: "The speaker is really in command," says Siegan. "Even people who are antagonistic to you defer to you—because they think you might make them look stupid. This occurs even when they ask the questions and disagree with you. They avoid getting too provocative."

As you become a more effective conferenceman, you will progress to more-sophisticated techniques—such as "reactormanship." This is another branch of the art, which consists of responding to comments and criticisms by going beyond the original statements. A good "reactor," for example, always makes sure his comments are twice as long as the speaker's, and always ends up on a pet topic that is a mile wide of the issue. Says Greeley: "The good reactor . . . says very little about the paper to which he is reacting, save possibly to distort some of the assertions of the speaker, or to use them out of context in order to make him look like an utter fool."

No matter how proficient you become, however, it is unlikely you will ever match the conferencemanship of the young preacher whose continual speeches on the subject of baptism prompted his superiors in the church to request that one week he instead preach on "pills." They figured there could be no connection between pills and baptism.

The next Sunday, the preacher said to his congregation: "This morning I have been asked to preach on the subject of pills. There are all kinds of pills—big pills and little pills, red pills and green pills, bitter pills and sweet pills, cheap pills and expensive pills.

"Another pill is the gospill, and that brings me back to my real subject—baptism."

And *that's* conferencemanship. ■

Meet the Author

Dennis J. Chase, who covers the "energy beat" for McGraw-Hill's Chicago World News Bureau, has written about such things as coal strikes, the Midwest power picture, and utility financing, for McGraw-Hill's domestic and foreign publications.
He received his B.S. in journalism from Michigan State University and worked for several newspapers and a public television station before joining McGraw-Hill. His previous article for CHEMICAL ENGINEERING, "Thinking About Thinking," appeared in the Dec. 11, 1972 issue.

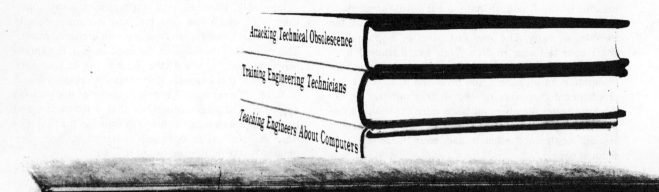

Attacking Technical Obsolescence

Training Engineering Technicians

Teaching Engineers About Computers

Running an In-Plant Course

Some firms are helping thier engineers staff off technical
obsolescence by organizing in-plant courses. Here's how they do it.

PETER J. BRENNAN, *Southwestern Editor*

I recently asked the chief process engineer at an isolated West Texas refinery and petrochemical plant how one can keep up-to-date in a place that is 100 miles from the nearest large city. His blunt answer: "You don't."

This reply suggests that, for most people, intensive self-education in subjects not immediately related to their jobs is usually quite difficult. This engineer subscribes to many journals, has a company library and his own technical library. He has a better-than-average opportunity to attend technical meetings. Yet he can't keep up.

What this man lacks is time and, perhaps more important, organized instruction. For it seems true that however strong the desire for more knowledge and the will to undertake self-instruction, most people do not gain facility with a subject unless they are taught by an instructor.

Realizing this, some companies have concluded that the best way to keep technical personnel up-to-date is via classes conducted either at the plant site or at a nearby institution. One simple approach (obviously feasible only when a plant is located near a suitable school) is the familiar tuition-refund plan. This has drawbacks, however, a principal one being that not all professionals desire to become part-time evening students, since this usually entails taking courses in a rather unstimulating atmosphere with other students of widely differing experience and motivation.

More ambitious, and probably more effective, are courses that are organized by the company and held on the firm's premises. One of the best known of these programs is that begun by Humble Oil & Refining Co. in 1946. Known as the Humble Lectures in Science and Engineering, the series has included more than 100 in-plant courses.

The series was started, says Humble, after "quite careful study of various methods for providing additional fundamental training to help technical personnel keep abreast of current developments in science." Note the word "fundamental." These are not job-oriented, vocational courses, nor are they refreshers at the undergraduate level, but rather are courses held on the graduate and postgraduate level. To ensure the highest level of instruction, Humble brings outstanding educators from all over the country to its Baytown, Tex., refinery.

The initial goal was to give each technical man the opportunity of taking one course every three years. In practice, each man has averaged one course every two years.

Engineers Have a Voice

The mechanics of setting up the lectures are actually quite simple and, more important, the plan is applicable to any plant, large or small, no matter how isolated its location.

Each spring, the lecture committee suggests a number of courses, and possible instructors, that appear pertinent and interesting. Technical personnel are then polled to indicate their preferences and are asked to suggest other possible courses and instructors. Seven or eight courses each year are selected on the basis of this poll.

To invite the guest lecturers, Humble sends each an introductory letter that describes the program, specifies the broad field the course is to cover, and discusses such matters as honorarium, travel and living expenses (paid by the company) and local transportation (furnished by the company). The instructor is given considerable latitude on the dates that he might give the course and complete freedom on method of presentation and selection of material.

If the instructor expresses interest in giving the course, a second letter describing the program in greater detail and firming up the arrangements is sent. In this letter, the company requests that the instructor agree to hold in confidence material concerning Humble's research program and plant practices. This agreement allows completely free interchange of ideas, and permits the students to discuss matters of immediate interest.

Occasionally the instructor may have a prior commitment—as a consultant to another firm, for instance—and cannot make such an agreement. In such cases, the secrecy clause is omitted from the letter and freedom of interchange of ideas is limited.

Restrictions on Attendance

Size of a class is limited to a maximum of sixteen and a minimum of nine. The average size has been fourteen. These numbers are usually considerably less than the number of those who would like to take the course and some applicants must be turned down. Selections are made on the basis of whether the course is pertinent to the employee's interests and duties, on his ability to handle the subject and on whether the man can be spared from his regular job. If a course is very popular, it will be repeated for those who missed it the first time around. Students are relieved of all duties for the period of the course—usually two weeks—and are expected to devote their full time to the lectures and outside study. Lectures themselves may consume as much as eight hours per day or as few as two or three, with individual consultations at the discretion of the instructor.

During the two-week period, the instructor usually covers the equivalent of one to two semesters' work on at least the graduate and often the postdoctoral level. The amount of material covered depends on the course and the aptness of the students who are enrolled.

Wide Popularity

The program is entirely voluntary, but 85-90% of the technical people at Humble's Baytown refinery have indicated a desire to take at least one course each year. Though voluntary, each student takes an exam at the end of the course and is graded. However, this is only to determine what the student got out of the lectures and his grade is not recorded.

Important to the success and high esteem of the Humble Lectures in Science and Engineering is the effort the company has made to obtain men of the greatest stature in their fields as instructors.

Among the lecturers have been: J. H. Hildebrand, University of California; Linus Pauling, California Institute of Technology; E. R. Gilliland, M.I.T.; O. A. Hougen, University of Wisconsin; R. E. Treybal, New York University; R. L. Pigford, University of Delaware.

The company's success in attracting such eminent people had little to do with its reputation. At the time the program was begun, Humble Oil & Refining Co. was only a domestic affiliate of the giant Standard Oil Co. (N. J.), and was mainly concerned with petroleum production and refining. It was well known only in the Southwest.

Outstanding teachers and scientists have come, and continue to come, to Baytown because they like to teach and know they will be addressing a willing and alert group, and because the company makes the arrangements as attractive as possible. Any other company considering such a program should not feel it is too low on the industrial totem pole to be able to obtain the very best men available.

For most companies, cost should not be a major factor in a decision to institute such a program. Considering the stature of the instructors and the amount of work that the instructor must do in preparing and presenting his course, the honorarium Humble pays is quite reasonable. Transportation, living expenses and so on also add to the cost. But these expenses are less than the salaries of nine to sixteen highly paid technical people who are given two weeks off to study.

Another Alternative

Smaller companies, without Humble's great resources, may feel that such ambitious in-plant courses are beyond the capabilities of their plant staffs to coordinate and supervise. However, it is possible for small firms to call on the services of outside consultants—and experts within their own organization—to conduct courses once or twice a week. These would be extended part-time courses, as contrasted with Humble's intensive, full-time two-week courses.

Where possible, such programs should be run in conjunction with a local college that can supply a course coordinator and instructors. Courses can be held on company premises and on the employees' time since we are speaking of plants that are too small to spare personnel from their regular duties.

The course coordinator (head of the chemical engineering department, for instance) can be given free rein to design the course, select instructors and make whatever arrangements might be necessary. The fee paid the coordinator would be about the same as he would receive for similar time spent on consulting work for the company.

A very specialized course could be conducted by one

or two instructors, with an occasional guest instructor for variety and a different point of view. Since the instructors would have to travel to the plant for each session, the choice of teachers would be limited by distance.

A broad survey course presents another problem. Since different lecturers can be used for each session, instructors can be brought from great distances to give one or two lectures; or a session can be scheduled to coincide with an instructor's trip through the area. The only requirement is that each lecture should fit into the broad outline of the course. Experts both from within the particular plant and from other company locations can also be used as occasional lecturers.

This approach presents a much greater problem in organization and scheduling, to prevent the program from becoming a series of disconnected seminars.

Success on a Part-Time Basis

A successful program of this type was recently completed at another Houston area plant, one much smaller than Humble's Baytown refinery and with far fewer resources.

This course, on systems engineering, was organized at the request of company management by a professor from a nearby university. The professor, who was a part-time consultant to the company to begin with, served as organizer, coordinator and occasional instructor but did not carry the full teaching load himself. The course ran for 16 weeks with two-hour lectures given twice a week. First lecture hour was on company time, the remainder on employees' time. Attendance was on a completely voluntary basis.

Two-thirds of the lecturers were specialists from outside the company, the remainder were employees. The course coordinator chose employee lecturers with the aid of company supervisors.

One of the disadvantages of the extended vs. the short type of course is the difficulty most people have in attending every lecture. Though every technical employee in the company participated to some extent, only half attended more than eight lectures out of a total of 32.

A complete set of lecture notes, running 500 pages, was prepared in advance and given to each registrant. The students could then dispense with note taking and give their full attention to the speaker. In addition, the notes provided a permanent record for future reference. Homework was kept to a minimum, though it was later felt that a greater amount would have helped in getting more of the material across.

Direct expenses of the course were the honoraria and expenses of guest lecturers and the course materials. By far the biggest indirect expense was that involving engineers' time, secretarial time and the coordinator's

time, though cost of the employees' time was minimized for the company since half of the class time was outside working hours.

Basic objective of the course was to familiarize engineers with the possibilities now offered by the systems approach. The program was definitely more job-oriented than most of the lectures in the Humble series, but was conducted at a graduate level.

What's the Payout?

Humble started its program with the feeling that the primary objective was a general upgrading of the technical proficiency of the staff. The company fully realized that immediate specific benefits could not be expected. However, it has observed that those who have participated in the courses have a better grasp of technical matters, as well as a better understanding of their problems and the methods of solution available to them. The program has exceeded the company's expectations in the degree to which it has renewed employees' interest in the basic sciences and in increasing their ability to apply such knowledge to their work.

Other companies echo similar sentiments. They say such programs boost employee morale since technical personnel are greatly encouraged when the company presents them with an opportunity to get advanced training. Employees not only learn about new techniques, but also have a greater interest in applying them.

If management in any firm feels that such programs could benefit its technical personnel, then neither the company's size or location, nor the cost of the courses, should be major obstacles.

Meet
the
Author

PETER J. BRENNAN, *southwestern editor for* CHEMICAL ENGINEERING, *is headquartered in Houston, although his assignments frequently take him far from his home base. Previously, he edited the Operations & Maintenance department for CE and has also worked for the General Atomic Div. of General Dynamics, Standard Brands, Inc., and Stauffer Chemical Co.*

How To Present A Technical Paper

Just about every engineer has heard
technical papers being read at meetings—
and been bored by them. If you want
to interest and inform your audience,
here's how to do it.

VINCENT VINCI, Lockheed Electronics Co.

The title of this article is really erroneous. Why?
Because technical papers should never be presented,
but technical speeches should. However, the erroneous
title has a purpose—to attract more attention to the
article because, in reality, engineers, chemists, bi-
ologists, pharmacologists, and many other scientists
do just what it says—present papers.

Standing before their fellows in the constant tide
of conventions, conferences and symposia, they read
their technical papers with all the equations, minute
details, intricate procedures, and endless tables and
graphs, pointedly disregarding the differences between
a speech and a paper. Returning to the beginning,
then, the title of this article should really be. How
To Present a Technical Speech.

Why are many technical speeches merely carbon
copies or shortened versions of a technical paper?
There are two major reasons. The first is that it is
the easiest way out. The second is ignorance of the
fact that technical papers, even good ones, do not
make good technical speeches, no matter how well
they are read or presented. Let us now consider the
differences in viewpoint, style, format, planning and
presentation.

The Difference

C. H. Woolbert has stated:

"A man speaking is four things, all of them
needed in revealing his mind to others. First,
he is a will, an intention, a meaning which he
wishes others to have, a thought; second, he
is a user of languages, shaping thought and
feeling by words; third, he is a thing to be
heard, carrying his purpose and words to others
through voice; and last, he is a thing to be seen,
shown to the sight, a being in action, to be noted
and read through the eye."*

The third and fourth items mark the significant
differences between writing a paper and making a
speech. A speaker must appeal to the auditory and
visual senses as the gateway to the audience's mind.
Even when he wants to appeal to any of the other
five doors to the mind—the motor, tactile, olfactory,
gustatory, or thermic†—entrance is achieved through
the eyes and ears of the audience. Furthermore, the
speaker's character and emotion can add strength and
believability to his reasoning and afford easier access
to the minds of his audience.

A speech, then, is more than mere words and
punctuation. A speech includes articulation, pronunciation, enunciation, rate, volume, pitch, intonation, emphasis, modulation, timing, resonance, and gestures.
In fact, a printed word may take on a different connotation once it is uttered. When you give a speech,
you breathe life into the thoughts, ideas, and analogies
of the presentation. Your presence lends it confidence,
sincerity, and enthusiasm. Since a speech is alive,
it is subject to change. A split second before a thought
is presented, you can rephrase it. You can emphasize
or de-emphasize through intonation, or even invert

---

* C. H. Woolbert, "Fundamentals of Speech," Harper and Brothers,
New York, 1920.

† Yeager, W. H., "Effective Speaking for Every Occasion," 2nd ed.
Prentice Hall, Englewood Cliffs, N. J., Jan. 1950.

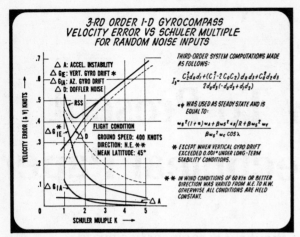

TYPICAL SLIDE generally can't be seen, and if seen, is almost impossible to comprehend—Fig. 1

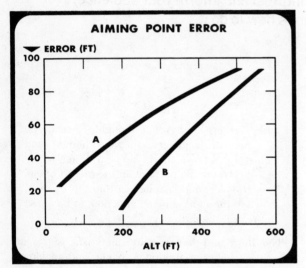

SIMPLIFIED GRAPH is quickly understood—Fig. 2

you told them," still pretty well sums up the use of repetition in presentations.

A speech unfolds only the highlights. To do this, the central ideas of a speech are held to a minimum because the audience lacks the time and the patience to absorb a surplus of main ideas. The listener, unlike the reader, cannot govern distractions, or the conditions under which he must understand and retain meanings and logic. The listener relies on memory, and the statement of too many ideas will cause him to give up. Furthermore, a listener can't dwell too long on a single thought without missing the speaker's next phrase and perhaps losing the continuity.

Although a speech and a paper may have the same objective, in essence they are quite different. Since the reader can reread a sentence, a paragraph, even the entire article, technical papers will and should contain more detailed supporting material than speeches. Methods of approach to research, equations, derivations, background, detailed test and performance data, and specifications can appear in a paper because if the reader wishes, he can analyze, reread and even perform his own calculations. For example, scholars have devoted lifetimes of study, research and meditation on such works as the Bible and Dante's "Divine Comedy," trying to fathom meanings, symbols and allegories; but a speech occurs at a given time and place and there's no chance to ponder as you listen.

Technical papers do not contain meaningful smiles, inflections, innuendoes, gestures, or other keys to a thought or visual underscoring. Even methods of presenting supporting material are different. For example, a typical illustration in a technical paper (Fig. 1) may contain elaborate equations, several curves (with many callouts) on a single graph, plus footnotes and other information. Similar data when used as a visual in a presentation must be simplified (Fig. 2) so the audience can read and grasp its meaning readily. You don't want your audience engaged in a reading session; if that's the case, you can save your energy and simply let them read your paper at their own pace.

What To Do About Your Talk

First, don't accept a speaking engagement unless you have ample time to prepare a speech or convert a technical paper into a speech.

Regardless of whether you convert or start from scratch, you must determine the main objective of your talk. Your primary objective will be the basis for organization—your foundation.

With your specific intent in mind, you now can select the main ideas behind the primary purpose. For instance, if your specific objective is "to establish that all chemical processing plants should be computer controlled," you might:

- State the control requirements of processing plants.
- Analyze the main control techniques or methods.
- Show how computer control best meets the needs of chemical plants.

the meaning. Each possible change is based on your interpretation of the audience's reaction to your previous ideas.

Aristotle in his "Rhetoric" distinguished between the language of writing and the language of speech. His reasoning was based on the knowledge that a speech is transitory while a written paper is permanent. On this basis, the speaker has one chance to accomplish his objective—right then and there while facing his audience. Therefore, the planning of a speech revolves around: a *specific* purpose, aimed at a *specific* audience, located at a *particular* place and presented in a *specified* time limit. A speech must unfold only the highlights, show their relationship to the overall objective, and keep the audience aware of how the pieces fit together. This awareness is accomplished through repetition; a must in speech-making, a transgression in writing. The old Army admonition to instructors, "Tell them what you're going to tell them, then tell them, then tell them what

Support Your Main Ideas

Once you have determined the main ideas (in effect, they form a speech outline). you must then select the supporting details. These may include statistics, comparisons, performance data, testimony, contrasts, facts, and personal experience. For example, statistics in the form of trends toward computer-controlled processes—relating the number of converted and new processing plants using computers, plus contrasting these trends with other control methods—would effectively persuade your audience. Statistics, in this case, would convince an audience more readily than testimony or anecdotes. Supporting material, therefore, gives life to your main ideas, adding credibility and conviction.

In choosing your supporting information, keep in mind "the big picture" and relate the meaning of the data to the overall or main objective.

Don't oversupport your main ideas; too much data may show everyone how much you know, but by swamping the audience with detail you'll only cause them to lose sight of the main purpose.

Spread your data, don't cram statistics into one portion of the speech. In addition, try to get a healthy mix of examples and numbers. Give your statistics life, don't just present a series of figures—tell the audience what's behind a particular statistic. In this way, they will not only feel the impact of the number, they will understand and retain its meaning.

Introduction and Conclusion

After establishing your main ideas and their supporting material, you are prepared to bring together all the strong points or highlights to form the conclusion of the speech. Your conclusion should match the type of speech. An informative speech requires a summary of the salient points, while a persuasive talk will need a "call to action" or an appeal in addition to a summary.

Usually written after the body of the speech has been written, your introduction is similar to a newspaper headline. The introduction should: create immediate interest; tell the audience what the speech is about; establish a rapport between you and the audience.

Get Help If You Can

In this age of high competition, with its emphasis on marketing and selling, speechmaking and communication have become sophisticated and necessary. Not only do companies now seek opportunities to present their knowledge, products, and capabilities, they have departments set up at the cost of good, hard cash, to help in the preparation and presentation of "papers" and "articles." Many companies draw upon the special talents of public relations and advertising agencies, package designers and management consultants. So why shouldn't professional aid and counsel be sought for speechwriting and speechmaking? Asking or getting assistance from a professional speaker or someone who earns his living at writing or editing isn't a reflection on your intelligence.

Remember, too, that the speech writer can assist you in researching, outlining, and developing your speech, as well as advise you as to expression and diction. He can act as a professional sounding board, a constructive critic, and a frame of reference, not only for the development and writing of the speech but also for presentation and platform manner. Many a speaker or engineer preparing a report or related document is wary of editors or technical writing consultants—he feels that his words or ideas will be distorted. This feeling is usually unwarranted, for if the editor has misinterpreted, it is very likely that the audience will have also.

However, you should know your man and what you can expect of him. In this light, a few words of caution: Know what you are looking for, know what you can expect from professional help, and be sure to give as much detailed information concerning the background and the speaking situation as you can. The returns you can expect depend on this knowledge. Often there's help around you—seek it, use it, but don't depend entirely on it.

In Summary

If you present a technical paper instead of a speech, you may write it off to experience, but the audience will see you as an inexperienced, ineffective speaker. In fact, they may find it downright insulting that you simply read your technical paper, thereby exposing your lack of desire to present your findings or theories concisely. It also shows that you are unprepared. In speechmaking, there is no alternative to preparedness. Presentation of an effective technical speech requires three elements: (1) preparation, (2) preparation, and (3) preparation. Remember as a speaker, not writer, you are appealing to an audience that have come to *hear* and *see* a speech and not a reading of a technical paper. The audience wants a finished product they can readily understand, retain and use. Keep in mind that a technical speech is transitory, a technical paper is not . . . and you'll always present technical speeches. ∎

Meet the Author

Vincent Vinci is Manager of Public Relations for Lockheed Electronics Co., U. S. Highway 22, Plainfield, N. J. Before joining public relations, he was supervisor of presentations, proposals and reports. He is a graduate of Seton Hall University, and has been a member of its staff, teaching courses in speech. He has also taught effective writing at Newark College of Engineering.

Going to a Meeting? Why?

Technical meetings can be really informative, even enjoyable. With these tips, you can make them so—whether you attend as a speaker or listener.

HOYT S. GRAMLING, Boyd Brace Associates

Do you attend meetings? If so, then quickly—what was the last one about, and where did it take place? Can you answer these questions without too great a pause? All right, here's another query: What were three of the talks about?

If you can very quickly answer that question, I'd say that either (1) you go to very, very few meetings or (2) the meeting was probably held within the last two weeks.

My point? Perhaps I'm trying to ascertain with you how much benefit meetings yield and, possibly more important, whether indeed it is the formal talks at the meeting that provide most of the benefit.

Speaking to the Speaker

Attending a meeting is, after all, not as rewarding or even pleasurable a matter for some as it is for others (notwithstanding the often very rich food). While I know of no actual polls that have been taken about "how well one goes to a meeting," I feel certain that many go not so well at all.

What should you do as a potential speaker to make a meeting worthwhile? First of all, and I'm sorry if this seems either obvious or facetious, weigh whether your talk will provide something of value, and if it won't— don't give it; be in the audience and learn from someone else. Outraged about that? Then answer this question: Have you ever heard a worthless talk delivered at a meeting? Weren't you outraged about that? !

Second, take good time to think out the title for your talk. Don't just put down the first thing that comes to your mind. Many a talk has been ill attended at a multi-session meeting simply because the speaker has dully labeled his presentation. Now by this I am not at all advocating sensationalism—certainly if you can't produce after promising much, you (and I mean *You* and not your talk) will be less regarded than if you promised very little to begin with. But I do recommend attractiveness. Pompous, multisyllabic abstract words do little to set the spark of interest going. Such words as Characteristics, Factors, Parameters, Developments must be used most carefully lest they turn the prospective audience com-

102

pletely off. Of course, I am not speaking out against label titles—which reveal your exact subject—such as "Heat Transfer in Catalytic Reactors"; I am referring instead to the leaden obtuseness—or even "redundant tautologies"—of very many of the abstract words. For example, "Effecting Optimization," "Inherent Characteristics of . . . ," etc.

Third, and also in terms of abstract words, your talk itself should be as free of them as possible. The more specific you can be, the more concrete your points and examples, the better you will be remembered as a sharp person with something important to say, rather than a dullard trying to blow his own horn. Also, I'd urge you as much as possible, no matter to what degree your paper is technical or nontechnical, to drastically curtail use of platitudes—such astoundingly deadly generalizations as, "the path of the economy lies upward (or downward)," "the sophistication of instrumentation keeps climbing," and so on. Be specific: name names, places; state dimensions; present case histories. Even if you're theorizing, give examples, ·make suppositions, etc. Over years of conference going, I tend to remember very specific types of statements, talks that dealt in specifics, and the people who presented these.

Fourth, before starting your talk, and probably even before the entire session begins, check out your audio-visual aids—or, if it is more diplomatic, ask the chairman to do so. I have seen too many otherwise intelligent people appear absolutely duncelike as they joggled malfunctioning microphones, groped for pointers in the dark, or after much searching pulled the *proper* box of slides from their pockets while a bored audience silently prayed for the coffee, lunch or dinner break.

Fifth, and many books have been written about this of course, speak distinctly, with some enthusiasm but without overexuberance, pomposity or arrogance. Your audience has attended to learn from you and, at the moment, you are (or certainly should be if you have anything worthwhile) a teacher, and this is your attentive, eager-to-learn class.

Some Competition

Now these five pieces of advice are obviously not all there is to say about a speaker's role at a meeting. There's much involved that is intangible, including some psychological aspects.

For example, I think an interesting, perhaps amusing, study could be made about what are the best times and worst times for a speaker's talk. I mean, just how good is it to be the first of five speakers at the morning session of the opening day of a three-day meeting? Conversely, just how bad is it to be the last of five speakers at the afternoon session on the closing day of this same meeting? (Incidentally, if you have something quite important to say, wouldn't it be worth trying to get good placement at a session?)

Perhaps you haven't thought about it much, but you do have an awful lot of· competition for the listener's awareness, you know. And I don't mean squeaking or banging doors, low-flying planes, or screaming fire-engines, either. I'm talking about your listeners' own thought processes. They can never be completely subjugated to your oratory. Put yourself in your audience's place (where you have certainly been on occasion).

You as Listener

When you are part of the audience, do you sometimes think that everyone is hanging on to each word of the speaker's talk except you yourself? Do you feel guilty when thinking that you are the only one who hasn't caught or understood the last sentence or sentences of the speaker?

Relax, you've got lots of company. People all around you are at times thinking of when the next train, bus, plane leaves; of when it will be time for lunch; of a dash to the restroom; of a possible failure in attempting to get theater tickets; of phoning the family; of quitting a job, or being fired, and so on. Even when not that divorced from the realities of where they are and what they are listening to, these same people, at different times, have drifted off the speaker's main track, to spur on their own branch-line of thought about the subject at hand. And in so doing, before they get back to what the speaker is actually talking about at the moment, quite a few sentences may have gone by, and whole chains of reasoning may have been broken.

While sitting through a long-winded presentation, I sometimes picture a sharp-minded gentleman suddenly rising and saying: "Will the meeting please stop." After momentary confusion, he addresses the audience: "Each of you has a piece of paper and a pencil. Please do two things. First, duplicate or paraphrase the last five sentences the speaker has delivered. And then, write a paragraph on what these sentences mean."

The question is, how much did you really derive overall from the ten talks you heard today? Can we invent here a parameter called "percentage of something really useful"? What will it be for any given talk? What will it be for the ten-talk session as a whole? How strongly will the dis-attention aspect weigh?

I ask this because I think that far and away the main value of most meetings accrues both after and around the formal presentations, and that these formal presentations are but preliminary aspects of more-meaningful things to follow: i.e., the question-and-answer sessions in an open meeting, the inter-panel disputation and, better yet, the private after-the-meeting discussions between speakers and listeners, which sadly are all too often bypassed or not taken full advantage of. The most rewarding moments in terms of knowledge-gaining I have ever enjoyed have taken place in private or small-group tete-a-tetes after the formal meetings—exactly when one sees countless numbers of meeting-attendees blithely strolling away from, or maybe studiously avoiding, such encounters. I can only feel sorry for these people. What an amazing amount of detail they will have failed to make themselves privy to. ∎

Meet the Author

Hoyt S. Gramling (a pseudonym) is executive director of Boyd Brace Associates (also a pseudonym), a management-consulting and public-relations firm. His earlier contribution in Chemical Engineering was "Acquiring the Executive Demeanor" (part of "Handbook for Executive Success"), which appeared in the Jan. 20, 1964 issue, p. 150.

PART IV

Making Reports Work for You

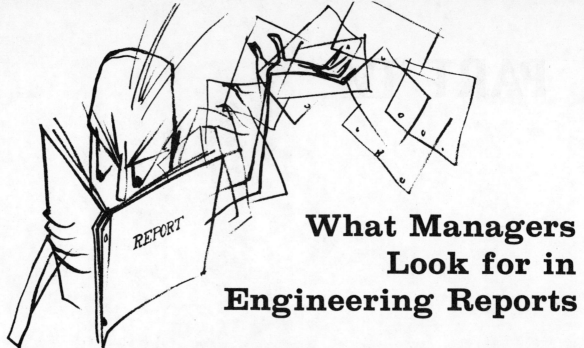

What Managers Look for in Engineering Reports

By knowing in advance the types of questions that managers always ask, you can organize your report to assure that your message gets across.

When a manager reads a report, he looks for pertinent facts and competent opinions that will aid him in decision-making. He wants to know *right away* whether he should read the report, route it, or skip it.

To determine this, he wants fast answers to some or all of the following questions:

- What's the report about and who wrote it?
- What are the conclusions and recommendations?
- What are their importance and significance?
- What's the implication to the company?
- What actions are suggested?
- Why, by whom, when, and how should the actions be carried out?

The manager wants this information in concise terms, in a summary form, at the beginning of the report.

Such summaries should contain three kinds of facts: (a) what the report is about; (b) the significance and implications of the work; (c) the action called for. To convey a clear understanding of what the report is about, the problem must first be defined, then the objectives of the report set forth. Next, reasons for doing the work must be given. Following this should come the conclusions. And finally, recommendations.

Subjects of Interest

In addition to the facts that a manager looks for in a report, studies at Westinghouse have shown that he is interested in five broad technological areas:

1. Technical problems.
2. New projects and products.
3. Experiments and tests.
4. Materials and processes.
5. Field troubles.

This material is excerpted from an article in the *Westinghouse Engineer*, July-Sept., 1962, which was based on an extensive study of management reading habits made at Westinghouse Electric Corp.

The things that managers want to know about each of these areas are shown in the table on the next page. Each set of questions can serve as a check-list for report writers.

In addition to these technical questions, a manager must also consider market factors and organization problems. Although such topics are not the primary concern of the engineer, he should furnish this information to management whenever technical aspects provide special insight into nontechnical problems. For example, here are some of the questions about marketing matters that a manager will want answered:

- What are the chances for success?
- What are the possible monetary and technical rewards?
- Can we be competitive in price and delivery?
- Is there a market or must one be developed?
- When will the product be available?

And here are some of the questions about organization problems that must be answered before a manager can make a decision:

- Is this the type of work the company should do?
- What changes will be required in organization,

How managers read reports

	Relative frequency of reading, %
Summary	100
Introduction	60
Body	25
Conclusions	55
Appendix	15

Relative frequency of reading, %

manpower, facilities and equipment, or procedures?
- Is it an expanding or contracting program?
- What will suffer if we emphasize this project?

Level of Presentation

Most readers—and certainly this is true for management readers—are interested mainly in the significant conclusions, and in the general concepts that grow out of the details. Consequently there is seldom real justification for a highly detailed presentation.

Usually the management reader has a different background from that of the writer. *Never* does the management reader have the same familiarity with the specific problem that the writer has. Therefore, the author should write at a technical level for a reader whose background and education differ from his own. If the report writer is a chemical engineer, his report should be made comprehensible to an industrial or mechanical engineer. If highly detailed material is necessary, it can be placed in an appendix.

Attention to some of these basic questions—before ever attempting to put words down on paper—can yield big dividends in the form of more effective reports.

Questions managers always ask . . .

About: Technical Problems
What is it?
Magnitude and importance?
What is being done? By whom?
Approaches used? Thorough and complete?
Suggested solution? Best? Consider others?
What now? Who does it? Time factors?

About: New Projects & Products
Potential? Risks?
Scope of application?
Commercial implications? Competition?
Importance to company?
More work to be done? Any problems?
Required manpower, facilities and equipment?
Relative importance to other projects or products?
Life of project or product line?
Effect on company technical position?
Priorities required?
Proposed schedule? Target date?

About: Tests & Experiments
What tested or investigated?
Why? How? What did it show?
Better ways?
Conclusions? Recommendations?
Implications to company?

About: Materials & Processes
Properties, characteristics, capabilities? Limitations?
Use requirements and environment?
Areas and scope of application?
Cost factors?
Availability and sources? What else will do it?
Problems in using?
Significance of applicaton to company?

About: Field Troubles, Special Design Problems
Specific equipment involved?
What trouble developed? Any trouble history?
How much involved?
What is needed? Who is responsible?
Special requirements and environment?
Who does it? Time factors?
Most practical solution? Recommended action?
Suggested product-design changes?

Fast, Functional

To start off, here is how a new writing-sequence concept—and a Report Highlights form of the type shown below—can help you . . .

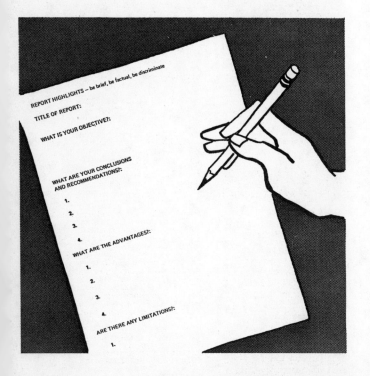

Organize the Report for Fast Writing, Easy Reading

THOMAS P. JOHNSON, Writing Consultant

Not so long ago, the conversation reprinted below took place in the administration building of a large company. The participants: an engineer (E) and an iconoclast (I). The setting: alongside a coffee-dispensing machine, located in a closet exactly halfway between the engineering laboratory and the front office.

E: Have you finished reading my report?

I: Yes, I'm afraid I have.

E: Well, what's the verdict?

I: I'll give you the pleasant part first. You're a pretty good writer, it seems to me. I had no trouble understanding what you had to say, except for a few technical terms here and there. I'm glad you didn't

Writing

imitate the typical business writer and drown your main points in a sea of pompous, abstract statements.

E: Thanks. Now let's get to what you really want to talk about. Where did I go wrong?

I: My friend, you did what too many other technical writers do. You produced an 80-page report that is a nightmare of disorganization. In other words, the outline you followed was a slap in the face of logic.

E: Explain.

I: Well, I read through your report the same way I would go through any other piece of writing—a novel, a newspaper story, a magazine article. I started at the beginning and read right through to the end.

E: Of course. What other way is there?

I: There's the old tried-and-tested "how to read a technical report" approach, which I deliberately chose to ignore here. You first turn to the *final* section—the one entitled Conclusions—so that you can get the main point of the report. Once you know what the author's pitch is, the course of action he recommends, you go back to the beginning and start plowing through the mass of historical detail that appears in Section One.

E: Wait a minute! I put my recommendations up front. You apparently didn't read my one-page summary right at the beginning of the report.

I: I certainly did. In fact, I read it three times—closely. So far as I can see, all it contains is a series of general statements. You state that the company is thinking about starting a new project, the one you're reporting on. Then you state that the results of your study are subject to the "advantages and limitations discussed in Sections IV, VI and VII"—whatever they are. You estimate "certain material and labor ex-

Thomas P. Johnson wrote the first section, which offers help on report organization and related matters. He is a consultant in technical and business writing, residing at 251 W. 89 St., New York City. During the past dozen years, he has taught writing courses to engineers, editors, and advertising personnel. Published in 1966 by Harper & Row, his book "Analytical Writing: A Handbook for Business and Technical Writers" has become an established text.

Auren Uris authored the second section, which focuses on the timesaving aspects of dictation, and examines the merits of machine- vs. secretarial dictation. Mr. Uris is on the staff of the Research Institute of America, 589 Fifth Ave., New York, N.Y. He is a widely known author and commentator on management problems; his most recent book is "Mastery of Management," subtitled "How to avoid obsolescence by preparing for tomorrow's management today," published by Dow Jones-Irwin.

James R. Fair wrote the third section, which gives advice on the special dictating problems of engineers, with emphasis on the dictating of technical and mathematical material. Dr. Fair, one of the recipients of *CHEMICAL ENGINEERING's* Personal Achievement Awards last year, has made many contributions to the engineering literature, and has authored next issue's report on sorption techniques. He is Manager, Engineering Technology, in Monsanto Co.'s Central Engineering Dept., 800 N. Lindbergh Blvd., St. Louis, Mo.

Herbert Popper is responsible for the final section, which passes along a variety of time-conserving hints garnered from his own experience and from that of others. Since joining *CHEMICAL ENGINEERING's* editorial staff in 1961, Popper has not only commissioned, developed and edited articles on a wide range of topics, but has done considerable writing himself, including such "You & Your Job" pieces as "Mission: Chimerical," "Death of an Engineer," "The Clam-Up Concept," and "Diary of an Engineer's Wife."

penses," then refer the reader to several formidable charts in your report appendix. You hint that something wonderful will happen to your company—maybe—if the project is feasible. In short, you don't convince the reader, because you refuse to come to grips with your subject.

E: I'm not supposed to do that in the summary. After all, isn't the summary a general statement that indicates the scope of a report?

I: That's not quite correct. A summary should be more specific than that. Theoretically, it should be a clear, concise record not only of the report's scope but also of the conclusions and recommendations reached. But what actually happens is almost always far different. Given a blank page labeled "Summary," the typical report writer invariably produces the same sort of cautious, overly general prose you've dished up here.

E: By the way, I'd like to point out that I didn't begin writing my report with my eyes closed. To make sure that I'd be correct on procedures, I dug out my old college text and followed the outline it recommended. I don't suppose you're familiar with Professor Jones' "Technical Reports I Have Known"?

I: Yes, I know that textbook and twenty others just like it. They all say the same thing: "When you submit your report to higher management, you should preface it with a short summary. Then you should discuss your subject in the following order: (1) introduction to the subject, (2) discussion of the subject, and (3) conclusions and recommendations. Appropriate appendices round out the report."

E: Right. And what's wrong with that?

I: Let me answer you by asking a couple of questions. If you do recommend that your company begin the project, you're asking it to make a sizable investment. Now, what's the first thing your boss wants to know when he picks up your report?

E: That's easy. He wants to know whether we should initiate the project and, if we do, what it's going to cost the company.

I: Where in your report do you answer this question?

E: Well, I touch on it in the summary, of course, but I spell it out in detail in my conclusions.

I: On pages 78 through 80, to be exact. What you've done is adopt the technique of the mystery novelist, keeping your reader in suspense by withholding your most important information until the very end. Here's another question: Once your boss knows whether your recommendation is "yes" or "no," what does he want to know next? Think hard about this.

E: If you remember, I recommend that we do begin the project. Considering this, I suppose he wants to know why we ought to begin it, how I arrived at my conclusions, how the project will benefit the company—that sort of thing.

I: Precisely. He wants to be sold on your recommendation. He wants to know the advantages of the new project, together with the limitations. He wants

concrete figures on things like cost savings, production increases, sales possibilities, and labor savings. All these things do appear in your report, but they aren't discussed until pages 39, 56, 63 and 72. Why not pull them all together and put them at the beginning of your report, preceded by your "yes" recommendation, so that these will be the first things he sees?

E (triumphantly): I'll tell you why! It's because I'm not allowed to. I can see the point you're trying to make, and I tend to agree with you. The only trouble is, our company policy is to follow the same academic outline that you object to. I couldn't deviate from it even if I wanted to.

I: That's an old engineer's tale, and it amounts to a sorry state of affairs. To put it bluntly, I think your company is wrong. If I didn't, I wouldn't be an iconoclast. There is a better way to organize a report, a much more logical way, and I'll be glad to show it to you.

E: Don't show me, show my boss.

Needed: A New Approach

In the above conversation, as well as in what follows, I am appealing to anyone who has to write technical reports, but especially to those who determine what the report format shall be. My contention is that today most reports fail to make the impact they should, simply because they are not logically organized. In the age of the computer, the report writer is still doggedly following precepts laid down in the 19th century. Usually he's doing so because he has been ordered to do it that way.

What is needed is a new approach to report organization, one that differs radically from the traditional form. Because it is senseless, however, to suggest change for the mere sake of change, I want to emphasize that the new approach should bring at least two benefits. It will help the report *reader* by directing him more quickly and more naturally to the main ideas in the report. And it will help the report *writer* not only to make his writing an easier task but also to sell his recommendations to the reader much more convincingly.

The conventional structure of technical reports, as prescribed by most textbooks and company style-manuals, is this:

A. Summary.
B. Text: 1. Introduction.
        2. Discussion.
        3. Conclusions and Recommendations.
C. Appendices.

Briefly, the new approach to organization suggests the following changes:

• The "Summary" is eliminated and is replaced by the section "Conclusions and Recommendations." The physical appearance of this new section is a form similar to the one reproduced in the cartoon on the previous page.

• The section "Introduction," which consists of

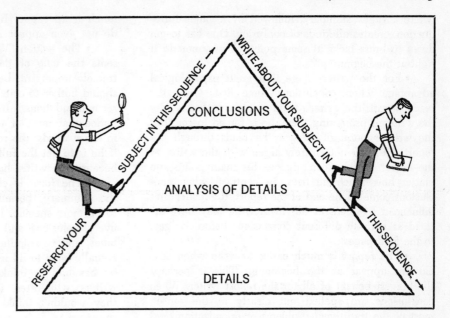

INVERTED-PYRAMID approach assures that the main ideas in the report—what the reader most wants to know—are at the beginning, not at the end.

background material and historical detail, is eliminated. (This material does reappear at various places in the new report structure, but not as a monolithic block.)

• The section "Discussion" is eliminated and replaced by detailed expansions of the conclusions and recommendations that appear on the "Report Highlights" form.

Where Reports Go Wrong

When a technical report is poorly organized, the writer is usually guilty of this fault: He has written his report in the same sequence he followed in researching his subject matter. Let's examine this statement in detail.

The research that precedes the actual writing of a report can be divided into three separate steps. First, the writer gathers all the details on the subject that are available to him. In this broad investigation, he collects background material, technical data, production details—anything that has any bearing on his subject. His second step is to analyze all this detail, separating it into logical groups that point the way to the conclusions he will reach. Finally, he arrives at those conclusions, which are accompanied by his recommendations.

The structure of this three-step research project is like a pyramid (see the diagram). And the most important part of this pyramid is the apex, where the main ideas (the *what* and *why*) of the author stand out clearly and boldly.

What happens when the researcher writes the report in the same sequence? The most obvious fault is that the reader does not have a full grasp of the *what* and *why* until the final pages. But there is another, equally insidious, fault: By following this academic approach—introduction, discussion, conclusion

—the writer forces the reader to go through all the spadework and trivial detail he himself had to endure while researching his subject matter. Nothing is more frustrating to the reader at that point.

The pyramid structure mentioned above highlights what should be a key axiom of technical writing: *When you write a report, don't make the reader climb your pyramid; he may have trouble getting to the top.* Such an axiom carries this message to the report writer: When you actually start writing your report, flip-flop the sequence you followed in doing your research. Put your conclusions and recommendations at the beginning of the report. And put all those details down in the base of the pyramid, where they reinforce your main ideas, not precede and dominate them.

The Inverted Pyramid

This structure, which has been called the inverted-pyramid approach to report organization, is far and away the most logical for any technical report, because:

• At once, the reader learns what he wants to know. For instance, if several copies of a research report are distributed, some of the most important recipients may have neither the time nor the desire to examine every page; all they may want is a clear picture of the conclusions that emerged from the research—and the inverted-pyramid form can give this to them without their having to hunt for the right pages.

• Conclusions are usually concrete, rather than general. Thus the writer avoids a notorious trap when he begins with his conclusions. He is not forced to begin with a lengthy, general introduction before coming to grips with his subject matter. This is a major fault of the academic approach to organization, where a vague summary, followed by a vague introduction, creates all kinds of confusion. One has to get down to brass tacks at some point, so why not do it right at the beginning?

• For the writer, there is a great psychological advantage when conclusions come first. Once the reader grasps the writer's main points, and learns why the writer is promoting them, he is forced to consider the writer's point of view as he reads through the report. He may not entirely agree with the writer at the outset, but he can't ignore his main points, no matter how much he tries. In contrast, when conclusions come at the end of the report, the reader isn't influenced by them at all; in fact, he may have arrived at entirely different conclusions before he gets to the final pages.

• The report is much easier to write when conclusions appear at the beginning. This is perhaps the biggest benefit of all for the report writer. When conclusions are spelled out clearly at the outset, most of the traditional problems of organization tend to disappear. The remainder of the report simply becomes an expansion of the conclusions and recommendations. And quite frankly, the organization after this can be atrocious, yet the reader is not likely to object so vociferously. Why? Because the first part of the report gives him clues or guidelines that make it much easier to interpret the mass of detail that follows.

A Specific Proposal, and Its Benefits

As mentioned earlier, I strongly recommend that the traditional report summary be eliminated, and that it be replaced by a standard printed form. Such a form, filled in to represent a typical report, is reproduced on the opposite page, along with the conventional summary for this report. In the discussion that follows, it will be helpful to refer from time to time to both the filled-in form and the summary.

Why a form? Admittedly, few people really enjoy filling out forms. As I am writing these lines it is early April, only a week or so before that most infamous of all deadlines, for taxpayers. Yet let us be honest with ourselves: If anything could be worse than having to fill out an income-tax return, it would be having to furnish the same information with no form at all.

What the report form does is force the engineer to spell out his main ideas clearly and concretely. It gives him a set of guidelines to follow, which are far more helpful than a blank piece of paper. One of the most frequent complaints of engineers is that they find it very difficult to get started on the task of writing reports. The form makes this task a little less formidable.

Several improvements come when the printed form replaces the blank page:

• The section "What Are Your Conclusions and Recommendations?" presents the *what* of the report in detail. Notice that the conventional summary is

much more vague. In fact, some of the conclusions do not even appear in the summary.

• The section "What Are the Advantages?" presents the *why* of the report in detail. This is extremely important, because it shows why the reader should bother to consider the writer's conclusions and recommendations. In the conventional summary, notice that most of these points are only hinted at; in other words, the reader has to do the interpreting if he is to get the full significance of the conclusions, because the writer has done little interpreting.

• The form is considerably more detailed than the summary, because the form forces the writer to be more specific. It makes him consider including five conclusions and recommendations, four advantages, and two limitations. (In the end, he may not actually have to fill in every blank space, but at least he has had to think about doing so. Thus, report writers will often include important details that they wouldn't think of putting into the traditional summary.)

• On the form, the writer must separate the various elements of his *what* and *why*. In other words, he must be more discriminating when he lists his main ideas. On the conventional summary, there is little of this discrimination, unless the writer is a far more skilled word craftsman than the typical report writer. As a result, the impact on the reader of these important ideas isn't nearly as strong as it should be.

• The form compels the writer to be more concise in his choice of words. Notice that the numbers on the form are arranged in a way· that the writer is forced to state an idea in no more than three or four single-spaced typewritten lines. (See blank form on p. 108.)

• Finally, the form encourages the writer to introduce figures on costs, savings and the like. The writer can't simply say to the reader, "Buy my recommendations because they are bigger, better, and more wonderful," which he is likely to do in the traditional summary. Such a statement may help to sell soap or hair sprays, but it doesn't convince the reader of technical reports.

Selecting the Form

In a few enlightened companies today, forms like the one suggested here are producing impressive results. Of course, the forms in use vary considerably, because reports of individual companies or departments vary widely. But whatever the physical format, the best forms do compel report writers to arrange their main ideas in an orderly fashion. The chaos of the traditional summary is kept to a minimum.

Anyone who is responsible for selecting the format of his company's reports should seriously consider replacing the summary with a form. You are welcome to appropriate the form given here if you find it meets your needs. (An alternate form is shown on p. 113.) Usually, though, you will want to devise

Summary

This report examines the capacity of the bottling lines for Chemical Specialty XYZ, relative to projected demand over the next ten years. (The demand projections are based on Market Research Study No. 46 (1968), and are detailed in the Appendix.) It is concluded that the present theoretical capacity is adequate to meet demand until 1975, assuming certain additional warehousing facilities can be obtained for seasonal peaks. However, unless the present efficiency of the lines is increased so that they operate closer to theoretical capacity, it is likely that shortages will occur by 1971, unless a considerable amount of overtime work is engaged in. This report therefore examines a program of preventive maintenance, foreman and employee training, minor line modifications and other measures whereby the efficiency of the lines might be improved. Other benefits of this program are also examined. A discussion of costs and a proposed timetable are included on pp. 24–28. (It is anticipated that the costs of this program will be confined to operating expenses; no capital appropriation is being requested at this time.)

HIGHLIGHTS PAGE (right) is only slightly longer than conventional summary (left)—yet is much more specific, and gives the reader a clearer grasp of the significant ideas in the report. The format can save writing time.

your own form. Here is some practical advice on this:

First you should make a survey of past company reports. This study should give you the answers to questions like these: How numerous are the *what's* and *why's* of past reports? What headings should be included? Should conclusions and recommendations be included as separate sections? When your survey is completed, you should have a pretty good idea of what form will work best for your own company.

Try to avoid oversimplifying the form. Make it as detailed as possible, so that your writers will have to consider all the things you feel are important.

Sometimes a form may have to be longer than the one-page form suggested here. You should try, however, to get everything on one page, adding at the bottom a phrase like "continue on reverse, if necessary." Incidentally, it's a good idea to reproduce each filled-in form and put the reproduction into a master file. Such a file would then become available to anyone in the company who wanted a clear, concise record of the *what* and *why* of any company report. If he then needed more information, he could always go to the report itself.

REPORT HIGHLIGHTS – be brief, be factual, be discriminate

TITLE OF REPORT: Chemical Specialty XYZ -- Bottling Capacity vs. Demand

WHAT IS YOUR OBJECTIVE?: To determine whether the bottling line for XYZ can meet demand over the next 10 years.

WHAT ARE YOUR CONCLUSIONS AND RECOMMENDATIONS?:

1. Capacity should be adequate until 1975, if we undertake programs to increase line efficiency from the present 75% to 90%.

2. A preventive maintenance program will account for 10% of the increase in efficiency.

3. Modification of the capping station (total cost, $10,000) will increase line efficiency another 5%.

4. Another 25,000 sq. ft. of warehousing space should be made available in 1971, to take care of seasonal peaks.

5. The new Tabor bottling process, which won't be on the market until 1974, remains the best candidate for future capital expansion.

WHAT ARE THE ADVANTAGES?:

1. No capital appropriation is necessary at this time. Program costs, an average $7,500 a year, will be absorbed by operating expenses.

2. On a per-unit basis, direct-labor costs will decrease in line with the 15% increase in line efficiency.

3. Increases in indirect costs will easily be absorbed by reduction of overtime premiums.

4. Adoption of a preventive maintenance program is long overdue. Here is an excellent opportunity to put some of our long-held theories into practice.

ARE THERE ANY LIMITATIONS?:

1. Overtime work may be necessary by 1971 if program proves inadequate.

2. Preventive maintenance must be rigorously enforced; to ensure this, a special training program must be set up for foremen.

After you have devised the form, have copies printed and insist that every report writer fill one in. If anyone objects, complaining that "it won't work for this particular report," have him prepare the traditional summary and then show him how the form will work. Most writers will be grateful for the form, and there should be few objections. If complaints do become too numerous, don't despair. This is a good indication that the form itself isn't

```
REPORT HIGHLIGHTS — be brief, be factual, be discriminate

TITLE OF REPORT:  Polymerization Study:
Catalyst ABC vs. XYZ

OBJECT OF RESEARCH:  To study the feasibility
of replacing catalyst XYZ, costing $5/lb.,
with catalyst ABC, costing $1/lb., in the
polymerization of phlegiston.  Current net
usage of catalysts XYZ is 10,000 lb./yr.

FINDINGS AND CONCLUSIONS:

   1. Catalyst ABC can produce equivalent
yields if temperature and pressure are main-
tained 15% higher than for catalyst XYZ. This
would reduce potential savings from $40,000/
yr. to $20,000/yr.

   2. If temperature and pressure were kept at
present levels, the loss in yield would more
than offset the savings in catalyst cost.

   3. Catalyst life, net quantities needed,
and regeneration economics are roughly
equivalent for the two catalysts.

NATURE AND SCOPE OF STUDY:

   Economic evaluation based on 25 bench-
scale tests under pressures of 500 to 1,000
psi. and temperatures of 200 to 300 F.

RECOMMENDATIONS FOR APPLICATION
OR FURTHER RESEARCH:

   1. Study temperature/pressure requirements
for modified version of catalyst ABC, costing
$1.50/lb.

   2. Compare process-control problems by run-
ning pilot-plant test.

   3. Make detailed end-product quality study
to confirm interchangeability.

   4. If outcome of above two items is favor-
able, run full-scale plant test in Eastern
Div. plant prior to July 1 turnaround.
```

RESEARCH PROGRESS REPORTS could adopt this type of format for the Highlights Page.

properly designed, that it should be reworked and reworded to take care of the objections.

The Rest of the Report

Once the report writer has filled in the form, he has an excellent guide to what the organization of his report should be. In effect, the filled-in form becomes the outline for the report; everything that follows is a detailed expansion of the main ideas stated on the form.

To illustrate, consider once again the filled-in form on p. 113. Part One of the report would consist of a detailed explanation of the report's objective, together with an explanation of the most important conclusion (here presumably the first one written on

the form). To support these, material from the "Advantages" and "Limitations" sections on the form should be introduced, along with any introductory background material that relates directly to the objective and conclusion.

Part Two of the report should be a detailed expansion of the second conclusion: Establish a preventive maintenance program. Again, this part of the report should be reinforced by advantages, limitations, background material, and the like. Part Three would give all the details on modifying the capping station. And so forth.

At the end of his report, the writer can sum up his case by including the traditional "Conclusions and Recommendations" section if he likes. But this is strictly optional, because this information is already available on the form.

Question: What happened to the conventional "Introduction" section that appears in most reports? Answer: As already noted, it no longer exists; that is, it is no longer a monolithic block designed either to bore readers to tears or to give them information they already know. Instead, it has been broken up into numerous little pieces, and each little piece has been put somewhere in the report where it will be more effective.

In the new approach to organization, background material is inserted to reinforce the main ideas, not to precede and dominate them. Definitions, historical data, and the like are thus subordinated to the main ideas. They are of course present, but they don't have a chance to obscure the conclusions and recommendations the writer is trying to sell to his readers. Every writer of technical reports should be required to memorize this key rule for effective organization: Always keep the *new* of your report (your conclusions and recommendations) uppermost in the mind of your reader; don't eliminate the *old*, but always use it to reinforce the new, not precede and dominate it.

Final Words to the Writer

Every aspect of business has its "don't rock the boat" champions. The format of technical reports is no exception. If you do consider this suggested approach to organization a logical one, but meet with violent resistance from higher authority, consider something further: Adopt the form anyway (secretly) and make the best use of it before you revert to the tired old academic approach to organization.

I'm suggesting that the next time you have to write a technical report, you should first fill out the form. This should bring three immediate benefits. First, it will help you to overcome the initial block about writing, which almost everyone experiences at times. Secondly, it will help you to organize your conclusions and recommendations more clearly and concisely. And finally it will help you to write a much better summary than you would have written otherwise.

Six Guidelines for Fast, Functional Writing

Here is how you can get more writing done in less time, without becoming sloppy—in fact, some of these toil-saving suggestions actually improve the informativeness of reports, letters and memos.

HERBERT POPPER, Chemical Engineering

Some types of improvement in the quality of one's writing can only be achieved at the expense of quantity—for instance, by spending more time on the editing of drafts. However, regardless of whether you use longhand or some form of dictation, there are several areas where quantity and quality go hand in hand, and where it can actually take less time to produce an effective piece of communication than an ineffective one. The six guidelines that follow take aim at that area.

Because writing problems vary in kind and degree from person to person, you may find that some of these suggestions either don't apply to you or appear self-evident. However, "fast, functional" writing skills are so important to most engineers and technical managers that even if you only find one or two of the suggestions really useful, this should more than repay you for your reading time.

1. Know What Your Audience Expects

A vice-president of operations was making his annual tour of the company's outlying facilities. At one plant, he chatted with the assistant manager about the upcoming labor negotiations with the local union.

"I wish you'd send me a fairly detailed report of those negotiations," asked the vice president. Flattered by this request, the assistant plant manager resolved to do an outstanding job of reporting. By the time negotiations were over, he had more than 50 pages of handwritten notes, which he decided to amplify with background information on some of the points the union or the management team had raised.

It took him two weeks after the close of negotiations to organize this material into a rough handwritten draft. Because of a secretarial bottleneck, it took him two more weeks to get this draft typed and edited, and then another two weeks to get the massive document typed up in final form. Nevertheless, as he signed the letter of transmittal in which he apologized for imperfections in the typing and commented on the shortage of good secretarial help, he felt rather proud of himself: The report read like a courtroom drama, and had a great degree of polish.

Unfortunately, before the report could even reach headquarters, the vice-president had made an acid phone call to the plant manager. Apparently, what the vice-president had really wanted was brief, day-by-day reports that he could review while negotiations were still in progress, and that he could pass on to another plant that started negotiations a week later. When he finally got the assistant plant manager's monumental opus, a lot of the information was old hat, the key points having been already passed along by the plant manager in a lengthy, long-distance phone call just before the close of negotiations.

Next year, the plant manager decided to handle the job of reporting himself; at the close of each day's session, he dictated his notes into a recorder—his secretary would type them up on the next day, so that he could ink in some comments and send them out as soon as he finished that day's negotiating. Since he didn't use a draft, his daily reports were not particularly polished; the inked-in comments and corrections looked rather informal—and yet these reports were acclaimed by the vice-president.

Moral of the story: Make sure you know what the audience wants. Don't be afraid to ask. There are times when speed, rather than quality or quantity, may be of the essence. In the example above, which is based on an actual situation, the assistant plant manager could have saved himself hours of toil by finding out what sort of details the vice-president did or did not want to know about, and whether quick dictation without a draft was acceptable.

Failure to find out or to really understand the audience's expectations is perhaps the single biggest time-waster in technical writing. An example of such inefficiency involves the engineer who uses exactly the same writing approach regardless of whether his report is primarily intended for the departmental archives, his immediate supervisor, or a financial executive on the appropriations committee.

If the report is just intended for a supervisor, for instance, there is nothing wrong with using technical jargon, and for keeping background information very brief. But if the report is to go to a financial executive—particularly one who lacks any sort of technical background—the engineer must avoid technical jargon, and explain some things that he would not need to explain to his boss, while leaving out technical details. In such a report, it is particularly important to make the first page or two tell the bulk of the story, in terms that are meaningful to the administrator.

If you are writing a dual-function report—say, one intended for both a financial executive and your boss—by all means get squared away with the latter on how the two approaches can be reconciled (e.g., by eventually giving your boss additional sections or informal notes that are omitted from the administrator's copy, by coming up with a preliminary version of the first two pages that you and your boss can review jointly before finalization, etc.).

When writing for publication, rather than for internal use, finding out the audience's expectations can be an equally great timesaver. Many magazines have booklets that discuss their "expectations" in regard to such things as writing style, quality of drawings, compatibility with readers' interests[1]—and are further prepared to conserve the author's time by reviewing outlines in some detail so as to minimize the need for revision of the final manuscript.

2. Mobilize Your Subconscious

Legend has it that on the day the opera "The Magic Flute" was scheduled to get its first performance, someone reminded Mozart that there still wasn't any overture, whereupon the composer calmly sat down and dashed off the magnificent overture just in time to give the score to the orchestra before the curtain went up. Actually, I think if this legend is true, the chances are that Mozart must have "precomposed" the overture in his mind days before he set it down on paper, so that leaving the actual writing until just

before the deadline may not have been as risky as it seemed to others at the time.

Unfortunately, many of us tend to display a Mozart-like confidence in being able to meet a last-minute deadline regardless of whether we have done any precomposing or not.

If you have a writing project with a far-off deadline, and you don't feel like starting the actual writing right away, then don't. But I would still suggest that you draw up a rough outline as soon as you can, see how much information you already have available and how much more you will have to dig out, decide when you should start this digging out so that the information will be available at the proper time, and discuss the outline for the project with your boss or with a colleague. That way, you will not only get a feel for the emphasis needed (as discussed in the previous section), but you will be giving your subconscious mind a chance to come up with ideas while the project is incubating.

To come up with useful ideas, your subconscious should have some sort of framework—that way, perhaps some of the framework will be filled in for you while you shave in the morning. But if you wait till the last minute, even to prepare an outline or think about an approach, all your subconscious can do is to provide you with a feeling of anxiety.

Another constructive use for the prewriting period is to do some preselling. People hate shocks—which is what may happen when your recommendations based on a full year's work are coldly dropped on your de-

Got a minute to review the outline for that "brief engineering report" you asked me to prepare last year?

partment head's desk. It is fairer to him, and kinder to you and your writing time, to use the "let's let him in on part of the secret" technique. So, give your boss some inkling of what your report is going to recommend. Don't try to do a complete job of selling, but do give him a chance to get some exposure to your ideas. From his initial comments, you may also be able to obtain pointers on how to best link your ideas to his, and to the current objectives of the department. This can save a great deal of writing time in the long run, and will often let you get the constructive involvement of the reader much sooner than if you use the "This may come as a shock, but . . ." approach.

3. Build Up and Exploit Your Momentum

"I sit down with a fountain pen and paper and the story pours out. However lousy a section is, I let it go. I write on to the end. Then the subconscious mind has done what it can . . . The rest is simple effort . . . going over a chapter time and time again until, though you know it isn't right, it is the best you can do." That's how W. Somerset Maugham said he got his thoughts down on paper. If you have trouble getting started and building up momentum on a writing project, then the Maugham approach of putting down your thoughts in any old undisciplined way and eventually going back to polish them up, has a lot to recommend it. Note that this is also the basic approach to combating writer's block that Auren Uris suggested in his "How to Be a Great Dictator" section, page 193.

What do you do if you still don't succeed in unplugging your thoughts, regardless of whether you are using pen, pencil, stenographer or dictating machine? Here are a few additional pointers:

• Go over your outline (or Report Highlights Sheet, as suggested in an earlier section) and pretend a good friend asked you to explain each point to him. If he were to ask questions such as "Why don't we just stick with the old process?" or "How does this gimmick work?," the chances are you wouldn't be at a loss for words—you would just say it like it is. So, pretend your friend is asking you questions that correspond to your outline, and write it like it is.

• Pretend that this is an examination, and that you have five minutes to get something down on paper for each thought on your outline—i.e., that if after five minutes you have nothing down on paper on the first point, you have nothing that you can be graded on, and you would thus get zero. (A couple of years ago, I took an aptitude test in which I was given a cast of two or three characters and had to shape them into a plot for a short story within ten minutes; then stop and shape another cast of characters into a new plot; then do this a few more times. Not considering myself a really fast writer, I was amazed at how much I could get down in ten minutes when the pressure was on, and when I knew I would be graded on content rather than style. It occurred to me that if I could pretend that I was in a similar situation when starting on a writing job, it would get me going—and it works!)

• Pick the best time to get started on a tough writing project. For most people, this may be the very beginning of the day, before things have come up to distract them. Others work best right after lunch. Still others find that the best time to unlock their thoughts is after dinner at home, and that once they get started that way, they can continue the project at work without much difficulty. If you haven't already done so, try to find a time pattern in the daily periods during which you feel sharpest and loosest; then exploit these periods to get started on tough projects.

Of course, getting started does not necessarily mean writing a brilliant beginning; it means getting started on the "meat" of the project. Very often a meaty fact-filled beginning is the most brilliant one anyway. But if you do feel the urge to think up something particularly striking or original, you may be better off doing this after most of the project is down on paper, rather than letting it be an initial stumbling block.

Once you have built up your momentum, how do you keep it?

First of all, try not to stop. Let someone take your phone messages. If you see a chance to finish the project by working late, do so. Resist the temptation to take a break until you start slowing down. (Personally, I find that sipping coffee or puffing on a cigar while doing difficult writing is preferable to running the risk of getting sidetracked by taking an unnecessary break.) Putting it into industrial engineering terminology, make sure you have a long enough production run to justify the setup time.

If you can't finish the project by working late, then it is usually better to leave it in the middle of a paragraph than to try and finish the particular section or thought. Finishing the thought the next day will be relatively easy, and this will serve to prime the pump for the next thought. I used to make the mistake of staying up until whatever hour was necessary to get a major section finished, only to find that it would take me all the next morning to stop resting on my laurels and to uncork my thoughts for the next section. Conversely, when I don't try so hard to come to a logical stopping place, I can usually continue the section without any difficulty the next morning and then launch right into the next section. (I can't take full credit for this approach; someone named Hemingway recommended it in a book called "A Movable Feast.")

4. Watch Out for Time-Wasting Verbosity

Not everybody has the uncoiling problems dealt with in the previous section. In fact, some people who can uncoil most of the time at the drop of a pencil encounter the opposite type of problem: How to avoid the verbosity that wastes their own time as well as that of the reader, so that they can make the most of their fluency as writers.

The section starting on p. 6 gives some excellent guidelines for ways to recognize and avoid destructive verbosity. Although that section was aimed at making writing more informative, most of the suggestions can also lead to faster writing. For instance, the writer can usually save time by cutting down on passive verbs, abstract nouns, and prepositional phrases. (Obviously, it would have taken me longer to write the previous sentence had I said "Time can be saved by the writer if proper consideration is given to a reduction in the use of passive verbs, etc.")

Here are a few additional suggestions:

• Don't be legalistic in a nonlegal piece of writing. Lawyers have to be extremely careful to cover every possible contingency—hence they may feel justified in using strings of words that may differ only very slightly in meaning (e.g., null, void, of no legal force, etc.). But engineers are seldom justified in coming up with a phrase like "The *development, establishment,* and *implementation* of process-control *philosophies* and *policies* must take place at an *early* or *incipient* stage in a project." There just isn't enough difference between the italicized words to warrant using more than one of each; if you say "philosophies," 99 out of 100 readers will assume that this includes "policies."

• Don't waste time on excess hedging. For instance, when you say "Based on bench-scale experiments run at ten different temperatures, 300 F. produces the best yield," you have clearly indicated on what you base your conclusion, and there is no need to add hedge phrases such as ". . . 300 F. may tend to produce the best yields, assuming that these bench-scale results are freely applicable to commercial conditions . . ." Putting it another way, readers generally realize that almost any technical, business or philosophical statement that can be made is subject to limitations and qualifications; if you insist on pointing out limitations that are either obvious or unimportant, you are wasting time (and probably producing dull writing). Particularly wasteful and deadly is the "triple hedge"—e.g., ". . . may, under some circumstances, tend to . . ."

• Use more tables, illustrations and in-text listings to cut down on verbosity. Earlier in this report, Johnson pointed out how a "1, 2, 3" approach to the Report Highlights page can avoid the verbose generalities that sometimes go into report abstracts; the same sort of item-by-item approach can result in tighter writing of all kinds, including the body of the report. (At the risk of appearing to disregard my own "hedging" caveat, I should point out that itemization can be carried to dull extremes, particularly once the triple sub-indentation stage is reached. But if you haven't been doing much itemizing, the technique can save you a lot of words in reducing generalities to specifics.)

• Consider leaving out some details altogether. Resist the temptation to tell the reader everything you know about the subject—just tell him what you think he needs to know. The latter is quite different from just telling him what you think he would like to hear— or from using a dual standard whereby you exclude all unfavorable details while including all those that are favorable. The memo or report that burdens the

Memo to department heads: It has been established that time has been wasted and misunderstandings may have been given rise to because use of the passive, impersonal construction has been overdone in technical communications. It is hereby suggested that use of the active, personal construction be not necessarily frowned on by engineering supervisors. . .

reader with every conceivable detail has not only taken the writer much more time than necessary, but suggests that the writer was unsure of himself because he left it to the reader to decide which of the details were significant. (If you are afraid that a short report won't adequately reflect the work that went into a particular study, you can always indicate the *type* of additional data that can be supplied on request.)

Of course, the classic example of detail elimination involves the man who got a letter from his landlord asking if he intended to vacate his apartment. The answer consisted of "Dear Sir: I remain, Yours Truly, Henry Smith."

Unfortunately, it's not always that easy to combine succinctness with politeness in handling one's correspondence, particularly when one is dictating it. Things that can waste the dictator's (and the reader's) time include:

• Marathon sentences. An occasional long sentence can supply useful variety, and may be needed in order to relate ideas to each other, but strings of runaway sentences impede efficient communication.

• Ditto for marathon paragraphs.

• Shotgun or overkill attacks on the topic, whereby the dictator, not being sure he has said what he really wanted to say, goes on to re-attack the topic in several other, equally roundabout, ways.

• Tendencies to throw in cliches and meaningless phrases just to keep the dictation process going. It is less wasteful to keep your secretary waiting for a minute while you find the right phrase than to dictate a phrase that adds nothing.

5. Save Time via the "Example" Technique

Most of us find the going slow when we write on an abstract, philosophic level for any length of time. True, the amount of such writing can be minimized by translating abstract concepts into dollars and cents, but this cannot always be done. For instance, if you are trying to change the attitudes of foremen towards some community or labor-relations problem, neither payout time nor discounted cash flow is going to be of much help to you. But this does not mean that your communications with the foremen must be entirely on an abstract philosophic, level.

Good philosophy is hard to write. There are all sorts of pitfalls: failure to define terms, or to relate them to the reader's frame of mind, failure to avoid either oversimplification or obtuseness, etc. But fortunately, you can write about an abstract topic—e.g., a desired change in attitude—without staying on the abstract level for very long. The idea here is to translate the abstract into the specific by using analogies, miniature case histories (either actual or hypothetical), projections of what might happen if the status quo were maintained, etc.

Of course, this "example" technique is not limited to communications that deal with corporate philosophy but should also be used when generalities and abstract concepts crop up in technical writing. Here, a one-sentence "for instance" can often take the place of a much longer explanation; a liberal sprinkling of such sentences can keep the discussion on the ground, and can result in an easier-to-write yet more-informative communication than one in which all abstract technical concepts are explained or promoted in only theoretical terms.

6. Know Thyself, and Thy Writing

The difficulty in many articles dealing with improving your writing is their generality; they presuppose that all writers have the same problems. This report has tried to be more specific—for instance, by showing how *less* discipline can be a timesaver for the engineer who has trouble uncoiling, whereas *more* discipline can be an eventual timesaver for someone whose problem is verbosity or poor organization rather than lack of writing fluency.

Where do you fall within these two extremes? Should your prime emphasis be on boosting your writing output or on boosting its quality? If you have difficulty answering that question, you can get help quite readily.

On p. 6-11 are some simple tests whereby you can evaluate the informative quality of your writing. If your score is low, perhaps your prime goal should be to make your writing more informative. At the beginning, this may reduce your page output because you will be spending more time on editing and rewriting. However, if you try to learn from your editing, you will find that output will eventually increase along with quality. This means spending a few minutes reviewing an edited draft to see what type of corrections are prevalent, and to think about ways of min-imizing the need for these types of corrections in subsequent writing.

Discuss your writing with your boss. Some bosses are reluctant to initiate such a discussion because they have found that it takes almost as much tact to constructively criticize a subordinate's writing as it would to constructively criticize his wife or family. But if *you* initiate such a discussion (I mean about your writing, not your wife), the chances are that overly defensive postures can be avoided, and that you and your boss will both gain a better insight into problem areas.

Ask your boss whether he thinks you are spending too much or too little time on writing. For instance, based on samples, would he settle for draftless dictation on some reports in order to give you more time for engineering?

If one of your writing problems is that interruptions are always breaking your train of thought, ask your boss about ways of getting more privacy, or about occasionally working at home to make headway on difficult writing chores.

In order to discuss other aspects of your writing, you may want to go over a sort of writing-inventory checklist, such as the one published in the *Harvard Business Review* article "What Do You Mean I Can't Write?"[3] This can be a good starting point in getting your supervisor's views on such matters as whether you sometimes present too many opinions and not enough supporting data (or vice versa), whether you tend to under- or overestimate his familiarity with your work, etc.

A concluding thought: The engineer who progresses in his company tends to do more writing every year. Eventually, he may also have to supervise the writing of subordinates; many of their reports and memos will go out over his signature and will reflect on the caliber of the work done under his supervision. Thus the engineer who becomes adept at fast, functional writing is in an enviable position—he can save a significant and increasing amount of time, establish his credentials as an efficient communicator, and eventually help his subordinates solve their own communication problems. We hope that the suggestions in various sections of this report will help point the way, and will let you apply the "work smarter, not harder" principle to your communicating. ∎

Acknowledgement

Some of the ideas in this final section stem from various members of CHEMICAL ENGINEERING's editorial staff, and also from Manny Meyers of Picatinny Arsenal, and Peter J. Rankin of Basford Inc.

References

1. See, for instance, "How to Write for CHEMICAL ENGINEERING," a booklet available from CHEMICAL ENGINEERING, 1-221 Avenue of the Americas, New York, N.Y. 10020.
2. Fielden, J., *Harvard Bus. Rev.*, May-June 1964, p. 147.

Creative Report Writing—Part I

If your approach to report writing is creative, your mastery of the subject matter will be more complete. You will discover fresh viewpoints and see conclusions not otherwise apparent. Even some of the drudgery will disappear.

H. M. QUACKENBOS, Union Carbide Corp.

Why do we engineers write reports? Four reasons are usually cited: to influence decisions; to incorporate a project and its results into a reference source; to impart an impression of industriousness; and to display professional skills.

But we ought to consider a fifth reason: the creative stimulus that comes from writing when it is done properly.

Better Writer, Better Engineer

The engineer who writes, which is nearly all of us, is often only vaguely aware of the creative aspect. He notices that his mind becomes clearer after writing, and he has a more-focused view of the subject matter. The report has enhanced his engineering work; indeed, it has become an integral and exciting part of it, if the creative aspect of writing has been fully exploited, as will be explained in this article.

If you approach report writing creatively, you can expect to deepen your mastery of the subject matter, even discover fresh viewpoints and expose hidden conclusions. And there are other benefits: a lot of the boredom and hard work of writing disappears; your language becomes more direct, so the message is clearer and the reference value of the report is improved; and, finally, less time is required for writing.

The creative approach will be illustrated in terms of a report that would follow several weeks, even months, of engineering work. Such a "big" report, by taxing one's writing ability to its limit, affords the fullest opportunity for using the principles that are involved; principles that, nevertheless, also apply to shorter reports, and even to other types of technical writing, in ways that will be indicated.

The Prewriting Stage

Much of the work of producing a creative report must be done before any writing is started. In fact, the preparation may take longer than the writing itself. In the prewriting stage, you take two steps: (1) You carefully review your work to achieve both a synthesis and a complete grasp of it; and (2) You prepare tables and graphs in rough form and begin an outline of the way in which you will discuss them.

The method advocated here for writing a large technical report, or indeed almost any communication, consists of three principal sections. First, there is a prewriting stage, in which the engineering work is reviewed and organized, an outline is prepared, and tables, graphs and other illustrations are assembled. Second, a fast "scribble" writing is undertaken, which entails retaining a flexible viewpoint with regard to the best arrangement of the material. Third, a first draft is dictated, typed, and revised into final form.

The Report Format

Industry-report formats, which are established by edict or custom, vary from one company or plant to another, but are essentially not much different. They usually consist of the following sections:

Summary
Introduction
Discussion
Appendix

The Summary concisely presents the entire work being reported on in about one typewritten page. It may or may not be divided into parts, such as Background, Conclusions, and Recommendations.

The Introduction is chiefly an enlargement of the background statements made in the Summary. However, whereas the Summary stands by itself—serving those readers who may have neither the time nor the inclination to read further—an important function of the Introduction is to lead the reader into the Discussion.

The Discussion is, of course, the heart of the report. It is here that findings are presented at length and conclusions are made and evaluated. In the creative approach to report writing advocated, this section should be written first because the others can be more advantageously shaped afterwards.

The Appendix contains anything too detailed or cumbersome to be included in the Discussion, such as highly technical data, which may not be of much interest to most of the readers but nevertheless constitutes valuable support for points made in the Discussion.

Prepared mentally and armed with pictorial and tabular aids, you will be ready for the subsequent writing in a way that will probably be new to you—for you will write without distracting interruptions to refer back to the original data, and you will write with speed and fluidity.

The rigorous prewriting preparation advocated conflicts with the way most engineers write. Usually, analysis and preparation is combined with the writing, to the detriment of both. By separating the functions, you fortify, yet make each more flexible. Moreover, you free a large corner of your mind for creative thinking.

A similar process was recently recommended by a distinguished professional writer concerned with handling many complex themes. Describing the writing of his five-volume "The Master, The Life of Henry James," Leon Edel said: "I try to write without consulting my material; this avoids interruptions and prevents me from overloading my text with quotations. In this way I establish a comfortable distance from the mass and pressure of data. It helps the narrative flow; it is a guard against irrelevancies."*

*New York Times Book Review, Feb. 6, 1972.

The Prewriting Review

Some engineers may object to the careful review that constitutes the first of the two steps in the prewriting stage, saying: "I've just finished a piece of engineering work and surely have a firm grasp of what's been going on for the three months of the project."

Such a comment overlooks the often tortuous path of how engineering work progresses. As you go from point A, the start of your project, to point Z, its end, you rarely traverse an easy, straightforward path. The path is more likely one in which side branches represent dead ends that were approached, recognized as dead, and retraced.

After such a journey, you will have arrived at Z with a perspective that has changed materially from the time you started at A. Your basic assumptions, methods of investigation, and the nature of your goal may all have changed. Therefore, you need to review, to travel again over the path from A to Z.

In your review, you will stand at point Z and look over everything that happened after you left point A, in these steps:

· Critical appraisal of all results—You may have to discard some earlier results as unreliable, and you may discover errors of determination or calculation at any stage. You may find that your results are not as complete as you expected, and that you need another week to fill in the gaps. But you might recall that the boss wants the report by next Friday, and, though you've made him ease up on that demand, you don't want to push him too hard. So you compromise for a day, or an evening, or two, on your own time.

· Special attention to errant findings—Some of the results may not fit the pattern of, or be as reproducible as, the bulk of your findings. Although it is tempting to simply exclude these, it is better to examine them carefully, for they may provide valuable insights.

· Consolidation of all results—Often, your findings are scattered through notebooks and many pieces of paper, and part of your mental energy is consumed in remembering their locations. You will save time later if you first prepare summary tabulations and plots, with references to primary sources. This preparation will fix your results firmly in your mind.

· Review of the literature—By "literature" is meant all relevant information, whether published or confidential. Your reading should have been done early in the project and summarized on file cards. Now you scan these cards, keeping two questions in mind: first, how do your conclusions and results agree with already existing ones, and second, what advances have you made? You should list the latter, for when you begin formulating your conclusions.

· Early organization—By now you will have noticed several groupings into which your findings naturally seem to fall. You should make brief written notes on these groupings, adding any thoughts regarding organization and presentation that may be in your mind.

As you go through these review steps, keep your mind consciously open. Don't become wedded to a set of conclusions or commit yourself to a certain way of organizing your report. By remaining flexible, you should have already generated several fresh viewpoints and insights. More of these will break through if you stay open-minded.

How long will the review take? For a lengthy project of the sort being discussed, about 5% of the total engineering time is appropriate, so prepare yourself mentally to spend this much time laying a good foundation for the subsequent writing.

These same principles of review can be adapted to any writing you expect to do—even for letters that present only a few calculations and a limited analysis.

Prewriting Outline

At this stage, you expand the beginnings of organization that you've already started. Your aim is to produce an outline from which you can begin to write, and to prepare the principal tables and graphs as they will actually appear in the report.

As you now approach the actual writing, you must think more and more of your readers. Start such thinking now, rather than after the report has been completed and the boss says: "Now whom should we send this to?"

A practical way of confronting your readers is to prepare a circulation list, and to consider the backgrounds and interests of the people on it. An industrial report sometimes goes to a readership having a surprisingly wide range of interest and skills—from a highly technical colleague to a sales manager who may be ignorant of engineering refinements. At other times, the readership is more uniform and of a higher technical caliber. You must adapt your report to the average technical level of your readers. At the same time, the technical complexity of your report can rise from start to finish, and so satisfy a spectrum of readers. The initial sections should be comprehensible to all, the middle sections digestible by most, with your most technical sections possibly placed in an Appendix.

"Discussion"—The Middle Section First

The middle section of a technical report is usually called the Discussion. It is here that you present your findings at some length and arrive at conclusions regarding them. The other sections of the report can be shaped more advantageously at a later stage.

For the Discussion, start with the groupings of your results that you made in the review step. Each grouping can become a section of the Discussion, but only if such a breakdown is convenient for the reader. A very long section, one that dominates the others, may give the reader indigestion, so you might try dividing it into two or more sections.

Consider also the order of presentation. Sometimes the order is dictated mainly by logic, with one section unfolding logically into another. A second consideration is the difficulty of subject matter. The most easily understood section should come first, and the most difficult, last. Your reader may be too tired by the time he reaches the last and most difficult section; but if it is placed earlier there is the danger that he may stop reading altogether.

These sections will not constitute all of the Discussion. You will need introductory remarks that prepare the reader for the several sections, and a closing section that briefly summarizes conclusions and recommendations. Of these fore and aft portions, the ending is likely to be the part that is better defined at this point. You have some conclusions and recommendations in mind and can note them in brief form. Conversely, the introductory portion may not crystallize until the core of the Discussion has been written.

On other occasions, the path is clearer. If, for example, the sections of the Discussion that deal with experiments comprise different sorts of results all obtained from the same piece of equipment, then a suitable introduction to the Discussion would be a simple sketch of the equipment, a brief description of the operation, and a sample result (possibly in graphical form). Your outline should then include brief notes on the remarks you might make, along with the necessary drawings or sketches.

When completed, your outline of the Discussion should consist of: (1) section titles plus a few more detailed notes or reminders; (2) all the graphs and tables you need for each section; and (3) any additional aids for the introductory and closing portions.

Furthermore, you may have a few miscellaneous jottings. It is good practice to have a jotting sheet on top of the desk on which you can record thoughts on the Summary that pop into your head while you're thinking about the Discussion. This way, you can make a rapid note with only minor interruption to the main activity.

Now, what results should go into each section of the Discussion? You have three choices for handling results: They can be included in the appropriate section of the Discussion; if too detailed, they can be placed in an Appendix; if even too detailed or too confusing to be fully included in the Appendix, they might be discussed there qualitatively. Which method you choose will depend on the technical level of your readers and on the requirement that the Discussion should be digestible by most of your readers. Ways of shaping your report to appeal to a broad spectrum of readers will be more fully developed in Part II of this article.

In the process of adapting your tables and figures to the Discussion, you are viewing your findings through the eyes of your reader. From that viewpoint, you will inevitably see several useful and more practical applications of your work than you had realized before. These conditions are propitious to creativity. Be alert to them and exploit them. ■

Meet the Author

H. M. Quackenbos is a senior research scientist with Union Carbide Corp. (River Rd., Bound Brook, NJ 08805). After receiving a B.Sc. in general science from the University of London and an M.S. in chemical engineering from the Massachusetts Institute of Technology, he spent 29 years in Research & Development, mostly with Union Carbide.

A member of ACS, IChE (England), American Institute of Chemists, and the American Soc. for Engineering Education, he has published 25 papers on the properties of plastics, and has written manuals for Union Carbide.

Creative Report Writing—Part II

You have gone through your preparation by following the creative approach.
Now you are ready to speed through the actual writing. The first step is
a fast scribble writing of the sections of your report in a selected sequence.

H. M. Quackenbos, Union Carbide Corp.

Whether you are writing a major report, or one only a page or two long, a creative approach to your writing can deepen your insight into the subject matter, speed up your work and make your message clearer.

Part I of "Creative Report Writing" (p. 120) expounded on these and other benefits of the creative approach. Part I, besides explaining the creative approach, discussed its first stage, the preparation for writing.

Part II now moves on to the second and third stages, which are concerned with the writing itself.

The Writing Stage

The best way to start your writing is to prepare a Summary—a brief presentation of your entire work in about one typewritten page. You hope it will be read and understood by everyone on the circulation list.

The exact form of the Summary will vary from one organization to another, because it is usually established by custom or edict. It may sometimes be broken into smaller parts: Background, Conclusions, Recommendations. Even so, its length should still be about one page.

Whatever the format, the first section should cover points that answer the questions: why, how and what?

Why you started the project; *how* you did it; *what* you found, and *what* should be done?

When starting the Summary, begin with a few rough notes under the headings why, how and what. Pay special attention to the "why" and the "what should be done," because through most of the work you've been concentrating on the "how" and the "what you found." Engineers mistakenly tend to assume that any reader can readily see why they started something, and that surely the implications of the work are obvious.

Your Summary at this stage will not be a final draft, so write it quickly, with little concern for legibility, for only you will read it. Don't search long for the exact word or the right sentence structure; you can polish later.

This draft is a test. Written in rough form, it should flow freely and rapidly if your preparation has been done well. If you have serious trouble with the writing, your preparation may need more attention. Occasional trouble may call for a more-selective review. Writing difficulties often arise simply because you don't know *what* to say—you haven't decided yet, the findings are contradictory, or you don't trust some of the data. Your writing rarely dries up because you don't know *how* to say it.

At this point in your writing, you are poised for fast progress; you have: (1) a Summary that expresses your firm grasp of the major points; (2) an outline of the Discussion backed by tables and figures; (3) minor pieces that will go into the Appendix. Now within your grasp is the entire report.

Principles To Follow

Write the big piece of your report—the Discussion—now. Write it as you wrote the Summary, rapidly and freely as a rough draft that will afterwards be transformed into something fit for typing by techniques that will be treated later. Follow these principles.

• Write rapidly, using abbreviations and not being concerned with legibility.

• Do not interrupt your flow to refer back to data. Leave blanks to be filled in later if numbers escape you.

• Do not hunt for elusive words or stop to polish sentences.

• Keep your jotting pad at hand for noting thoughts on other sections. For example, you may wish to refer your reader from the Discussion to the Appendix for further details on experimental procedure, methods of calculation, etc. Just note in your text that further details are in the Appendix and scribble on your jotting pad a comment like: "Appendix—details of vacuum system."

• Find your best writing quantum. Mine happens to be about two hours at a time. If I string together episodes of only a few minutes of writing, the report acquires a discontinuity. On the other hand, after two hours, I tire and lose inspiration, which is perhaps fortunate because plant activities rarely allow more than two hours without a major interruption. If you have developed a firm grasp of your material before you start to write, such interruptions can be tolerated, but they are almost fatal if they come when you are trying to organize, interpret and write all at once.

• Be consciously adaptable. If you have scribbled a page in a few minutes, you will not have a large investment in it. So it will be easy to exchange paragraphs and to delete or add. Try to be like an artist blocking in his canvas with charcoal: he can still change some of the main lines.

• Use a conversational style with active voice and present tense for readable, direct statements. Granted that your audience has reading skill and a capacity for inference, you should prefer the second paragraph below to the first:

"The samples were placed in an oven at 100 C. and weight-loss was followed. The plot of weight-loss versus time is shown in Fig. 1. A loss of 5% was reached after two weeks."

"In a 100 C. oven, the sample loses 5% weight in two weeks, Fig. 1."

The painful progress from one sentence to another in the first paragraph suggests slow writing, with an interruption to draw Fig. 1. Preoccupied with his art work, the writer cannot help referring at undue length to Fig. 1 and the underlying experimental procedure.

After the draft of the Discussion is finished, proceed to the other major sections of the report, leaving the Appendix for later because it can be readily shaped to hold desirable but more-detailed material that is left over.

The Sections of the Report

The order of a report generally is:
Summary
Introduction
Discussion
Appendix

The Introduction can be described as an enlargement of the introductory material stated very briefly in the Summary. It deals with (1) the reasons for starting the project; (2) the condition of technology at the start; and (3) the advances needed to solve the problems at hand. It should be brief, probably one page at most.

These three elements of the Introduction make it a neat bridge between the Summary and the Discussion. The first element expands the brief statement of need in the Summary. The second passes over to a consideration of the technical tools available for solving the problem. The last presents the lines of investigation that constitute a logical attack. These lines point straight into the Discussion, where you will continue them in terms of what you did, what you found, and what it means.

Completing the Rough Draft

You now have in hand a rough draft of the Summary, Introduction and Discussion. In addition, you have some material for the Appendix and some notes as to additional sections of it. Your hardest work is over. How do you complete the rough draft? These steps are suggested:

Read your pages from the broad point of view, as an architect looking from afar at the building you have created. But retain the freedom to demolish and reassemble sections. You may find parts of your Summary may no longer be valid, in which case, they should be rewritten to embody the fresh insights and ideas you have generated while writing. This means that your writing has been creative.

Now, rewrite the Summary, using the rapid scribble method. Sometimes much of the old Summary will still look good but at other times you may feel impelled to completely rewrite it. Be sure that your Summary is tailored to those people who will base a decision on your report, and to those whose support for the decision will be valuable. Point plainly to the decision that you feel your work supports—to continue your project, whether or not to enter a market, to buy certain equipment, to adopt a new control test, etc.

Next, read again your Introduction and Discussion in a more detailed way (the architect walking through the rooms of his building). Modify awkward sentences, improve the choice of words, and fill in small blanks.

Now prepare a draft for the secretary to type from your scribbled and only semilegible pages. One way is to rewrite in a neat and readable hand, but this is recommended only for brief communications. For a lengthy report, the cost in time is exorbitant and by dictating onto a tape you can shorten the time four- or fivefold, even when speaking slowly and distinctly for the secretary's benefit. Ask for a double-spaced draft and save her time by permitting her to leave blanks for words that she cannot understand.

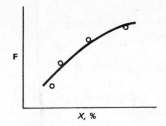

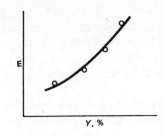

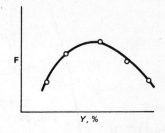

Properties as a Function of Composition—Table I

Composition	A	B	C	D	E	F
I Control, 2,463	1,427	1,862	1.72	242,800	14.18	16.15
II Control + 2%X	1,414	1,891	1.63	254,600	14.20	23.27
III ...	...	...	...	...	...	...

Improvement in Formulation 817—Table II

Property	Old Formulation	New Formulation
A	1,430	1,450
B	1,860	1,830
C	1.7	1.6
D	240,000	250,000
E	14.2	21.6
F	16.1	23.3

When the typed draft returns, take advantage of the several days that will have elapsed to reread the report with a fresh eye to improvements. Because you can continue to make improvements indefinitely, you must arbitrarily limit yourself as to how much time you will allow for this. Nevertheless, major changes will still be possible. You can quickly reassemble the order of sections of the Discussion, using scissors and stapler. And you can add paragraphs and sentences, and supply special sentences to bridge gaps. Yet, never allow yourself the time to polish your style, as some authors recommend, to a state of almost painful brilliance. Too many people will be pounding on your door if you're late; besides, you'll usually begin to become tired of the whole subject.

Lastly, complete the Appendix, which will include Details of Procedure, Sample Calculations, Literature Review, Detailed Results, etc. A somewhat telegraphic style will save time and sometimes allow dictation onto tape.

After all this, submit the draft for approval. Incorporate the good suggestions that are made and oppose the bad ones. Draw the figures in final form and submit the whole thing for the last typing.

Appendix—Appealing to a Spectrum

Problems that arise when you must shape your Discussion to be understood by a readership having a broad spectrum of technical training can be best solved in the prewriting stage, when you are preparing tables and graphs. If these were properly gaged to your readership, most of your writing will be easy.

A portion of a table having six columns of figures, **A** through **F**, and eight rows, only two of which are given, is shown in the box. All 48 numbers would constitute an indigestible mass. Such a table can be included in the Appendix but should be excluded from the Discussion.

Yet, suppose that this study of compositions (I through VIII) vs. properties (**A** through **F**) is a vital portion of your work. How can you best adapt the findings to the Discussion, keeping in mind all your readers?

It can be done in the following manner:

"Variations in additive X had little effect on any property except **F.** "(This Discussion statement is then referenced to the Appendix for supporting evidence.) "The relationship with **F** is shown in Fig. 1. Variations in additive Y principally influenced properties **E** and **F** (Fig. 2 and 3)." (See box.)

"Levels of X and Y were adjusted in a new compound to an optimum, which is compared in Table II to the old compound." (See box.) "Note the distinct improvement in properties **E** and **F**."

Thus, the development of the new compound is presented in a way that can be easily followed. Table II makes the vital comparison between the old and new formulation with only 12 numbers, which is within the suggested limit of 15 numbers for a table in the Discussion section of an industrial report circulated to a mixed readership. Note also how the numbers in the condensed table have been sensibly rounded off.

The easier course would have been to include Table I "as is" in the report and explained it at length. If, on the other hand, you instead made up Fig. 1, 2 and 3 and Table II for your outline, (which would of course take up more space), your results would be presented in more-digestible bites.

How many graphs should be included in the Discussion? Suppose that in your treatment of the original data you had compiled Table I and also plotted each of the six properties (**A** through **F**) against the range of X and Y contents. You would end up with a large table and twelve graphs! Twelve graphs are too heavy a load for the Discussion. So you should select only Fig. 1, 2 and 3 and the shortened Table II for the Discussion, and place the remaining graphs or the original table (Table I), but not both, in the Appendix. ∎

Acknowledgment

The comments of Charles F. Pitt did much to improve the cohesiveness of this article and the aim of several of its sections.

(Only significant contributions of this sort— and not routine cooperation—should be acknowledged in an industrial report.)

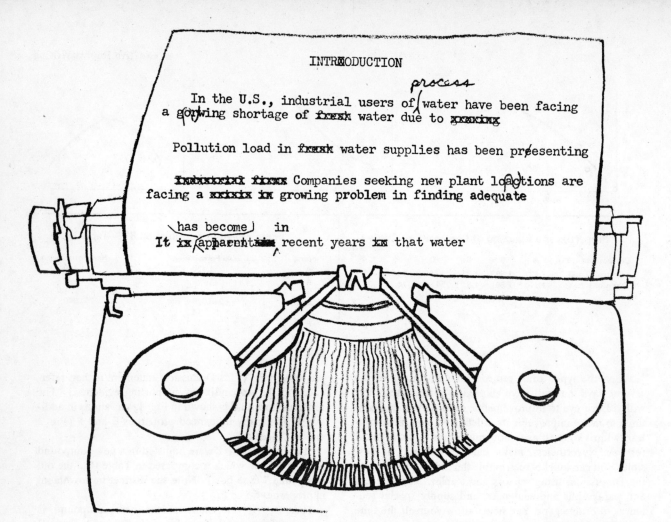

INTRODUCTION

In the U.S., industrial users of /water have been facing
a g̶o̶w̶ing shortage of f̶r̶e̶s̶h̶ water due to x̶x̶x̶x̶x̶x̶x̶

Pollution load in f̶r̶e̶s̶h̶ water supplies has been presenting

I̶n̶d̶u̶s̶t̶r̶i̶a̶l̶ f̶i̶r̶m̶s̶ Companies seeking new plant locations are
facing a x̶x̶x̶x̶x̶ i̶n̶ growing problem in finding adequate

has become) in
It i̶s̶ apparent̶t̶i̶m̶ recent years i̶n̶ that water

Ten Common Weaknesses In Engineering Reports

Although there are numberless books about technical writing, many engineers still commit basic writing errors. Here's an expert's examination of the most common mistakes.

JAY R. GOULD, *Rensselaer Polytechnic Institute*

One company that I recently worked with had become concerned over the quality of the reports being turned out by its engineers and scientists. After examining more than 100 of these "problem" reports, a pattern of common errors began to emerge. These ten common mistakes are outlined below.

If you feel that your report writing could stand improvement, these ten points can be used as a handy checklist. The next time you write a report, look over your first draft to see if you can improve on any of these specifics:

1. Abstracts

The abstract is a vital part of the report; it will probably be read by more people than read the report itself. Abstracts are also valuable for indexing and filing.

The fault with most abstracts is that they are skeletal outlines; they only define the subject matter. Here is a skeletal abstract:

This report describes and compares some of the less orthodox processes used in the manufacture of salt. It contains a historical review of older processes together with their advantages and disadvantages.

This abstract is so short as to be noncommital. It contains very little that is specific; the author has staked out some territory and that's about all.

To correct: Go through your data, pick out the salient facts, and especially conclusions and recommendations, if any. Make the abstract fit your piece of writing. Here is an *informative* abstract for the same report:

This report describes and compares some of the less orthodox processes used in the manufacture of salt: (1) the Alberger Process in which a fresh brine feed and recycle brine is heated in a number of shell and tube exchangers; (2) the Morton Process, similar to the Alberger Process, except that only one heater and one flasher are used; (3) the International Process in which all heating is by direct injection of steam into the brine; and (4) the Richards Process in which hot brine is flashed under vacuum in a closed flasher instead of being cooled in contact with an open pan. Advantages and disadvantages of the four processes are discussed.

2. Introductions

If you find that the beginnings of your reports are disjointed, forget the word "introduction" and think of what you should be doing for the reader. Remember, he may think in almost opposite terms from you.

To correct: This check list should help:

1. Relate the introduction to the needs of the reader. Try to imagine what he will want to know first. It may be the cost of the project, the competition involved, or how the project came about.

2. Show the purpose and scope.

3. Identify the subject matter.

4. Relate the subject matter to other projects.

5. Show the basic method and procedure followed in carrying out the project.

This excerpt from an introduction combines many of these features:

Steady business improvement during last year's final months enabled most companies in the chemical process industries to make a good showing in the year-end financial reports. Sales and profits hit close to the high figures reported for the previous year.

This report gives the sales and earnings for five process industry groups: chemical and allied products; paper and allied products; petroleum refining; rubber products; and stone, clay, and glass products.

3. Headings and Titles

Uninterrupted pages of text make much technical writing difficult to read, and equally difficult to retain the information.

To correct: Don't hesitate to break your report into headings. Headings serve at least three purposes:

• They organize the material into logical units and force you to stick to your subject matter.

• They make reading easier by letting in some air and white space.

• They make it easier for the reader to refer back to particular sections.

4. Paragraphing

Faulty paragraphing stems from haphazard arrangement of items within the paragraph as well as an apparent lack of knowledge of what a well-constructed paragraph can do. Faulty paragraphing is the cause for at least one-third of reports being turned back for revision. Keep these two things in mind:

• Each paragraph is a unit. If the main idea in a paragraph can be expressed in a single, highly compressed sentence, you have done a good job.

• Paragraphs can be constructed according to function. For example, perhaps the most useful device for paragraphing is the topic sentence. This is a preliminary over-all statement that can be followed by details inherent in the topic statement.

If your writing lacks good structure, look to your paragraphing. Pay more attention to your topic sentences and the supporting details, as in this example:

Some accidents are caused by a combination of laziness and ignorance. An operator may lack the energy and personal drive to find out the governing circumstances and not have the technical knowledge to appreciate some special requirement.

5. Listings and Tabulations

The example below shows how a set of instructions might look if written in a straight narrative form:

To operate the digitally controlled tube tester, you should first turn on the main switch and wait for the green light. Then you insert the tubes from left to right. After that, you move the calibrate switch to run position, the socket switch to manual position, and the test switch to automatic position. Then you push the start button.

To correct: Take your rough copy and see how you can clarify it by adding listings and tabulations. Don't ask the reader to dig out the information. Help him by numbering the various steps, by underlining, italics, capitalization, spacing, and other devices.

Here is how the author of the instructions on the tube tester could reorganize his material:

THE DIGITALLY CONTROLLED TUBE TESTER

OPERATION

1. Turn on MAIN switch and wait for green light.
2. Insert tubes from left to right.
3. Move switches:
   a. The CALIBRATE switch to RUN position.
   b. The SOCKET switch to MANUAL position.
   c. The TEST switch to AUTOMATIC position.
4. Push START button.

6. Point of View

Examine this piece of writing:

We are glad to provide you with information about the coloring of negative slides. A copy of your completed report would be greatly appreciated when you are through.

You should do the coloring process in three steps: Apply a water-insoluble lacquer; after the lacquer has dried, we always paint the enclosed area with a water solution; after the dye has dried, the lacquer should be removed.

When you examine this section closely, you find that the author has used various approaches. He starts out by assuming a "you" attitude then he editorializes with his use of the pronoun "we." He runs through a gamut of styles: active, passive, personal, impersonal, and conditional. He has been guilty of a shift in *point of view*.

To correct: Adhere to a single point of view, as in this corrected example:

We are glad to provide you with information about the coloring of negative slides.

We find that the coloring process is done best in these three steps:

1. Apply a water-insoluble lacquer immediately around the lines or letters to be colored.
2. After the lacquer has dried, paint the enclosed area with a water solution of an aniline dye.
3. After the dye has dried thoroughly, remove the lacquer with a suitable solvent.

7. Transitional Material

Industrial writing should be sparse and to the point. But it's possible to be so sparse and so lacking in guides and signs that you are practically unintelligible. For example:

The construction of a technical paper is essentially the same as the construction of a report. The paper usually consists of a main presentation plus a short abstract. The technical paper does not contain the separate elements of the formal report. It should be broken up into logical sections. Many technical papers follow the outline of abstract, purpose, conclusions, and procedure.

It is difficult to follow through the author's intentions in such a condensed piece of work.

To correct: Supply phrases and guide words that lead the reader from one thought to another—and provide headings, listings, and tabulations when needed. Here is the same paragraph with the addition of a few such devices.

The construction of a technical paper is essentially the same as the construction of a report. But the paper usually consists of one main presentation plus a short abstract. Although the technical paper does not contain all the elements of the formal report, it can usually benefit by being broken up into logical sections. As a result, many technical papers follow this outline:

(1) Abstract
(2) Purpose
(3) Conclusions
(4) Procedure

8. Figures and Tables

Improper positioning of tables and figures in the text can create confusion in the mind of your reader.

To correct: Determine whether the tables or figures should be placed in the text itself or should be reserved for the appendix.

An *internal* table is one that must be used closely with textual material. In such a case, place it in the report proper as close as possible to the reference in the text.

A *record* table contains supplementary material, helpful but not necessary to the discussion at hand. Place it with all other supplementary material in the appendix or other terminal sections so that it doesn't distract from the main presentation in the central body of your report.

9. References and Bibliographies

Many writers are inconsistent when recording references and bibliography.

These citations came from an engineering report I read recently.

Kunin, R., and Myers, R. J., Ion Exchange Resins. New York: John Wiley and Sons, Inc., 1950.

Smith, H. R., and P. D. Jones, Elastic Creep of Automobile Tires, Holt, Rinehart, and Winston, 1958.

Two items, and two methods of recording.

To correct: Pick a system and remain faithful to it in any given report.

10. Keep the Reader in Mind

This check is really an over-all test of the effectiveness of your reports. After you have completed the first draft, see if you have aimed at the reader in these three particulars:

(1) Have you devised a method for getting the reader to start reading? This points up the importance of a good introduction.

(2) Have you devised methods to keep the reader reading? That is, is your organization and structure as clear and logical as possible?

(3) Have you decided what you want the reader to retain? This will be a guide to how you should emphasize material in abstracts and summaries, appendixes, tables and graphs.

Meet the Author

Jay R. Gould is director of the Technical Writers' Institute at Rensselaer Polytechnic Institute. Besides his extensive experience as a teacher of technical writing, Prof. Gould has authored several books and magazine articles on this topic and has acted as a writing consultant for many industrial firms.

Guidelines for R&D Reports

The author delves into his experience in product and process development, as well as editorial work, to suggest how various kinds of R&D reports can be written with maximum effectiveness.

ROY V. HUGHSON, *Chemical Engineering*

Recently, the American Society for Engineering Education asked engineers who graduated between 1955 and 1957 to name the subjects in which they felt a personal need for additional study. Of the 4,057 respondents, 64% chose technical writing, putting this topic in a virtual tie for first place. (The only equally popular topic was "management practices.")

While this study did not break engineers down into specific work functions, it is likely that engineers engaged in research and development work felt a particularly strong need for technical writing courses. After all, a research laboratory seldom produces anything except information. The information itself is of little use until "packaged" into a report. The reports—and, perhaps, a few accompanying samples—are the lab's only justification for existing, so the reports had better be informative.

The young engineer soon finds that there is a big difference between the reports he wrote in college and the ones required of him now. Even his older counterpart frequently complains about the time it takes to write good R&D reports, and wishes there were ways to improve the "acceptability" of reports without increasing the time required to write them.

Before discussing some approaches that may prove helpful, a quick word about order of presentation in R&D reports.

Most colleges tell the student to start his report by explaining his objectives. He is then told to list the equipment he used and discuss his experimental techniques. After several pages of data and calculations, the student finally states his conclusions.

In industry, it's what's up front that counts. The beginning of an R&D report should not be devoted to introductory generalties, broad background or chronological narrative but rather to results and conclusions. Specific recommendations (if any) come next. The rest of the report is merely an appendix that justifies the conclusions and recommendations.

Progress Reports: Optimism vs. Realism

In all research reports, the ultimate basis is the laboratory notebook. As I have pointed out in another article,* reports will come much easier if you keep them in mind while the notebook is being written up. For example, when you do library research, full bibliographic data should go into the notebook. So should diagrams or photographs of experimental setups. Such practices save an enormous amount of report-writing time and energy.

Perhaps the most common research reports are progress reports. These are usually issued at definite periods, and are intended to be read as part of a series. Hence, each one doesn't generally go into such things as objectives and background.

Optimism is a usual characteristic of these reports. Even if most of the research during the period consisted in finding things that didn't work, the report will concentrate on the few bits of progress that really were made.

One of the problems of the progress report is how to handle the "progress" that you don't really believe in. I remember one project that I was working on in which we got an absurdly high yield in one of our experiments on the day before the progress report had to be written. The month's research hadn't produced much of note, and my supervisor insisted on my including the great news. I can still remember how I hedged the statement—"Preliminary experiments tend to indicate that it may be possible to realize yields as high as X%." Most of my weasel words were edited out, but my caution was justified: We never did equal that yield (and we never found out what went wrong).

Of course, the best way to handle results that you are dubious about is to omit them from that particular report until they can be checked. If you have an enlightened management, you can be blunt and include

*Hughson, R. V., How to Keep Laboratory Notebooks, p. 132.

the finding, noting that you question its reliability and are rechecking. But some managers hate to admit that uncertainty exists and that mistakes may have been made—in such cases, all you can do it to use the most cautious language. It is therefore a good idea to save such language for the times you really want to sound cautious. (If you use ultra-cautious language for all your writing, the reader cannot judge your degree of confidence in *anything* and will become frustrated.)

Coping With the Project Report

Because of its length, the Project Report is often the hardest research report to write; sometimes it covers years of work and contains enough pages to fill several books. Nonetheless, the problems are much the same as for any report, although on a much grander scale.

Companies differ as to what goes into a project report. (And, if it is being written for someone, outside the company—such as a governmental sponsor—you have their wishes to consider, too.) Sometimes the report is simply a summary of what was accomplished, giving only the most significant results, and discarding the rest. If this is the case, you're lucky. Just sit down with the various progress reports, and you'll have little trouble.

The big problem lies in the kind of project report that is intended to detail all the work that was done, explain the reasons for each particular experiment and the conclusion drawn from it, and even to include all the data. The idea behind this detailed approach is to see that nothing is ever lost, and that work once done is never repeated. The idea fails, however, if the resulting report is so voluminous that it is never read.

A really good index may help your report escape this fate, but making a good index is a difficult and time-consuming job.

Another possible way of including all the data without making a very bulky report is to provide a list of references to the notebook pages on which the data may be found. If all completed notebooks are filed in some central place, this could be very adequate for any future researcher. (However, I know of no organization that actually follows such a scheme.)

If you do have to compile a complete tome, first use the progress reports to write a summary of the significant results, and then go over the lab notebooks for the rest. Generally, the organization will be historical, starting at the beginning and tracing the development through to the ultimate analysis.

Most projects actually consist of a number of simultaneous trains of development, and the final report will be much more readable if each of these is treated separately. A few connecting paragraphs can link these developments with each other at appropriate places in the report.

Handling Data

Deciding just what data to put into your report is always a problem. You certainly don't want to tran-

Getting started on the report

It is possible to start writing an R&D report with only the roughest of outlines, or one that exists only in the mind. In fact, there are times when a very detailed, inflexible outline may become more of a hindrance than a help. As you write the report, you may see that the sequence of ideas should be changed in order to emphasize the important points. Or you may find that the act of writing the report—ond having to think about the entire project—may change your previous conclusions. In such cases, you may make up a new outline, or merely rearrange your already written report to make it serve as an outline for the next draft.

Sometimes there are so many ideas to get across that you don't know just where to start. One approach that I often find useful in such situations is to start anywhere. I write out a paragraph or two on a page and then start a new page. Sometimes I continue on the same theme, and sometimes I start on a new thought that occurred while I was writing the last paragraph.

After a while, I find myself with a thick sheaf of pages. I stop, and start sorting them out and arranging them. As I work, new thoughts occur, so I stop and write these up on some more sheets. It becomes obvious that certain bridging paragraphs are needed to lead from one idea to another. I write these, put them in the proper places, and I have a rough draft of my report. The rest is just a matter of polishing.

scribe the entire contents of your lab notebook. On the other hand, data are useful in supporting your conclusions and recommendations.

That last line contains the key. Include only such data as are really necessary to support your conclusions and recommendations. The rest should stay in your notebook.

There are three common ways of presenting data. One way, which is best for limited quantities of important information, is to include them in the text—e.g., "We consistently obtained yields of 78 to 80% when running at 300 F. and 120 psi."

For large quantities of data, you are forced either to tables or graphs. When your intent is to show a trend—for example, the effect of temperature on product yield—a graph is always preferable. Tables are best used when the actual numbers will have to be used by somebody else; for instance, by the mathematician in making a statistical analysis of the data.

Polishing Makes the Difference

The main difference between a good report and a poor one is often the amount of work that goes into polishing. It's a tedious process, but even the best writers have to endure it. (In fact, attention to details of this kind is one of the marks of a good writer.)

The first thing to do is, of course, to read the manuscript through and correct errors of fact, as well as grammatical errors involving tense, number, and the like. Next, read the manuscript aloud. If you stumble, or hesitate, it often indicates a need for some kind of punctuation, or perhaps you have come on an awkward phrase that needs rewriting, or a sentence that

doesn't hang together and needs to be split up. As you make revisions, remember the suggestions that T. P. Johnson made in the earlier section, "How Well Do You Inform?"

This is about the minimum that you can get by with. To go further, read through the manuscript and ask:

• Can I eliminate this phrase, or sentence, or paragraph, or section, without really losing anything important?

• Is this too complicated or too elementary for the expected reader of this report?

• Would an example help here?

• Have I used an unusual term, symbol or abbreviation without defining it?

• Am I consistent? (If, for example, you use the abbreviation "Btu." in one place, it should not be "B.T.U." somewhere else.)

After you finish, take a few minutes to review the revisions you have made, and also to think about those you would have made if you had the time. Jot down some pointers that will act as personal reminders when the time comes to write your next report. If you keep on doing this, the amount of polishing you have to do should decrease with each writing effort.

How to Keep Laboratory Notebooks

ROY V. HUGHSON, *Chemical Engineering*

Scribbled notes on scraps of paper not only hinder report writing but also destroy the legal proof that may be needed later to support patent claims.

The only product of a research laboratory is information. Running a research program without keeping adequate records is similar to running an expensive chemical processing plant and piping the final product through a very leaky line into the storage tank. In both cases, most of the work is wasted.

At the time a project is started, you have to realize that the research may result in a patentable invention, however unlikely it may seem at the time. Consequently the project should be written up in detail, paying particular attention to spelling out exactly what the problem is and how you intend to go about solving it. Of course, there will be changes in plan later—I've never seen a project that went from start to finish without changes based on information that came up during the experimentation.

As the work progresses, data, ideas and summaries should be entered as they occur, chronologically. Before each experiment, you should detail just what you expect to learn from it. At the end, you should summarize what you've learned.

As changes occur in the original experimental plan,

they should be detailed in your notebook. As you go along, you'll probably think of things that you'd like to try but aren't able to at the time. If you don't write them down, you'll probably forget most of them.

Progress Reports

Try drafting progress reports in your notebook. It's a good way to summarize the results of your work monthly, or at whatever interval reports are required in your organization.

Progress reports, written for management, generally tend to be optimistic and emphasize progress while minimizing setbacks and difficulties. Your original notebook draft can be more candid and more comprehensive—it can be easily edited to provide the formal report.

Library Research

In addition to descriptions of the experiments that you perform, your notebook should also include other

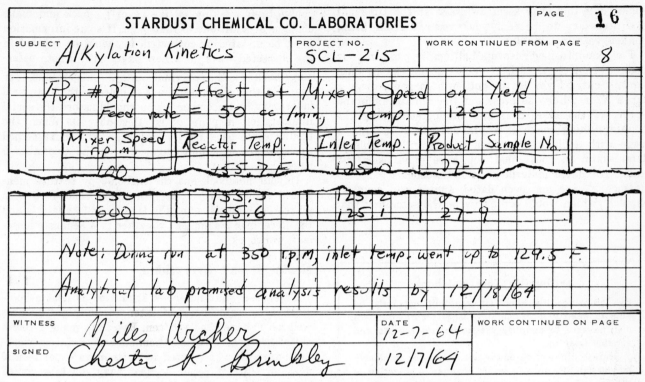

Ideal notebook page includes more than laboratory notes.

data that you get from your reading and formal library research. Full bibliographic data (exact title, author, publisher, date) should be included, since you will probably want to list them when it comes time to make your final report, or you may want them for one of your progress reports.

The Notebook Itself

Your notebook should be a chronological record. And it may in time have to be a legal record. This means that it must be bound (not loose-leaf) and the pages must be numbered, preferably by the printer. There must never be any question as to whether a record has been added or changed at a later date. Perhaps the CIA has facilities for forging and inserting a page in a bound notebook, but the average person hasn't and the courts know it.

Each page should be dated and signed by the notebook's author, and your company lawyers will probably like it better if it's signed and dated by a second person. In the overwhelming number of instances, this will never be needed, but in the rare circumstance when it is, it will be invaluable.

Incidentally, it is always a good idea to have your lawyers (particularly your patent lawyers) periodically review the way in which notebooks are kept. They may want to make changes based on their knowledge of the latest court decisions.

An excellent notebook page is shown in the figure above. This is based on the format used by one of the writer's past employers.

Since a notebook is kept in strictly chronological

sequence, the experimental data will frequently be interrupted by pages of summaries, ideas, or other kinds of data. Hence each page carries boxes to indicate of what page it is a continuation and on what page the particular topic is continued.

In the notebook pictured, the numbered pages are interleaved with perforated yellow pages that are punched for a loose-leaf binder. In use, a sheet of carbon paper is inserted between the numbered page and the following yellow page. When a numbered page is completed, the perforated yellow sheet is torn out and placed in the author's loose-leaf workbook. Here, the pages devoted to various phases of each project can be rearranged and kept in the proper order. When the bound notebook is full, it is returned to the laboratory file room for permanent filing, while the yellow carbon copies are retained as a working file.

The main area of the notebook page has a light grid printed upon it. This makes it easy to sketch in diagrams of apparatus and the like.

If a Polaroid camera is available, you may also want to make photos of your lab setups and paste them in the notebook. They can be very valuable later in showing details of equipment arrangements that have been left out of your sketches. Check with your company lawyers, though. They may want you to sign and date anything that's pasted in the notebook (in addition to signing and dating the page itself).

Preserving the Chronological Record

Because your notebook is supposed to be a day-by-day record of research activity, you have to follow some rules that may seem awkward at the time but are necessary to prevent your records from being challenged at a later date.

For example, never leave a half-empty page in your book when it is signed. If your calculations or data haven't carried you to the bottom of a page, draw a large X or otherwise cross out the remaining blank space. If the researcher and the person doing the countersigning make it a practice never to sign a page with a blank area, then no one will be able to later claim in court that you have gone back and added postdated material to your notebook.

Once a page has been dated, signed and countersigned (which would ordinarily be the same day that you've been working on it) never go back and make changes or additions to that page. If some information must be updated or corrected, it should be entered in the corrected form on a new page, with a note referring back to the original entry. This means, for example, that if you send out samples to the analytical laboratory on December 9, you should record the serial numbers on a page dated December 9. When the results come back on December 16, you must record the analysis on a new page—not on the December 9 page.

If your notebook has the carbon-copy feature mentioned above, however, it is a simple matter to keep all related material (i.e., the December 16 analysis and the December 9 samples) together in a separate loose-leaf workbook.

Neatness Isn't Everything

Of course, your notebook should be as neat as possible. If it can't be read later on, it might just as well never have been written. But don't make a fetish out of neatness. I've had chemists and engineers working under me who wanted to write down experimental data on slips of paper so that they could be copied oh-so-neatly into the notebook.

But you should put the data directly into the notebook, even if it doesn't look quite as pretty that way. Each time data are copied, there's a chance for errors to creep in. Besides, a notebook is much less likely to be lost than a slip of paper.

Closing Out a Project

If you've kept your notebook properly, the final report will be easy to write. Everything will be at hand. You'll be able to show just how the original objectives of the project were carried out. You will easily be able to point to what the project uncovered that was new or of potential importance. You'll be able to make suggestions for future work, if it should be needed.

It's best to make a first draft of your project report right in your notebook. The final version can then be edited directly from it.

Setting Up Your Notebook

By following this checklist you will not only be able to keep a more-complete legal record, but will also be able to simplify the writing of reports and articles later on.

√ State the objective of the entire project as clearly as you can. Be sure to record changes in objective as the project develops.

√ For each experiment run, be sure to record:
- Objective.
- Equipment used and procedures.
- All raw data written directly into notebook.
- Calculations (be sure to define all symbols and nomenclature so that someone else can follow your procedures step-by-step later on).
- Results and conclusions.
- Suggestions for further work.

√ List decisions that affect the course of project work, the alternatives considered, and reasons for rejecting them.

√ Include any standard operating procedures developed for equipment being used. Record and date any changes subsequently made in these procedures.

√ Sign and date each completed page. A countersignature will strengthen your records as a legal document.

√ Take snapshots of all equipment setups (Polaroids are the easiest) and paste them into your book with date and signatures. If regular prints are used, note where negatives can be found.

√ Carefully note the serial numbers of any samples sent to the analytical lab.

√ Include full reference citations for any books or articles used as sources of information.

√ Make note of memos, reports and other pertinent project documents, and where complete copies can be found.

√ If you must make a cost accounting at the end of the project, record the cost of all supplies, equipment (with model and serial number) and miscellaneous expenses.

Meet the Author

Roy V. Hughson is an associate editor of *Chemical Engineering*, with primary responsibility for Corrosion Forum. Prior to joining the editorial staff, he spent 8½ years in process and product development in the central research laboratories of Standard Brands, Inc. His last position was that of head of a research division specializing in instant coffee.

He received his B.Ch.E. and M.A. from New York University, and is a member of AIChE and ACS, as well as several other societies.

PART V

Producing Visually Effective Reports

Dress Up Your Technical Reports

Many executives know an engineer only through his technical reports.
Remember that your reports can be used to impress people as well as express ideas.

G. FREDRIC HOLDEN, Adolph Coors Co.

From the company's standpoint, a technical report is a means of permanently recording information and opinion. To you, the author, it has another important quality—the report is your product, your output! It sums up the reasons that you were paid over a certain period of time.

Remember that reports can be used not only to express but also to impress.

Getting the Report Written

Obviously, before you can begin to dress up your report, you first have to get it written. Report writing can be sheer drudgery. The job that you are reporting on is completed, and there's a new and interesting problem waiting for you. But you're chained to your desk. Report writing isn't romantic or demanding, but it is necessary.

The routine writing of monthly progress reports and the periodic issue of project and other engineering reports serve a number of purposes. The obvious purpose is the communicating of the data and understanding that were the original quest of the investigation. Once written down and distributed, it is available for management and technical men to use in planning and decision-making. The technical report is—or should be—as much an action tool as a recording tool.

From the author's viewpoint, the report is his knowledge materialized on paper. As such, it can serve as an advertisement to his peers and superiors of his technical skills and accomplishments. Also, once the report has been completed, it can serve as part of the engineer's personal portfolio,[1] for future use in describing his technical career.

Making an Impression

You want to have the right pair of eyes review and appreciate your efforts. If you are going to make an impression, it ought to be a favorable one.

There are a number of techniques used by book and magazine designers and commercial artists that can contribute to better ways of presenting reports—techniques of format and presentation.

Topics such as content, sentence structure and syntax will not be covered here. They have been adequately dealt with in many articles; some in this magazine.[2]

Space: There's Plenty Available—Use It

From the advertising man, we can borrow the concept of "white space." You remember the eye-catching appeal of the 6 × 6 in. advertisement that says in tiny centered letters, "Do you have bad breath? Bad breath is better than no breath at all—but if you care, use Sparkl." Because of the white space, the ad caught your eye—and then you got the message. Careful use of white space can give your report an almost artistic quality. Do you remember seeing a report whose pages were jammed from edge to edge with long sentences, multisyllabic expressions and formulas? How appealing was it to you? Did you want to lengthen your eye span and exercise your attention span poring over it? I doubt it. It was probably a distasteful experience, and either done half-heartedly or not at all. But with a little white space, the same report could be made eye-catching and appealing to the reader.

Break it Down

From the analytical chemist, we can gain a fresh idea for report writing. He takes complex molecular structures and must determine what's in them. To find out, he breaks them down into smaller and smaller components, until he knows just what the original compound was made of.

We can apply a similar concept to report writing. Most companies have a standard report format that has been established for uniformity and ease of expression of technical concepts. This framework must, of course, be maintained. But there is some latitude as to detailed presentation within those major boundaries. If it is at all possible, it is desirable to break up lengthy sections and long paragraphs for ease of comprehension. This can be done easily by reviewing the content, and interjecting appropriate subheadings. Such logical divisions ease the concentration of the reader, and make the report more readable. They also provide logically located "thinking points." And you are incorporating more white space to enhance the report's eye-appeal.

Therefore, instead of one complete section titled only "Discussion," you can use underlined subheadings, such as "Problem Background," "Problem Description," "Theoretical Explanation," "Approach Description," "Preliminary Observations," etc. You have applied the principles of programmed instruction to the written explanation of your technical investigation. Were you a bit more bold, you could create more-lively and descriptive headings, while remaining within the bounds of accepted format and good taste.

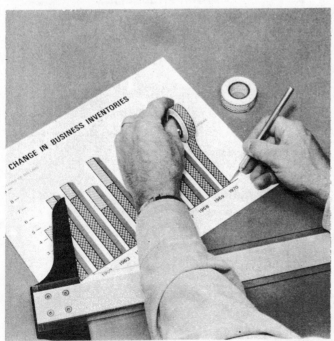

COLORFUL-pattern tapes make striking graphs—Fig. 1

Don't Fence Me In—Or Should You?

From the artist, we can appropriate a concept that helps to make a good first impression. He can spend hours or even weeks painting a picture. When it is finally done, does he hang it up? No, he'll usually wish to display the picture at its very best, and mount it within an appropriate frame. Engineering reports, too, can be framed.

A special title page, for instance, can give the report title, author and date, along with the company name and location. However, a black-lined border, about ⅜ to ½ in. from the page edge can dress up the title page, and give it a more finished appearance. To highlight the title, author and date, one or all could be emphasized in a smaller boxed outline, centered within the box, and with the box placed above the center on the bordered title page.

A similar application can be used to "finish" graphs, photos or other illustrations. And data tables in the body of the report can also be placed within a border, to separate them from the surrounding prose.

Dress It Up—Right

The marketing man knows the importance of packaging his product attractively. Eye-appeal and product appeal are closely related. Packaging for a report is simple, and usually available. If it is a permanent research or process-investigation report, you might consider a cardboard binder—especially for file copies and those to the men in charge. Also, photographic and other illustrative material can be placed in clear, protective, plastic-sheet holders. The permanence and importance of the report will determine the extent to which you bind, protect and reinforce it.

Tools of the Trade

As a final idea, from the professional illustrator, we have the professional illustrator's tools. Most of us are not artists, and artistic talent is usually not needed, or even desired, in a technical report. But some of the artist's tools can be used.

For instance, tape plays a big part in "quick fixes," as the engineer knows so well. Properly used, tape can also help you to dress up your technical reports.

There are special tapes available just for the purpose of making graphs or "drawing" borders.[3,4,5] They are available in many hues, widths and finishes. You can obtain tape in all the colors of the rainbow, shiny or matte finish, and in almost any width. In addition, it can be striped, slashed or varied in design.

To use this tape, the engineer sets up his graph and plots the points. Instead of inked lines, he can use tape for the axes of the graph. Narrow tape can be used for constructing the actual curves—the tape is surprisingly flexible and can follow even sharp curves. Special applicators—sometimes called "tape pens"—make the job even easier. The width of the tape can serve to indicate the accuracy and reproducibility of the data—narrow for exact data and wide for data with less certainty.

Even-wider tape can be used for constructing bar

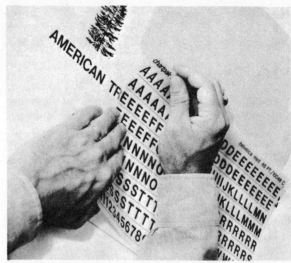
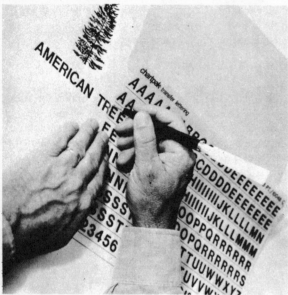
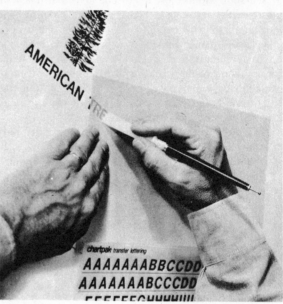

DRY-TRANSFER lettering is easily applied. a. Fold backing sheet out of the way. b. Position letter. c. Rub over letter lightly with soft pencil or ball point pen. d. Lift off carrier sheet; burnish letter down—Fig. 2

graphs, as shown in Fig. 1. Colored and patterned tapes are particularly effective for this use.

Do you have difficulty with lettering? Commercial artists use dry-transfer lettering to solve many of their problems. These are something like decals and are printed on the back of a transparent carrier sheet. The proper letter is positioned over the place you want it on your paper, and transferred by rubbing the back of the carrier sheet with a soft pencil or ball point pen. The four photographs of Fig. 2 show the process. The letters are available in a wide variety of styles (or type faces) and sizes.

In addition to letters and numbers, special symbols can be obtained for such things as flowcharts and PERT diagrams.

You can buy these special tapes and dry-transfer letters at any large art-supply store, or write to the manufacturers[3,4,5] to find the location of the dealer in your area. ■

(Photographs from "Chartpak," Avery Products—Graphics Div.).

References

1. Holden, G. F., Your Personal Portfolio: A Job-Hunting Tool, *Chem. Eng.*, Sept. 7, 1970, pp. 88-92.
2. Fast, Functional Writing, *Chem. Eng.*, June 30, 1969, pp. 104-122 (Reprint No. 69), or Efficient, Effective Writing, *Chem. Eng.*, Feb. 26, 1966, pp. 145-162, (Reprint No. 295) are good examples.
3. Chartpak Rotex, Div. of Avery Products Corp., 2620 South Susan St., Santa Ana, CA 92704, and One River Rd., Leeds, MA 01053.
4. Datak Corp., 85 Highland Ave., Passaic, NJ 07055.
5. Letraset USA, Inc., 2379 Charleston Rd., Mountain View, CA 94040.

Meet the Author

G. Fredric Holden is a chemical engineer who works for Adolph Coors Co., Golden, CO 80401. He was formerly data processing supervisor for a medium-sized chemical company. He has a B.Ch.E. from the University of Colorado and is a graduate of the Alexander Hamilton Inst.

Illustration Techniques For Technical Reports

Poor illustrations can spoil an otherwise excellent technical report. What should an illustration do? When should one be used? What type best fills a particular need? These are only a few of the questions that are answered.

GARY A. SMOOK, MacMillan Bloedel Ltd.

Few technical reports consist exclusively of the written word. In most instances, the engineer must use illustrative material to elucidate and amplify on the results of his investigations.

Somewhat surprisingly, therefore, much of the illustrative material in technical reports is poorly conceived and executed. Frequently, it is not of the same quality as the written word and does not augment and complement the text as it should. An otherwise excellent report still makes a poor impression on the reader when the graphs and figures appear to have been given only haphazard attention. One engineering manager has reacted to the variance in illustration quality by referring to illustration preparation as "the forgotten chapter in the book of technical report writing."

What are the reasons for the inconsistency in illustration quality that most supervisors see every day? Much of the blame can probably be placed on the supervisor himself for not setting standards on illustrations. Apparently many companies do not provide any direction for this, even though they issue otherwise complete guidelines for the preparation of technical reports.

When To Use Illustrations

In general, illustrations are used to show what words cannot tell quickly and accurately. They support and augment the text, and make the descriptions and comparisons more vivid. They also serve as a summary of what has been detailed in the text, and show the particulars of those aspects of a subject that have been discussed perfunctorily or passed over altogether.

An illustration can be a "bridge to understanding" or a "bridge to logical reasoning." If the reader has become

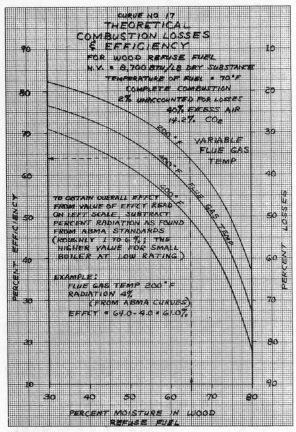
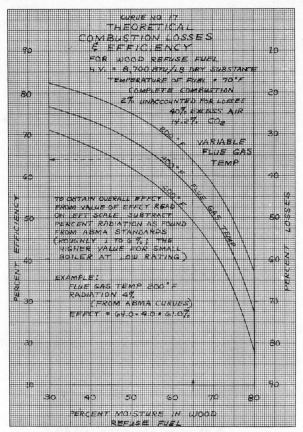

COPYING PROCESS may reproduce grid lines so heavily that deciphering a graph could be difficult—Fig. 1

lost at one point through the lack of such a bridge, the writer may have lost an opportunity to sway him to a particular viewpoint or enable him to accept a hypothesis. Sometimes an illustration that restates a point made in the text may seem needlessly redundant, but if it assists the reader in recognizing an important point, its inclusion may be worthwhile.

Readers appreciate an attractive and interesting presentation of intrinsically dry material. Even a reader technically trained does not lose a liking for form, variety and color. As far as is reasonable, therefore, technical illustrations should be artistic as well as useful.

There appears to be widespread disagreement on how frequently illustrations should be used in technical reports. At one extreme are those who say that illustrations should only be used to portray information that cannot be conveyed in any other way. On the other side are those who advocate including many an occasional figure to break up pages of print for the sake of visual variety that will maintain reader interest, even if the illustrations are not essential for conveying the message.

Perhaps the middle ground is best. If an illustration will make a report more effective, it should be included. If, on the other hand, it is completely superfluous and intended only as "window dressing," it should be omitted. Generally, illustrations should be used more often, rather than less, in technical reports.

Available Techniques

A large number of illustration techniques are available to the report writer (see box). Whether he avails himself of a particular technique probably depends on how comfortable he works with it. However, he should try to inject variety into his illustrations.

A perspective drawing can be advantageous in many instances, but is rarely used by engineers in reports because they seem to feel they are stepping into the domain of the artist. Perspective drawings are used to project a real-life appearance, but are less suitable than engineering drawings when detailed dimensioning is necessary.

The "box," another illustrative tool too little used in technical reports, is especially useful when it is necessary

---

Examples of Illustrative Material

Lists	Tabulations	Sample calculations
Tables	Nomographs	Plots
Graphs	Reference boxes	Equations

Charts—bar, directional, range, organizational, distribution.

Diagrams—logic, arrow, PERT, CPM.

Engineering drawings—orthographic, isometric, oblique.

Pictures—photographs, half-tone reproductions, perspective drawings, maps, layouts, patterns.

Ideas for Better Illustrations

Plan your illustrations for your readers' convenience.

Fully label all illustrations. An illustration should be self-explanatory, even if removed from the context of the report. Titles should be brief but descriptive. There should never be any doubt as to how an illustration relates to the text. When the text says "as shown in Fig. 2," the figure must fully clarify the point being made.

Cite every illustration in the text. Never assume that the reader will go to a particular illustration on his own.

If there is a "gimmick" to understanding an illustration, provide a full explanation. When only one or two illustrations are involved, an explanatory note can usually be affixed to each. When there are a number, include an explanation in the report (usually in the Introduction), such as a subsection entitled, "A Key to Understanding the Graphs."

Plan the illustrations first. They should not be placed in a report only as an afterthought.

Illustrate any equipment described in the report that may be unfamiliar to the reader.

The scope of a single illustration should be restricted by how speedily it can be comprehended.

Do not necessarily be limited to one illustration per page. Nothing may be lost by reducing the size of some graphs, charts, plots or sketches so as to include several on a page. This will lessen the size and copying costs of a report. Also, a composite illustration can sometimes replace several smaller ones without becoming overly complicated.

Avoid multicolor illustrations if the colors cannot be reproduced.

Do not clutter illustrations with too much or irrelevant detail. (The drawback of photographs is that they show too much.)

Provide illustrations with ample margins. This space improves visual impact and avoids the cutting off of figures in copying and binding.

When possible, run the base of an illustration along the bottom of the page, with the titles and notes oriented the same way. This makes viewing the illustration more convenient.

When an illustration must be referred to frequently, append it in the back of the report in such a way that it can be folded out and left wholly visible while the report is being read and pages turned. When an illustration is referred to only once, place it on the back of the page preceding its mention if possible.

Use a larger page for an illustration only when it cannot be placed on the standard-sized page. If this is not possible, try having only one dimension longer. In this case, make the fold about ¼ inch inside the right-hand edge so it will not extend and become worn with fingering. When both dimensions must be longer, make the folds at both the top (this one first) and right edges. Insert extraordinarily large illustrations in a pocket at the back of the report, from which they can be removed and unfolded for reference.

Make the data used as the basis for a figure or table available to the reader. This is usually done in an appendix, but sometimes a reference to the source will suffice.

BLUE-LINED GRID

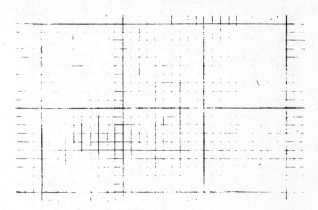

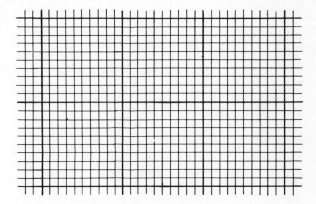

GREEN-LINED GRID

GREEN grid lines reproduce darker than blue—Fig. 2

to repeatedly refer to a set of points, questions or a general listing. In such cases, the box should be included in the form of a foldout page.

The box can also be used for a sideline discussion that is useful for reference or background but is not part of the "meat of the report." Such a device is called an "illustrative writing" because it can be read out of context, or with the text for a change of pace. It is similar to the appendix, except for being part of the body of the report.

When illustrating data within a technical report, there is sometimes a question of whether to use a table or a figure. The criterion here should be accuracy. And when extreme accuracy is required, there is little choice but to use a table. Figures are usually more effective for showing totals, trends, directions and distributions, and for dramatizing comparisons. If precision is secondary, a graph or chart is usually preferable.

Although variety is desirable, there are certain representations that do not belong in a technical report because they lack precision and so can too easy mislead the reader. One of these is the pie chart. Another is the symbolic, or pictorial, chart (for example, one bag equals 1,000 bushels).

It is unfortunate that economics prevent the wider use of colored illustrations in technical reports. Color would undoubtedly help readers grasp some of the more complex descriptions of apparatus and equipment and their workings. However, some of the same advantages can be

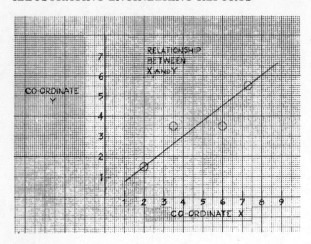

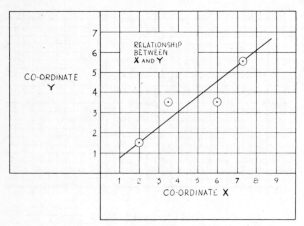

PLOTS on wrong type paper may be hard to read—Fig. 3

gained to a lesser degree by judicious use of cross-hatching in black and white illustrations.

Planning Illustrations

The choice and planning of technical illustrations (see box p.141) should be guided by the reader's convenience, not the writer's.

Many of the problems with technical illustrations arise from not anticipating how they will look after they have been copied and bound into a report. For example, the grid lines in Fig. 1 copied darker than the curve and notations, making the graph difficult to decipher. Obviously, some knowledge of available copying processes is necessary so that reproduction limitations can be compensated for. For example, every user of a Xerox copier should be aware that green, red and orange grid lines reproduce heavier than blue lines (Fig. 2); therefore graph paper must be selected with such characteristics in mind. If there is any doubt about how an illustration for a report will look after it is reproduced, it is a good idea to check this out before the report is passed to the typist.

Other problems with illustrations arise because report writers feel constrained to use only materials readily at hand. For example, if the wrong type of graph paper is used, the result might be a figure with too many and too thick grid lines, lack of margins and poor composition (Fig. 3). Poor choice of tabular paper will contribute to

Guidelines for Tables and Graphs

TABLES

Do not overload a table. If possible, divide the material into several smaller tables.

Arrange data in a logical order. Independent variables are usually shown in the left-hand column, with dependent variables listed appropriately along the top row.

When a long, complex table is necessary, include it as an appendix, and insert a condensed version in the text.

GRAPHS

Do not be limited by the graph paper at hand. With modern copy machines, graph paper can be tailor-made for a specific job. The types of graph paper available commercially should be reviewed periodically, and those that may be useful should be stocked.

When the abscissa, or time base, must run along the long side of a page, always face the graph toward the right-hand side when including it in a bound report.

Reserve the heaviest lines for the data curves, and moderately thick lines for the axes. A minimum weight and number of lines should be used for the grid. However, the 2nd, 5th, or 10th line, or other convenient subdivision, of the grid can be made slightly darker to facilitate reference to the scales.

Indicate data points by variants of circles, squares and triangles. All symbols should contain approximately the same area to avoid the impression of weighting certain sets of data.

Show all titles, notes and scales on unlined areas of a graph for best visibility. (Open areas can be added to commercial graph paper by placing strips of blank paper in the appropriate areas.)

When scales contain discontinuities or do not begin at zero, indicate the breaks on the coordinate axes.

With chronological plots, choose a scale for the dependent variable that will illustrate differences without distorting or magnifying the relative effects. Use an appropriate time scale, such as 12 hours, 24 hours, 1 week, 1 month, 1 quarter, 6 months, etc. Avoid such scales as 17 hours or 5 months.

Use templates to show data points and to delineate equipment on a line sketch. Unless the freehand printing is professional, the lettering should be typed or done with a template.

Do not place too many curves on the same figure, especially when the curves intersect at acute angles.

Avoid too many scales on the same plot. Usually two or three scales should be maximum for the coordinate axis.

If possible, use curve labels instead of a legend. This practice saves the reader the time of referring back and forth between the curves and the legend.

poor layouts of tables—and no report writer should expect the typist to rearrange his tables.

In most cases, the report writer will be well advised to tailor-make the graph paper and tabular paper he needs. Because most report writers have access to a copying machine, once a specialty sheet has been designed, it can be duplicated to any extent desired.

Arranging Tables and Graphs

Some guidelines for presenting tables and graphs are listed in the box on p. 142.

A major irritation to many managers is the recurrent need to physically reorient a report in order to read graphs. For a graph that is facing the right-hand side of the page and has the Y coordinate labeled along the axis, it is necessary to rotate the report by 180 deg. in order to read the ordinate label.

Imagine the vexation involved in reading a 100-page report with, say, every other page containing an illustration oriented toward the right-hand side. When possible, it is always preferable to plan figures so they can be read comfortably as pages are turned, without the need for contortions on the part of the reader.

A common error in graphic presentations is to show data that represent the average level over a considerable period as a single point. In the case of a chronological plot of monthly or annual averages, it is better to show data as a step chart rather than as a sawtooth plot.

As nearly as possible, data should be shown in a representative fashion. For example, consider a plot whose area between the points and a target level is likely to be mentally integrated or weighted on an area basis. Clearly, the use of points may give an erroneous impression, so a step-type representation is preferable.

When data are extremely variable, step charts may also be chosen, because they tend to give better resolution to the points (Fig. 4).

Whenever possible, templates should be used for depicting data points, making line sketches, and drawing process flowsheets. Unless the illustrator's hand-lettering is excellent, it is also advisable to use either a typewriter or a template for titles and notes. Although freehand figures may be legible, they will not convey the desired impression unless they appear crisp and professional.

Another problem in preparing graphs concerns the choice of ordinate scales for time-base plots. If a scale is too compact, it will be difficult to observe the changes that occur. On the other hand, an overly expanded scale may misrepresent the magnitude of the changes, or may give an exaggerated sawtooth appearance to the data (Fig. 5).

Drawings and Photographs

It is sometimes expedient to include more detail in an illustration than is needed. For example, there is always a temptation to use an available drawing, perhaps a working drawing, to illustrate a particular point. But because the drawing has been made for another purpose, it will show many other features as well. The good expositor will abstract the drawing and show only the features

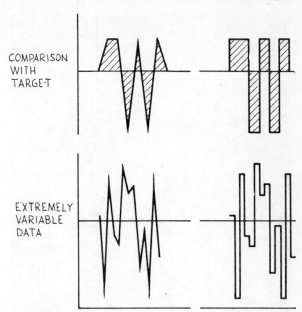

STEP CHARTS are clearer than point graphs—Fig. 4

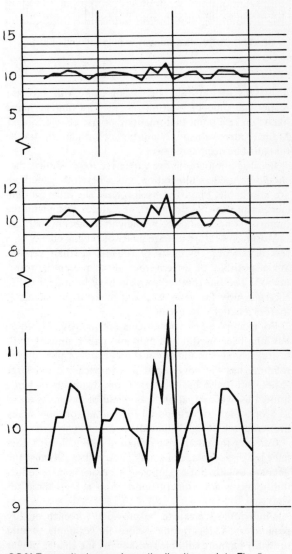

SCALE magnitude can dramatically alter a plot—Fig. 5

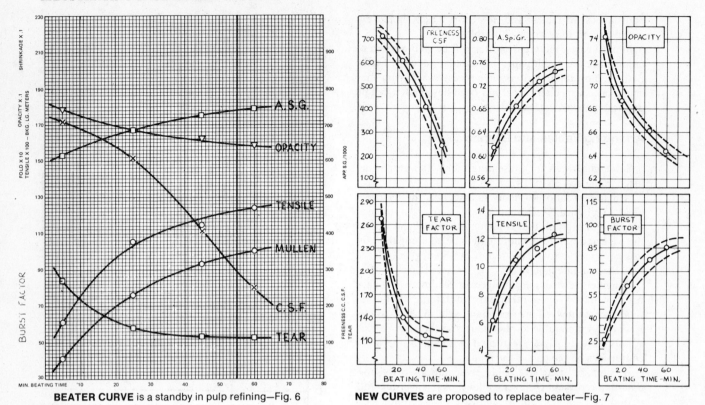

BEATER CURVE is a standby in pulp refining—Fig. 6

NEW CURVES are proposed to replace beater—Fig. 7

he wishes to illustrate. In so doing, he will save the reader the time of figuring out the drawing or, more likely, make a point that might otherwise be overlooked. Many readers will simply not bother with an illustration that must be deciphered.

Because photographs are expensive to reproduce, they should be used as illustration only where other methods are unsuitable. Photographs also have the inherent deficiencies of showing unimportant features along with the important ones, and of being difficult to label properly.

Most technical writers are guilty of relying chiefly on a few dependable methods of illustrating their reports. When possible, be adventurous about presenting information! The fact that certain data have been depicted in a certain way for years does not make them sacred. If there is a better way, use it.

For example: The "beater-curve form" (Fig. 6), which has long been used in the pulp and paper industry to illustrate changes in the physical properties of pulp during refining, has the advantages of compactness and large scales. But it also has the serious disadvantages of being limited to two compatible scales, and of having as many as 8 or 9 plots superimposed (depending on how many properties are being evaluated).

Consider the alternative proposed in Fig. 7. This does have the disadvantage of smaller graph sizes (because the data are usually not of sufficient accuracy and reproducibility, this is not critical). But it offers at least three advantages:

• Individual scales can be provided for each quality parameter. A logarithmic scale, for example, would probably be more suitable for showing the change in tear factor during refining.

• Each parameter plot is separate. Up to six plots can be shown on a letter-size sheet, and up to nine on a legal-size sheet.

• Limit-lines can now be included, showing the normal spread of data for each pulp grade.

Final Word

Any technical illustration will probably succeed if you keep in mind exactly who your reader is, and plan your illustrations for his convenience, in terms of understanding, readability, professional impact, clarity and conciseness. Do not be limited by the materials at your desk, or confined by the accepted methods.

Remember that management personnel usually comprehend illustrations far better than technical terms, mathematics or chemistry. So, especially when your report will be read by a wide cross-section of people, you must use many "bridges to understanding." Illustrations can be an effective tool for this purpose. ∎

Meet the Author

Gary A. Smook (No. 303, 4465 Michigan St., Powell River, B.C., Canada) has spent 15 years in process and project engineering, and production supervision. With MacMillan Bloedel, he has served as technical specialist, assistant to the vice-president of manufacturing, and sales technical-service representative.

Holder of a B.S. in chemical engineering from the U. of Calif. (Berkeley), he is a member of ACS and Tech. Assn. of the Pulp and Paper Ind., and a registered engineer in the Province of British Columbia.

Preparing Better Flowsheets

A flowsheet can be accurate and complete, but yet so hard to follow that valuable reading time is wasted and misinterpretations become almost inevitable.

EUGENE GUCCIONE, *Chemical Engineering*

It has already been said that a report, to be truly informative, must be easy to understand. This certainly applies to flowsheets.

As the graphic representation of an over-all system, flowsheets spell out an entire process with all its inputs and outputs, energy flows, and component units. As such, they are the best vehicle to transmit engineer-

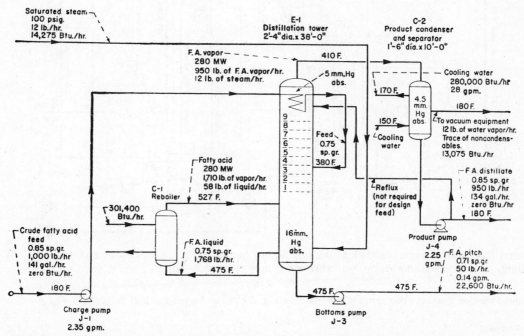

Material and energy balance is the starting point for a process flowsheet; this preliminary diagram has sacrificed simplicity in order to parallel the physical arrangement of the distillation unit.—Fig. 1

Revised diagram of same unit is easier to follow and to use as basis for detailed drawings.—Fig. 2

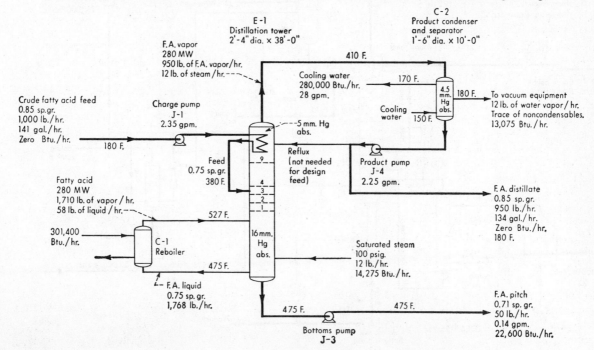

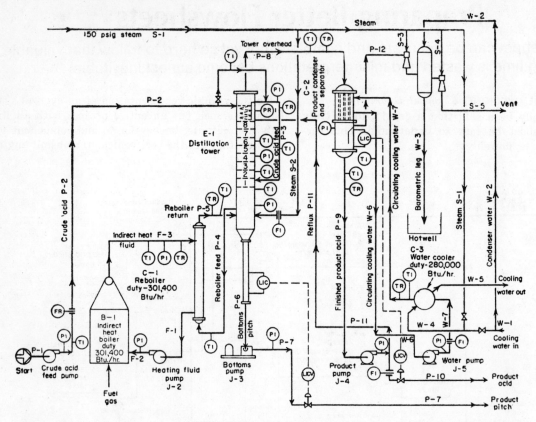

Control flowsheet of same distillation unit has 40 line bends and 16 crossovers that slow down reading and unnecessarily clutter an otherwise simple diagram.—Fig. 3

Revised version contains the same information as Fig. 3 but can be read in half the time.—Fig. 4

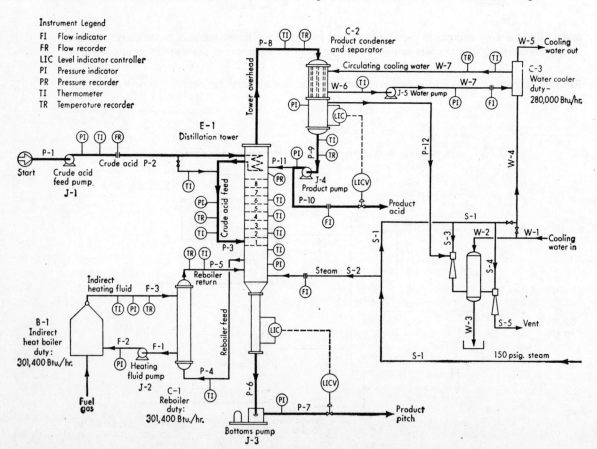

ing data accurately and completely. But unless they are judiciously drawn up, they will present a forbidding maze of tortuous lines that defy one's patience and understanding.

Obviously, flowsheets require something besides completeness and accuracy—and that is clarity. Otherwise understanding even a simple processing sequence can become a time-consuming chore. So, to be easily understood, i.e., to be informative, flowsheets need redrawing just as much as a technical report needs rewriting. In fact, even more so.

Whereas a report or interoffice memo usually goes to a small number of people, flowsheets feed information to practically everyone in the organization—from vice presidents and department heads, to R&D people, project engineers, designers, purchasing men, equipment fabricators, plant superintendents and various operating personnel. On the basis of data transmitted in flowsheets, various people working on the project will proceed to develop all subsequent drawings (e.g., for control and instrumentation, equipment design, plot plan, foundations, piping and utility layouts, wiring diagrams) as well as cost estimates, conversions and yields, and operating and maintenance manuals for training plant operators.

Considering all the people involved, even a slight improvement— one that chops a few minutes off the time necessary to grasp the basic information from a series of flowsheets—will save untold hours of work for the whole company. If it also prevents a misunderstanding or two, so much the better.

Flowsheet Pitfalls

At the start of any new project, exploratory calculations or pilot-plant data provide the material and energy balances for the process. These data are usually presented in tabular form and constitute the first step towards constructing a flowsheet. In many cases, the first flowsheet rendition of, say, a simple distillation unit has a somewhat garbled look because of tight work schedules and poor supervision in the drafting room. An example of this is shown in Fig. 1; this is an actual flowsheet that appeared in the literature. Although accurate, the flowsheet is harder to follow than the redrawn version in Fig. 2.

Once the wrong precedent is set, the felony gets compounded in subsequent more-detailed drawings, and Fig. 3 (also from the literature) shows what happens when the control instruments and a few auxiliary lines are added to the first flowsheet.

In Fig. 1, for example, the reflux line is interrupted and bent three times before entering the distillation tower. In Fig. 3, it is interrupted five times before getting to the tower; and in the same drawing, the cooling-water line bends eight times and crosses five times before returning to the overhead condenser. These flaws may seem petty, but note how they give an unnecessary cloak of complexity to what is, after all, a very simple diagram.

Figs. 2 and 4 show the same unit, and provide the identical data. The rearrangement in flow pattern is

minor, yet it halves the reading time for the two redrawn diagrams.

This example, of course, illustrates one of the most common types of processing units. But in a slightly more complex process there might be, say, six or seven fractionators, a few absorption towers, exchangers, compressors and so on.

In such cases, the process engineer—whether he works for a large or small firm—would be well advised to spend a few minutes of his time revising and simplifying the rough sketch of the flowsheet he sends to the drafting department, or else give the draftsmen a few lectures on how a good flow diagram should be put together. Unless he does that, he will keep on getting hard-to-read diagrams, with lines (process, recycle, utility and byproduct streams) that relentlessly bend, twist and cross over in elaborate branching throughout yards and yards of drawings.

The only advantage that such garbled diagrams offered in the past was that various types of equipment were grouped and lined up in neat rows. For example, all pumps and compressors were shown at the same elevation so that a designer could quickly spot a particular pump. But today there is no reason why a flowsheet should not be drawn clearly and with a minimum of effort. Computers are relieving the load of producing piping isometrics, bills of materials, pipe routings, valve locations, and design of standard parts. And with the help of even crude plot-plan models and planning models, well-drawn flowsheets are invaluable for determining quickly the best possible piping layout.

How to Improve Flowsheets

What can be done to improve flowsheet drawings? In the first place, the flowsheet should have only essential equipment, and should show the material flow sequence as developed from the material and energy balance.

Next, it would be advisable—even when working on simple processes—to make a separate drawing to show process controls and instrumentation.

Then there is the obvious suggestion of finding alternative ways to eliminate as many line bends and cross-overs as possible. Note how this has been done in the illustrations. The control diagram of Fig. 3, for instance, was greatly simplified to Fig. 4 by just placing the product pump and water cooler above the barometric condenser—thus shortening the reflux line to about one tenth of its original length, without any bends or cross-overs—and by a minor rearrangement of the steam line.

Flow diagrams should dispense with items that add nothing to accuracy, completeness or clarity. Some of the common pitfalls include: "gilding the lily" by showing pump motors, drives, standard furnace tubes, double lines, equipment internals; repeating names and specifications (instead of referring to standards); hand lettering (instead of typing); routine drafting of standard equipment instead of using templates.

Drawing Effective Flowsheet Symbols

Confusing, difficult-to-understand flowsheets waste much time and money.
Here is practical advice on how to select standard and nonstandard flowsheet
symbols, and how to use these symbols to readily communicate information.

RUSSELL G. HILL, *Scientific Design Co., Inc.*

The engineer who makes the effort to use effective symbols in his flowsheets will find that he is amply repaid by improved communications with his readers.

Engineers prepare flowsheets to communicate process designs to their superiors, other engineers, mechanical designers, startup crews, etc. Those receiving the flowsheets may use them for reviewing the design, making economic evaluations, preparing more detailed or specialized flowsheets, making piping drawings, planning operator duties, or for any other activity that is based on the engineer's work. If the flowsheet reader is not given a clear and unmistakable picture of the design, communication is impaired. At the very least, time will be wasted while he questions or puzzles out the flowsheet; and in many cases, he may make serious mistakes based on an erroneous interpretation of the flowsheet.

In what follows, we shall: (1) present those flowsheet symbols that have already been accepted as standards or are commonly used in the chemical process industries; (2) show how the engineer should draw his own symbols, when standards do not exist; (3) propose basic symbols (where standards do not exist) for chemical equipment and accessories used throughout the CPI; and (4) list sources of standard symbols and sources of nonstandardized symbols that the chemical engineer may find useful.

Selecting the Symbols

Chemical engineers have many commonly accepted symbols available, which because of their time-proven effectiveness should be used whenever possible. When an appropriate symbol does not exist, or when an existing one does not completely fill the need, a new symbol must be created. Most engineers will find the latter to be frequently true because of the diversity of flowsheet functions and the increasing variety of chemical-plant equipment.

Selecting or creating effective symbols may seem to be a difficult task involving abstract considerations of perception, recognition, interpretation and comprehension. Fortunately, in recent years much has been learned from studies of the problems of nonverbal communication so that, by observing the following principles, it is not difficult to improve the effectiveness of flowsheet symbols.

Communicate Concepts, Not Images

A flowsheet is a tool for communicating special information for particular purposes. Almost all chemical plants are built from drawings based on the concepts communicated by the flowsheets, but not from the flowsheets themselves. Symbols, therefore, do not have to be graphic representations of physical items; their purpose is to communicate a concept of the item and not a photographic image.

The words *thermodynamic steam trap*, for instance, do not resemble the physical form of a steam trap, yet they communicate to the reader the concept of a piece of equipment that performs a certain function and that has certain strengths and limitations. It is unlikely that an exact pictorial representation could deliver the message as efficiently.

Pictorial symbols are quick to draw, easy to understand, and transcend language barriers; this is why they are used for flowsheets. But, as shown above, there undoubtedly are situations in which a few well-chosen words will be more effective than any pictorial symbol could be. It is also frequently convenient to incorporate alphabetic or numeric characters.

Table I shows a recommended nomenclature list for instruments, and Table II, recommended nomenclature for various plant services and materials.

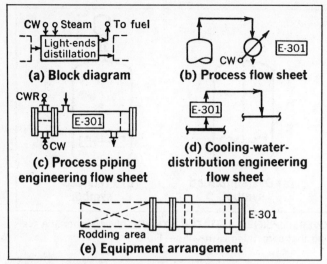

(a) Block diagram

(b) Process flow sheet

(c) Process piping engineering flow sheet

(d) Cooling-water-distribution engineering flow sheet

(e) Equipment arrangement

VARIOUS FORMS of condenser symbols such as are used for different-purpose flowsheets—Fig. 1

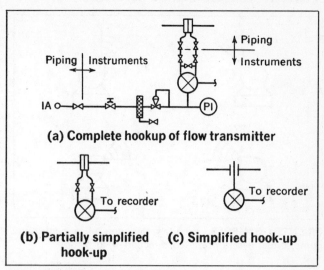

(a) Complete hookup of flow transmitter

(b) Partially simplified hook-up

(c) Simplified hook-up

SIMPLIFICATION of a flow transmitter symbol in accordance with particular purpose of flowsheet—Fig. 2

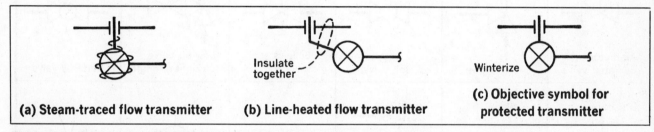

(a) Steam-traced flow transmitter

(b) Line-heated flow transmitter

(c) Objective symbol for protected transmitter

FREEZE-PROTECTED FLOWMETER can be represented in different ways, according to need—Fig. 3

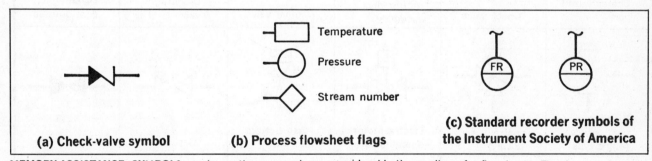

(a) Check-valve symbol

(b) Process flowsheet flags

Temperature

Pressure

Stream number

(c) Standard recorder symbols of the Instrument Society of America

MEMORY-ASSISTANCE SYMBOLS such as these speed up considerably the reading of a flowsheet—Fig. 4

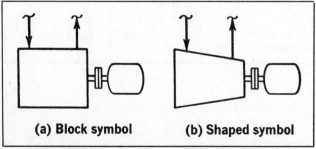

(a) Block symbol

(b) Shaped symbol

EYE MOVEMENT speeds up through shaping of symbols. Note how this is accomplished in (b) by reduced size at outlet of centrifugal compressor—Fig. 5

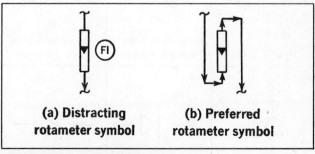

(a) Distracting rotameter symbol

(b) Preferred rotameter symbol

IMPOSSIBLE SITUATIONS distract reader. Sketch (a) is simpler, but downward flow in rotameters is impossible. Sketch (b) is better choice—Fig. 6

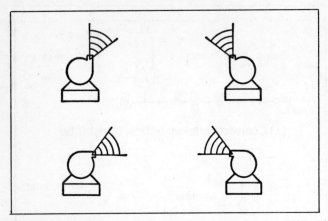

ORIENTED SYMBOLS, such as this one of a centrifugal pump, direct eye in preferred direction—Fig. 7

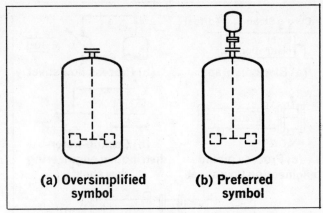

(a) Oversimplified symbol **(b) Preferred symbol**

OVERSIMPLIFIED AGITATOR SYMBOL gives reader the feeling that something is missing—Fig.8

Air-motor-operated valve	Angle valve	Ball valve
Bellows seal valve	Blow-off valve (straight or angle)	Butterfly valve
Characterized port	Check valve	Combination relief valve and rupture-disk assembly
Damper valve	Diaphragm valve	Diaphragm control valve
Diaphragm control valve (angle type)	Diaphragm control valve (3-way)	Electric-motor-operated valve
Flush bottom tank valve	Gate valve	Globe valve
Needle valve	Non-return valve (straight or angle)	Piston-operated valve, air or oil
Plug valve	Plug valve, 3-way (4-way plug valve)	Quick-opening valve
Safety relief valve (vacuum breaker)	Slide valve	Y valve

MOST VALVES are represented by the gate-valve symbol in general flowsheets. Specific symbols, such as those others suggested here, are used whenever required in other types of flowsheets—Fig. 9

					CSC/CSO
Main lines	Auxiliary lines	Instrument lines	Instrument capillary lines	Instrument electrical lines	CSC= Car seal closed CSO= Car seal open*
Figure 8-type blind	Hose connection*	Jacketed pipe	Line blind	Material furnished by others*	Open drain to sewer
Reducer	Reversible elbow	Sample connection*	Sample connection with cooler*	Steam traced pipe	Valve requiring throttling adjustment or frequent operation*
Vent or drain (plugged or blinded)*					

*Note: Appropriate valve symbol should be used, as required.

PIPING AND PIPING-SPECIALTIES SYMBOLS are used when additional detail is needed—Fig. 10

Symbols Must Be Flexible

Create or select your symbol to suit the purpose of the flowsheet. Do not force a symbol on the reader just because it will be used on other flowsheets, but which for the particular flowsheet being drawn conveys more detailed information than is appropriate.

Fig. 1 shows the various ways in which a condenser for a fractionation column might be shown. These flowsheet designations are not necessarily universally accepted, but have been chosen to illustrate one way in which a symbol can be varied from one flowsheet to another to communicate the essential ideas.

The block diagram in Fig. 1a shows only that the fractionation step includes a water-cooled condenser. The process flowsheet (Fig. 1b) adds the information that it is a shell-and-tube condenser that is physically independent of the column and the reflux drum. The process-piping engineering flowsheet (Fig. 1c) shows, in addition, that the cooling water is on the tube side (depending on the conventions followed, this might not have been explicit in the process flowsheet); it also shows that the exchanger is a fixed tube-sheet type, with removable channel covers and two tube-side

passes; and that the cooling water flows upward, etc.

In the cooling-water-distribution engineering flowsheet (Fig. 1d), used for showing the layout of the cooling-water headers, the condenser can be shown once again as a very simple symbol. The equipment-arrangement drawing (Fig. 1e) is concerned only with physical layout and not with process details; it is the only drawing that shows the condenser in scale and that includes supports and maintenance requirements.

Another possibility in the selection of a symbol is to make one—which ordinarily stands for a specific item—represent a class of items. This, however, applies only when distinction between the members of the class is not required. For instance, the gate-valve symbol (Fig. 9) is often used to represent any type of valve for the few times that it is necessary to indicate a valve on a process flowsheet. This is acceptable, because it is rarely necessary to know the type of valve intended in order to understand the concepts of the flowsheet.

Symbols Should Be Simple

A simple uncluttered symbol is not only quicker to draw; it is also more easily understood. Fig. 2 shows various ways a differential-pressure signal transmitter for an orifice plate might be shown on an engineering flowsheet. (On a process flowsheet, the transmitter would be eliminated and only the flow recorder would be shown.) Although it is unlikely that anyone would show this much detail on a flowsheet, it is given here to point out the fact that the commonly used symbol of Fig. 2b is not complete, and that there is no reason for not simplifying the symbol even further, as shown in Fig. 2c.

Where a simplified standard symbol is used (such as Fig. 2c), it should be explained and shown complete with detail, either as a note on the flowsheet or as one of the mechanical design standards.

The enforced use of standards improves communica-

tions in two ways: First, the function being performed is emphasized by eliminating the distraction caused by detail; and second, the possibility of error that is likely to occur when a detail is repeated many times is virtually done away with.

We will not discuss here whether or not antifreeze protection requirements (e.g., for steam and water lines in the northern U.S.) should be shown on the engineering flowsheet or on a separate document. However, if this information is shown on the engineering flowsheet, it should be in the simplest fashion.

Fig. 3 shows several possibilities for a steam flow meter. Two possible mechanical solutions to the problem are shown in Fig. 3a and 3b. Since the selection

(Cont. on p. 156.)

ACCESSORIES SYMBOLS for piping and equipment are used in special-purpose flowsheets—Fig. 11

Basket strainer	Bellows-type expansion joint	Continuous blowdown assembly	Duplex strainer (valve integral)	Exhaust head	Eyewash fountain
Flame arrestor	Flexible hose	Flexible joint	Gage glass	Lifting trap	Line filter
Mixing nozzle	Restriction orifice	Rupture disk, in line	Rupture disk on line or nozzle	Safety shower	Sight flow indicator
Silencer	Separator, steam, oil or water, etc.	Standard steam-trap assembly	Steam or air trap	Tank breather vent (conservation vent)	Temperature connection
				Thief-hole cover	Y-type strainer

Letter symbols used for identifying instruments and instrument components*—Table I

	Measuring Devices				Controlling Devices			Alarm Devices			
Variable	Primary Element	Record- ing	Indicat- ing	Trans- mitter	Record- ing	Indicat- ing	Blind	Record- ing	Indicat- ing	Blind	Control Valves
Analyzers..............	AE	AR	AI	AM	ARC	AIC	AC	ARA	AIA	AA	ACV
Conductivity..........	CE	CR	CI	CM	CRC	CIC	CC	CRA	CIA	CA	CCV
Density...............	DE	DR	DI	DM	DRC	DIC	DC	DRA	DIA	DA	DCV
Flow..................	FE	FR	FI	FM	FRC	FIC	FC	FRA	FIA	FA	FCV
Hydrogen ion..........	pHE	pHR	pHI	pHM	pHRC	pHIC	pHC	pHRA	pHIA	pHA	pHCV
Level.................	LE	LR	LI	LM	LRC	LIC	LC	LRA	LIA	LA	LCV
Moisture (humidity)...	ME	MR	MI	MM	MRC	MIC	MC	MRA	MIA	MA	MCV
Pressure..............	PE	PR	PI	PM	PRC	PIC	PC	PRA	PIA	PA	PCV
Pressure, differential..	DPE	DPR	DPI	DPM	DPRC	DPIC	DPC	DPRA	DPIA	DPA	DPCV
Speed................	SE	SR	SI	SM	SRC	SIC	SC	SRA	SIA	SA	SCV
Viscosity..............	VE	VR	VI	VM	VRC	VIC	VC	VRA	VIA	VA	VCV
Weight...............	WE	WR	WI	WM	WRC	WIC	WC	WRA	WIA	WA	WCV
Special...............	XE	XR	XI	XM	XRC	XIC	XC	XRA	XIA	XA	XCV

Other Symbols

LG	Level-gage glasses	RO	Restriction orifices	SV	Solenoid valves
RV	Relief valves and safety heads	SS	Selector switches	TW	Thermowells

* Expanded version of standard nomenclature of the Instrument Society of America

Nomenclature for various services—Table II

A	Plant air (utility)
B	Brine
BW	Boiler-feed water
C	Catalyst
CW	Cooling water
DW	Distilled water
FG	Fuel gas
FO	Fuel oil
GO	Gland or seal oil
HM	Heating medium
HS	High-pressure steam
IA	Instrument air
LS	Low-pressure steam
MS	Medium-pressure steam
N	Inert gas
PW	Portable (city) water
RW	Refrigerated water
SC	Steam condensate

Sources of standard and other symbols—Table III

For Standard Symbols

Instrument Society of America, 530 William Penn Place, Pittsburgh, Pa. 15219:
RP5.1, Instrumentation Flow Plan Symbols (1944)

USA Standards Institute, 10 East 40th St., New York, N. Y. 10016:
Z32.13-1950, Abbreviations for Use on Drawings
Y32.2-1962, Electrical and Electronics Diagrams, Graphic Symbols for, with Supplement No. 1
Y32.2a-1964, Supplement No. 1 to Y32.2-1962
Y32.4-1955, Plumbing, Graphical Symbols for
Y32.9-1962, Architectural and Electrical Layout Drawings, Graphic Electrical Wiring Symbols for
Y32.10-1967, Fluid Power Diagrams, Graphical Symbols for
Y32.11-1961, Process Flow Diagrams in the Petroleum and Chemical Industries, Graphical Symbols for
Y32.16-1965, Electrical and Electronics Reference Designations
Z32.2.3-1949, (R1953) Pipe Fittings, Valves, and Piping, Graphical Symbols for
Z32.2.4-1949, (R1953) Heating, Ventilating, and Air Conditioning, Graphical Symbols for
Z32.2.6-1950 (R1956) Heat-Power Apparatus, Graphical Symbols for

For Other Symbols

"Special Report 30—Design Manual—Chemical Engineering Process Design Symbols," Dryden, C. E., Parkinson, R. W., and Bigley, P. R., Engineering Experiment Station, Ohio State University, Columbus, Ohio (1961).

"Chemical Engineering Plant Design," Chapter 3, Vilbrandt, F. C., and Dryden, C. E., McGraw-Hill, New York (1959).

Adsorbers	Agitator, turbine	Agitator, propeller	Agitator, anchor	Agitator, scraper (jacketed vessel)	Bagger
Blender, double cone	Blender, ribbon	Blender, roll	Blower	Centrifuge, horizontal basket	Centrifuge, disk
Centrifuge, solid bowl	Centrifuge, vertical	Classifier, air	Classifier, rake	Compressor, centrifugal	Compressor, reciprocating
Compressor, rotary	Condenser, barometric (contact, spray)	Conveyor, bucket	Conveyor, screw	Conveyor, vibrating	Cooling tower
Crusher, gyratory	Crusher, roll	Crystallizer, pachuca	Crystallizer, Oslo	Cyclone	Decanter (with surge chamber)
Drum, horizontal	Drum, with water drawoff	Dryer, batch (shelf)	Dryer, rotary	Dryer, rotary shelf	Dryer, spray
Electrolytic cell, parallel	Electrolytic cell, series	Ejector	Extruder	Feeder, rotary	Filter, bag

Stm=steam ; CW=cooling water ; Cond=condensate   **BASIC SYMBOLS FOR EQUIPMENT** commonly used by the chemical

154

Filter, leaf	Filter, oil bath	Filter press	Filter, rotary	Furnace, arc	Furnace, fired
Flaker	Gas holder	Grinder, ball mill	Heat exchanger, air cooled	Heat exchanger, bayonet	Heat exchanger, kettle
Heat exchanger, shell and tube	Heat exchanger, spray	Hopper	Kettle	Kiln	Kneader
Mist eliminator, brink	Mist eliminator, mesh	Mixer-settler	Montejus (blowing egg)	Prill tower	Pug mill
Pump, centrifugal	Pump, gear	Pump, in line	Pump, proportioning	Pump, reciprocating	Pump, submerged
Scale and truck	Scale and hopper	Screen	Sphere	Stack	Tank, cone-roof
Tank, floating roof	Thickener	Tower, disk and donut	Tower, packed	Tower, tray	Turbine

process industries. References listed in Table III give additional symbols—Fig 12 may depend on the piping configuration—which may not be known at the time of the flowsheet preparation —again, a simple symbol that shows intent rather than method (as in Fig. 3c), solves the problem and improves communication.

Assist the Memory, Emphasize the Important

As with almost every technical communication, in preparing flowsheets it is also highly desirable to help the readers sift the important from the detail. One way of doing this is to eliminate the unimportant by following the above principles; that is, by remaining flexible and keeping the symbols simple.

Where the detail cannot be eliminated, it can be suppressed by using small symbols or light-weight lines.

Since each project requires the use of many symbols, the flowsheet reader cannot concentrate on the message if he is constantly referring to a table of symbols. Memory can be assisted in many ways:

• Use commonly known and accepted symbols wherever possible. (see Table III for a list of sources).

• Have the form of the symbol follow the function of the item. Most check-valve symbols exemplify this; they give an impression of being a strong barrier to reverse flow (Fig. 4a).

• Draw the symbol in a way that approximates the shape of the item it represents. This is particularly useful for data presentation on process flowsheets where the pressure flag resembles a pressure gage, and the temperature flag resembles a glass thermometer (Fig. 4b).

• Use initials from standard nomenclature as part of the symbol. ISA (Instrument Society of America) symbols for instruments use such nomenclature for recorders (Table I); even though a common symbol is used for all the various recorders, they are differentiated by the letters written on them: FR, for flow recorder, PR for pressure recorder, etc. (Fig. 4c).

Move Reader's Eye Forward

Comprehending a flowsheet involves a process of moving from concept to concept, first seeing how each fits into the whole scheme, and then moving ahead to the next concept. Symbols that naturally lead the eye in the direction of the next concept facilitate this movement and free the reader for the more important task of understanding the flowsheet.

Some symbols, such as those for steam turbines and centrifugal compressors, lend themselves to shaping in a fashion that directs eye movement. Fig. 5 shows two ways of depicting a centrifugal compressor. Note how the shaped symbol in Fig. 5b causes the eye to follow a natural path from suction to discharge. In addition, in the course of following the flow through the symbol, the shape itself reinforces the concept of compression.

Apply the following techniques:

• Arrange the symbol to comply with mandatory flow patterns. The rotameter symbol in Fig. 6a, for example, gives as much information as that in Fig. 6b; however, the former disturbs and distracts the knowledgeable reader, because downflow through a rotameter is impossible. There is, in addition, the grave possibility that a careless or ignorant piping draftsman might design the piping to match Fig. 6a, if that symbol is used.

• Orient the symbol to start the eye in the correct direction. Centrifugal-pump symbols can be oriented in four ways that are consistent with general-flowsheet practices (Fig. 7). Each of these orientations starts the eye moving in a definite sector, as shown by the shaded areas. Obviously, another four orientations are possible, if the discharge nozzle is located below the center line; but these orientations are generally avoided, because centrifugal pumps are seldom installed that way, and such unnatural symbols disturb the reader.

Avoid Esthetic Shock

Sometimes it is necessary to have minor violations of the foregoing principles to avoid giving the reader the nagging feeling that something is not quite right. We have seen with rotameters and centrifugal pumps how otherwise-preferable symbols should be avoided because of this.

In other instances, it may be necessary to add useless detail to give the reader a feeling of completeness. The agitator in Fig. 8a gives all the information that is necessary (electric motor drives are assumed if no other drive is shown), yet most flowsheet engineers would find it desirable to add the motor, as in Fig. 8b, to complete the picture.

Fig. 9 shows symbols that can be used for valves; Fig. 10 shows symbols for piping and piping specialties; and Fig. 11 shows piping and equipment accessories. May of these symbols are already commonly accepted, but some are unique. However, any engineer or designer who is acquainted with the items depicted could quickly learn the meaning of all the symbols that are new to a project. Suggested basic symbols for equipment have been grouped together and are given in Fig. 12.

Meet the Author

Russell G. Hill is assistant vice president, project engineering, Scientific Design Co., Inc., 2 Park Ave., New York, N. Y. 10016. His work has included design, project management, and startup of chemical plants. He has a B.Ch.E. degree from Rensselaer Polytechnic Institute, and is a licensed professional engineer in New York. Mr. Hill authored the chapter on Project Engineering and Management in "The Chemical Plant" (Landau, R., ed., Reinhold, 1966), and is a member of AIChE.

Putting Technical Illustrations to Work

Illustrations can be made to function like any other discrete tool, when the engineer learns to use their content to serve the over-all purpose of his technical report.

Relative Ease in Solving the Four Problems for the Presentation of Tables, Figures and Equations — Table I

Type of Illustration	Problem			
	To be correct	To be accurate	To emphasize	To be easy to read
Tables	Easy to do	Relatively simple	Usually difficult and time consuming	Easy to do
Figures	Extensive thought required	Care needs to be taken	Easy	Quite a few simple principles
Equations	Usually a lot of work	Usually easy	Easy	A few simple concepts

DONALD R. WOODS, *McMaster University*

The chemical engineer who is to succeed in the environment of contemporary technology must be able to formulate his technical thinking — his ideas, data and know-how — within the disciplines imposed by the conventional technical report. An essential feature of such technical reports is the illustrations.

However, the choice and design of illustrations for technical reports is rarely treated as a discrete tool which can be mastered as part of the requirements of the profession. Too often, when the design of an illustration is separated from the rest of the thought content, engineers will regard that design as something outside the scope of their interest. Yet technical illustrations are more easily mastered when thus separated. The engineer needs only to identify what the illustration is to do, as well as what it is to say—to identify its primary purpose correctness, accuracy, emphasis, or ease of comprehension.

These four purposes of a technical illustration can usually be accomplished to a greater or lesser degree through one of three general types of illustration— tables, figures, and equations,—depending on the contents of the report, as indicated in Table I. Since the thought-contents are only sometimes suited to the author's purpose, the main effort required in the design of any type of illustration is overcoming its weaknesses. Thus the main effort required for tables is that of incorporating the table into the text for emphasis; for figures it is that of making them accurate and not misleading; and for equations it is that of making them correct and easy to comprehend.

Tables

Tables are perhaps the most useful method of presenting data. They give exact numerical values and are not limited by the number of variables. The development of the digital computer has added a new dimension to the use of tables; data are fed to, and received from, typical computers in tabular rather than graphical form. However, tables do present discontinuous information rather than continuous information, which makes them less suitable to demonstrating those relationships necessary for making a point.

Correctness

It is easy to tabulate correctly. Simply label the rows and columns with name, symbol and units; assign a number and title of the table; and for record tables, include the original data as well as the calculated or corrected results.

Accuracy

It is also relatively simple to make tables that are not misleading: (1) keep the number of significant figures within the uncertainty of the data, (2) report values less than 1.0 with a zero before the decimal, as 0.25; (3) use a consistent set of units; (4) indicate whether the entries are calculated or measured, and (5) avoid expressing very small and very large numbers as powers of 10, which presents confusion as to whether the entries have been multiplied by this factor.

Emphasis

It is frequently difficult to make a table prove a point. In this regard, tables may be classified according to two types: integral and record. Integral tables appear in the body of the report; all data are not necessarily included; and the table is used as supporting evidence for the discussion of the work. Record tables should appear in the appendix and include all data. Whereas integral tables demand a lot of attention, record tables are relatively easy to arrange.

The first step in devising integral tables is to tabulate all of the measured data plus the pertinent calculated information in a record table, which will be appended to the report. This information is then interpreted; trends are noted; a decision is made on the points that the data can be used to support; appropriate data are selected for these points and these data are included in the integral table. This may mean that the record table is divided into small integral tables (or graphs) to prove several points. Also, the same data may appear in more than one integral table, since direct reference should not be made in the body of the report to data reported only in the appendix record table.

Following this approach, tables often illustrate better than a graph, when the percentage error is too small to be shown on a curve. And they may be used to emphasize points by grouping similar items together. Consider, for example, two tables from the body of a report:

How decreased cone angles increase calculated collection numbers in centrifugal-type cyclones — Table ABC

Inside Body Diameter Cm.	Cone Angle Degrees	Collection Number %
60 ± 1%	30 ± 2%	81 ± 2%
	20 ± 2%	90 ± 1.5%
20 ± 0.5%	10 ± 1%	84 ± 3%
	5 ± 1%	93 ± 2%

Effect of increased Reynolds numbers on the flow behavior inside pipes, for water and methanol at 25 C — Table XYZ

Fluid	Observed Flow Pattern	Calculated Reynolds Number
Water	Smooth	830 ± 10%
	Wavy	1780 ± 8%
	Continuous-break	1810 ± 10%
	Diffuse	2100 ± 9%
	Diffuse	2800 ± 7%
Methanol	Smooth	300 ± 12%
	Smooth	700 ± 11%
	Diffuse	2160 ± 10%
	Diffuse	2380 ± 8%

Ease of Comprehension

Follow four rules: (1) put the principal comparison in columns, rather than rows, (2) try to eliminate ditto marks by grouping similar items together, (3) avoid vertical rulings, and (4) try to locate the title caption above the table.

To summarize, tables are most useful in presenting multivariable, discrete information; and they are easily made correct and accurate. They can also be used to prove a point, as integral tables in the body of a report.

Figures

The word "figure" is a general term that includes drawings, sketches, photographs, maps, graphs, histograms, bar charts, pie diagrams, flow diagrams and balance sheets. Some general characteristics shared by all these various types of figures are worth noting. Figures . . .

• work best with specific yet simple titles that tell what is interesting.

• need to be related to the text by a reference number.

• are more effective when placed near the text that refers to them, but never before that text.

• are more conveniently attached as a foldout to the last page of the report when they are referred to repeatedly.

Graphs

The primary function of graphs is to show trends in a set of data; they usually do this more effectively than tables. However, it is often difficult to construct graphs for systems with more than three variables; and unless the search for a trend is an important aspect of the report, it is often best to first try a table for complex systems. Even if the table is not entered directly into the body of the report, its time of preparation is not wasted, for the table then serves as a reference in the appendix.

Correctness: Certain conventions should be observed with respect to graphs. The dependent variable is plotted on the ordinant (y-axis) with the independent variable along the abscissa (x-axis). Both the coordinate axes are clearly shown and carefully labelled with the name of the variable, its symbol, and the units. For reports, the graph is completely identified by the name of its originator and date drawn. (This is particularly important when personnel are shifted from one project to another, since the information may need clarification, and one can then seek out the originator for details.) All the data points are clearly identified; and if there is more than one set of points a code key is used to identify the sets of points. All pertinent data points representing experimental results are included, except perhaps when a calibration line is presented. Finally, no data should appear on the graph, unless they are tabulated in the appendix or otherwise stored for reference.

Accuracy: Graphs are easily misleading. The same variable should not be included on both axes. Dimensionless groups should not be used for only two or three changing variables, unless a note specifies that this has been done. Both ordinate and abscissa are dimensionless, when a dimensionless group is used. In choosing dimensionless groups, the following order of preference is suggested.[5]

1. Those derived from fundamental equations such as Reynolds, Euler, Cauchy, Froude, Weber, Peclet, and Strouhal numbers.
2. Those used as dimensionless methods of expressing experimental data, such as friction factor, drag coefficient, dimensionless, torque coefficient, catalyst effectiveness, dissipation coefficient, Nusselt, Power and Sherwood numbers.
3. Dimensionless combinations of physical properties, such as specific heat ratio, Prandtl and Schmidt numbers.
4. Simple dimensionless ratios, such as particle-to-tube diameters, lengths to distance ratios, density difference to liquid density.
5. Groups derived from combination of other dimensionless groups, such as the Stanton number.

In selecting the important dimensionless groups, the choice among various methods should proceed in the following order of preference.

1. Normalization of fundamental equations, including the equations of change.[1, 2, 3, 4]
2. Similitude of ratios of forces used to indicate the important phenomena.[3, 4]
3. Dimensional analysis.

Different plotting papers can yield misleading results. Linear-linear, logarithmic-linear, logarithmic-logarithmic, isometric, triangular, polar coordinate, linear-probability, logarithmic probability, Cox, Poisson—these are some of the plotting grids available on graph paper. For most applications, linear-linear, logarithmic-linear (semilog) and logarithmic-logarithmic (log-log) graph plots are used. Fig. 2 shows how lines that are straight in one type of plot become curved when replotted in another. Also, uniform error bands on linear-linear plots are no longer uniform for semilog or log-log plots. If a plot is selected so that the line is as near straight as possible, and the slope near unity, equal accuracy is more probable in all regions of the graph.

To select a plotting paper that will not mislead, first plot the data on linear-linear paper. Any relationship that appears among the variables may then be used as a guide to the choice of a more appropriate plot. All too often log-log plots are made first to smooth out variations, and it has been suggested that log-log paper should only be used to find the constants for equations of the form $y = ax^b$, and to present all data clearly on one graph when the data range over several orders of magnitude.[5]

Scattered or "rogue" points that are far removed from a proposed theory or correlation must not be suppressed. Sometimes there is a temptation to discard these data. Sometimes the graph misleads by placing a coordinate axis, title, or an information box so close to the "rogue" data that they are not easily noticed (Fig. 3). Rogue points are very important because they can warn of a correlation that does not accurately describe the data and of other variables that may be significant. Fig. 4a presents a reasonable correspondence between data and theory, with the exception of one rogue point; it contrasts sharply with what a detailed literature search revealed for Fig. 4b.

Also, the correlating line should not extend the range of the data through implication. Nor should trends of the data be exaggerated. The smallest divisions of the plot should approximate the experimental errors.

The zero point tends to aid accurate interpretation

Effects of plotting on curves—Fig. 2

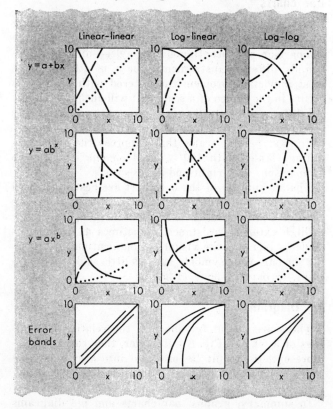

How concealed points mislead—Fig. 3

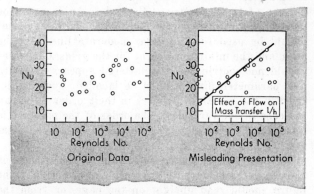

How one rogue point can reveal deviant phenomena—Fig. 4

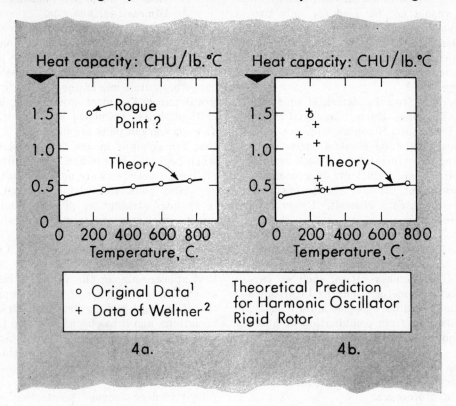

4a.

4b.

and should be shown where practical. Scales should be easily subdivided for accurate interpretation and reading. All the data should refer to the same phenomenon, and when there must be exceptions, care should be taken to point out the differences. Powers of 10 should not be used in the label for an axis. Any factor should be directly associated with a number and not with the units. Finally, the calculated, theoretical, and measured data should be clearly distinguished.

Emphasis: A graph is used for a reader to quickly visualize the relationship among the variables, and it is thus very effective in proving a point. This function of the graph should not be interfered with by too many lines, particularly when some of these lines might duplicate data of an integral table. Data that do not belong to the set should be omitted. Also, when nonarithmetical plotting is used to obtain a straight line, the text should point out the effects of the particular plot.

Ease of Comprehension: Several techniques can be used to improve the appearance of graphs. Heavy lines should be used for the data, moderate lines for the axes, and the minimum weight for the grids. Grid lines should not contribute to a cluttered appearance. Data and parametric lines should be labelled. Symbols defined in the key should reflect in their order either an increase in one variable or the order of the parametric lines. Data points should be indicated by conventional symbols, such as $\bigcirc, \bigtriangledown, \triangle, \square, +, \odot$, and $\times$.

Multicolor figures should be avoided, unless there is a technique for adequately reproducing the colors. The figure should read upright on the page, or from the right-hand side. The graph should be surrounded by a box that excludes explanatory details, scales and captions. And there should be plenty of space.

Bar charts

A bar chart is a simple and useful tool for making one-dimensional comparisons. Its main function is the comparison of discontinuous variables—different compounds, different instruments, years, months, etc. The most important problem encountered with bar charts occurs in the choice of a scale that will adequately show the differences without exaggerating the results. Three common devices that misrepresent in this fashion are (Fig. 5): partial scales that suppress the zero, percentage scales with 100% based on one item in the comparison, and right-and-left sections.

The advantages of the bar chart are best illustrated in Fig. 6, which effectively shows the change in the relative characteristics of meters in going from low to high external resistance. Sometimes an attempt is made to increase the visual communication by replacing the bars with symbols, such as little soldiers, dollar-signs, or bags of flour (Fig. 7).

Pie Diagrams

These are useful for showing the relative percentages of a whole (Fig. 8). However, they can also misrepresent, if the pie is converted into a cylinder and part of the wedge removed, since the wedge does not then represent the correct proportion of the whole.

In summary, graphs, bar charts and pie diagrams

Three bar charts that mislead—Fig. 5

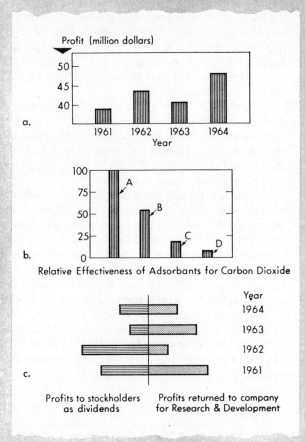

a.

Profit (million dollars)

b.

Relative Effectiveness of Adsorbants for Carbon Dioxide

c.

Profits to stockholders as dividends   Profits returned to company for Research & Development

Correct use of a bar chart—Fig. 6

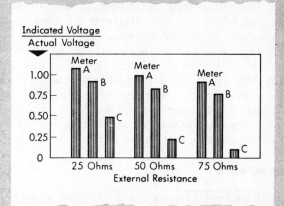

Indicated Voltage / Actual Voltage

External Resistance

How symbols give emphasis—Fig. 7

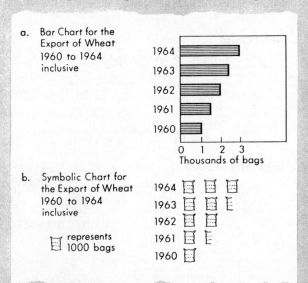

a. Bar Chart for the Export of Wheat 1960 to 1964 inclusive

Thousands of bags

b. Symbolic Chart for the Export of Wheat 1960 to 1964 inclusive

represents 1000 bags

How a pie diagram can mislead—Fig. 8

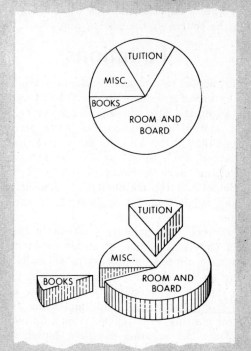

are powerful tools for making a point, but care must be taken to prevent these figures from misleading.

Also there is that class of illustrations called flow diagrams, which will not be discussed here fully. Two classes of flow diagrams are commonly used: Schematic and detailed engineering flow diagrams. Schematic flow diagrams illustrate the general system and its components, without comprehensive details. Detailed engineering flow diagrams show everything necessary for applying the general system to a specific installation. These differences in the amount of detail indicate how and where the flow diagrams are used in communication. Schematic flow diagrams are used in the body of reports like annual reports, company descriptions, etc. Detailed engineering flow diagrams appear with field construction instructions, exhibits to contracts, etc.; they lie intermediate in function between illustration and engineering design drawings; and some companies use detailed engineering flow diagrams to show relative elevations of critical equipment.

Photographs

Although photographs are inconvenient to reproduce in a technical paper, there are times when they become invaluable for lending reality to abstract concepts. Some guiding principles: Unnecessary background should be removed. Some means of identifying scale should be included in the photograph to give the reader an appreciation of size. Use identification labels where possible. Equipment should be photographed from the point of view of its operator or tender. The captions should aid in bringing out the point for emphasis. Interesting features might be identified by arrows or other pointers superimposed on the photograph. And finally, the source of the photograph should be given.

Equations

Experimental results and conclusions are best illustrated by use of graphs or tables. When further calculations using the data are required, however, it is convenient and often necessary to have mathematical equations that fit the data. As far as technical writing is concerned, such equations are valuable for neatly summarizing large amounts of tabulated or plotted data. Sometimes the mathematical form of the equation may suggest useful application or extension of the data.

Correctness: The primary problem in the applications of equations is that of obtaining correct representation. A three-step process is normally used for deriving an equation. First, an expression is evolved, which appears to describe the data—an expression chosen from theory, or found empirically from trial-and-error plotting, or developed from a finite-difference study. Once the equation has been found, values are

assigned to its constants. Five common techniques for assigning constants are the slope-intercept method from a straight-line plot, the selected points method, the method of averages, the method of least squares, and the polynominal fitting method. Finally, the equation is checked for a fit between correlations and the data. Methods of checking are: (1) minimizing residual differences, (2) the Gauss residual, and (3) statistical techniques.

Accuracy: To prevent an equation from being misleading, it should be accompanied by a statement of percentage accuracy and range of application. Final equations are classified as being theoretical, approximate solution, numerical solution, semi-empirical correlation and empirical correlation.

Emphasis: Equations alone do not prove a point without some text to complete them. When the point is simply that the data can be represented by the equation, then standard deviations should be offered as evidence; the equation by itself is not evidence.

Ease of Comprehension: Ensure that the assumptions, initial conditions and boundary conditions are clearly stated for every working equation. Definitions of the symbols should be clearly set forth. Chemical equations or complicated equations describing a phenomenon should be aided by words that identify terms, as for example, the equation of motion in fluid dynamics:

$$\frac{\partial \rho v}{\partial t} = -[\nabla \cdot \rho vv] - [\nabla \cdot \tau] - \nabla p + \rho g$$

$$\underbrace{\qquad\qquad}_{\text{Internal Forces}} \quad \underbrace{\qquad}_{\substack{\text{Surface}\\ \text{Forces}}} \quad \underbrace{\qquad}_{\substack{\text{Body}\\ \text{Forces}}}$$

Finally, the appearance is improved if the report does not end a paragraph or section with an equation. More text should be added, as here.

References

1. Bird, R. B., W. E. Stewart and E. N. Lightfoot, "Transport Phenomena," Wiley, New York (1967).
2. Bird, R. B., W. E. Stewart and E. N. Lightfoot, *Chem. Eng. Prog.* Symposium No. 58, Series Vol. 61 (1965).
3. Johnstone, R. E., and M. W. Thring, "Pilot Plants, Models and Scale-up Methods in Chemical Engineering," McGraw-Hill, Toronto (1957).
4. Kline, S. J., "Similitude and Approximation Theory," McGraw-Hill, Toronto (1965).
5. Rowe, P. N., "The Correlation of Engineering Data," *The Chemical Engineer,* No. 166, p CE 69 (1963).

Meet the Author

Donald R. Woods is an Assistant Professor at McMaster University, Ontario, where he has taught courses in technical communications for several years. Before coming to McMaster, he received his Ph.D. and M.Sc. (1961 and 1958) at the University of Wisconsin. He received his B.Sc. at Queen's University, Kingston; and he is a licensed professional engineer in the Province of Ontario.

PART VI

Communicating Within the Company

Effective Communication: Key to Promotion

Studies have shown that "Ability to Communicate" has long ranked highly as a skill important to advancement. You can make your communications clear, concise, well organized—and the springboard for your next promotion.

NORMAN B. SIGBAND, University of Southern California

Somewhere along the line, the engineer sold himself a bill of goods that "I'm an engineer, an analyst, a guy who understands math and computers—I'm no literary giant!"

But—think a moment—whoever said you had to be?

Of course, you do have to communicate—but being a good communicator is really no more complicated than remembering a few principles and practicing a few ground rules.

But, before we get into these, some of us may need a little convincing that communication really is a key to promotability. For a start, let's look at a *Harvard Business Review* article, based on a survey of U.S. corporations that asked what factors influence managerial promotion.*

Part of the study consists of a listing of personal qualities and their importance in advancement. Of 22 attributes, "Technical Skill Based on Experience," surprisingly, placed fourth from the bottom. Such traits as ambition, maturity, capacity for hard work, ability to make sound decisions, getting things done with and through people, flexibility and self-confidence, all ranked higher. At the top was "Ability to Communicate."

Many other such studies have reached essentially the same conclusion. And engineers who have been working for several years will readily attest to the importance of communications in their jobs.

If your ideas are to reflect credit on yourself, you must communicate them effectively to others. So long as your idea remains in your mind, or on a project sheet in your desk, it will have little value. It must be communicated so it will be understood and accepted if it is to be implemented.

The engineer, or engineering manager, must secure his objectives through people, and it is only through communication that he can motivate other people to help achieve objectives. Research has conclusively revealed that monetary rewards or fear of losing a job are not

*What Helps or Harms Promotability, *Harvard Business Review*, January 1964.

long-term, positive motivators, whereas recognition of achievement and responsibility—in the form of oral and written communications—are. Thus, it is imperative that the engineer be a good communicator.

And in most cases he is!

Communication Is a Complex Function

Perhaps one of the major problems in communication is the speaker or writer's assumption that whenever he talks or writes, he is communicating effectively. And this is understandable, for the communicator (encoder) always knows what he wants to say; and when he says, or writes, it (or thinks he is saying or writing what's in his mind), he reassures himself that he has communicated effectively by asking for a response (feedback), such as,

---

How Not To Get Promoted

Stan T., a petroleum engineer for a large corporation, was recently being considered for promotion to Division Manager. One major point bothered his boss.

"Stan is a brilliant man, but it takes me hours to wade through his reports—oral or written—to figure out what he's trying to say and what his recommendations are. Neither our president nor board chairman has the time, or the inclination, to do that with reports they receive from division managers. They want all staff studies, proposals and reports to be clear and concise, with any recommendations properly substantiated; these are vital to decision-making. Stan's reports don't even come close to these few simple criteria."

The conclusion to this real-life case: Stan was not promoted to division manager, and probably never will be until he has learned to follow his boss' suggestions on report writing.

"Do you understand how that works?" And the listener or reader (the decoder) may reply, "Oh, yes," even if he doesn't understand.

Let's look at a simple communications model and see some of the problems that can arise:

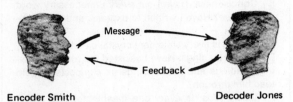

Encoder Smith   **Decoder Jones**

It looks elementary, doesn't it? And that is where the problem lies: the assumption that effective communication is simple.

Smith thinks of an idea; he sends it to his mouth (or to his fingers), where it is verbalized (or written); it goes out into the air; Jones hears it and sends it to his brain, where it is decoded; and then he feeds back a response that Smith (the original encoder) hears.

Problems usually start with the encoder, because the idea that began in his brain is not often the one that comes out of his mouth (or onto his memo pad), for he is frequently heard to comment, "I didn't mean to say that," or "Did I really write that?"

Even if the message is transmitted as intended, there are many possible barriers between encoder and decoder:

Distractions—such as clattering typewriters, pounding punch-presses, disturbing odors, poor ventilation—serve to impede the clear transmission of ideas.

Biases, whether the sender's or receiver's, can be major barriers. How does one communicate when he has already been told, "I don't care what you say; I've been in chemical engineering for 23 years and I just know your idea won't work." Where does one go from here? To attack bias head-on only serves to reinforce it. Perhaps a completely different type of presentation is in order, but the first step is the recognition of the barrier itself.

The *personality* of an individual sometimes drowns out his words and his message. With personality, as with so many barriers, it is vital that one looks at himself as well as the other person.

Word interpretation brings us to the enormous field of semantics and the principle that meanings are not in words but in people! "I need this spec early tomorrow" seems clear enough. But "early" may mean 8:15 a.m. to the chief engineer and 11:00 a.m. to the design engineer. Words make symbols and pictures in people's minds but the representations are often quite dissimilar for the same word.

Competition for the attention of the receiver is a major problem for all of us. We live in a world constantly inundated by words. Words spewed out in conversations, over radios and telephones, in conferences and interviews, at meetings, through records, tapes and projectors. The paper blizzard keeps getting worse. Reports increase, documents proliferate, memos and letters multiply, computer-printout stacks mount higher and higher.

The solution?

There is only one, and it is the same for overcoming

any competition: make a better product! Your reports must be clearer, more concise, yet more complete, if they are to beat out the competition. And the same must be true of your letters, your conference presentations, your interviews and your speeches.

The *emotions* of either the sender or receiver often create communication problems, especially if the atmosphere is charged. Of course, this barrier rarely exists by itself, because personalities, biases, and other obstacles quickly enter into the situation. When, however, emotions are the result of enthusiasm and excitement, they can be positive factors.

Differences in perception or frames of reference can prove to be a barrier. You may look upon Smith's job as vital to the completion of a highly specialized project, but he may see it as a means to a paycheck. To secure an open line of communication, it is not necessary that you agree with his perception, but it is important that you see his point of view and tell him that you do. Once common ground has been established, effective communication may be carried through.

Different levels of knowledge may cause communication breakdowns. Your knowledge may be so thorough that you may be misled by an affirmative response when you ask, "Do you see what I mean?"

Why do so many of us say we understand when we really don't? Perhaps our ego leads us to think we understand when we really don't. The only solution here is for the sender to measure feedback—both oral and written—as carefully as he can.

But let us assume that our message encounters none of these barriers. We must still accept the fact that decoder Jones will see or hear the message and then "filter" it in his brain on the basis of his background, perceptions and desires. And when he feeds back (and so becomes an encoder, and you a decoder), the entire process starts all over again.

Our belief that we are communicating effectively when we talk or write may be real, but it may also be an illusion. So you must first recognize that communication is a complex process. You must keep in mind that effective communication does not take place when you send a message but only when the decoder receives it, when he receives essentially the same message you sent. It isn't the communicator who communicates, but the decoder when he receives.*

Once you accept that you must take care in designing a piece of communication, you will be well on your way to success. You must first plan and present your communication to overcome all, or most, of the barriers within yourself and the decoder, as well as those that may arise between you and him.

Written Communication

What is left now is to observe some mechanics in written communication, person-to-person and person-to-group.

Many of us write easily and quickly. But how effectively do we communicate? We usually won't make an

*Peter Drucker states that, unless the decoder receives, the communicator is only "making noise." See his "What Communication Means," *Management Today*, March 1970.

incorrect assumption of our effectiveness if we appreciate the reader's perceptions and if we apply a few checks, such as:

Is it clear? Reread your report, memo, letter or proposal. Is every sentence so clear it not only will be understood but cannot possibly be misunderstood!

What do you mean by, "If the new formula for the plastic sample is acceptable, send it at once?"

Send what at once? The new formula? The plastic sample? Obviously, if the formula is sent, and the correct choice was the plastic sample, time and money will be lost, and the people involved will be irritated. The fault, of course, lies in the statement's lack of clarity.

A revision to achieve clarity is simple: "If the new formula is acceptable, please send us a sample of the plastic."

Clarity is again lost in, "The engineer told the supervisor about his error." Whose error? The engineer's? The supervisor's? To what does "his" refer? It could just as easily be the engineer as the supervisor. Here again, a little thought will turn a confusing sentence into one that is clear. "The supervisor's error was told to him by the engineer."

"When you encounter a phrase or a sentence in your writing that isn't crystal clear, don't attempt minor surgery by moving a word here, a phrase there. Excise the entire statement mercilessly and rewrite it completely.

Is it complete? Check your piece of writing. Have you recognized and dealt with the problem from every reasonable angle? Have you answered all facets of the inquiry? Have you supplied all the necessary data? Reread your message with a reader's perception; have you answered all the questions asked?

Is it concise? Use your editing pencil with abandon. Cut every extra word or phrase. If you have five paragraphs, cut them to three, but retain your key ideas. If you have ten pages, cut them to five, yet lose none of the gist. Select words that are direct and simple. Keep sentences relatively short. Most important, write to express, not to impress!

Is it reader oriented? Before you write, ask yourself what your reader's interests, perceptions and expectations are, then write to these. Will he be impressed if you tell him your firm was founded 80 years ago, has 5,000 employees, has increased production 50% this year . . . or will he be more interested in how your product will fill his needs, increase his profit, conserve his efforts and please his customers. Selling your idea is very much like selling your product. The old saw still holds true:

> To sell John Smith
>
> What John Smith buys
>
> You must see John Smith
>
> Through John Smith's eyes

Is it well organized? Will your reader feel that he is following a well-planned presentation as he reads? Does every topic follow the preceding one logically? Have you related cause to effect, effect to cause.

Almost no engineering activity is carried through without a plan: a blueprint or set of specifications. So, too, with a piece of writing. An outline is essential, and must be carefully constructed before the task of writing begins.

Does it have reader direction? Assist your reader in every way possible. Begin your report with an overview, clearly identify your sections, and indent and number key points.

Transfer your outline into topic headings, which should be used generously throughout the paper as signposts to assist your reader.

With topic headings and subheadings, you guide him in his reading and thinking. Furthermore, if he is only interested at that moment in your comments on, for instance, "training activities for management personnel," don't force him to read through all the pages to find them. Assist him by using a topic heading for that and every other section.

Be sure your topic headings are also meaningful. There is little value in a heading like "Discussion" (discussion of what?), "Analysis" (analysis of what?). More useful would be a major heading, "Training Activities and Cost, 1972," with subheadings of "Management Training," Supervisory Training," "Hourly Employee Training," "Instructional Techniques," "Training Costs," "Training Facilities," "Training Projected," and "Recommendations."

Lastly, remember that the effectiveness of your communication is important to you because your report frequently becomes the reader's image of you. ■

Everyone Is Busy . . . Especially Your Reader

☐ Use this checklist on your next piece of writing:

☐ **Conciseness:** Have I cut every unnecessary word and phrase? Have I written to express, and not to impress?

☐ **Clarity:** Is every statement crystal clear?

☐ **Topic Headings:** Have I assisted the reader by using headings and subheadings as signposts to help lead him through?

☐ **Visual Aids:** Is every one meaningful and clear? Can I replace three paragraphs of mind-boggling data with one clear table or chart?

☐ **Conclusions:** Do they logically follow from what is presented?

☐ **Recommendations:** Are they specific, brief and thoroughly substantiated?

☐ **Appearance:** Is the report visually attractive? Are margins for notes wide, headings clear, and tables and charts meaningful?

Meet the Author

Norman B. Sigband is a professor of business communication in the Graduate School of Business of the University of Southern California (University Park, Los Angeles, CA 90007). His newest book, "Communications for Management," has already been widely adopted by colleges and universities and in industry. Listed in "Who's Who in American Education," he has received several citations for his teaching and contributions to higher education. In addition to being a teacher and author, he is a widely recognized industrial consultant. He received his Ph.D. from the University of Chicago.

Psychology in Your Communications

The industrial psychologist can offer several useful suggestions for engineers who find that their attempts at written communication within the company are not as successful as they would like them to be.

JAY R. GOULD, *Rensselaer Polytechnic Institute*

Engineers who must write a great deal, and writers who must deal with engineers, could solve many of their communication problems if they would take a few tips from the industrial psychologist.

For here is a professional man whose job it is to figure out how people act in certain situations, how they are motivated and how predictable their responses will be. Yet the industrial psychologist is seldom consulted in communication problems—in situations where engineers must write reports, or communicate with others within their companies, or even edit the writing of other people.

The engineer frequently does not think of himself as a writer, and therefore does not bring to writing projects the knowledge of psychological relationships he ordinarily uses in human relations.

A Lack of Response

Where the engineer, and the technical writer as well, so often falls down is in obtaining the proper response from other people within his own organization. Readers just do not always react the way writers think they should—and the message doesn't get across.

Yet, this challenge in communication can be met and to some extent alleviated if we think of communication as not only the physical act of speaking or writing but also as a problem in psychology and human factors.

Experimental work in industrial psychology has already raised some possibilities for improving the quality and effectiveness of technical and engineering publications. Here are a few examples:

Hostility Breeds Lack of Understanding

The industrial psychologist tells us that if there exists a serious negative relation between the reader and the writer, there is little chance of getting the message across.

As a consultant in industrial writing, I am often asked by engineering firms to help improve the writing of their engineers. For many supervisors, to "improve" means to give a refresher course in English composition—and in many cases, this is the last thing needed. What we so often find is a varying degree of apathy and even hostility existing between the person who is putting out various communications and the person or persons for whom the messages are intended.

In one company, I discovered that rivalry had been whipped up over a possible promotion. Actually, this was ill-founded, for the writer in question was not qualified for the new job and knew it, whereas his reader was. When this fact was pointed out to the second engineer—and his fear of competition had been removed—he became much more responsive to the written instructions and directives he had been receiving from the first man.

A Professional Relationship

Such blocks to communication illustrate an important truth. If you are on poor terms with the person with whom you are trying to communicate, you may have a tough time convincing him of the validity of anything you say or any action you wish him to take.

The industrial psychologist points a way to improvement. If you are having trouble getting the results you want, try to establish more of a professional relationship between you and your reader. Play down personal relationships, use more persuasion, and offer better reasons to get the message across.

A lack of cordial relations between the engineer and his readers within the company should be taken seriously by company supervisors. They should recognize that attitudes are as important as words in the communication process.

Communication Requires Interaction

The industrial psychologist says that the ideal of communication is *interaction*, not action alone.

The engineer writer should develop a sixth sense about his reader. He must possess, or cultivate, enough imagination to be able to put himself in the other person's shoes.

Supplementing this approach should be some method of providing feedback in communication. It is too easy for a person to read a memo or a report and then forget about it. But if certain devices can be used that force him to respond, then the entire communication process can be strengthened. Interaction and feedback can be obtained in various ways:

Stating Objectives

We can get interaction from our readers by first of all stating our objectives and how the things we are describing will benefit them.

A skillful engineer-writer, then, will pay particular attention to introductions in his writing and present his objectives from the point of view of the reader. Try to imagine what the reader wants to know first. Time may be an important factor to him, or the cost to his department, or the number of new employees he must hire. The point is that by aiming at the reader's interest rather than at your own, you will have forced him to interact with you. He may not like what you say, but you will undoubtedly have attracted his attention.

Make Readers Do Something

Interaction can also be achieved by asking your readers to do something actively; in other words, by putting some responsibility on them. This might be in the form of a short questionnaire or an evaluation sheet, or a suggestion that they pick up the telephone and talk the matter over with you.

An experiment in industrial psychology carried out several years ago produced this statement: "Zero feedback is accompanied by low confidence and hostility." A group was asked to perform a task without any questions asked or answers given. The task was accomplished up to a point, but the results were not encouraging. In a follow-up experiment, the group was permitted to ask questions both before and after the writing was performed. A decided improvement in both content and accuracy resulted. Free feedback, then, whether requested or volunteered, will give better results. Any opportunity for involving your readers should be seized.

Needed: Education in Reading

Companies should educate their engineers as *readers* of technical material in addition to educating them as *writers*.

I have yet to see a company training program in which any time was given to teaching employees how to read professional documents, how to interpret and criticize what has been written. Such training would surely result in better interaction by preventing the reader from jumping to conclusions, by showing him

how to pick out the important points in any communication, and by forcing him to appreciate the writer's point of view. Above all, it would force the writer to be on his mettle, if he knew that his statements would be so carefully scrutinized.

These three points of interaction, then, emphasize that industrial communication should not be a one-way road.

The Language of the Group

The engineer-writer should develop a knowledge of group behavior.

According to the industrial psychologist, every group made up of specialists in the same field will act and react according to a behavior pattern set for that field. However, if someone enters that group from another field, he probably will not react with the group but rather as an individual. A well-known communication specialist has another way of saying it: "People learn and retain material better if it conforms to their attitudes, background and training."

To give an example: you may have distributed a set of directions to a group of chemical engineers, and the directions have been well received. But in that group are two or three physicists. From them you may receive a particularly poor response. The reason? Because you are asking the physicists to act and think like chemical engineers.

The Readers' Roles

Similar difficulties may occur with your communications when you attempt to write cover-all messages to be read by engineers, technicians and management people. Such a weakness has been defined as a breakdown in *role expectation*—some of your readers will be irritated because they have not been treated according to the image they have of themselves.

One of the best-known technical writers in the business said this at a conference: "A communicator can probably never convey the exact message he intends. What a burden, then, does he place upon himself when he has little idea of the way his readers will react, either as a group or as individuals."

This knowledge of group psychology is often applied to conferences, case discussions and other situations where the speaker is brought face to face with the group. But how seldom are the lessons of group behavior and role expectation carried over into written communications.

Timing Is of the Essence

Communication is seldom simple. A past president of the Speech Assn. of America points up this complexity by listing these barriers to communication: poor attitudes on the part of both writer and reader; conflict between writer and reader; vagueness in the wording of a message; and timing of the communication.

This last barrier, timing, together with another

one, ambiguity of authority, may constitute another breakdown in communication.

The industrial psychologist says: "The reader may have too many jobs piled on him, that is, too many for him to sort out the messages he receives from other people. Or there may exist too rigid an organizational structure within a company."

A man may not only be a vice president of his company, but sales manager as well. As vice president, he may be interested in corporate ideas along with other administrators. As sales manager, however, his interests may be entirely different as he turns to an outside audience and tries to make it buy his company's product.

When a report or a memo hits his desk, in what capacity is he functioning? Can the message make headway with a man who is far from being single-minded? And just as a salesman must decide the best time to call on a customer, so the memo writer should judge the best time to approach the man who is acting in several capacities. The reader himself should help solve the situation. It's probable that he should delegate some of his responsibilities as a reader to other people who do not have multiple responsibilities.

The psychologist is aware of what happens when a piece of writing is forced to go through too many hands for approval before it reaches its objectives. With many people involved, the lines of communication between the writer and reader become vague and indistinct—and the piece of writing ends up anonymous, improperly motivated, and ambiguous in authority.

Choosing the Right Words

The industrial psychologist also tells us: "The interpretation of every word is affected by the company it keeps."

What he is pointing out is *contextual breakdown*, which comes about through unfamiliarity with words and not recognizing that the reader will interpret such words in his own way unless he is told definitely otherwise.

A recent magazine article described contextual association in everyday terms: "A husband greeted at the door by 'I bought some electric bulbs today' will do more than interpret the statement literally. He understands that he should go to the kitchen and replace a burned-out lamp."

Such free association is good up to a point. But in professional writing it can result in specific meanings being lost. For example, breakdowns can result by the thoughtless use of a word in two contexts in two sentences closely related. Here is a sample: "The lawyer asked for a postponement of the trial because he had not time to prepare his *case*. This was brought out in a *case* study."

Avoiding Inexactness

Here are another couple of sentences that emphasize inexactness of expression: "It is best to start with a *coarse net*, even though a *fine mesh* is the ultimate goal. Successive trials bring the *grid lines* closer and closer together." This writer thought that he was providing exact synonyms when in effect he was providing very inexact ones.

Another engineer wrote, "The macroscopic surface area of a cube of *any bulk material* can be measured by using *devices such as* a micrometer." Because the italicized words are not particularly concrete, the reader is permitted to use his imagination to too great an extent and to indulge in too much contextual association. The remedy, of course, lies in using words in their most limited and denotative sense.

The Effective Industrial Writer

This attempt to point out some of the techniques that can be learned from the psychologist and the communication specialist, confirms the professionalism of the effective industrial writer. Such a writer should possess these qualities, among others:

• An effective writer achieves his purpose in the best possible way. He should know the difference in format demanded by a report, or a manual, or an article.

• An effective writer knows what he is capable of doing. He experiments and learns from other writers and from other specialists who must also deal with people.

• An effective writer tries to get some feedback for his communications. He realizes that writing is by no means a one-way affair.

• An effective writer knows that the actual physical part of setting words to paper is only part of the writing process. He must find out how his readers are motivated and how they will respond to certain situations.

Meet the Author

Jay R. Gould, who helped found the Technical Writers' Institute at Rensselaer Polytech, Troy, N. Y., is now its director. For a number of years, he was in charge of the undergraduate course in technical writing; at present, he is advisor for the graduate program in communication and technical writing that leads to an M.S. He has published several books and articles on technical writing and has acted as a consultant. Next spring, Prof. Gould will conduct a technical writing workshop in Nice, France.

How to Write Better Memos

Company executives and those in other company divisions
get to know you through your memos. Write them right.

HAROLD K. MINTZ, RCA Corp.

Memos—interoffice, intershop, interdepartmental—are the most important medium of in-house communication. This article suggests ways to help you sharpen your memos so that they will more effectively inform, instruct, and sometimes persuade your coworkers.

Memos are informal, versatile, free-wheeling. In-house they go up, down or sideways.* They can even go to customers, suppliers, and other interested outsiders. They can run to ten pages or more, but are mostly one to three pages. (Short memos are preferable. Typed single-space and with double-space between paragraphs, Lincoln's Gettysburg Address easily fits on one page, and the Declaration of Independence on two pages.) They can be issued on a one-shot basis or in a series, on a schedule or anytime at all. They can cover major or minor subjects.

Primary functions of memos encompass, but are not limited to:

- Informing people of a problem or situation.
- Nailing down responsibility for action, and a deadline for it.
- Establishing a file record of decisions, agreements and policies.

Secondary functions include:

- Serving as a basis for formal reports.
- Helping to bring new personnel up-to-date.
- Replacing personal contact with people you cannot get along with. For example, the Shubert brothers, tyrannical titans of the American theatre for 40 years, often refused to talk to each other. They communicated by memo.
- Handling people who ignore your oral directions. Concerning the State Dept., historian Arthur Schlesinger quoted JFK as follows: "I have discovered finally that the best way to deal with State is to send over memos. They can forget phone conversations, but a memorandum is something which, by their system, has to be answered."

Memos can be used to squelch unjustified time-consuming requests. When someone makes what you consider to be an unwarranted demand or request, tell him to put it in a memo—just for the record. This tactic can save you much time.

Organization of the Memo

Memos and letters are almost identical twins. They differ in the following ways: Memos normally remain in-house, memos don't usually need to "hook" the reader's interest, and memos covering a current situation can skip a background treatment.

Overall organization of a memo should ensure that it answer three basic questions concerning its subject:

1. What are the facts?
2. What do they mean?
3. What do we do now?

To supply the answers, a memo needs some or all of the following elements: summary, conclusions and recommendations, introduction, statement of problem, proposed solution, and discussion. Incidentally, these elements make excellent headings to break up the text and guide the readers.

In my opinion, every memo longer than a page should open with a summary, preferably a short paragraph. Thus, recipients can decide in seconds whether they want to read the entire memo.

Two reasons dictate placing the summary at the very beginning. There, of all places, you have the reader's undivided attention. Second, readers want to know, quickly, the meaning or significance of the memo.

Obviously, a summary cannot provide all the facts (Question 1, above) but it should capsule their meaning, and highlight a course of action.

When conclusions and recommendations are not applicable, forget them. When they are, however, you can insert them either right after the abstract or at the end of the memo. Here's one way to decide: If you expect readers to be neutral or favorable toward your conclusions and recommendations, put them up front. If you expect a negative reaction, put them at the end. Then, conceivably, your statement of the problem and your discussion of it may swing readers around to your side by the time they reach the end.

The introduction should give just enough informa-

* We will return to this sentence later.

tion for the readers to be able to understand the statement of the problem and its discussion.

Literary Qualities

A good memo need not be a Pulitzer Prize winner, but it does need to be clear, brief, relevant. LBJ got along poorly with his science adviser, Donald Hornig, because Hornig's memos, according to a White House staffer, "were terribly long and complicated. The President couldn't read through a page or two and understand what Don wanted him to do, so he'd send it out to us and ask us what it was all about. Then we'd put a short cover-memo on top of it and send it back in. The President got mad as hell at long memos that didn't make any sense."

Clarity is paramount. Returning to the asterisked sentence in the second paragraph of the introduction, I could have said: "Memoranda are endowed with the capability of internal perpendicular and lateral deployment." Sheer unadulterated claptrap.

To sum up, be understandable and brief, but not brusque, and get to the point.

Another vitally important trait is a personal, human approach. Remember that your memos reach members of your own organization; that's a common bond worth exploiting. Your memos should provide them with the pertinent information they need (no more and no less) and in the language they understand. Feel free to use people's names, and personal pronouns and adjectives: you-your, we-our, I-mine. Get people into the act; it's they who do the work.

Lastly, a well-written memo should reflect diplomacy or political savvy. More than once, Hornig's memos lighted the fuse of LBJ's temper. One memo, regarded as criticizing James E. Webb (then the head of NASA), LBJ's friend, infuriated the President.

Another example of a politically naive memo made headlines in England three years ago. A hospital superintendent wrote a memo to his staff, recommending that aged and chronically ill patients should not be resuscitated after heart failure. Public reaction exploded so overwhelmingly against the superintendent that shock waves even shook Prime Minister Wilson's cabinet. Result? The Health Ministry torpedoed the recommendation.

Two other courses of action would have been more tactful for the superintendent: make the recommendation orally to his staff or, if he insisted on a memo, stamp it "private" and distribute it accordingly.

Literary style is a nebulous subject, difficult to pin down. Yet if you develop a clear, taut way of writing, you may end up in the same happy predicament as Lawrence of Arabia. He wrote "a violent memorandum" on a British-Arab problem, a memo whose "acidity and force" so impressed the commanding general that he wired it to London. Lawrence noted in his "Seven Pillars of Wisdom" that, "My popularity with the military staff in Egypt, due to the sudden help I had lent . . . was novel and rather amusing.

They began to be polite to me, and to say that I was observant, with a pungent style. . . ."

Format of the Memo

Except for minor variations, the format to be used is standard. The memo dispenses with the addresses, salutations, and complimentary closes used in letters. Although format is a minor matter, it does rate some remarks.

To and From Lines—Names and departments are enough.

Subject—Capture its essence in ten words or less. Any subject that drones on for three or four lines may confuse or irritate readers.

Distribution—Send the memo only to people involved or interested in the subject matter. If they number less than say, ten, list them alphabetically on page 1; if more than ten, put them at the end.

Text—Use applicable headings listed after the three questions under *"Organization."*

Paragraphs—If numbering or lettering them helps in any way, do it.

Line Spacing—Single space within paragraphs, and double space between.

Underlines and Capitals—Used sparingly, they emphasize important points.

Number of Pages—Some companies impose a one-page limit, but it's an impractical restriction because some subjects just won't fit on one page. As a result, the half-baked memo requires a second or third memo to beef it up.

Figures and Tables—Use them; they'll enhance the impact of your memos.

Conclusion

Two cautions are appropriate. First, avoid writing memos that baffle people, like the one that Henry Luce once sent to an editor of *Time*. "There are only 30,000,000 sheep in the U.S.A.—same as 100 years ago. What does this prove? Answer???"

Second, avoid memo-itis," the tendency to dash off memos at the drop of a pen, especially to the boss. In his book, "With Kennedy," Pierre Salinger observed that "a constant stream of memoranda" from Professor Arthur Schlesinger caused JFK to be "impatient with their length and frequency."

Meet the Author

Harold K. Mintz is Senior Technical Editor, RCA Corp., P.O. Box 588, Burlington, Mass. 01801. He has worked in publications since 1956 but at this stage of his career, he would prefer full time university teaching and free-lance writing. He has a B.S. in economics from Tufts College, Medford, Mass., and and M.S. in journalism from Boston University (where he now teaches English and engineering writing, part-time). He is a member of the American Business Communication Association.

Writing Appropriation Requests

These guidelines apply to engineers requesting funds for any worth-while project.

W. J. DODGE, *Socony Mobil Oil Co.*

What is an appropriation request? Is it a form to be filled out? Is it a sales pitch? Is it a statement of facts? Is it a summation of alternatives? Is it a demonstration of persuasive writing?

The answer is yes. It is all of these. Yet, it is easy to compose if you know the facts, have examined the alternatives, have arrived at a conclusion—and know how to present them.

Almost every company has a standard form, accompanied by a written procedure explaining how to fill it out. Some forms are better than others. No doubt each has been established by the controller's department and contains a spot for each bit of information that is considered necessary for accounting and record purposes. It is not this form that we wish to discuss but rather the requirements for an effective over-all presentation.

Consider Your Reader

In preparing this presentation, you are convinced that the appropriation should be approved. You have made thorough studies, examined all of the details and are sure that your recommendation is the right one. In conveying this information to those who must make the final decision, you must put yourself in their shoes. If, for example, you were a member of the Board of Directors, what would you want to know about the project? This mental transformation sounds elementary. Yet it is one of the keys to preparing a good presentation—or to good salesmanship, for they are much akin.

You are asking your management to make an investment, whether it be ten thousand dollars or ten million. If it were your money that was being spent, you would want to know the alternatives available, the risk involved, what the consequences would be if things went wrong, and what the profit would be if they went right.

Furthermore, you are busy. You do not want to search through unnecessary details, yet you want them available if needed. You want the information clearly stated and easily understood (you have enough complicated and ambiguous material to wade through during the day).

Having these thoughts clearly in mind, let us prepare a presentation to meet those requirements.

The Outline

Hanging on the wall in the office of a colleague of mine is a plaque that reads as follows:

"In any oral or written communication intended to sell or inform:
- State the purpose of the exercise.
- Give some background to set the stage.
- Explain the alternatives considered.
- Isolate and support the alternatives selected.
- Describe the next action to be taken or being recommended."

In organizing a presentation, I know of no better outline that can be prepared. In fact, as the heading indicates, the outline can be used for any exposition prepared to convince the reader and get your ideas across.

The "purpose" should always include the benefits the reader may expect. Never keep the reader in suspense as to what these benefits are or he may not read far enough to find out. To illustrate how this outline can be effective in even a five sentence presentation, consider the following:

Purpose: "The cost engineering section is requesting two additional desk calculators to improve its efficiency." (Note that the second part of this sentence contains the benefits.).

Background "Due to staff increases, it is now necessary to shift calculators from one office to another, causing delays and waste of an estimated 7 man-hours worth $70 per month."

Alternatives: "A survey was made to determine whether calculators could be released from other sections."

Alternative Selected: "No calculator being available, we will need to purchase new ones if we are to have maximum efficiency."

Recommendation: "We therefore recommend that an expenditure of $2,000 be approved for this purpose."

Expanding the Outline

Adopting this five-step outline to the preparation of a more-complex appropriation request, you may expand your outline somewhat as follows, with each of the subheadings further broken down as necessary:

1. Purpose.
2. Background.
3. Alternatives considered:
   A. Description of alternatives.
   B. Relative costs.
   C. Economic comparisons.
   D. Intangible differences.
4. Alternative selected:
   A. Project definition.
   B. Project plan.
   C. Investment cost.
   D. Economics.
   E. Effect of project variables.
5. Recommendation.
6. Appendix.

In the preparation of your outline, list at random all of the subjects you wish to cover. Then arrange them as subheadings under one of the five major headings of the outline. You will find that they will all fit appropriately under one or another.

In writing the report around this outline, continuously keep the reader in mind. Supply the answers to those questions that are apt to arise in his mind, but do not include explanations merely because you know them. Many presentations lose effectiveness by including too much; it is often better to relegate some of the borderline material to the appendix. Sometimes, one need merely state that certain data are available in the files if they are needed. Like cost estimates themselves, reports and papers are more apt to over-run than under-run.

The Summary

Every presentation or report more than two or three pages long should contain a summary. This should be composed with great care, since it may be the only portion read by some of the top executives. It should follow exactly the same outline as the presentation itself.

Many report writers prefer to insert the summary right after the "purpose" section. If this sequence is followed, the summary, of course, will not need to repeat the purpose. Most writers find it easiest to prepare the summary last, even though it precedes the presentation when assembled.

To save space, most of the illustrative examples that follow will be extracts from typical summaries rather than from the full reports.

Section 1: Purpose

This section will cover in words many of the items that appear on the company's standard request form. It introduces the reader to the magnitude and location of the proposed investment, and the subjects to be discussed in justification of it. For example:

This appropriation request is for the installation of a new 80,000-lb./hr. waste-heat boiler, to be erected in the catalytic cracking area of the Richmond refinery. The estimated cost is $600,000. A rate of return of 14% discounted cash flow and a three-year payout after taxes are expected to result.

This presentation, submitted in support of the above request, covers background, steam requirements, alternates considered, description, timetable, and economic justification for the project.

Section 2: Background

In this next section, a summary is given of what has happened in the past, leading to the presentation of the appropriation request. Although some of your readers are already aware of the background, it must be repeated for any who are not. It also serves to refresh the memory of the others, and to get this information into the record. The extent of detail to be included needs careful consideration. On a large proj-

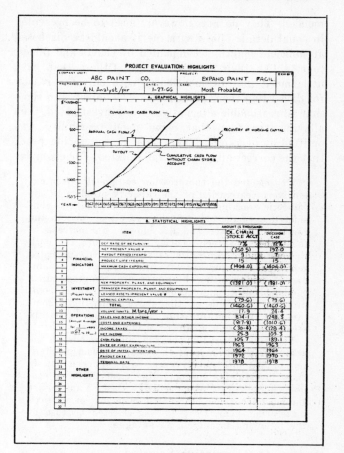

This form summarizes the highlights of a project evaluation, and helps justify the alternative selected.

ect, much may have happened in the past. Only by placing yourself in the position of the reader can you properly assess what he will want to know of this background. For example:

This company recently acquired the XYZ Soap Corp. in order to participate in the anticipated rapid growth of the biodegradable detergent industry. Our aim was to make profitable use of the skills and know-how this acquisition afforded, and to establish an additional outlet for our products, as raw materials for the detergent industry. To achieve this aim, we have evolved a broad development strategy in which the Midwest, with its dynamic industrial and agricultural economy, is the key area.

Recent surveys reported to you show the following situation in the Midwest:

1. Detergent consumption is large and increasing rapidly.

2. A new producer could find room because current production facilities are uneconomic or likely to become so, and there is an existing or anticipated production short-fall.

3. We have an established nucleus around which a strong marketing organization can be built.

As agreed in the Board of Directors meeting of Aug. 17, 1965, we have developed a concrete proposal by which the outlined aims can be implemented.

Section 3: Alternatives Considered

In this third section, all of the alternates that were considered are discussed, including the one recommended. They do not, however, need to be presented in equal detail. Those with merit should be discussed at sufficient length, accompanied by charts and tables, to establish their relative values. Others that have little merit may be mentioned, with only the reason for discarding them being given. The object is to show that all reasonable alternatives were investigated, thus allaying the fear that some good possibility was omitted by oversight. There must be convincing proof that the correct alternative was selected. For example:

> We selected the compression equipment after extensive investigation of the capacity problem in the catalytic cracking area. Among the possibilities considered were the electrification of either or both the combustion blower and lift blower, an increase in the number of reciprocating compressors for both the low- and high-pressure stages, a low-pressure centrifugal compressor with an increase in the number of reciprocating high-pressure compressors, a combined first- and second-stage centrifugal compressor, operation of the above centrifugal compressors by backpressure steam, mixed-pressure steam, condensing steam or electric drives.
> There are over 100 possible combinations of the above. With the help of the local engineering staff, ten of the most likely cases were worked out to show investments and operating costs. Relative economics are shown in Appendix II. Cases 9 and 10 are the most favorable, both having a payout of approximately one year. Case 10 was selected because of the following intangible advantages: . . .

Section 4: Alternative Selected

This section goes into greater detail in explaining the proposed project. After defining the scope of the job, and its limitations, the section discusses project timing, including the expected date of completion. The project cost is given, with an indication of its degree of accuracy, and a reference to a breakdown by major components contained in the appendix. The other assumptions used in making the economic evaluation are also described, i.e., raw-material, operating and maintenance costs, product prices, sales volume, etc., also with references to appendix material. Each assumption must be qualified to indicate the degree of confidence attached to it.

The economic evaluation of the project follows, indicating the payout, rate of return, present worth or other criteria of profitability. These must then be qualified by tables or curves, included here or in the appendix, showing the sensitivity of the economics to changes occurring in any of the assumed values. Where a high degree of sophistication is practiced, these changes may, in turn, be assigned probabilities, and the resultant over-all probabilities stated.

An excellent form for summarizing the project evaluation highlights is illustrated on the previous page.

Section 5: Recommendation

The recommendation is normally the shortest but most forceful section of the presentation. A typical example is:

> Modernization of the Alabama plant presents an opportunity for the company to invest $13 million in a project expected to yield a 21% discounted cash flow rate of return. All significant technical problems have been resolved. We recommend that the appropriation be approved.

The recommendation portion of the appropriations request is generally followed by the Appendix; this presents the detailed data that may be needed to support statements made in previous sections.

Physical Form

Although the physical appearance of a presentation does not necessarily reflect the quality of the contents, it does have a psychological effect on the reader. A workmanlike appearance implies a workmanlike job, whereas a sloppy appearance may give a good presentation a bad start.

Letter-size paper ($8\frac{1}{2} \times 11$ in.) should be used. Allow ample margin on the left for binding (at least $1\frac{1}{4}$ in.). It is most annoying if part of the typing is concealed in binding. Double spacing is preferred; not only is it easier to read, but it permits the reader to jot down notes as he studies the contents. Tabulations may, of course, be single-spaced to conserve room.

Except in a short presentation on a minor project, a cover is recommended. When in doubt, favor its use, because it adds to the report's prestige. Most companies have one or more standard cover designs, some of which are quite elaborate. Often the more elaborate ones are used for external distribution. The author should determine the appropriate quality of cover, erring, if at all, in favor of the better one. The cover should always have the title, date, and name of the originating organization imprinted on it.

Short presentations may begin on the first page inside the cover. This page should have a heading repeating the information given on the cover.

In long presentations (approximately eight pages or more), the first page should be a title page, and should have a table of contents immediately following. In very long presentations, section dividers with appropriate tabs are desirable, to permit quick location of the sections.

If the body of the presentation is to contain frequent references to tables or graphs, they should be located in the handiest place—for instance, within the appropriate page of the text, or as a separate page immediately following the reference. Or they can be bound on the right side of the sheet and placed opposite the printed copy.

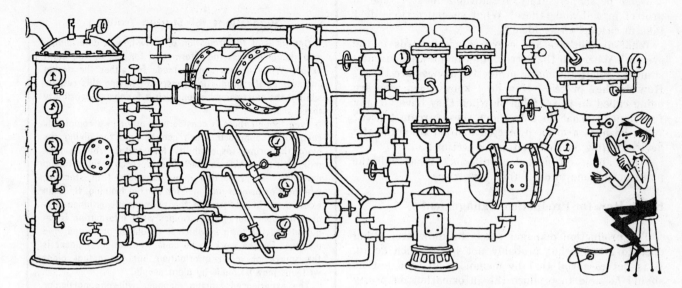

Even a brilliant engineering feat may prove a commercial disappointment unless you . . .

Communicate Your Designs

This article is addressed to the engineer who has been involved in the design of a process unit and who has an interest in helping a plant organization get that unit on stream. Operating and maintenance engineers should find it stimulating.

R. D. HULTGREN, *Procter & Gamble Co.*

Your "baby"—the process unit that you have helped to design—is being entrusted to its permanent guardians. How will it fare in their hands? Will it achieve its potential?

Obviously part of the answer depends on the quality of your design and on the competency of the production and maintenance people. But there is a third important factor; it involves the transition of know-how across the design-operation interface. For a successful transition, everyone in plant operations and maintenance who will be concerned with the equipment must learn enough about it to do his particular job properly —knowing what to do, when to do it, as well as what not to do.

You, as design engineer, are the prime source for much of this equipment information. The design organization can significantly help the operating organization take over the process and master it.

Mastery occurs when improvements and refinements in operation and in hardware are routine experiences

The ideas expressed in this article are the author's and do not necessarily reflect the policies of Procter & Gamble Co.

for the production people. It also implies a situation where the profit potential of your design is being maximized. The alternative is wasteful indeed, as we shall see.

The Needs of the Production Operator

While the organizational structure may vary from company to company, the needs of the different types of operating people tend to fall into a rather general pattern.

For a start, let's see what the production operator needs to know about the equipment in order to do his job. His requirements might read something like this: What are the pieces of equipment that I must work with? What does each piece do? How does its operation relate to the rest of the equipment?

What do I have to do to each piece of equipment to start it, to shut it down for short periods, to restart it, to shut it down for long periods, to adjust its performance? How can I tell whether it is doing what it is supposed to? How far can performance deteriorate before I should take corrective action? What do I do when the equipment doesn't seem to be running properly and I can't correct it? What are the limits of its performance, and how can I tell when they are reached?

Where are the controls and indicators? What does each one do? What can it tell me? What does it say. normally? How much do I adjust it, to get a desired change? How does this feel? Sound? Look? What adjustments and valves should not be used? Why? How can I tell whether the controls are set where they should be?

What are the cleanouts required? When? How? What lubrication is required? When? How? By whom?

175

What personnel safety precautions must I take to protect myself and others? What special actions do I take in case of an accident?

What are the fire and overpressure hazards in the system? Where do they occur, and under what circumstances? What automatic protective devices are there? How do they protect? How do I know when they are being called on to function or when they have already functioned? What do I do under these circumstances? What hazards are not protected against by automatic devices? How do I effect this protection?

What about off-normal conditions? What will the plant permit me to do if the need arises?

Know-How for Production Management

The production manager needs to know everything operators know, but probably not in as much detail. It is not essential that he memorize all this, but he should be able to produce the information on pretty short notice. In addition, the department manager needs to know:

How can I get more capacity from the unit? Where are my bottlenecks? What are the approximate dollar and time costs to remove them? How can I figure out methods for operating in ways that were not in the original design?

What are the downtime and cost consequences if I decide I must maintain production and run her till she busts?

Where are my probable high-deterioration spots? What provision has been made for rapid, economical correction at these points?

Know-How for the Maintenance Mechanic

The maintenance mechanic needs to know some of the rudiments of operation. In addition, for each system and piece of hardware, he needs to know:

What is proper performance? How do I test for it? What do I do if performance is not normal? How do I adjust what? How do I take the equipment apart? What special tools do I need? What should I expect to see inside? What do I repair and what must I completely replace? How do I reassemble?

What must I order to get a part that looks like this? What are the material specifications? How can I get production back on stream quickly?

Know-How for the Maintenance Manager

The maintenance manager, like the production manager, needs to know all that his mechanics know (with the same provision as to the speed and detail in producing the information). In addition, he should know:

Is the equipment being asked to perform beyond its design capabilities? How can I test to determine this? Do I have any equipment I can transfer from non-critical service, in times of emergency, to restore production? What equipment substitutions can I make under these circumstances? What are the cost and time consequences of doing this?

Suggestions for Startup Training

One facet of the transition of know-how is determining who should process the information for use by the plant people. While a case can be made for either the design engineer or the production supervisor having this responsibility, the most common approach is for the responsibility to be shared.

Even though there is considerable merit in a completely cooperative approach, much can be said for giving the plant the prime responsibility for startup training (i.e., making it the senior partner). One approach is the "startup manager"—a production man, experienced in startups, who acts as project manager for startup training. He is an extra man, in addition to the permanently-assigned production supervisor. He determines what information is required and the form in which it should be presented, and arranges for the work to be done. The design engineer is the source of much information but the actual plant writeups may be made by plant people.

The experienced startup manager will pay particular attention to the training of maintenance people, and to the preparation of their "reference information" package. This is an area often neglected in startup training. The plant cannot be started up without trained production people but this does not hold true for the maintenance people. Design people and construction people usually are on hand and can handle minor maintenance work along with their normal debugging duties.

Unless care is taken to insure that the maintenance people have the opportunity to learn during the startup period, they will have to do their learning in breakdown situations, six to eighteen months after startup.

One good approach to maintenance training is to have the maintenance organization contribute the bulk of the manpower required for pre-startup checkout of equipment. Here they act as assistants to the design engineer. They help him determine whether the installation conforms to his design. This gives them an opportunity to work on the hardware, and to quiz the expert. Experienced maintenance people welcome such an opportunity and will really try to exploit it.

The Designer as Educator

Having covered who-needs-what in the way of specific information, we now come to the question of who should do the informing.

While most of the operating requirements will have to come from the process development people, most of the equipment information will have to come from you, the designer. If you want your design to achieve its goals, you must do a good job of information dissemination, and this may require your enthusiastic participation in pre-startup training.

A good job is the one that will enable reasonably qualified and properly motivated plant people to run the equipment in such a way as to maximize profits today and over the years.

"Profits today" implies that the startup will be

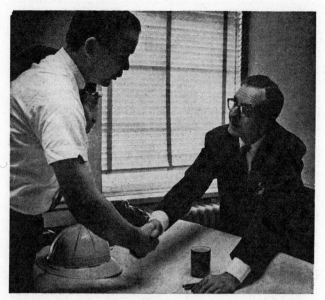

Everything may seem pretty simple to the production man during the calm, pre-startup days . . .

But when the production pressure is on, will he be able to remember all you told him?

smooth and rapid, and that design capacity and efficiency will be reached, and hopefully exceeded, in short order. No matter how good, your design will make profits today only if it is used intelligently and energetically by the plant organization. So this means training.

"Profits over the years" implies two important things: (1) that the production department will be able to maintain indefinitely, or improve, its skill in operating the process, even with changes in personnel and (2) that the plant will be able to avoid equipment abuse and, at the same time, detect and correct deterioration in the performance of the equipment.

What does "profits over the years" have to do with you? The plants can take care of that, can't they?

Usually, but not always. On too many occasions, equipment design experts have visited a plant several years after startup and have noted evidence of slipping profits. Production efficiencies and rates have slipped, and the designer's brainchild has been flagrantly abused.

So what? Isn't this still a simple problem of a crackdown by plant management? After all, the design engineer was the one who detected the situation; what more is there for him to do, other than to urge the plant management to get going?

Here the picture begins to get fuzzy. The answer to these questions must be qualified. And it goes something like this: Yes, this *is* a plant responsibility, and the profits can be restored by the plant management, provided (and here's the qualification) that, in turning over your design to the plant you delivered the means of maintaining the high level of training and qualification over the years.

Before going further, let's examine what has happened over the years since startup. When you revisit, you find that almost all of the people are new. Moreover, your few remaining startup pupils seem to have

forgotten some of your carefully-implanted teaching.

Musical-chair type of personnel changes represent a long-established way of life in plant operations. In the absence of formal qualification standards and written training materials, the plant may have had to use the "each one to teach one" process when bringing in replacements. In this form of communication, the average receiving and retransmit efficiency are each about 90%. This means, unfortunately, that as few as three replacements can produce a qualification as low as 49%:

	Cumulative Percentages	
	He Learns	He Teaches
Pre-startup instructor	——	100%
Pre-startup trainee	90%	81%
First replacement trainee.................	73%	66%
Second replacement trainee..............	60%	54%
Third replacement trainee...............	49%	etc.

But what about your start pupil, the production manager, who has been on the job since startup but doesn't seem to be nearly as sharp as he was? Here's what may have happened:

When you were training him before startup, his main job was to get trained, and he was eager. He listened intently to your pearls of wisdom, and seemed to follow with great understanding, your lucid explanations of the flowsheets and drawings. He could answer your probing questions with ease, alacrity and precision.

The situation now is a little different. Here he is, trying to get out production, and yet handle the myriad things that his boss and a host of staff people have thought up for him. The zone industrial engineer has just asked him why his wage performance six weeks ago was 2% less than it was in the same period in 1962, the utility man has just dumped $10,000 worth of good stock down the sewer, the plant manager's meeting started ten minutes ago—and here comes that bright-eyed college kid whom he's supposed to give a recruiting pitch to! . . .

It is reasonable to expect the production manager to show the same "ease, alacrity and precision" that you drummed into him ages ago by much efficient explanation and arm-waving?

So, perhaps the "How?" of pre-startup training needs a close examination. We can conclude that informal, undocumented training at startup (done by you) does well then but that when this is done by plant people later on it is done very poorly. In addition, we can conclude that memory can cope with only so much, and that easy-to-use reference information is a practical necessity.

Material for Pre-Startup Training

What can be done about this? Somehow you must provide the plant with material that it can use with good effectiveness long after you have departed. And you might as well do it when developing the pre-startup training. Then you can use it for training and then pass it on to the plant.

Here are some pointers for developing reusable training material:

1. Put it in writing. And remember that a piece of paper can't wave its arms to drive in a point. So, don't just outline—create a document that will do the full job of teaching.

2. Say it in plant terms. This means tell the pupil, in full detail, what he is supposed to do or not to do, and when. Remember—plant people are busy and are not as interested as you in getting a deep understanding of principles of operation. They want to *do*, not reflect on principles.

3. Provide a management yardstick. Prepare a performance-type technical qualification exam for each job. Cover all the aspects you can think of. This gives the plant management an absolute standard against which it can measure the readiness of a trainee to take over his job. Better include the answers, too, in case the teacher has lost some of his know-how.

4. Recognize that there is a difference between design information and the information a plant needs to operate and maintain a system. Be sure to meet the plant needs.

A design package is very complex, and necessarily so. This is because you must tell other people what to buy, where to put it in reference to buildings and equipment that do not yet exist, and how to hook it up. This requires models, engineering flowsheets, assembly drawings, and so on—to such an extent that

the non-specialist sometimes marvels at how anyone can make his way through the mountain of information.

The plant has little need for most of the design package. The system exists. It has all been put together and checked out. Except for system schematic drawings, and occasionally a specification or two, there is not much in the design package that the operating people require. If the whole undigested mass is turned over to the plant, this provides much "static" in the process of communicating the essential information.

Earlier, we discussed the type of information that is needed by various types of plant people. Providing them with this material can sometimes be done by working smarter, not harder. More often, however, extra effort is needed. While the costs of this effort may seem considerable at pre-startup time, they pale into insignificance when compared with the benefits that will accrue from them not only at startup but over the years.

Therefore, don't regard information processing and dissemination, or participation in startup training programs, as a marginal or extra pursuit. Look on it as part of your job as design engineer. Sound engineering judgment, imagination and enthusiasm are as important here as in any other phase of design work.

A Concluding Perspective

The division of responsibilities for process development, plant design and plant operations varies widely in industry today, both at corporate and plant levels. This may affect the degree to which the design engineer participates in the actual preparation of operating manuals, the conducting of pre-startup training, and the processing of design information for reference use in the plant. However, the design department can never separate itself entirely from these functions, since it is the primary source for so much information about the hardware of a process.

Meet the Author

Ralph D. Hultgren is currently on special assignment in the production engineering department of Procter & Gamble Co.'s Engineering Div., Ivorydale Technical Center, Cincinnati. Since joining P&G in 1941, his work has involved him in the design of electrical control systems and instrumentation, as well as in engineering administration and, particularly, technical training.

An electrical engineering graduate of Purdue University, he is a registered professional engineer in Ohio.

Communications Between Maintenance, Design and Production

The systematic interchange of ideas and experience between maintenance, design and production, or between parallel groups at different plants, can bring some very tangible benefits. Pennsalt uses a six-point approach to maximize these benefits.

JAMES W. TRACHT, *Pennsalt Chemicals Corp.*

Waste of information can be just as costly as waste of materials or man-hours.

Consider this example, which involved specifications for a new installation:

The material chosen for the pipe-joint gasketing was claimed to withstand the corrosive and very hazardous chemical being handled. Unfortunately the claims were not borne out; numerous leaks developed. A substitute gasketing material was installed by the plant maintenance group, and it proved to be satisfactory. This change was never referred back to the design group.

Several years later, an expansion of this facility was undertaken. Not knowing that the original gasketing material had proved defective, the design group again specified it. Fortunately the error was detected prior to startup, but all of the piping had to be dismantled and the proper gasketing material inserted, at considerable expense and some delay.

This is but one instance of what happens when information that is known to someone within an organization goes to waste instead of being disseminated. Other examples could involve operating as well as maintenance information, and the improvement of existing facilities as well as the design of new ones.

Our Company's Approach

I would like to describe how our company has attempted to meet these problems. To help orient your thinking, the Pennsalt Chemicals Corp. employs a total of 3,500 people in 18 chemical plants coast-to-coast. The plants range in size from one that has a 200-man maintenance department to several plants that have just a small group of maintenance men.

The central engineering department does all of the design engineering for most of the plants, participates in their major construction projects, and handles all construction work at new plantsites. A maintenance section is part of the central engineering department.

There are six facets to our efforts at improved communications:

1. Cooperation (without splintering the responsi-

bility) between maintenance, design and production in solving repetitive-repair problems in existing facilities.

2. Indoctrination and training in the needs of maintenance and operations among the group responsible for the design of new facilities.

3. Provision of design checklists and construction standards.

4. Reviews of plant designs by maintenance personnel.

5. Review of the initial operating and maintenance experience of a new process.

6. Inter- and intraplant dissemination of maintenance information through an internal publication ("Maintenance Engineering News"), and through company-wide meetings.

Problems in Existing Facilities

In existing installations, the maintenance engineering group at the plant is the key to corrective action. It studies the areas of high maintenance costs, with particular emphasis on those involving repetitive repairs. This approach, of course, requires a cost system that permits identification of the troublesome areas; such a cost system is mandatory in every successful maintenance operation.

When a problem area is detected, a maintenance engineer is assigned to investigate. He consults with design, operating and maintenance people to obtain the complete background on the problem. A solution is then proposed for consideration. When approval is obtained, the corrective action is formalized by the same maintenance engineer. Working with the plant engineering design group, the project is designed, specifications are established, and a cost estimate is prepared. Justification of the project is also stated. Depending upon the expenditure involved, formal approval through the appropriation-request procedure may be required.

Having received this approval, the maintenance engineer follows the project to completion. After a period of operation, usually six months, he analyzes operations to date and submits a performance report for comparison with the claims made when the project was proposed. The case histories of such projects, successful or unsuccessful, may be recorded in the "Maintenance Engineering News," to be discussed later.

We stress the importance of responsibility resting in one individual, from the original analysis of the problem to successful completion of the corrective action.

Proposed Construction

Where construction is still in the design state, we have the opportunity to apply the benefits of maintenance experience in full.

First, as regards personnel, our construction projects are headed by a project manager, who is the key man on the job and therefore necessarily the key man

in the communication of maintenance problems back to the designers. He has been trained to keep maintenance constantly in mind while the project is being designed.

This applies also to the design-group engineers and draftsmen assigned to the project. These men, at the first opportunity after joining Pennsalt, are provided actual experience on construction work in the field, by serving as engineering assistants during actual construction. Even more important, they participate during startup operations, which is the period when most design problems are first encountered. When transferred back to the central design group, these men bring with them a good appreciation of maintenance and operating problems, and we find that this remains with them.

The project manager is actively associated with, and preferably in charge of, the startup operations, including maintenance. In this way, responsibility for design, initial operation and maintenance are grouped within the control of one individual, which greatly improves the probability of successful feedback of maintenance experience.

Design Checklists and Construction Standards

General checklists for review of designs from a maintenance standpoint are provided to the designers and draftsmen. These include such reminders as: Is proper access for maintenance work provided? Are provisions for rigging facilities required? Are materials of construction suitable, based on all the information that is available?

In addition, standards for construction are used where these can be justified. These standards are particularly useful in helping bridge the gap resulting from changes in personnel. Much maintenance and production experience can be built into these standards, and thus made a matter of record.

Reviews of Design by Maintenance

In handling new construction, we have already discussed the importance of indoctrinating personnel employed in the design of the project—from the project manager to the draftsman—in the importance of the maintenance function. As the design progresses, general-arrangement drawings, equipment specifications and material selections are reviewed by maintenance supervision and maintenance engineers, to insure that design for effective low-cost maintenance has been taken into consideration.

This review begins in the early stages of design and is particularly useful in avoiding the use of equipment or designs with poor maintenance records. The maintenance engineers and supervisors, in effect, look over the shoulder of the designers for this purpose.

Supervision of Construction

Close supervision of construction is maintained to see that the design is followed and that good work-

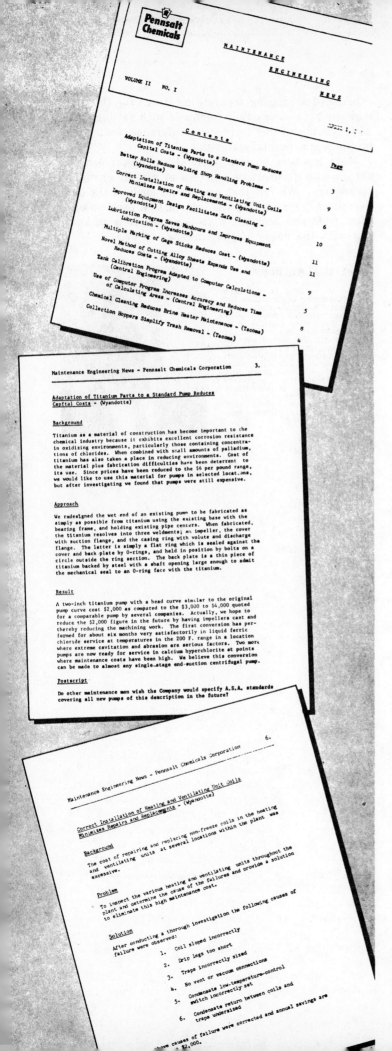

manship is practiced. The importance of this cannot be overstressed, as the best design can be substantially weakened if good construction practice is not used. Where design or layout changes are made in the field, careful records of as-built conditions are kept. This is particularly important for underground and similar installations not easily available for inspection, in order to facilitate future maintenance and design work. The as-built information is transmitted back to the design groups.

As previously mentioned, assistance to the construction supervisor and participation during startup are excellent training grounds. Here the key man is the construction supervisor, who has the opportunity to communicate his wide experience to the less seasoned personnel.

Review of Initial Experience

After six or more months of operation of a new process, a review is held at the plant for discussion of maintenance and production problems experienced to that date. Production, maintenance and design people are present at this review. On site inspections of these problems are conducted, as required. After thorough discussion and evaluation, procedures that will help solve the problems are agreed upon.

Copies of the report of this meeting are distributed to all concerned. Progress on the corrective action is closely followed until satisfactory conditions are reached. If necessary, additional meetings are held after twelve months of operation, and even later.

One prime advantage of these meetings is that they provide a sounding board for production and maintenance personnel, who all too often are not given the opportunity to pass along and discuss their particular problems.

The "Maintenance Engineering News"

Not all communications problems are confined to the construction of new facilities. We have found that there can be failure to communicate maintenance experiences among various groups within a single large plant, as well as among groups in different plants. Several methods of disseminating information on maintenance problems have been tried by Pennsalt with very little success.

We are currently using a new approach—an internal publication called "Maintenance Engineering News," the idea for which was borrowed from the Krummrich plant of Monsanto Chemical Co. (The people there kindly provided us with copies of their similar publication "Engineering Digest.")

Information for subject material is solicited from our larger plants and incorporated in the publication, which is issued twice a year. The history of each maintenance problem is described, together with the solution. Emphasis is placed upon cost reduction, and information on costs is included wherever available.

Shown at the left is the contents page of a copy of

"Maintenance Engineering News," and reports on the solution of two of the maintenance problems. These two examples have been selected to demonstrate the range of problems covered and the way they are written up.

Excellent response has been received, and some 325 copies of each issue are now distributed throughout all divisions of the company. These are sent to management and supervisory people at all levels, beginning with the first-line foremen of the production, maintenance and staff groups. Interest is continuing, and the number of items being submitted has increased, with more and more plants of all divisions participating.

Interplant Maintenance Meetings

The "Maintenance Engineering News" is supplemented by meetings of plant engineers, maintenance engineers and maintenance supervisors from the various plants. These meetings are held to discuss common problems and to establish contacts for future exchanges of information. To avoid the time and expense of arranging separate meetings for this purpose, we have successfully combined such get-togethers with visits to the technical conference that these people would normally attend.

Much has been written lately about the problems of information feedback in this era of rapidly changing technology. We feel that procedures such as the ones described, for attacking the information problem on a plant-wide and company-wide level are fully in keeping with the needs of the times. ∎

Meet the Author

James W. Tracht is manager —maintenance of facilities for Pennsalt Chemicals Corp. Before assuming his present position in Pennsalt's central engineering department at King of Prussia, Pa., he served successively as electrical engineer, power engineer, chief plant engineer, and assistant plant manager — maintenance and power. An electrical engineering graduate of Wayne State University, he has taken graduate work in mechanical engineering and is a registered professional engineer.

Communicating Better in Research and Engineering

These guidelines on how to resolve work-goal confusion and prevent other communications problems are presented in an R&D setting —but many apply to almost any technical/managerial area where ideas, directions or results must pass from person to person.

E. M. KIPP, Research Management Consultant

Even when R&D is riding high, chemical engineers and other researchers are under a variety of personal and group pressures. But when R&D is under the gun (as is frequently the case when budgets are tight), the pressures increase substantially—all converging on the same personal and professional concerns:

· Is my job threatened? Am I about to be demoted or have my salary cut back?

· Will my opportunities for advancement be more limited?

· Does my present assignment command good corporate visibility? Is it related to objectives regarded as important and timely by top management?

· Who is at fault in regard to poor R&D productivity, and who is going to be the judge of my role? Will I have a day in court before fairminded superiors?

· How is my performance to be judged—factually or emotionally?

These concerns are common to all, though they may vary in degree with each individual. The highly regarded man assigned to a real "dog" of a project may worry whether he can afford to recommend that the project be terminated or whether this would tarnish his reputation at a critical time. Even researchers with the good fortune of working on sure winners seem to worry more than before—i.e., as to how long their good fortune will continue in an environment of retrenchment and an adverse corporate climate for R&D.

All researchers have become concerned about the quality of communications between R&D management and company management across the board—particularly as to whether the Director of R&D really enjoys the confidence of corporate management, and whether he is included as a welcome member of the inner-circle power groups. Is he really communicating effectively with his counterparts in the corporate family? Do they have a realistic understanding of R&D as related to the particular company needs and objectives? Or do they say things such as "let's deemphasize commodity chemicals and emphasize proprietary products" without realizing what this means in terms of R&D?

Although a little stress can sometimes improve performance by preventing complacency, the net result of all these stresses and worries upon R&D has been coun-

terproductive. Individual and group communications have become more guarded. There is less frankness and trust, and a greater tendency to go all out in protecting one's short-range personal interests rather than saying what should be said if the best interests of R&D and of the company are to be served. Areas where unselfish teamwork or cooperation—or intelligent risk-taking—are essential, suffer accordingly. What to do?

A large measure of the answer will be found in a concerted dedication by each person in R&D to greatly improved communications at all levels. I realize that this may sound like a rather abstract goal, but I will try to translate it into specific skills—particularly in regard to identification and carrying out of work objectives.

Let us consider the case of a section manager, Thurston, and one of his subordinate group leaders, Smith. (The general approach will be equally effective at any other level in the R&D structure, although some of the specifics will differ.)

Smith's productivity record will largely determine the course of his career. A person's productivity can be defined in many ways; let me define it here as his ability to attain assigned work goals and related objectives within agreed time and costs. Furthermore, should the results of his work indicate that assigned objectives can probably not be achieved within stated limitations of time, monies and other allocated resources, a truly productive person must learn on his own initiative how to communicate the situation effectively to his boss—in this case, Thurston—and how to work out with him appropriate modifications of the original work objectives.

By the same token, as Smith's work progresses, it may develop that the objectives will be attained at lower costs and sooner than expected. Or, Smith's results may suggest early modification of the original assignments. Quality of communications in these circumstances will bear importantly upon his productivity.

Let us consider typical factors leading to communications gaps between Thurston and Smith, and how these may be successfully bridged to the benefit of all.

Setting Work Goals

Thurston should first prepare a draft outline of the proposed job assignment. This outline should be based

I know that Gormley believes in simplicity rather than elegance of communication, but he could have permitted himself the luxury of a "Eureka"!

upon specific goals and should cover the:
• Statement of the problem, and background information.
• Target dates for total-project completion and completion of each component work-goal.
• Project budget and other resources to be allocated.
• Scheduled project-review dates.
• Economic parameters for monitoring work progress.
• Proposed roles for other R&D or corporate groups.

Thurston should briefly discuss this first draft outline with Smith, emphasizing that it is a first draft. He should ask Smith to study the proposal carefully, and to make any suggestions or other comments that might improve the proposal. Thurston should make certain that Smith understands he will be judged in part on the quality of his response, and he should then:
• Set a date with Smith for detailed discussion of project work goals.
• Modify the project if necessary, based on Smith's inputs.
• Ask Smith to summarize, in writing, his understanding of assigned work goals. If this checks out, Smith is ready to go to work.

By proceeding in this fashion, both Thurston and Smith will have avoided most of the potential communications problems about work goals. As an equally important bonus, Smith will have participated in setting these goals and the approaches to attaining them, and begun to learn how to do so effectively (something that will stand him in good stead when he himself becomes a section chief). He will better understand why the specific work is to be done, how it will tie in with other work, and how the whole project will contribute to the welfare of the company. This provides the all-important opportunity to obtain meaningful job satisfaction and fulfillment, and to advance professional growth. Smith will work harder on "our" project—i.e., one to which he contributed significantly before it was finalized—than he is likely to on "Thurston's" project.

Reaching Work Goals

R&D being what it is, agreement on goals and reaching them are often quite different problems. The goals may be unrealistic, or the resources allocated may prove inadequate. As work progresses, new information will often dictate substantial revisions or even termination of the project. Let us assume that work goals are intrinsically sound and that, given adequate professional competency, success is attainable. How can we make the odds even more favorable through superior communications?

First, group leader Smith should prepare a personal timetable for reaching his various work targets in order of priority. He should review these daily for himself, and on a weekly basis with section chief Thurston—or as frequently as Thurston may require. At these review sessions, Smith should tell his boss whether the various phases are on schedule. For any that are not, he should discuss the reasons, whether he expects to get back on schedule, and how.

If Smith is confronted by a problem and is at a loss for a solution, he should not hesitate to tell Thurston, and to ask for help. Researchers are too often unmindful of expertise available among R&D colleagues, most of whom are glad to be of help if asked. Thurston can also assist by making other inhouse or outside resources available.

In addition to informal weekly meetings, formal reviews on the project work goals should be scheduled. These reviews provide the best opportunity for coordinating work goals within R&D and with other interested corporate groups, and for applying the data developed. Smith should prepare himself to supply the following inputs to the project progress reviews:
• Project status re scheduled target dates.
• Plans for getting off-target phases back on schedule.
• Current total expenses vs. budgeted costs.
• Current major problems (if any), and proposed approaches to solving them.
• Status of the economic-control targets—whether these are being met, or whether the quality of the project is deteriorating as an investment opportunity.
• Proposed work program and other activities in preparation for the next scheduled progress review.
• Recommendations for any management action that may be required to ensure successful completion.

A written report on the project-review session should be issued, with emphasis on decisions made as a result of the review. Minority as well as majority views should be covered.

The foregoing communications techniques will virtually ensure successful reaching of the assigned work goals—if they are in fact attainable.

Modifying Work Goals

The most common reasons for revising work goals are:
• Unexpected increases in budgeted R&D costs, re-

flecting greater effort than originally forecast to solve scientific or technical problems.

• Indications that the processes under development will be more costly or less efficient than had been targeted.

• Significant revisions in estimated raw-material, distribution or marketing costs.

• Competitive developments, such as lower prices for competing products serving the targeted markets.

• Pressures from other R&D projects.

These factors, singly or in various combinations, may reduce the profit potential of the project below the pre-selected values necessary to justify investment of company funds. The only alternatives then are to change or reduce the scope of the work goals or to terminate the project. Poor communications at these critical times will almost certainly lead to the wrong decision.

The communications game plan already outlined in the section on "Reaching Work Goals" lays the groundwork for early recognition of signals justifying modifications of the original plans. Once these signals are recognized, Thurston and Smith should schedule a detailed project review with top R&D management and representatives from other company groups that are most involved with the project, to alert them to the new developments.

Another objective of the review is to identify whether there is a pivotal problem among those related to work goals—i.e., a problem having a dominant impact upon the economic-indicator targets. If so, the scope of the project should immediately be reduced to this one problem. There should be agreement as to how much of the total project money will be provided to solve the problem, and an understanding that if it is not solved by the time the funds are spent, the project will be dropped.

Another approach is to develop and review possible alternative approaches that, if successful, would bring the economics of the project back on line. Creative researchers can usually develop a number of paths to solving a given problem. If there is a strong consensus that there are viable alternative approaches to the pivotal problem, management may be well-advised to modify the work objectives accordingly, and to allow the modified project to continue. At this stage, a new set of economic project-control indicators should be developed, limiting commitment of additional resources to levels that will permit the project (if successful) to meet corporate economic criteria.

Modifications in work objectives may be necessary even when work toward the original objectives is progressing smoothly, and within allocated budgets and resources. These cases usually stem from development of new technology that may have broad implications well beyond the scope of the original project. For instance, if a catalyst being tried for a certain process shows promise of versatility (based on bench-scale work), perhaps the work objectives should be broadened so that a modified version of the catalyst is tried on other processes (e.g., while the original process is being pilot planted).

Thurston and Smith must be alert to such developments, and be prepared to communicate effectively with higher management as to the implications of the new knowledge for the current project and for possible other projects. Some of the most profitable R&D ideas often stem from leads developed in pursuing an original objective that itself may not be reached.

In such instances, communications with higher management will be better when management is first provided with a draft of the why's and wherefore's of proposed changes in work goals. In a subsequent review, Thurston and Smith can provide additional details such as budget changes, time schedules, etc. If Thurston and Smith take the trouble to think the thing through—committing the new action proposals to paper in logical sequence, and checking justifications for each proposed work-objective modification—they will have less trouble selling their modifications to higher management than if the proposal appeared to be a hastily conceived response to a managerial request for a progress report.

Terminating Work Goals

The approach outlined above can lead to a prudent decision as to whether to modify or terminate a project. But there can be serious communication problems if management decides to terminate in face of strong resistance by the project leader and his group. These researchers may feel very sincerely that, given additional time, they can still solve the problem and they will submit idea after idea in trying to do so.

The best way for management to communicate in this situation is to rely upon the harsh but realistic dictates of impersonal technical economics—i.e., to point out that if the cost of the research effort, even if technically successful, exceeds a predetermined limit, the project can no longer be sufficiently attractive to justify further investment of corporate funds and other resources.

If the project is a major one, the most effective way to communicate this is for the Director of R&D to set up a meeting with the project members. At this meeting, he will briefly address himself to each of the specific factors leading to the termination decision. While the people may not necessarily agree with management's analysis, they are entitled to know why management acted the way it did. They will react much more constructively when the problem is handled in this manner (and when they are given some indication of what the ensuing project is going to involve, as discussed further in the next section).

Setting New Work Goals

Managers often complain about researchers' traditional reluctance to stop any project once it is started. But this type of research attitude is seldom prevalent when there is a good backlog of high-quality project proposals in reserve. Any R&D director worth his salt must have the capacity and resolve to develop an attractive reserve of exciting ideas clamoring for attention. Those that fail to do so are shortchanging themselves and the company.

The director can draw on his entire staff for these ideas during the course of work (e.g., by encouraging his researchers to evaluate "spinoff" ideas as soon as a project's main priorities have been met). Also he can draw on inputs from the Marketing Dept., from the patent and trade literature, from manufacturing people that he talks to, and so on.

A detailed discussion of sources of R&D ideas is outside the scope of this article—I just want to emphasize that when a reserve of potential new projects is available, the transition to new work goals is more readily accomplished, and the recently deceased project soon forgotten.

Examine Your Communications

Whatever your job may be in R&D—bench worker, group leader, or section chief—check the health and vigor of your communications as they relate directly to your work. Use the items that I have briefly talked about as a checklist, one by one. How do you stand in regard to these—in particular, would your boss agree with your versions of the communications inputs in each case? Are you satisfied that you have all the primary information you need to perform productively? If not, do your homework.

If you identify with group leader Smith, get together with your boss, go over each area listed in the sections on the setting and attaining of work goals, and apply this approach to your current projects.

If you identify with section chief Thurston, follow the same steps, so that your talks with group leaders and researchers will be productive. In addition, take the initiative, if circumstances seem to suggest doing so, to work out modified work goals, new work goals, or a termination and redeployment plan. Then, you would be well-advised to follow the same sort of communication procedure that group leader Smith uses when he is communicating with you.

Let us now turn to a broader aspect of communication—one involving the interaction between corporate management, R&D management, market research, and chemical technology. To avoid talking in generalities, let me introduce a case study.

Demoralizing a Product-Development Team

The events described below constitute a real-life composite, and are based partly on personal experience and partly on extensive communications with R&D people in a number of companies.

Although the case study involves errors of omission and commission by management, its purpose is not to lambaste management, but rather to stimulate constructive thought about how some of the errors could have been avoided—and how they *can* be avoided in future situations of this kind.

The Start of the Project

The project involves a fiscally conservative firm that we shall call the Bulwark Co., and will center on Bulwark's effort to develop a novel chemical feedstock that one of its customers would use to make a new line of consumer products.

R&D's assignment was to develop a process flowsheet for this feedstock, and establish technical and economic feasibilities at various levels of production.

The assignment came about as a result of the activities of Dr. Driver—an ambitious, aggressive, self-confident project chief in the commercial development section of Bulwark's R&D department. He had learned, through his commercial intelligence activities, that the Consummit Corp.—a major, highly regarded company—was strongly committed to the manufacture of a series of new products with unique functional properties.

Furthermore, according to Driver's information sources, (1) Consummit had firmly decided not to manufacture the key chemical feedstock for these new products, because it did not have access to the necessary raw materials; (2) Consummit had fully developed the process technology for the manufacture of the products; and (3) many of the production units were installed, and manufacturing costs well firmed up. Driver therefore felt sure that if Bulwark could produce the feedstock quickly enough, Consummit would snap it up at a price that would produce a good profit.

Driver's informal discussions with the boys at the bench in Bulwark's organic chemistry group were most encouraging, and convinced him that the process chemistry required for the feedstock should present no serious problems.

Next, Driver convinced Dr. Eager (an R&D project supervisor who reported directly to the vice-president of R&D) that here was a golden opportunity to break Bulwark's long drought on new-product investment opportunities generated by R&D. Eager (who had recently been hired from another company, where he had developed a reputation as a real hotshot and a man proud of his executive decisiveness) okayed the project, proceeded to form a project team, and appointed a team leader.

The team quickly held its organizational meeting, developed a well-conceived arrow diagram, checked out individual assignments, and agreed to meet every ten days. The first meeting was adjourned in a climate of enthusiasm and "can do" attitudes.

The team leader reported to Dr. Eager on the plans developed at the first meeting, stressing that in the team's best judgment a minimum of eight months to a year would be needed to discharge the assignment. This did not sit well with Eager, who told the team leader that the final report was due within three months.

Trying To Meet the Deadline

The team proceeded with its work, finding that the flowsheet would require six separate unit processes as well as some sophisticated catalysis technology. Chemical engineering problems needing further R&D were identified. Approaches to solving these problems were developed in detail, with careful estimates of required funds, time and manpower. Team consensus at this point (and even at the end, incidentally) was that the probabilities of technical success were favorable and that the economics of the process would be well within target.

As the team leader conscientiously reported each ten days to Dr. Eager how matters were going, Eager expressed increasing concern over the "large number" of individual boxes in the process flowsheet. But he did not express concern for what were more-critical factors, such as the risk attitudes of top management, the market forecasts of the proposed customer, or the desire of top management to enter what would be a new and unfamiliar product area.

As for Dr. Driver, he kept on telling Dr. Eager and the members of the team how important it was for Bulwark to waste no time in supplying Consummit with sufficient samples of the feedstock chemical to further validate Consummit's own production development, marketing research and promotional activities.

Concurrently, certain peripheral corporate kibitzers began to vocalize skeptically on the reliability of Driver's inputs as to Consummit's manufacturing technologies, market forecasts, and so forth.

The deadline for the team final report was almost at hand. It had become clear that the team's original eight-month-plus time schedule for proper execution of its assignment had been quite realistic: But Dr. Eager refused to revert back to that timetable, or to try and obtain top-management approval for some sort of extension of the moved-up timetable.

To the credit of the team, all members were still highly motivated, and determined to construct a positive and realistic recommendation to management—one that would keep the new-product opportunity active, and that would mitigate the incomplete status of the process technology and economic data.

Discrete inquiries by the team leader indicated that the vice-president for R&D had not been in close contact with his counterparts and superiors; he did not know how they felt about supporting a new-product venture that involved an unfamiliar market and relatively unfamiliar chemical processes.

To forestall possible misgivings by higher management, the team decided to develop a low-risk commercialization strategy—one that would minimize the initial investment while continuously increasing the amount of available information at the critical points of decision, and simultaneously providing support for the customer's own program.

The strategy was the construction against a time-money projection of several escalated production-levels of the feedstock chemical. The initial level was a modest bench-scale production, followed by a small-scale pilot-plant operation, followed then by production on a semi-commercial scale, and culminating in the final decision as to whether to proceed with full commercial production (i.e., of several million pounds per year). A feature of this strategy was that commitment to each successive escalation would not have to be made until all feedback from each preceding stage signaled a go-ahead.

Dr. Driver reviewed these plans with his contact at Consummit, and was delighted to find that the proposed schedule of sample production would meet Consummit's needs satisfactorily.

At this point, the team happily and expectantly completed its final report, well before the deadline. All hands felt they had handled a controversial assignment rather well.

The Word Comes Back

In rather untypically quick time, feedback arrived from the vice-president of R&D: "Kill the project!" Reasons given included strong doubts as to whether the Board would support "such a risky" venture, lack of confidence in Consummit's technology and cost data, skepticism as to Consummit's market forecasts, and misgivings about the lack of fully developed answers to all of Bulwark's potential processing problems (answers that the team had been denied the time to develop).

Apparently, all these were personal misgivings; the team later determined that the v.p. had not indulged in any but the most superficial of discussions with his superiors or counterparts. (It later turned out, however, that some misgivings about the whole project had been relayed to him by an "elder statesman" in his R&D department who, although not a member of the team, took it on himself to query an old friend at Consummit. This friend was less optimistic about the sales projections for the new product than Dr. Driver's contact.)

The reaction of the team members was indeed bitter. There was a clear loss of confidence in research and corporate management, serious doubts as to the quality of communications between R&D's top boss and top corporate management, fear of further loss of corporate regard for R&D, and confusion about market-development's role in the fiasco.

There was concern by each team member that his standing and career prospects had been damaged as a participant in a failure project—indeed, there were strong indications that the failure would be blamed not on managerial confusion or breakdowns in communication, but on a "technically incompetent" team.

The project leader felt he had been let down by his superiors and made to lose face with his peers and team members. The sharp edge of his commitment to Bulwark's R&D department was eroded.

The team's organic-chemistry-section chief filed a strong protest. Some years earlier, he had been hired away from another company on the basis that Bulwark was firmly committed to product diversification and was prepared to assume the risks involved. He now privately vowed to refuse appointment to any new-product team (by subterfuge, if necessary) unless it was clearly destined to be a sure thing from the beginning.

Dr. Eager shrugged off his own role in the failure, and swore that any new product-diversification leads he would come up with would involve the licensing or purchase of fully developed technology, rather than R&D.

Lessons To Be Learned

Most of the lessons contained in this case study are quite obvious and we need not belabor them. Let me just make some brief comments:

The study shows what happens when a technically competent, risk-oriented R&D department has to deal with a corporate management that has an entirely different threshold of risk orientation. In a situation of this kind, it is particularly important that the vice-president of R&D be a good communicator, so that he can either persuade management to tackle an occasional high-risk/high-reward project, or at least point out to management what is going to happen to the future viability of the company if such projects are never approved.

For instance, if it is corporate policy that "a venture team will only be formed when sufficient data are available to confirm a very high probability of technical success, a good margin of favorable economics, and a strong set of market parameters," it is safe to say that very few venture teams will be formed. Does management really

have enough faith in the indefinite profitability of existing products to impose such rigid restrictions on the exploration of new ones?

If the vice-president of R&D cannot bring about an immediate harmony in risk-taking philosophies, he must at least try to make the best of the situation by getting the word to his men as to what type of project is doomed from the start.

At a propitious time—when management gets sick and tired of a steady diet of such projects and starts asking "Why can't we come up with something more exciting?—the v.p. of R&D can try again to persuade management to undertake some high-risk/high-reward projects.

On another matter, we mentioned that an "elder statesman" in the R&D department went directly to the vice-president with word that his contacts at Consummit were less optimistic than Dr. Driver's contacts. Which contacts had the true perspective? I don't really know, but if Dr. Driver and the elder statesman had "pooled" their contacts in the first place, the chances are that a true picture could have been obtained before too much damage was done. This illustrates the pitfalls of failing to use all available communication channels at the beginning, particularly in regard to marketing information.

Finally, I hope the case study has illustrated at least some of the areas in R&D where communications can make the difference between success and failure. Actually, in this case, technical communications within the group were good—it was a failure in other communications that frustrated a competent project team.

But this is not to say that intragroup technical communications are *always* good. And this is why it is necessary to emphasize the areas relating to work goals discussed at the start of this article, as well as basic communication skills such as writing informative research reports, presenting information effectively via oral presentations at staff meetings, and digging out the data you need to provide as well-rounded a picture as possible. Space does not permit detailed how-to advice in this area; many hints by various authors are contained in the sections on communications, information-gathering, and career building in "Modern Technical Management Techniques" (Popper, H., editor, McGraw-Hill, 1971).

Research is more dependent than most functions on the interchange and evaluation of information between individuals and groups. While better communications may not solve *all* of R&D's problems, I cannot think of any single more-fertile area for improving R&D's productivity.∎

Meet the Author

E. M. Kipp, 204 Devon Blvd., Devon, PA 19333, is a consultant in R&D management and human resources. He is a former Associate Director of Research and Development for the Sun Oil Co. His earlier industrial experience includes service with the Aluminum Co. of America and the Foote Mineral Co. Dr. Kipp has a B.S. degree from Wesleyan College, an A.M. from Boston University, and a Ph.D. in physical chemistry from Pennsylvania State University. Besides having many patents to his credit, he has authored a number of articles on management subjects.

PART VII

Working With a Secretary

Operating Manual: Secretary

If you don't know how to operate a secretary—and a lot of engineers don't—here is an operating manual. It was written for you by a certified professional secretary.

YVONNE LOVELY, Oak Ridge National Laboratory

The secretary to an executive today is more than his status symbol; she is a part of management. Executives may be away from the office for days and business will go on as usual. But if the secretaries were absent for equal periods of time—chaos!

There are many college and university courses, certificates and degrees, training programs, seminars, and study groups, some sponsored by business and industry, others supported by the secretaries, that all deal with "how to be a good secretary." A familiar complaint from the graduate of such a course, however, is "My boss doesn't know what a secretary is for."

A top executive knows what a secretary is for, and he uses her, to free his time for the creative thinking necessary to his own responsibilities. He depends on her to relieve him of all routine of operating his office, to know intuitively the telephone calls or visitors he wants to receive and to get rid of the others tactfully. He realizes that she will help him plan his time, keep him on schedule, and see that the office atmosphere is one of tranquility.

"When all else fails, read the instructions." Every item on the market today, from automobiles to Xerox machines, comes with instructions for its use, maintenance, and repair. Not so for a secretary! Bosses need instructions on how to use this human office machine. For the benefit of junior executives and others who don't know how to operate a secretary,* here are some basic instructions:

How To Operate a Secretary

1. **Select Your Own Secretary.** Don't take pot luck from the secretarial pool! An intelligent boss won't put up with an incompetent secretary, and an intelligent secretary won't work for an incompetent boss. The boss and secretary are a management team, and for any team to work effectively, there must be mutual respect, cooperation and capability.

Be as particular in choosing a secretary as you would a wife. Chances are, if you pick a good one, she will be with you as long as your wife (if not longer, considering the present divorce rate); furthermore, the executive who spends more time at the office than he does at home may very well spend more time with his secretary than he does with his wife.

To keep your wife happy and your mind on your work, choose a woman who is neat and attractive rather than a sex bomb. If you prefer a secretary with looks *instead* of ability, you're reading the wrong magazine.

In selecting your secretary, consider her qualifications with regard to the type of responsibilities you want her to assume and work with her for a few months on a temporary basis before you commit yourself to a permanent business association. Decide during this temporary period whether her personality is attuned to yours and if there is reason to believe that you will be able to work effectively together over a period of time, perhaps years. The right secretary can contribute to your peace of mind in the office; the wrong one can put you on the analyst's couch.

2. **Communicate With Your Secretary.** Review with her, preferably at the beginning of each day, appoint-

---

* The feminine gender is used in the following manual because the majority of secretaries are women.

Certified Professional Secretaries

The National Secretaries Assn. (International) has over 25,000 members. Obviously, only a small proportion of this country's 2.5 million secretaries belong.

The Institute for Certifying Secretaries, a department of NSA, has issued to more than 5,000 women, and a few men, the Certified Professional Secretary certificate, which is based on a two-day examination. This comprehensive examination tests knowledge in six areas of business: environmental relationships, business and public policy, economics of management, financial analysis and the mathematics of business, communications and decision-making, and office procedures. Skills in typing and shorthand are tested in only one section.

---

ments, meetings, and correspondence that will require a part of your time, so that you will both know how best to plan the rest of the day. Discuss with her your own responsibilities, company policy or procedures, and how to get the job done. Trust your secretary—she should know how to keep her mouth shut. She will give to other people, even within the company, only enough information to serve the purpose. Seldom will you have to tell her that something is confidential—she will know it—but if a matter is especially sensitive, she will not resent a word of caution.

Don't hesitate to ask her opinion. Remember that she is a part of your job and your company, and she may have some good ideas that have not occurred to you. You may find that discussing a particularly knotty problem with her will help you to clarify your own thinking.

Whether you give her instructions concerning a one-time task or a full-time future responsibility, give her adequate information—but don't overdo it. She will appreciate an opportunity to use her own initiative, and detailed instructions will only frustrate her.

3. **Don't Handle Your Secretary.** The boss and secretary must have respect for each other. If you want to show your appreciation for a job well done, don't pat your secretary on the head, or anywhere else for that matter. A word of praise when she deserves it will keep her happy for quite a while. If you're carried away by her performance over a period of time, nothing gets the point across like money—raise her salary.

The successful boss and secretary relationship is strictly professional; official business and monkey business don't mix, in or out of the office. Whether or not the company frowns on hanky-panky among employees for moral reasons, it usually objects if it happens on company time. Don't get mixed up in her private affairs and you'll be able to stay out of her personal problems.

4. **Don't Play Hide-and-Seek in the Office.** A worldwide complaint by secretaries is "I can't keep up with my boss." You don't have to ask her permission to leave your own office, but your best interests will be served if you let your secretary know whenever you will be away for more than a few minutes. When *your* boss is looking for you, he doesn't want to hear from your secretary that you are not in, she doesn't know where you are, and has no idea when you'll be back.

There could be an urgent call within the company, or from your wife, or from a business associate ready to sign a million-dollar contract. Even if you don't want anybody *else* to know where you are or what you're doing, keep your secretary informed—she won't tell, but she will know when and how to get an urgent message to you whether you're on the golf course or having a sauna bath. For anything less than urgent, she will take care of it herself or stall until your return to the office.

5. **Don't Be Your Own Secretary.** You're not paid for expertise in office routine—your secretary is, so let her handle it. Let her answer the telephone; she may

be able to take care of the call without disturbing you. Let her open the incoming mail; she will attach any pertinent correspondence or reports and she may compose and type a reply for your signature so you need see the material only once. Don't keep a mass of correspondence on your desk; let her keep track of the paper. She knows how to file it and how to find it.

Save yourself for your own area of expertise; delegate to your secretary as much additional responsibility in the office as she is willing to accept. Don't be afraid she will try to take over your job; she won't assume any responsibility or authority that you have not specifically assigned. Let her do some of your library research, abstract reports, or accumulate statistical data for reports.

Let her make appointments for you; knowing your schedule, she will remind you before you forget one. Let her handle the details of a meeting, such as preparing and distributing the notice, preparing an agenda, taking the notes at the meeting, and writing the minutes.

Give her the gist of a message to be conveyed and let her compose routine or nontechnical letters and memoranda for your signature. Encourage her to design forms and develop procedures to expedite the work of the office. Let her determine the priority of her work; even though everything must be done immediately, it can't all be done simultaneously. Leave her alone and trust her to get everything done as "immediately" as possible and in the proper order.

6. **Don't Make a Slave of Your Secretary.** Your secretary was hired, not bought. She is a part of the management team, and her job is one of personal service, but within limits. A topflight secretary is too valuable to the company to spend her time as your personal slave.

Don't ask her to shop for your personal friends—check with the personal shopper at a department store. Don't ask her to take care of your personal correspondence unrelated to company business—if she is willing, pay her to do the work for you outside the office, or let your wife address her own Christmas cards. Don't expect her to baby-sit your children in the office while Mama goes shopping—tell Mama to hire her own baby sitter. A secretary will perform willingly any reasonable task assigned by her executive if it is company business, but who wants to clean a guppy bowl in the office for a boss whose hobby is tropical fish?

Don't accept a job in a community organization and expect your secretary to do all the paperwork on company time. Duties performed during office hours should be for the benefit of the company. If company money is being spent for your personal convenience, this should be reported to the Internal Revenue Service as "income other than cash."

7. **Respect Your Secretary's Personal Time.** When your secretary accepted the job, she agreed to work reasonable office hours, normally about forty a week.

She expects the rest of the time to be hers. In case of an emergency, any good secretary will make arrangements to stay overtime at the office, if the emergencies don't happen too often. Plan your work so that there is seldom any need to ask her to stay after hours to get a job done. She may have to make special arrangements for transportation home, her husband and children may have to eat out, or she may have to cancel a personal engagement.

Encourage her to take the scheduled time out for a meal at noon; she will accomplish more after a break and a change of scene than she will if she works through lunch nibbling on a sandwich at the desk. Manage without her when it's time for her vacation, and be agreeable about it; she needs an occasional respite from the office as much as you do. Be understanding if she must be away from the office because of a doctor's appointment or illness; the best secretary is a well secretary, and it's to your advantage to see that she stays that way.

8. **What To Do If Your Secretary Isn't Working Properly.** The instructions on how to operate a secretary assume that you have shopped carefully and selected a good one. If your secretary isn't working properly and if you have carefully followed the preceding instructions, first determine if she has a salvage value.

Discuss with her where you believe she fails to measure up to your requirements. Suggest that she investigate the Certified Professional Secretary Program (see p. 191) and encourage her to follow through to successful completion of the examination. Preparation for the examination is an excellent means for improving secretarial performance. She may need to enroll in evening courses offered at a local educational institution; perhaps there is a company policy that would provide at least a part of the expense. The best way to get a Certified Professional Secretary is to "grow your own"; there are few, if any, CPS's in the secretarial market.

There are many so-called secretaries who aren't. If your secretary is one in name only and is unwilling to make an effort to meet your requirements, accept her resignation with regret and proceed with Instruction 1 on p. 191. ∎

Meet the Author

Yvonne Lovely is secretary to Lewis Nelson, Director, Education and University Relations, Oak Ridge National Laboratory, Union Carbide Nuclear Div., Oak Ridge, Tenn. She is a Certified Professional Secretary (CPS), and has a B.S. in business administration from the University of Tennessee where she is also currently enrolled in the graduate program in industrial management. She is a member of the honor societies Phi Kappa Phi and Beta Gamma Sigma, and of the National Secretaries Assn.

To help you get more writing done in less time, via a secretary or dictating machine, here is practical advice on . . .

How to Be a Great Dictator

AUREN URIS, Research Institute of America

This article has been dictated. A dictated draft was completed in 1 hour and 15 minutes. Subsequently, it required 1 hour of editing by the author. Total time required to produce the manuscript, in the final form to be sent to CHEMICAL ENGINEERING: 2 hours, 15 minutes. Estimated time if dictation had not been used: one working day.

There's no doubt that the engineer or technical manager who can dictate not only observations, memos and letters but also reports and manuscripts can save himself hours of toil. For anyone who wants to make it in print, learning to dictate can be a major step in a time-saving "writing" skill.

Potential Dictators All

Anyone who can speak can dictate. And few people in industry would have any qualms about using a stenographer or a machine to dictate simple letters and memos. For example:

Pete Bramble, holding a written query he has just received from the front office, gets his boss's secretary to take a letter. He says, "All right, Gladys, here it is: 'To C. R. Castor. In reply to your question about the drums piled up in the hallway of Building B, comma, I'm happy to report that they've just been removed, period. Signed, Pete Bramble.'" He doesn't have to bother adding the date or departmental location. Gladys will take care of that. Then he goes on to dictate a couple of other short notes.

But suggest to Pete Bramble that he dictate a five-page report, and he'll think you're crazy, because everybody knows that lengthy communications, such as reports or an extensive written presentation, must be written out in longhand, or pecked out laboriously on a typewriter. But as often happens, what everybody knows isn't necessarily so. Practically everyone can develop a reasonable dictating skill sufficient to cut writing-time requirements by 50% or even more.

The potential to be gained in time is immediately evident when you consider: the man who sets out to provide a report in longhand can probably produce the finished product at the rate of about 30 words a minute. If he dictated to a capable stenographer, he would be able to triple that speed. And if he used a machine, he could get down his thoughts almost as quickly as he could find the words for them.

The advantages of being able to dictate are so extreme that it's worth the while of every professional to at least give this technique a trial.

Obviously some people will be more successful than others. Interestingly enough, however, it doesn't necessarily follow that the fluent speaker is the one who makes the better dictator. In some cases, the man who is less fluent and even stumbles over his words may actually be dictating "harder" copy: If his thinking is orderly, his dictation may be more concise than that of the man who speaks easily but whose thoughts meander.

There's no mystery in how to go about mastering the dictating skill. These points can help you:

What to Dictate

While almost anything that is to be written can be dictated, there are some types of writing that effect greater time savings by dictation than others. Reports, for example, are particularly worthwhile for dictation since they tend to be lengthy; undictated they represent large investments of time.

Letters and memos, of course, are also prime communications to be handled by dictation. As a matter of fact, a trained stenographer can often compose an entire letter when her boss simply dictates one or two key sentences and leaves it up to the secretary to fill in the usual formalities of address, greeting, closing and so on.

Unsuitable for dictation are names or other proper nouns, numerical tabulations, and highly mathematical copy (i.e., where more than half of the copy is comprised of equations).

Girl or Machine?

As already indicated, the dictator may have a choice between a stenographer and dictating machine. Recent years have seen dictating equipment refined. Machines are lighter, operate more easily. Some companies have dictation systems where one dictates into a mouthpiece or telephone: a recording tape or other medium, in a centralized location, records the dictation, which is subsequently handled by a typing pool.

Regardless of particular mechanism, machine dictation and dictation to stenographer have advantages and disadvantages. The chart on the opposite page compares the two.

Getting Started

"My trouble in dictating," says one technical manager, "is to just get off the ground."

It's a common problem. But there are several preparatory moves that can help beat the hangup:

Gather your information, background material, and so on, in advance. Don't start your dictation and be forced to interrupt yourself because you are missing a piece of reference material. Have available all the backup material you will need—if possible, in the order in which you will use it.

Make a rough outline. An outline has the virtue of giving a track to run on, a framework on which to build your final product. And, except for lengthy or complex projects, you needn't get involved in the kind of elaborate outlining that is sometimes taught in school. At a minimum, a number of words or phrases that give you a logical sequence of ideas will do the trick. For example, here is the outline that was used in dictating this article.

Introduction: Benefits
    Everyone can do it to some degree
1. What to dictate
2. Girl or machine?
3. Getting started (after the preparation steps)
4. Common hangups and how to overcome them
5. Improving your copy
6. Reviewing your weak and strong points and improving your technique
Conclusion: Byproduct benefits

Other preparations such as physical arrangements for convenient working—a comfortable chair, a table or desk for notes and background materials, a comfortable chair for your stenographer, or a convenient location for your dictating apparatus, round out the preparation steps.

Common Hangups and How to Overcome Them

Discussions with individuals who have attempted to dictate material other than letters or memos reveal some common problems:

• "Writer's block." Some people say that when faced by the need to start dictating, they freeze. This is similar to the paralysis that occasionally stops even the professional writer in his tracks. To counter this problem, check back and make sure that all your preparations have been made. In some cases, the feeling of not being ready to dictate may be the obstacle. Then, start! Throw hesitation to the winds. Don't worry about finding the "right" word, phrase or sentence. Plunge in! In other words, an effective way to end a starting problem is simply to *start*. Another way is to begin with a brief or "easy" piece of dictation. This bit of pump-priming usually gets you going.

• "I can't get down to brass-tacks. I ramble and digress." The solution here lies both in having and *following* an outline. If you find you're straying from it, go over it to make sure it covers your subject adequately. Then stick to it, forcing yourself to stop when you seem to be digressing.

• "It's disconcerting to have a stenographer waiting for me to grope for an idea." Try using a machine; or, change stenographers; or make some disarming or humorous comment, letting your stenographer know that you don't expect to talk smoothly and incessantly. If you have not been doing much dictating, it is no disgrace to admit it, and to imply that your stenographer will have plenty of time to catch her breath while you gather your thoughts or grope for the phrase you want.

• "I never liked gadgets, and talking to a lifeless machine is disconcerting." Try a stenographer. Or, the particular make or model of your dictating machine may be a poor choice for you. In today's market, one can find a wide variety of dictating equipment, involving everything from tape to plastic sleeves. If you are having trouble with a machine that you have tried, a trip to an office supply company will make it possible to test various types of equipment. You should be able to come up with one that overcomes the problem.

• "I lose too much time searching for a word or phrase or even an idea." This is a common and major hangup for many people. To overcome it, bull it through—put down any word or phrase that will get you over the hurdle, knowing that you will be able to improve the word or phrase or idea later on.

The important thing is to work for a *rough draft*, because once you have your copy in black and white, you have something to work with. The professional writer will often push on to complete his draft regardless of how many word gaps or idea gaps there may be in his copy. He knows that these points can be rectified later on. "Finish the draft" is the slogan of the goal-oriented professional.

Improving Your Copy

The greatest misconception about dictation is that you say it once, and that finishes the job. It's true that *neither* the dictated nor written copy is "right" the first time. Every potential writer will tell you that the *rewriting* is an essential part of the operation.

So consider the typed pages you get either from your stenographer or from the typist who has worked from your machine-recorded material as merely a draft, a preliminary version. What you should strive for is to turn your first rewrite into what professional writers call "final copy." In some cases, you may have to do two rewrites; that is, revise your copy twice before you have a final draft.

It's in the editing or rewriting that you can eliminate any oral habits that are objectionable. The repetition of the words "you know," for example, and such stilted phrases as "to be sure," which in verbal communication go unnoticed, may become objectionable when written. Count on your editing to eliminate and tighten up.

Improving Your Technique

After you have tried dictating once or twice, review your technique. Use the above discussion of hangups as a kind of checklist to spot your weak points. Then, try to improve your technique via practice. Even someone very much used to dictating letters cannot expect to undertake longer communications without some preliminary difficulties.

If first attempts are discouraging, try again, dictating material on which you have a good grasp. Don't give up too quickly, because the rewards of success can be substantial. Repeated attempts can help you score a breakthrough.

Further, although we have mostly emphasized timesaving, some dictators claim that the *quality* of their writing improves when they dictate: "I find I can think more clearly when I talk than when I type or write out my ideas in longhand," says one manager. "My correspondence sounds less stilted and more readable when I dictate it," says another.

You may be the greatest dictator of all times—but you can't know just how great until you try.

Stenographers vs. Machines: How They Stack Up

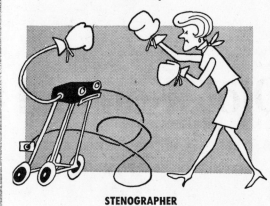

STENOGRAPHER

Advantages	Disadvantages
Useful rapport can exist between steno and dictator.	Usually works 8-hr. day or less, and may resist overtime.
Can make corrections and insertions on the spot, and supply quick readbacks.	May tire after an hour or so.
Can be helpful in giving instant feedback to dictation (in terms of reaction to wording, ideas, etc.). Can ask questions immediately if something is not clear.	If steno is absent from work and has not completed transcription of her notes, chances are no substitutes can read her shorthand. This means a delay until steno returns to work.

DICTATING MACHINE

Doesn't complain, has no personal habits or traits that can irritate you.	Can lend themselves to corrections, but some people find machines difficult in this respect.
Available 24 hours a day, and is tireless.	Cannot help supply a missing word or phrase.
Some people are less selfconscious when they dictate to a machine. There is no need to apologize for pauses or interruptions.	If transcriber has difficulty in discerning some words or phrases dictated, the dictator may not always be available to be asked.
Conserves secretarial time, and can be taken along on a business trip without precipitating office gossip.	Transcriber might feel it's a waste of time to listen to the entire recording before typing from it, preferring to take it down in shorthand to facilitate transcription of corrections, changes, and punctuation.

Dictation and the Engineer

A selective approach to dictation,
with special attention to
technical material, may be necessary
to reap full benefits and avoid pitfalls—
particularly if the secretarial situation is
less than ideal.

How do you spell $C^*(j\omega) = \frac{1}{(j\omega)^2} \int_0^\infty \sum_{k=1}^{\gamma} a_k u_l\,(t - l_k)e^{-j\omega t}\,dt$?

JAMES R. FAIR, Monsanto Co.

In principle, I fully agree with the previous author's premise that most of the writing needs of engineers as well as of nontechnical people can be satisfied by dictating to a girl or machine. And the time- and effort-saving advantages of dictation can be tremendous.

In practice, however, many engineers face some special hurdles, especially in regard to technical material. My purpose here is to focus attention on how some of these hurdles can be surmounted.

Secretarial Resources and the Engineer

In order to gain some perspective, let's first consider two idealized situations involving the engineer-dictator. The first involves a prosperous technical consultant named Brown, who must prepare a 16-page typewritten report for a client. He gathers reference documents and data, prepares a detailed outline, and buzzes for his private secretary, Mrs. Green. After arranging for another secretary to take all calls, she settles herself in front of his desk, notebook in hand, and prepares to take down his report in shorthand.

Brown starts by dictating title, distribution, and table of contents. He then goes through the entire report, speaking carefully and distinctly to Mrs. Green. When he comes to a figure, he notes its place in sequence and dictates its title. When he comes to a table, he dictates title, column headings, and hands her the penciled figures to be inserted. He is careful about style, does not overuse certain words or expressions, and modulates his speaking so that Mrs. Green will have no difficulty in handling punctuation and paragraphing.

Mrs. Green has worked closely with Brown for many years. She is college-trained and does a bit of writing on her own. Thus, she takes the dictated material, types it up in final form, proofs it with another girl, and hands it to Brown. He, in turn, glances through the report, nods approvingly, and says "Send it out!"

The second idealized situation: Project Manager Gray dashes to the airport to return home from an all-day conference with an engineer-contractor. Aboard the plane, he finds that the seat next to him is not occupied, so he spreads out his papers, takes his lightweight dictating machine from his briefcase, and prepares to dictate his trip report. Airborne, he declines the drink offer from the stewardess, starts with a fresh tape in the machine, gives his secretary guidance on the format and distribution of the report· (e.g., telling her to type it up in final rather than in draft form) and then launches into an account of the conference while the details are still fresh in his mind.

Next morning, Gray hands the tape to his secretary at 8:30 a.m. Two hours later, the trip report has been distributed to key people in the building, and at 1:00 p.m. the document is being used by several of the recipients in a project review meeting. While the secretary was typing the report, Gray was concerning himself with other needs for the meeting.

Now, just to make the story complete, let's consider an unidealized situation—a fairly realistic one, I believe, in a number of firms. Engineer Black has to write to several companies for information on catalyst supports. He has been told by his boss that he should develop dictating ability, so he decides to give it a try. After thinking about what he wants to say, and perhaps actually scribbling out some parts of the letters, he attempts to locate a secretary.

The trouble is, Black shares the secretary, Miss Blue, with 9 other engineers. At the moment, she's on an errand for one of his colleagues. When she finally returns, he calls her in and starts dictating those letters. After several fumbles, mumbles, and other manifestations of inexperience, Black gets the job done—and Miss Blue swishes out of his office.

When Black finally gets the typed letters (let's not forget that Miss Blue has her own priority system), he finds that they look pretty bad. Sentence structure is poor, capitalization is wrong, and some technical terms are misspelled. He's not sure whether the letters really convey his desired meaning, and he doubts whether they would represent properly the image that he and his company want to present. He tries to edit the letters, but finally decides to do them over in longhand. In the end, he is disillusioned and Miss Blue is upset. "This business of dictating is for the birds," claims Black.

Developing the Skills for Efficient Dictation

The above three situations, which cover some typical communication needs of the engineer or technical manager, illustrate that conditions could be right—or wrong—for dictating effectiveness. If conditions are wrong, this does not mean that the engineer should stay away from dictation but rather that he should use it selectively at the start, and gradually expand the amount of dictation as his proficiency increases and as obstacles are overcome.

Materials to be communicated fall into these categories:

1. Notes for personal files, etc.
2. Office forms—e.g., for disbursements, supplies.
3. In-house memoranda.
4. Correspondence with suppliers, customers, etc.
5. Formal technical reports and papers.

It is easy to see that this listing follows a gradation of demand for dictating skill. To put it another way, even the novice can skip the rough-draft stage in dictating, for example, recollections of a meeting he attended if these recollections are intended for his personal files or as an informal note to a colleague. Conversely, even the accomplished dictator may want to go through the rough-draft stage for key portions (e.g., the summary, conclusions, recommendations) of a formal technical report, or for the first few pages of a manuscript for publication.

On a percentage basis, the biggest savings in dictating come about for work where you can skip the draft stage. Dictating memos and letters, and then just signing the finished product, can be several times as fast as writing them out longhand, as the previous author has pointed out. But if the material has to go through a draft stage, the total time spent in outlining, dictating and then later editing the draft may not always be very much less than typing and writing out the draft yourself, making corrections or erasures as you go along, and then giving it to your secretary for the final typing.

In my opinion, the engineer's goal should be to avoid the rough draft except in those cases where wording and style are quite critical. The basic approach should be "try to do it right the first time."

Dictating Equipment

The dictating system comprises the **dictating machine** and a compatible **transcribing machine.**

Dictating machines may be characterized by their portability and by the type of recording medium. A machine just for office use will weigh about 12 lb., cost about $400, and include features that emphasize clarity of recording and flexibility of operation. A machine emphasizing portability will weigh about 2 lb., cost $225-400, use battery power, and have limited flexibility of operation (for example, it will not serve well for recording conferences). And there are "hybrid" machines incorporating some features of both the fixed and portable types. All types can be adapted for recording telephone conservations.

Another method for characterizing dictating machines is the type of recording medium: disc, belt or tape. Discs give high recording clarity, accept rapid dictation, and are readily mailable. The grooves show the extent of dictation, but are not erasable for reuse. Belts give generally good clarity, are easily mailable, and can be erased if they are of the magnetic type. Tapes give fair clarity, are somewhat cumbersome to mail and, being magnetic, are erasable.

Belts and discs are easily scanned (by moving the needle), but tapes require relatively slow winding or rewinding. The reusability advantage of magnetic tapes and belts is offset by the difficulty of locating points where correction or playback is needed.

In line with this, the dictator should force himself to:

- Develop a detailed outline.
- Picture just how the type will look on the page.
- Use direct readback to cut out repetition or clumsiness.

I realize that there is much to be said for the adage "to write is to rewrite." Up to a point, the revisions are well worth the effort. I also realize that some people are very slow writers but fast dictators and fast editors—for them, dictating has advantages even if there are two drafts before the final version. But in general, I feel that *indiscriminate* use of the rough draft tends to be a crutch—it promotes sloppiness. Here is how you can use rough drafts more judiciously:

1. Start out by dictating notes for your own files; also routine paperwork and in-house memoranda. Dic-

---

Dictating Technical Material

Below are a few paragraphs from the manuscript for a report that CHEMICAL ENGINEERING edited and published in 1969 ("Design of Modern Distillation Columns," in the Apr. 22, 1969 issue). I chose these paragraphs not because they are particularly well written, but to illustrate what's involved in dictating technical expressions.

At right is a reconstruction of the way these paragraphs were dictated. The italics indicate nontranscribed material; my secretary distinguished between this and the material to be transcribed by noting my intonation and gestures.

I had made up a fairly detailed outline before starting to dictate. The material was transcribed directly, without a draft. About 25% of the 70 double-spaced transcribed pages in the manuscript needed corrections of some kind, but very few of these involved redoing the entire page.

PREDICTIVE MODELS FOR EFFICIENCY

Work sponsored by the AIChE Research Committee led to the development of the "AIChE Method" for predicting the mass transfer efficiency on a crossflow-type (bubble cap, valve, sieve)* distillation tray. The model is described in the AIChE Bubble Tray Design Manual, (1) and explained very lucidly by Smith (54). It is based on the two-film theory, and is directed toward the prediction of point efficiencies, with most of the experimental foundation work having been done in small columns where liquid mixing on the trays was essentially complete.

According to the film model, the point efficiency can be defined as:

$$E_{OG} = 1 - e^{-N_{OG}} \qquad (34)$$

where N_{OG} (the number of overall gas phase transfer units) is equal to an overall <u>conductance</u>, the reciprocal of which is the sum of the individual phase resistances:

$$\frac{1}{N_{OG}} = \frac{1}{N_G} + \frac{\lambda}{N_L} \qquad (35)$$

The phase transfer units are obtained from the general expressions:

$$N_G = k_G a' t_G \qquad (36)$$

$$N_L = k_L a' \tau_L \qquad (37)$$

It is immediately apparent that the effective interfacial area term a' is difficult to evaluate. Hughmark (32) has correlated it empirically with gas rate, weir height, liquid viscosity, liquid density, vapor density and surface tension.

*Tray or plate devices that force the frothy liquid to flow across each plate.

Now, Beverly, we completed the section on Plate Efficiencies. Today, let's start with the subheading PREDICTIVE MODELS FOR EFFICIENCY. *Capitalize and underscore all that, please.*

Work sponsored by the AIChE Research Committee led to the development of the *quote* AIChE Method *close quote—and capitalize method* for predicting the mass transfer efficiency on a cross-flow *hyphen* type *parenthesis* bubble cap *comma* valve *comma* sieve *close parenthesis, asterisk* distillation tray *period.* (*Now, Beverly, I would like to tie this footnote into that asterisk:* Tray or plate devices that force the frothy liquid to flow across each plate *period, and that should end the footnote. Now, back to the paragraph.*) The model is described in the AIChE Bubble Tray Design Manual *comma, parens reference* 1 and explained very lucidly by Smith *parens reference* 54 *period.* It is based on the two film (*hyphenated*) theory *comma* and is directed toward the prediction of point efficiencies *comma* with most of the experimental foundation work having been done in small columns where liquid mixing on the trays was essentially complete *period, paragraph.*

According to the film model *comma* the point efficiency can be defined as *colon (now, Beverly, leave space for equation* 34) where capital N *sub* OG *parenthesis* the number of overall gas phase transfer units *close parenthesis* is equal to an overall conductance (*underscore*) *comma* the reciprocal of which is the sum of the individual phase resistances *colon; space for equation* 35; *paragraph.*

The phase transfer units are obtained from the general expressions *colon (space for equations* 36 *and* 37) It is immediately apparent that the effective interfacial area term a' (*Beverly, that should be a lower case "a" with a superscript prime mark*) is difficult to evaluate *period.* Hughmark *H-u-g-h-m-a-r-k parens reference* 32 has correlated it empirically with gas rate *comma* weir height *comma* liquid viscosity *comma* liquid density *comma* vapor density and surface tension *period.*

tate these items carefully without asking for a draft. When you see the final version, ask yourself whether the writing is concise, whether the meaning will be clear to the intended audience, and whether the material seems to represent the work of a reasonably literate person. If some of the answers are no, you may correct the material if you feel necessary, but your main goal should be to avoid these shortcomings in future dictation. So make some mental or actual notes.

2. As you improve, start dictating most outside correspondence, and the noncritical portions of technical reports (e.g., the appendices, description of procedures, etc.), keeping in mind the pointers on handling technical and mathematical material discussed elsewhere in this article. Don't ask for a rough draft. When you get the typed material, some pages may have to be corrected or retyped, but if you have dictated carefully, many of them will be acceptable as is. (Keep in mind that dictated material will rarely reach perfection in the mind of the dictator; but carefully worded longhand may not always do this either.) Again, take note of pointers that apply to future dictating work, so that the percentage of pages that have to be corrected or retyped goes down the more you dictate.

3. As for particularly sensitive correspondence, and the critical portions of reports, you have your choice of dictating into draft form from a rough outline, trying to dictate into final form from a detailed outline, writing the draft in longhand or (if you are a reasonably fast typist) typing the draft. Personal preference can be the legitimate deciding factor: You may find you can do the best job of putting complex, crucial thoughts down on paper when you have a pencil in your hand and can see every sentence take shape. Or you may find that you can uncoil most easily by dictating these thoughts rapidly without worrying about style, and then carefully editing the draft. In other words, after you have developed the skills to dictate most of your material efficiently, use whatever seems to work best for really critical portions of your writing needs.

Engineers and the Office System

In recommending that engineers use dictation for more and more of their writing, I realize that the office system is not always ideal for engineer-to-secretary dictation.

Most engineers share a secretary with many others. So it follows that the secretary cannot handle all of "her men" on a demand dictation basis. Directly or indirectly, the men are encouraged to use longhand or a machine. There are cases where a secretarial pool makes possible dictation on demand, but under such circumstances the engineer may have a different girl almost each time he calls for assistance.

In most office systems, machine dictation does provide distinct advantages over laborious longhand, especially for noncritical work. Also, some companies are able and willing to supply their technical depart-

ments with additional stenographic help if the engineers can prove that this would boost their own productivity, and that the additional help would be used efficiently—in other words, that a girl earning a stenographer's or secretary's salary will not be used primarily to type up handwritten material. (The latter is not only inefficient but can cause discontent and high turnover among stenographers.)

Most secretaries working in a technical organization can learn to handle such esoteric terms as phthalic anhydride and contact catalysis quite readily. But they cannot be expected to clean up sloppy dictation or writing. And they probably will not understand the individualistic desires of the dictator regarding punctuation.

In most cases, the best approach is to dictate punctuation marks, paragraph designations, and unusual capitalization (see box, opposite page). Further, the dictator must be alert to words with alternate spellings. It may take some practice to do all this without losing one's train of thought, but it can be done.

Technical Material and Other Problems

When we discussed Consultant Brown, we touched on the special problem of dictating tabular material. There are similar problems with much of the material that an engineer is likely to be writing.

First, there are the mathematical expressions. They can be dictated directly if the secretary has a degree in mathematics, but one doesn't find such secretaries very often. The best plan is to write out the expressions and designate them so that the secretary will add them in sequence at their proper place in the dictated text. One might say "blank for equation 16," or words to that effect. If a rough draft is planned, the dictator can write in the equations himself.

Other special problems involve symbols, Greek letters, foreign words and phrases, and so on. The important watchword is understanding of the secretary and her capabilities. A scratch pad on the desk between dictator and secretary can be very helpful.

As for dictating equipment, p. 197 provides a fair sampling of what is available. In all cases, care must be taken to erase old dictation; to identify current dictation with subject, date, and instructions as to whether it is to be in rough draft or final form. The problem of advance notice of correction is especially difficult on some machines, and this must be recognized.

To sum up, engineers should not expect instant success in emulating Consultant Brown's "great dictatorship." In his case, the propensities of both man and system to dictation effectiveness are high. Such a combination is not often found, however.

I feel that the man, not the system, usually determines the degree of resistance. Almost every engineer has *some* secretarial support, and by exploiting it efficiently, he can lay the groundwork for more support.

The economic potential of effective dictation remains high. It's just another case where man/woman and man/machine interfaces need more exploitation. ∎

PART VIII

Getting Your Material Into Print

Pleasures and Problems of Being Published

Pleasures
Requests for reprints
Congratulatory letters
Increased stature
Job offers
Requests for speeches

Problems
Requests for reprints
"Crank" letters
Requests for detailed information
"Constructive" criticism
Complaints of lack of credit

Are you the potential author of an article? There are many advantages to being an author, but there can be some problems that you never thought about.

MANNY MEYERS, Picatinny Arsenal

Every engineer realizes that there are advantages in having one of his articles published in a trade professional magazine—recognition, stature and satisfaction.

However, to a first-time author, the publishing of an article can be a traumatic experience. This happens mainly to an author who has not foreseen the problems that can arise, and is not prepared to deal with them.

To prepare the potential author for the onslaught, therefore, here are some of the things that any engineer or scientist can anticipate after the publication of an article.* These situations are a synthesis of problems that are likely to occur; some may seem fanciful and some facetious, but none are really exaggerated.

Reader Response

The first common occurrence after the publication of an article is that the author receives requests for reprints. Such requests can be quite numerous. They may come (by regular mail, several weeks later) from all over the world. This is flattering, but it can also be time-consuming. Conscience dictates an immediate response and so the reprints are sent by airmail. In

* This article does not consider the professional writer or editor of technical articles, who has different reactions to his readers.

the light of what most magazines and journals pay by way of "honorariums" (and some do not remunerate at all), this can be expensive. However, for most authors, the mailing of reprints is one of the tacit obligations of publication.

The next type of request from the reader is usually for additional data, either without comment or noting that the respondents are working on similar projects and that the supplementary information would be valuable. Concurrently, there might be some letters to the author complimenting him on his technical acumen and offering comments and criticisms. These letters are usually objective and the author welcomes them as fair comment either on a neglected point or as a clarification of some aspect of the subject. (The editor also uses these letters in a subsequent issue to correct what might have been an editorial oversight or a typographical error.)

Incidentally, a flattering ploy by a reader requesting a favor is to use the form "Doctor" to an author who does not warrant the title (this particularly so from foreign readers who are uncertain and do not wish to offend). It is at this point that the fun or the aggravation—depending on the staying power and psyche of the author—begins.

The advantages of publishing an article (particularly for oft-published authors) are: recognition in the form of deferential letters or invitations to address symposiums or to give lectures; cash awards from their firms for having published; paid consulting work; a job offer; laudatory recognition by supervisors and coworkers; and the gratification of requests for counsel by readers.

However, some letters from readers can be termed "outrageous." Some readers will ask for reams of additional information, as if the author's time and attention were specifically allotted to providing services of this type. These are simply requests for work without compensation. Some authors have been induced into giving their time to corporations and firms on deliberately misleading assumptions; later they find to their dismay that they are having their brains picked. Other letters may suggest that the author pay the letter writer to do additional work in the author's special field.

The Crank Letter

Another, more unpleasant, type of reader response is the vituperative letter (there are cranks in the engineering and scientific disciplines as there are in other professions). This offensive letter can come from someone who either has done similar work but has never published or who is simply a maladjusted reader. He will contest every point on a personal basis, is rabid about his disputations and casual with his insults. One variety of this species is the type that will not let go: to answer his comments in a reasonable manner is to incite another barrage of invective. Another sort is the self-recognized wit who responds with inept attempts at ridicule and ends up by displaying his retarded sense of humor.

Another consistently vexing factor for the author is the "credit gap." It seems that credit is a commodity that, as in the financial world, there never seems to be quite enough of. This complaint of lack of recognition emanates primarily from immediate peers and overzealous public relations men or small-firm executives. The unkindest cut (since it is more personal) will come from a colleague who will ask: How come you acknowledge the contributions of so and so, but not mine.

Then there is the reader who will deprecate an author's innovation with the statement that he had the same idea or had done the same work a long time ago. Or if the author highlights a widespread fault that needs corrective measures, the hostile rejoinder will be: "You're an engineer. How come you hate other engineers?" Mention some product or give credit to a firm for performing a technical service or pioneering a concept and invariably a vice-president in charge of public relations and plant disposal services at another firm will respond that his own company had manufactured the item or contributed to the discovery of the process long before the author.

The Backbiter

The most wounding of all experiences for the author perhaps is the professional backbiting and dis-

paragement from his peers. Many authors will encounter petty, sometimes infantile, manifestations of jealously, ranging from accusations of stealing ideas to the most picayune criticism and to having adverse comments on their articles prominently displayed on bulletin boards or circulated within their working areas. A typical tactic of the spoilsport is to question not the validity of the subject matter, but the grammar. The snide comments and venting of spleen in the working environment are usually from equals or subordinates, and not from higher management levels, which almost always endorse the publication principle. In fact, in certain situations the publication of articles is considered essential to the maintenance of status; it both enhances promotional opportunities and improves the reputation of the writer's firm.

For the distaff side, all these reactions are applicable, with one additional annoying distinction: Female authors will often receive letters addressed to them as "Mr."

Despite the irritants, the consensus among authors is that there should be publication without tears. Most authors agree that their publication of material has been a professional elixir; they contend that exposure to a multiplicity of comments by their compatriots has made them sharper and more alert in all respects. (One author notes, "When you publish a high-flown piece, you had better be right or you are shot down in flames.") Publication also has supplementary bonuses; it relieves the routine of daily work and rejuvenates viewpoints. It can even have a humbling effect, since the constructive criticism of an article can dilute the supercilious attitude an author sometimes acquires.

Reader criticism—fair and unfair—should be expected by the author. Some authors consider that half the fun of publishing is the badgering they know they will receive from their readers. As one author retorted to a stinging letter: "Better to be damned with faint praise than not to be damned at all." Also, a pervasive euphoria can come from knowing that your professional colleagues all over the world are reading your creation.

An author finds it especially satisfying when someone from outside his immediate community recognizes his name solely on the basis of his articles. One author, who has published more than 130 articles in the past decade, was particularly articulate about enumerating the regrets he had in doing that amount of writing. He had been exposed to all the worst aspects of being published; and yet when he thought about it he succinctly stated the case for most authors with: "It's a great feeling to be published."

Meet the Author

Manny Meyers is Chief, Editorial & Publications Section, Ammunition Engineering Directorate, Bldg. 355, Picatinny Arsenal, Dover, N. J. 07801. His work there involves helping engineers produce readable manuscripts. He has a B.A. in journalism, an M.A. (and is presently a candidate for a Ph.D.) in American civilization. All his degrees are from New York University.

Writing for Publication

Thinking of writing an article some day? If so, the
suggestions below may save you time and effort; many of
them contain principles that apply to all engineering writing.

ROLAND A. LABINE, *Chemical Engineering*

Engineer Smith finds writing for publication to be
such a rewarding experience that he no sooner finishes
one manuscript than he starts thinking about another.
He enjoys the extra spending money that comes from
the honararia, takes pride in the added professional
recognition and company publicity, is stimulated by
the new insights that occur during the writing process,
and feels good about contributing something worthwhile to the engineering literature.

At the opposite end of the spectrum is engineer
Jones. He had what seemed to be a good idea for an
article, toiled painstakingly over every sentence in
setting it down on paper, drew diabolically detailed
diagrams, and then found that nobody wanted to publish what he had written.

Where did Jones make his mistake? Let's look at
some possibilities, and see how you can assure the
success of your own writing efforts.

Knowing Your Reader

If Jones's manuscript had something worthwhile to
say, the most probable reason for its seemingly cruel
rejection was that the information had not been presented in a reader-oriented manner. Jones may have
been writing as a technical specialist interested only
in communicating with those few who are well-versed
in his specialty. He may have had something of value
to say, but he didn't set it down on paper so that the
ordinary engineering reader could understand its significance.

If you want to produce a reader-oriented article,
your first job is to have a clear picture in your mind
of exactly the kind of man you want to reach.

To get this picture, you must first realize that there
are two basic types of technical publications that normally accept bylined articles from outside contributors:

1. Research journals.
2. Business publications (including those with society affiliations).

The objective of research journals is to communicate
the results of research to other workers in the same
specialty. The journals themselves usually accept no
advertising, use no editorial color, and publish the
manuscripts (including diagrams) in essentially the
form in which they are received. The number of potential readers of any of the articles is quite small, and
publication is viewed basically as a public service. In
the chemical field, the *AIChE Journal* is such a publication.

Business publications, on the other hand, strive to
communicate practical, technical information to men
in industry. These publications usually accept advertising and often, as in the case of CHEMICAL ENGI-
NEERING, turn a profit for providing this communication service.

Although business publications do not expect every
reader to read every article, the editors must constantly be wary of the manuscript that will interest
only a small fraction of the audience. The range of
potential readers for any given technical subject is
illustrated by the curve on the opposite page.

Take a topic like "Mixing." An author can write
a highly theoretical treatise that would interest only
those thoroughly familiar with the subject. These readers are represented by the right-hand portion under
the curve. An editor is on dangerous ground if he
attempts to cater to the specialized interests of this
sophisticated group. For in so doing, he may lose the
majority of other potential readers.

At the other end of the scale, the author of an article on mixing might start at the very beginning
and define all the basic terms for those completely unfamiliar with the subject. The editor must reject this

approach also, because the elementary style will offend all those who have even a passing acquaintance with the topic.

This brings us to the middle ground, the type of man we think is the reader of a typical article in CHEMICAL ENGINEERING. This middle reader might be the man who uses mixers in his plant but hasn't kept up-to-date on the latest advances. An article on mixing that will review the state of the art for him, and perhaps provide some guides for intelligent purchasing, will be of tremendous practical value. Such an approach will also attract the maximum number of readers.

A helpful device in planning your article is to imagine yourself sitting across the desk from another person who has only a nodding acquaintance with your subject. Try to imagine the kinds of questions he would ask; the answers to the questions frequently set the stage for the whole approach in writing the article. The most crucial questions are:

    • What kind of job does this potential reader have?

    • How much does he already know about your subject? (If you are a specialist, remember that what may seem commonplace to you may seem quite new to the general reader.)

    • Why should the reader want to know anything about your topic?

    • How much information can he profitably use?

Your Ideas Need Selling

Once you have identified your potential readers, you as a writer have a sales job. Your manuscript must first sell the editor on having something worthwhile to say. Then you and the editor must sell the reader.

No reader is going to devote an hour of his reading time to your article unless he is convinced you've got something of value to give him. And you've got to convince him of its value in the first few seconds he may devote to scanning.

How do you sell the reader? *Not* by spending hours looking for a catchy opening sentence. Chances are the editor will discard your opening sentence and provide his own opening anyway.

You sell the reader by telling him, in the first few paragraphs, *What* you are going to say and *Why* it is of importance. The rest of the article can be devoted to the "How."

It's often useful to start your article by giving your major conclusions and recommendations. Too many writers hide their major findings like a squirrel hides his acorns. The author imagines the sheer delight of the reader as he comes to the last paragraph and finds the conclusions that the author has been leading up to through six pages of closely reasoned logic. But most readers just aren't that patient. By telling the reader about your major conclusion first, you may convince him that the details are worth reading.

To fully explain why something is important, you may have to get into a little bit of history. This is fine, but don't start out with something like: "The origins of mixing equipment are lost in antiquity. The first records we have of commercial mixing operations are

Aim for the center—don't aim for the corners

The bell-shaped curve shows the range of potential readers for a technical topic. If you are particularly anxious to have some of your material reach the people in either corner, use the "box" technique. This means pulling out some particularly elementary or sophisticated material from the text, and making an "optional reading" section out of it. The editor will put this material into an appropriately labeled "box," so that it does not slow down the average reader, yet catches the eye of the novice or expert.

on Babylonian clay tablets over 3,000 years old. Then, in 205 B.C. . . . ."

By the time you finish with the ancient Egyptians and get around to what you have to say, the reader will be long gone and looking at the employment ads in the back. As a way around this, historical material can frequently be handled as optional reading in a box in the text of the article.

Writing the Article

You should have an outline, even if it's only a mental one. Know in advance the major point you are driving at, and shape the elements of the outline around this major goal.

If you know the publication in which you would like your article to appear, consult one of the editors of the magazine at this outline stage. He can tell you at the outset whether the subject is of any interest, and offer helpful suggestions.

There are two additional advantages to bringing the editor in at an early stage:

1. He gets an emotional involvement in your article and will most likely spend more time evaluating it and making suggestions for possible additions or revisions than if he just received the manuscript "over the

transom" and evaluated it on a take it or leave it basis.

2. The editor will usually ask you to commit yourself to a deadline, and this may provide the incentive you need to get the manuscript finished. How many of us have unfinished writing projects that we are going to complete "someday, when we have the time?"

After your outline is complete, you must set yourself to the task of putting all the information in your head down on paper in an understandable order. Write in a natural, conversational manner, as though you were telling a friend about your work. While not all sentences need be short, try to avoid very long ones (e.g., ones that take more than four lines).

Remember that you main job is to inform, and that this is best done in simple, direct statements. Your readers are as busy as you are, so they will be grateful if you make your point with the fewest words possible.

Avoid abstractions whenever possible—particularly ponderous, multi-syllable abstractions. The article on p. 6, "How Well Do You Inform," had several practical suggestions that will be of help. If you must use an abstract concept or a broad generalization, try to insert some specific examples or "for instances."

For instance, in an article about centrifugal pumps, such statements as "Proper design of the impeller is very important for severe applications," or "Materials of construction must be carefully chosen for abrasive service," are so general as to be almost meaningless. These statements should either by taken out entirely or else immediately amplified with examples of what you consider "proper design," "severe applications," "carefully chosen materials of construction," and so on.

As you write, keep in mind that you are communicating information to a broad spectrum of readers. This means making your conclusions as generally applicable as you reasonably can, avoiding the jargon of the specialist, and indicating where the principles might be employed in areas other than your own.

Tables, Drawings, Graphs, Photos

In organizing your article, always be on the lookout for elements that can be illustrated with a summary table, graph, photo or drawing. The reader who isn't inclined to plow through six or eight pages of solid text will frequently at least glance at the illustrations. And one might catch his fancy and start him reading.

Setting ideas down in a summary table is an especially valuable exercise. For example, if you were writing an article about conveyors for the chemical industry, most readers would want to see a summary table that showed all the major conveyor types, capacity ranges, mechanical features, limitations on materials handled, major advantages and disadvantages, and comparative prices.

Such tables are usually difficult to construct because there are always some missing data, or available data aren't on a comparable basis. A diligent author can usually find the needed information, however. And the result is that he crystallizes his own thinking in this organized form and performs a very valuable service for his readers.

Your illustrations don't have to be works of art. As long as they are clear and easy to read, most business magazines have art staffs that can redraw them to fit the magazine's style.

The Editor's Viewpoint

Let's see what goes through an editor's mind as he picks up the manuscript that you, the author, have just sent him. If he has not seen a previous outline, his mental checklist goes something like this:

• What's this article all about?

• Does it say anything new or provide a valuable interpretation?

• How many of my readers will be interested? (On CHEMICAL ENGINEERING, any article that we feel will interest less than 20% of our readers is a candidate for rejection, unless it appears to be of intense benefit to the small minority who will read it.)

• Are there any overlap problems with other articles? (Such problems can, of course, be prevented by letting the editor review your outline.)

• Does the author make his points logically?

• Are we getting this manuscript on an exclusive basis? (Most first-rate magazines won't touch a manuscript that isn't exclusive.)

• Is his writing style easy to understand (i.e., will it be much work for me to edit?).

Notice that writing style comes last on the list. An editor will work long and hard polishing up a manuscript once he is convinced the author has something to say.

The need for an author to say "something new" does not mean he has to be reporting new reseach results. Quite the contrary. We consider some of our most valuable articles to be those that survey the current state of the art, then review, interpret and evaluate the findings for those engineers who don't have the time to make a thorough literature search. The author who performs this invaluable review and evaluation function is saying "something new" when he adds his own comments—the results of his own experience and know-how—to the published work of others.

How Easy Is It For You to Write?

This varies not only from individual to individual, but also from company to company, as illustrated by the tearful tale of Taci-Turn Chemical Co.

HERBERT POPPER, *Associate Editor*

George Likely, the personnel manager of the Taci-Turn Chemicals Co., was lunching with Frank Venturi, the head of engineering.

"How's the college recruiting going this year?" asked Venturi. "I hope you're going to fill all those openings for young engineers before the vacation season starts. Our guys have been working pretty hard, and I'd hate to hold up any of their vacations."

"Well, you may have to," Likely warned. "The boys we want don't seem to want us. It's funny, but a lot of seniors just haven't heard of the work we are doing here at Taci-Turn. They know that we're a big outfit that has been around a long time, but when I asked a group at one college what else they knew about us, the most enlightening answer I got was, 'Aren't you the people who had that big reactor explosion that was in the papers last year?' One instructor told me he once asked Taci-Turn to supply a speaker who could tell his local AIChE group how our new plastics were developed, but apparently every engineer at Taci-Turn was busy that week."

Venturi scowled. He remembered the reactor explosion; actually it wasn't a big one at all—so small, in fact, that he had refused to talk to reporters about it, whereupon the reporters got their story from a rather excitable nearby resident. "I don't know why people remember our explosions longer than anybody

else's. And as for not getting a speaker for AIChE, I just can't understand that. You know that we encourage all our engineers to give talks and write papers—just so long as they don't give away our know-how, or fall behind in their work."

Likely didn't look impressed. "Maybe you don't encourage them hard enough. The last article you people published in a technical magazine was two years ago. Don't forget, those college seniors read the technical magazines, and if Taci-Turn isn't writing any worthwhile articles, they get the idea that Taci-Turn isn't doing any worthwhile engineering either. And then when the recruiter shows up and tells them that Taci-Turn is a great place for professional development, they don't buy it."

"Look," said Venturi, "all I can say is that I encourage all our engineers to write and give talks. Sure I had to hold up Charlie Meanwell's paper last year because it gave away too much information, but I did get him to revise it. It's not my fault that the revision still hasn't been cleared—someone in industrial relations is holding it up now. I think they want Charlie to tone down the bit about the labor-saving possibilities of the control system. And I think someone in quality control wants Charlie to change the part where he says the old control system used to give us purity problems. But once Charlie has made those revisions, the paper will be all set for the boss to look at. He'll pass it right on to public relations,

> *"Over the years, I have read many magazine articles that have helped me in my work as maintenance engineer. However, until last year, I never authored an article myself—partly because I wasn't sure of the procedure required to get my ideas into print.*
>
> *The ice was broken when CHEMICAL ENGINEERING, hearing of some of the work my company had been doing with vibration analysis, asked me to write a short article on the subject. I found that writing it was a stimulating experience, but even more gratifying was the response the article got. It was hardly published before I got a letter from a reader in Spain. Shortly afterwards, more correspondence and telephone calls started to come in—from Panama City, Houston, Chicago, New York, various spots on the West Coast, and elsewhere. While most of the people wanted to learn more about our experience with this or that instrument, or about some other facet of our vibration analysis program, the exchange of information was not a one-way street. I made some very fruitful contacts with people having maintenance problems similar to ours.*
>
> *I now realize that, in the world outside my own company, one useful four-page article can generate more recognition than years of hard work in themselves. And I don't think it is wrong to be pleased with such recognition—one of the marks of professionalism is supposed to be an interest in recognition among one's colleagues and counterparts.*
>
> *For all these reasons (and, of course, because I feel I have something more to say that may interest others), I am now working on another article."*
>
> R. H. Nittinger
> Maintenance Engineer
> Allied Chemical Corp.
> General Chemical Div.

and they usually don't take too long to clear it if there are no new revisions. When it's all over, maybe I'll encourage Charlie to write another paper."

The Cheerless Chores of Charlie

If Frank Venturi could have talked to Charlie Meanwell at this very moment, he would realize that Charlie is resolved never to write another paper again as long as he is with Taci-Turn Chemicals.

A number of things happened to Charlie earlier today. First of all, the industrial relations department returned his paper with the suggestion that he rewrite the section that deals with labor savings. "Perhaps," they noted, "you could say more about the quality-control advantages of the new control system, and less about the labor costs. We don't want trouble with the union."

Shortly after Charlie had got through mulling over this admonition, he got a call from Rex Ultra, the quality control manager. "I've been meaning to call you for a couple of weeks," apologized Rex, "but you know how it is. Anyway, Frank Venturi has showed

me a copy of your paper, and I think it's great—real great. I like to see our engineers writing for publication; it keeps Taci-Turn's name in front of our customers, and shows them that we're really alert to the latest improvements. There's just one thing—must you really show what our actual purity was before we installed the control system? Couldn't you just say 'Installation of the system led to a further gain in purity from its already high level'? You see, your purity comparison table might make some customers think that the stuff they were getting from us two years ago wasn't very good or consistent.

"By the way, I like your section on labor costs. Our customers like to know that we're keeping a lid on our staffing; it makes them feel we can make the stuff cheaper than they could themselves. So why don't you just rewrite the quality-control section, leaving out the actual comparison, and then I'll shoot the article in to the sales manager to make sure there's nothing in it that he doesn't like."

By a strange coincidence, no sooner had Charlie finished talking to Rex Ultra than he got a call from Herb Patience. Herb is the editor of a technical magazine, and he had expressed great interest in reviewing Charlie's article when he first heard about it. Every few months, Herb had been calling up to find out whether the project was dead or alive. This time, Herb's call was singularly ill-timed; his parting wish that the article would be cleared before the control system became completely obsolete didn't draw much of a laugh.

For his part, Herb wasn't smiling either; a year earlier, he had turned down an article from someone at Voluble Olefins Inc. because the subject would have overlapped Charlie's, and because Charlie should be coming through "any day now." The Voluble engineer wrote the article anyway, submitted it to another magazine, and had it published—and now there was still no way of telling when Charlie's article would be forthcoming, and whether it would still be useful enough to accept after everyone at Taci-Turn had made his own pet revisions and deletions.

Let us now take our leave of Charlie, who is wondering if he should join up with Voluble Olefins Inc., particularly since he allowed himself to say some rather heated things to the quality-control manager. And let us also bid farewell to George Likely and Frank Venturi, although they have just spawned a brilliant idea while waiting for dessert—they are going to ask Charlie Meanwell to give a talk to seniors at nearby colleges on the theme of "Why I Like Being a Taci-Turn Engineer," and they are going to try hard to get Charlie's talk cleared by all the people involved before the seniors graduate. (P.S.—They didn't make it.)

What Companies Can Do

Having taken our leave, let's get serious.

First of all, is writing a technical article or presenting a paper really worth all the bother? Aren't the advantages being oversold by program chairmen and by magazine editors who have axes to grind?

"When our program to encourage writing for publication was first started, I felt it would benefit both the company and individual engineers in several ways. Badger stood to gain from favorable publicity for one thing; for another, Badger might get away from the common impersonal corporate image and thus be better able to influence potential clients and potential employees. I believed publication would enhance the professional reputation of the engineer-author, and, as a sort of bonus, would force him to organize and consolidate his thinking in his special field. To at least some degree, all of these projected benefits to both company and individual have happened.

We are aware of other advantages we hadn't anticipated. They're small but they add up. Several authors have commented about a feeling of mental renewal they got after writing about a project and analyzing the results from all angles. Some said that writing had given them more confidence in themselves and in their work. One mechanical engineer said the experience was an eye-opener—he hadn't realized until he'd made the rounds gathering information how helpful and cooperative other types of engineers in his own organization could be.

Unanticipated company benefits? Well, there is evidence of closer Badger-client relationships as a result of some joint papers. Correspondence between authors and their readership has stimulated ideas and interest, too, and has probably been useful for both company and author.

There still seems to be no quantitative way to demonstrate just how valuable the program is in dollars, prestige, good will, or what have you. I can only repeat that while many of the benefits are intangible, we are convinced they're there."

Robert E. Siegfried
Engineering Manager
The Badger Co.

Well, since I might be accused of having an axe to grind myself, I won't answer that question directly, but will refer the reader to the quotations on these pages. To avoid repetition and save space, they have purposely been kept few and brief.

Second, if writing a paper or technical article is so beneficial to the company and to the individual engineer, why don't more companies pay more than just lip-service to the writing cause?

Actually, many companies *are* taking positive steps to encourage writing among engineers. For instance, about two years ago, the Badger Co. started a program, the five key points of which are:

1. Authors are paid an honorarium of $100 per article or paper, in addition to any author's fees from a publisher. There are qualifying stipulations which require that:

• The subject matter of a planned article be approved by the engineer's supervisor.

• Nothing be published that might violate secrecy agreements with a client.

• The writing shall reflect the company's good reputation.

2. Writing efforts will be respected and will not be mercilessly edited without the author's full knowledge and cooperation.

3. A reasonable amount of company time may be spent in preparation. To discourage possible internal moonlighting, however, it is made clear that the company-time privilege is not to be abused.

4. Since most engineers are not self-starters in the writing field, the company makes available professional assistance in organizing, outlining, and placing articles.

5. Each author is encouraged to appoint a younger engineer to assist in the preparation of the article, both to get him accustomed to writing and to have him help with the necessary research.

We asked the people from Badger what benefits the company and the individual engineers have gained from this program; the comments appear elsewhere on this page.

Other Positive Steps

Some companies have done fairly well in streamlining their clearance procedures so that the process involves fewer steps, less time, and is basically constructive.

Quick-acting, centralized clearance and review committees that operate for an entire division have often proved useful. At Monsanto, for instance, these committees serve to telescope almost the whole clearance process. It is one thing for an author to get a suggestion from such a committee as to how a certain section could be improved, and quite another for him to get five or six separate, delayed and sometimes conflicting suggestions from individuals who object to this or that passage.

Of course, there are clearance committees and clearance committees. Some pride themselves on the zeal with which they excise any tidbit of information that, by some stretch of the imagination, might possibly help or inform a competitor. As a result of this great zeal, the article or paper usually ends up being unwanted because the final version is so bland that it doesn't really help or inform anybody. Most committees, however, realize the harm that such a narrow attitude does to an author's morale, his professional development, and to the company's chance of reaping future rewards through publication.

Companies that have internal publications for professional personnel sometimes list all articles that engineers in that company have published in the period covered. This is a good way of giving inter-company recognition to the authors, and sometimes serves an even more tangible purpose—that of giving engineers a better acquaintance with the experts and specialists present within their own company.

This last point can be quite important in large firms. A plant engineer, for instance, who has just read a good pump article written by someone in central engineering will know where to get help if he has a

"Articles written by Allied Chemical people in publications such as CHEMICAL ENGINEERING are good both for our company and for the writer. Worthwhile articles help to foster wider understanding and appreciation of Allied Chemical's engineering and scientific efforts; they enable us to expose our company name in a favorable way to people who count—some of whom are potential employees. Our professional employment efforts are decidedly aided by such articles.

As for the writer, he has an opportunity to inform the technical community of his areas of activity. This offers a really positive element to his job satisfaction."

Gerald E. Ottoson
Director of Placement
Allied Chemical Corp.

pumping problem. And it also works the other way—people in central engineering have often benefited by reading articles written by people out in the plants.

Some companies encourage and stimulate engineers to write by asking editors of technical magazines to talk to a group of engineers at plants or design centers. For instance, CHEMICAL ENGINEERING has recently conducted a number of "Plant/Editorial Seminars"; these seminars show engineers that they have management backing in their writing efforts, and make them aware of the value of publication to professional development. In the individual discussions that conclude the seminars, the engineers have a chance to discuss ideas for articles with editors and their own management.

These, then, are some of the things that companies can do and are doing to encourage the output of meaningful papers and articles by engineers.

Writing for Fun and Profit

What can the engineer himself do to make his writing task as easy and rewarding as possible? Here are a few suggestions:*

1. Before you start, tell your boss what you propose to do. Give him a brief outline of your approach, tell him if there is any deadline for the project, and perhaps ask him for suggestions. That way, he becomes involved in the project at an early stage, and is more likely to go to bat for you if you hit a snag later.

2. Find out if there is an established procedure for

---

* Some of these thoughts are taken from "How to Write for CHEMICAL ENGINEERING."

clearing technical papers for delivery, or articles for publication. If your company has a public relations department, it is a good idea to contact it at the outset. Quite often, this department can smooth out the clearance process.

3. If you are writing for a technical magazine, give its editors an outline so that any suggestions they make can be considered before the article is in its final form. When you are ready for the writing itself, start off with a statement defining the scope of the article and the benefits the reader may expect to get from it. The bulk of the article will then be devoted to answering the questions of "how" and "why."

4. Let the style be in keeping with the purpose of your paper or article. If you are going to go before a learned body and make a formal presentation that will be written up in the transactions of that society, there may be certain formalities of style to be followed. For most technical magazines, however, it is best to write in a simple conversational style, as though you were telling a friend about your work. Use short sentences and short paragraphs. Avoid the temptation to put a "hedge" clause into every sentence. Don't be afraid of the first person singular or the first person plural. Make sure that the people who will have to approve your article know what type of meeting, society or magazine it is intended for; otherwise they may question your style or make needless changes.

5. If you are writing for a magazine such as CHEMICAL ENGINEERING, keep in mind that you are communicating information to a broad spectrum of readers. This means making your conclusion as generally applicable as you can, and showing where the principles described might be employed other than in your own special area. Short case histories are sometimes very effective for illustrative purposes or to pave the way for generalized recommendations, but if your whole article is one long, detailed case history, you may be limiting its appeal (and possibly creating clearance problems).

6. If you are having difficulty writing a certain section, go on to another, and come back to the tough one later. By that time, your thoughts may have fallen in place. If they haven't, talk it over with someone—a colleague, editor, or program chairman, for instance. Very often, just the talking process will suggest a way to resolve the snag. If you merely procrastinate, you may lose your momentum and end up being a drop-out author or speaker. Later on, you may regret becoming a drop-out—just like the person who wrote those posters currently on view in the New York subways saying "I quit school when I were sixteen." On the other hand, if you persevere, you may eventually become as proud as the person who, on one of those posters, scribbled the words "I didn't quit school—I goed on to college!" ∎

Engineers and the Technical Writer

Can't write right? Or perhaps you just don't have time to polish your output into readable, well-illustrated prose. In either case, the help of a good technical writer may be just what you need.

WILLIAM C. KAYSING, *Santa Barbara, Calif.*

Today's chemical engineer is increasingly involved in writing reports, preparing speeches, presenting papers, generating articles—in short, in technical communication.

Many firms now realize that few engineers possess the necessary skills to turn out a smooth finished publication and that, furthermore, it is an inefficient use of their time to try. These firms hire technical writers.

Who Are the Technical Writers?

Whether he is called a writer, editor, publications man, presentation specialist or communications expert, the technical writer is an individual hired to help control the rivers of written information that flow from all company departments. He must put basic units of communication into an orderly, presentable form with a minimum expenditure of time and money.

The most capable men for this job often have de-grees or training in English, journalism or other liberal arts. And they almost always show a greater-than-average interest in engineering and science. One of the most capable technical writers with a large West Coast aerospace firm is also a well-known science fiction author—his after-hours avocation.

Many technical writers began their careers as engineering students but changed majors after discovering a stronger penchant for writing. It is interesting to note that, while many engineers have become fulltime technical writers, few reverse the process.

There are several different types of technical writers in the chemical industries. They range from the modestly educated proofreader to highly qualified men who have degrees in both the arts and science. This latter group is capable of assisting in chemical research or process studies, while at the same time writing with erudition on these subjects. The great bulk of technical writers, however, fall between these extremes. Most of them can communicate technical information to an audience with clarity and vitality, while enjoying the work involved.

What Technical Writers Do

Organizationally, the technical writer may be attached to the company in a variety of ways. He may be a staff writer assigned to a specific group or groups, or he may belong to a separate publications unit. Sometimes he works for both the public relations and engineering functions but, in any case, his services are available to the engineering staff when required.

When not busy with specific assignments, the technical writer usually occupies himself with routine writing tasks such as monthly progress reports. During periods of high-priority activity, however, such as preparing bids and proposals, he may work around the clock.

Here are some examples of what a capable technical writer can do to assist the chemical engineer:

1. Minimal effort would require only a quick once-over of the material, followed by typing coordination, proofreading, final corrections, obtaining management approval and signatures, followup through the printing and distribution stages.

2. Moderate effort would include thorough editing for grammer and sentence structure, correcting technical errors, coordination and approval of illustrative material (graphs, charts, photos), supervising typing, proofreading, approvals, printing and distribution.

3. A major effort would mean that the writer would write all or part of the report from rough notes, laboratory data, specifications and the engineer's general outline. This would be followed by comprehensive editing and re-editing until approval of all concerned was obtained. The rest of the effort would include all the steps outlined above from typing or typesetting through distribution.

A single report might well involve the writer in all three levels of effort. To illustrate, he might write the standard sections such as foreword, abstract and summary, monitor the artwork, employ temporary typing assistance for a rush job, and then take a final hand in determining a mailing list.

Delegating the Responsibility

Just how much of the work the engineer can delegate to the technical writer depends on:

• The capability of the engineer as a writer.

• The extent to which the technical writer understands the field of chemical engineering.

• The type of subject matter being prepared.

If the engineer is more adept at chemical processes than he is at sentence structure, it would be advantageous for him to leave most of the writing to the writer. In this way, the engineer can pursue his own specialty and leave the grammar and graphic art details to a professional. Of course, the writer must be equal to the task. He cannot be the type whose knowledge is limited strictly to grammar and syntax.

For example, a chemical propellant engineer once wrote: "the propellant combination yielded a specific impulse of 235 seconds." An inept editor changed this to read: "specifically, the propellant combination impulse was 235 seconds." This kind of well-intentioned but clumsy meddling with the meaning of a technical sentence can only cause trouble. Thus it is most important that the chemical engineering knowledge of the technical writer be equal to the task.

The third element to consider is the material itself. For example, if the publication consists of pages of correlations and formulas, most of the work will be the responsibility of the engineer. However, if a corporate capabilities brochure is to be prepared, the technical writer may provide both rough drafts and finished material, as well as layouts, color choices, size and cost estimates.

In summary, the engineer can most effectively use his time in his own specialty by leaving publication chores to the technical writer. Conversely, the writer should hesitate to enter strictly technical areas, but be quick to assume as much of the load as he is capable of by virtue of his training and experience.

The Best Ways to Use a Technical Writer

A chemical engineer who has spent months, perhaps years, with a project likely has one of two feelings, or a mixture of both, about preparing his report. He may be tired of his stacks of data and piles of notes. In this case, he can simply turn the technical writer loose with instructions to come up with something presentable. Secondly, he may be so deeply involved with his material that he feels only he can prepared a document that will do it justice. Or he may have mixed feelings—fatigue with the data-gathering effort plus anxiety about proper preparation. He may want to do some parts and delegate the rest.

In all three of these cases, the technical writer can help. In the first instance, he can sit down with the engineer and work out an outline. He can explain what can be done with various pieces of information—some will be condensed into graphs, others into tables. Further, the writer might suggest that photos be taken of a pilot-plant installation to save words of explanation. In short, the writer will take over from the engineer and prepare the most effective presentation from the material available in accordance with the engineer's instructions. Obviously the writer in this case must have considerable technical know-how, as well as be a crack editor and graphics man.

Where the engineer feels that his personal attention to writing and editing is required, the technical writer can still perform many useful functions. He can help determine the scope of the report, its distribution, the quantity to be printed, preparation costs and whose approval will be required before the document leaves the company. All this information will be useful to the engineer before he starts writing. Furthermore, the writer's experience with many types of published material will help him act as a consultant to the engineer and guide his efforts to make maximum use of time and space.

In the third case, where the technical writer does various parts of the report, there are hundreds of ways he can help save time and money while at the same time producing an excellent report. Line drawings, for example, are essential to reader interest because pages and pages of unrelieved text are both unattractive and monotonous. A writer who has experience in graphic presentation can work as coordinator between the engineer and the technical illustrator to produce drawings, graphs, charts, process diagrams and other pictorial material that will clarify and embellish the prose. He can also take notebooks crammed with test data and shrink them to a few bar graphs or charts, thus saving time for both the company and the reader.

Sharply detailed photos are also important, and the technical writer with experience in this field can either take the pictures himself or arrange to have them taken. Then after the photos are developed and printed, he can supervise cropping and air brushing to achieve the best appearance.

It is interesting to note that there are many new photographic processes that have become available to aid in communications. For example, the Polaroid camera is highly useful in obtaining instant pictures that, if well planned, can be used to great advantage in reports. Although the Polaroid process is familiar, there is a step beyond it that is still little known and used. Key to this step is a ruled-screen insert that permits screening of halftoning the pictures as they are taken. This saves both time and money because the resulting screened photos can be considered as "line" copy and can be reproduced by the photo-offset process with no additional processing at the print shop.

If some of the terms used in the last couple of sentences are strange to you, I have made a significant point. Consider how difficult it is for the engineer to keep up with his own field, much less stay abreast of the advances being made daily in the graphic arts, publications and communications in general. This is the province of the capable technical writer, who spends his spare time becoming more familiar with the most modern techniques in his area of specialization.

The Range of Publications

A capable writer can help the chemical engineer to prepare almost any type of written material for in-ternal or external distribution. Here are some examples of material for internal use:

Interoffice reports	Maintenance manuals
Specifications	Safety procedures
Process instructions	House organ articles

And here are some typical publications intended for external distribution:

Contractual reports	Speeches and papers
R & D proposals	Data for advertising
Trade magazine articles	Press releases

These lists could go on at length and could include such diverse assignments as a slide or briefing chart presentation for a local university, preparation of an article for an encyclopedia, or even a complete text book.

It is appropriate that the chemical engineer spend most of his time accomplishing work in his own field. To do so, he must use as much qualified assistance as is available to him. A trained and dedicated technical writer can provide this assistance in a vital area—technical communications.

Meet the Author

William C. Kaysing has written articles on subjects ranging from motorcyle riding to how to use modern farm equipment. This article was based on seven years experience as a writer-editor with the publications group at Rocketdyne, a division of North American Aviation, Inc. A graduate of University of Southern California. Kaysing has done both free-lance and full-time writing. He is now director of sales and marketing for the Swivljig Co., Santa Barbara, Calif.

INDEX

Abstract words:
  and meeting papers, 103
  nouns, 9-11
Acronyms, 16, 17
Active verbs, 10, 11
Ad libs, 63
Advancement, job (*see* Promotions)
Analytical writing, 7, 8, 11
Appropriation requests, 172-174
Article writing (*see* Publication)
Audiences:
  analysis of, 55
  holding attention of, 54, 59-61, 80-89
  understanding, 54, 94
  (*See also* Conferences; Meetings; Talks)
Audio aids:
  audibility of, 68
  canned messages as, 70
  instruments, musical, 67
  pretesting of, 70, 71
  radios, 67
  records, phonograph, 67, 70
  tape recordings, 67, 70, 84
  voice, 67
  (*See also* Audio-visual aids; Talks)
Audio-visual aids, 66-71
  with meeting papers, 103
  movies, 84
  principles of, 69
  types, 69, 70
  (*See also* Audio aids; Talks; Visual aids)
Authorship (*See* Meeting papers; Publication)

Bar charts, 160, 161
Bibliographies, 128

Case histories, 56, 85
Catalogical writing, 6-8, 11, 128
Charts:
  bar, 160, 161
  pie, 160, 161
  step, 143
Communication:
  business, 14, 15
  failures in, 9, 14-19, 49, 186
  formal, 12
  with groups (*see* Talks)
  importance of, 48-50
    (*See also* Promotion)
  informal, 12
  and listening (*see* Listening)
  with maintenance, 179-182
  with management, 13
    (*See also* Promotions)
  with non-scientists, 13
  of operating information, 175-178
  oral (*see* Talks)
  problems in, 1-3, 9, 12
  and promotions (*see* Promotions)
  psychology in, 167-169
  in R&D, 183-188
  and reading, 1, 40-45
  and speaking (*see* Talks)
  and word choice (*see* Words)
  and writing (*see* Reports, technical; Writing)

Comprehension and listening, 28, 29
Concrete nouns, 9-11
Conferences:
  leadership of, 93-95
  listening at, 37
  and promotions, 93
  (*See also* In-plant courses; Meetings; Talks)
Courses, in-plant, 96-98
Cutaways, use of, 84

Dependent clauses, 7-9
  tests for, 8
Designs, communication of, 175-182
Details, handling of, 6-8, 11, 128
Diction, 14
Dictation, 1-3, 193-199
Drawings, 143, 144

Engineering reports, ideal, 9
  (*See also* Reports, Technical)
Engineers:
  as communicators, 1
  and dictation, 1-3, 193-199
  and poetry (*see* Poetry)
  and secretaries, 190-199
  as writers, 1, 20, 26
Equations, 162
Examples, use of, 118, 119
Exhibits, use of, 84, 85
Extemporizing, 60, 81, 82
Eye contact, 65, 82

Facial expressions, 64, 65, 89
Feeling:
  communication of, 21
  listening for, 28-33
Figures, use of, 128, 158-161
Filibusterers, 77
Flannel boards, 84
Flowsheets, 145-156
  pitfalls in, 147
  symbols for, 148-156
    sources of, 153
Fund requests, 172-174

Gestures, 35, 82, 83, 89
Graphs, 142, 143, 158-160
Group communication (*see* Talks)
Group participation, 85

Hecklers, 77

Illustrations, report, 115, 136-144
  bar charts, 160, 161
  copying, 140
  drawings, 143, 144
  equations, 162
  eye appeal, 137
  figures, 128, 158-161
  flowsheets, 145-156
  graphs, 142, 143, 158-160
  lettering, 138
  photographs, 143, 144, 162
  pie diagrams, 160, 161
  step charts, 143
  tables, 118, 128, 142, 143, 157, 158

Impromptu talks, 60
In-plant courses, 96-98
Initials, use of, 16, 17
Instruments, musical, use of, 67

Jargon, 18, 19
Job advancement (*see* Promotions)

Laboratory notebooks, 132-134
  and R&D reports, 129
Leadership:
  of conferences, 93-95
  of meetings, 90
Legal proof, notebooks for, 132, 133
Listening, 1, 2, 12, 28-39
  commandments for, 32, 33
  for comprehension, 28, 29
  at conferences, 37
  for feeling, 28-33
  and gestures, 35
  learning, 37-39
  and management development, 36
  nonverbal, 35, 36
  speed, 38
  at staff meetings, 37
  techniques, 33
  tests for, 39
  training for, 34-39
  what's new in, 28-36
Listings, 128
  (*See also* Catalogical writing)

Maintenance, communication with, 179-182
Management:
  and communication, 36, 183-188
  communication with, 13
  communication demands of, 26
  and engineering reports, 106, 107
Meeting papers, 99-103
  (*See also* Audio aids; Audio-visual aids; Talks; Visual aids)
Meetings:
  how to run, 90-92, 102, 103
  listening at, 37
  (*See also* Conferences)
Memos, 6-11, 115, 170, 171
Models, use of, 84, 85
Movies, use of, 84
Musical instruments, use of, 67

Name choosing, 23
Notebooks, 129, 132-134
Nouns, abstract and concrete, 9-11

Obsolescence, technical, 96
Opaque projectors, 70
Operations information, 175-178
Oral communication (*see* Talks)
Overhead projectors, 68-70, 84

Pad boards, use of, 84
Paragraphing, 128
Papers, meeting (*see* Meeting papers)
Passive verbs, 10, 11
Patent records, 132
Personal writing style, 11
Phonograph records, use of, 67, 70

Pie diagrams, 160, 161
Poetry:
    and impact words, 13, 26
    and word choice, 20-23
    and word order, 24-26
Posture and talks, 64, 65, 89
Production, communication with, 179-182
Projectors, use of, 68-70, 84
Promotions:
    and communication, 3, 164-166, 170, 171
    and conferences, 93
    and listening, 36
    and oral presentations, 49
    and technical writing, 119
Pronunciations, 64
Psychology and communication, 167-169
Public speaking, 78, 79
    (*See also* Talks)
Publication:
    problems of, 202, 203
    writing for, 204-213

Question-and-answer periods, 72-78, 92
    conducting, 74-77
    and filibusterers, 77
    and hecklers, 77
    planning for, 73

Radios, use of, 67
Reading:
    as communication, 1
    rapid, 40-45
Records, phonograph, use of, 67, 70
Reports, technical, 6-11, 108-132
    and details, 6-8, 11
    and examples, use of, 118, 119
    guidelines for, 115-119, 129-131
    ideal, definition of, 9
    illustration of (*see* Illustrations, report)
    and management demands, 26, 106, 107
    organization of, 108-114
    progress, 129, 130, 132
    style for, 118, 127, 128
    and tables, 118, 128, 142, 143, 157, 158
    weaknesses in, 126-128

Research, communication with, 183-188

Samples, use of, 84
Secretaries:
    and dictation, 1-3, 193-199
    vs. machines, 194, 195, 197
    working with, 190-192
Sentence variation, 8, 9
    test for, 9
Showmanship in talks, 83-85
Slides, use of, 68, 84
Speaking (*see* Talks)
Speech writers (*see* Technical writers)
Startup information, 175-178
Stenographers (*see* Secretaries)
Step charts, 143

Tables, 118, 128, 142, 143, 157, 158
Talks, 48-103
    and ad libs, 63
    analysis of, 51-53
    and audiences, holding, 54, 59-61, 80-89
    and communication, 1, 2, 12, 14
    extemporaneous, 60, 81, 82
    impromptu, 60
    mannerisms during, 60, 62-65, 82, 88, 89
    memorization of, 60, 81, 82
    and the Q&A period, 72-78, 92
    reading of, 60, 81, 82
    showmanship in, 83-85
    (*See also* Audio aids; Audio-visual aids;
        Conferences; In-plant courses;
        Meeting papers; Meetings; Public
        speaking; Visual aids)
Tape recorders:
    as audio aids, 67, 70, 84
    to practice talks, 82
Technical writers, 24, 101, 211-213

Verbs (*see* Active verbs; Passive verbs)
Visual aids, 66-70, 83-85
    criteria for, 67, 68
    portability of, 68
    preparation of, 69

projection of, 68-70, 84
types of, 66-70
    cutaways, 84
    exhibits, 84, 85
    flannel boards, 84
    models, 84, 85
    pad boards, 84
    samples, 84
    slides, 84
    rules for, 68
voice integration with, 70
(*See also* Audio-visual aids; Talks)
Voice, speaking:
    as an audio aid, 67
    and expressiveness, 63, 64
    tone and level of, 89
    and visual aids, 70

Words:
    abstract, 9-11, 103
    dual meanings for, 12
    feelings from, 22
    as a hobby, 12, 13
    impact of, 13, 26
    and poetry (*see* Poetry)
    psychology of, 167-169
    selection of, 14, 15, 169
    tailoring of, 12, 13
    technical, 18
Writing:
    analytical, 7, 8, 11
    of appropriation requests, 172-174
    catalogical, 6-8, 11, 128
    and communication, 14
    and dictation, 1-3, 190-192
    grammar of, 6-11
    of memos, 6-11, 115, 170, 171
    philosophical, 9
    publication (*see* Publication)
    and secretaries, 1-3, 193-199
    styles of, 11
    tests for, 6-11
    (*See also* Poetry; Meeting papers; Reports,
        technical)